QUALITY ASSURANCE in ANOTHER WORLD

01

MASAMICHI SATO

contents

Quality Assurance in
Another World

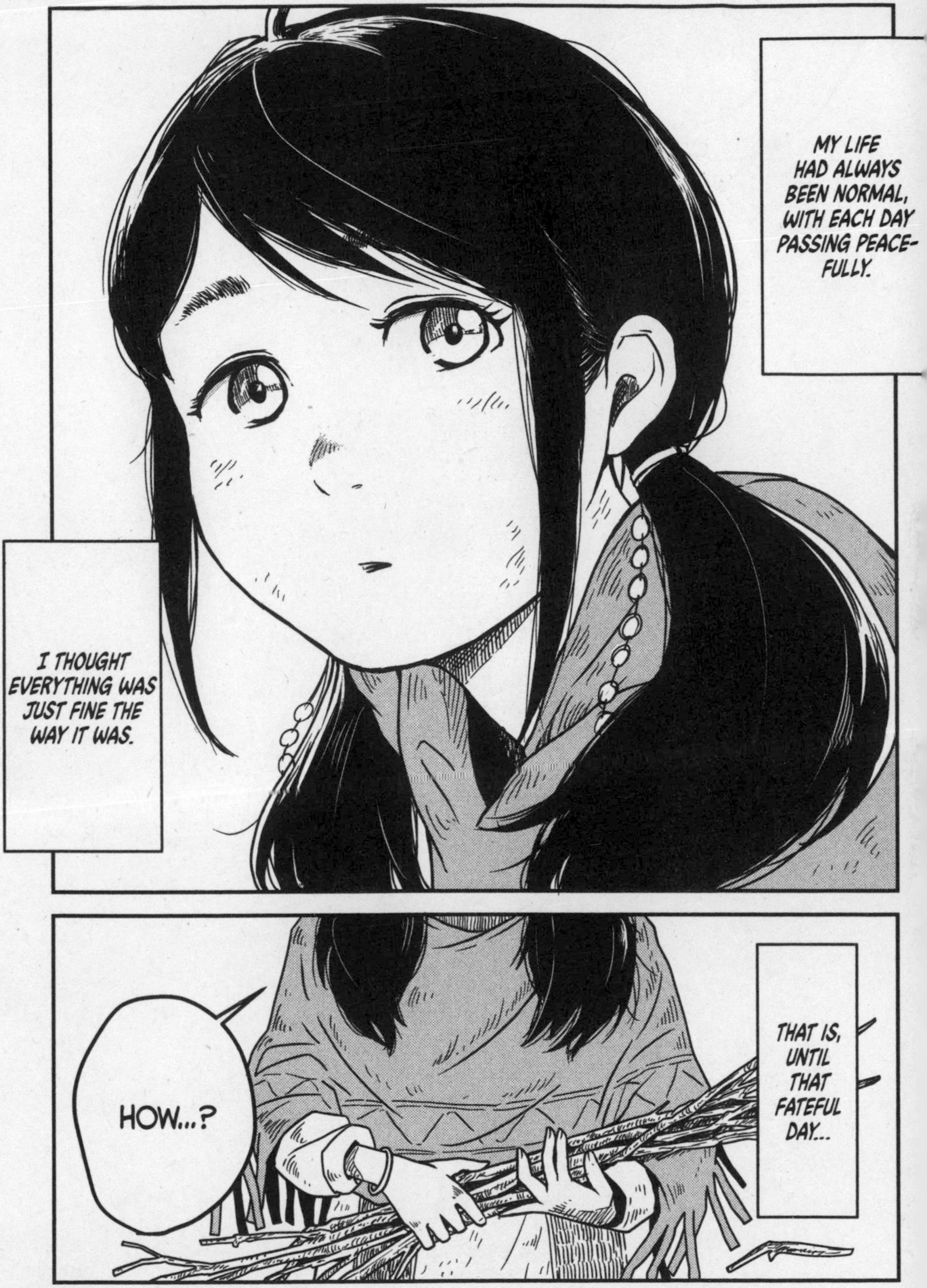
MY LIFE HAD ALWAYS BEEN NORMAL, WITH EACH DAY PASSING PEACE-FULLY.
I THOUGHT EVERYTHING WAS JUST FINE THE WAY IT WAS.
THAT IS, UNTIL THAT FATEFUL DAY...
HOW...?

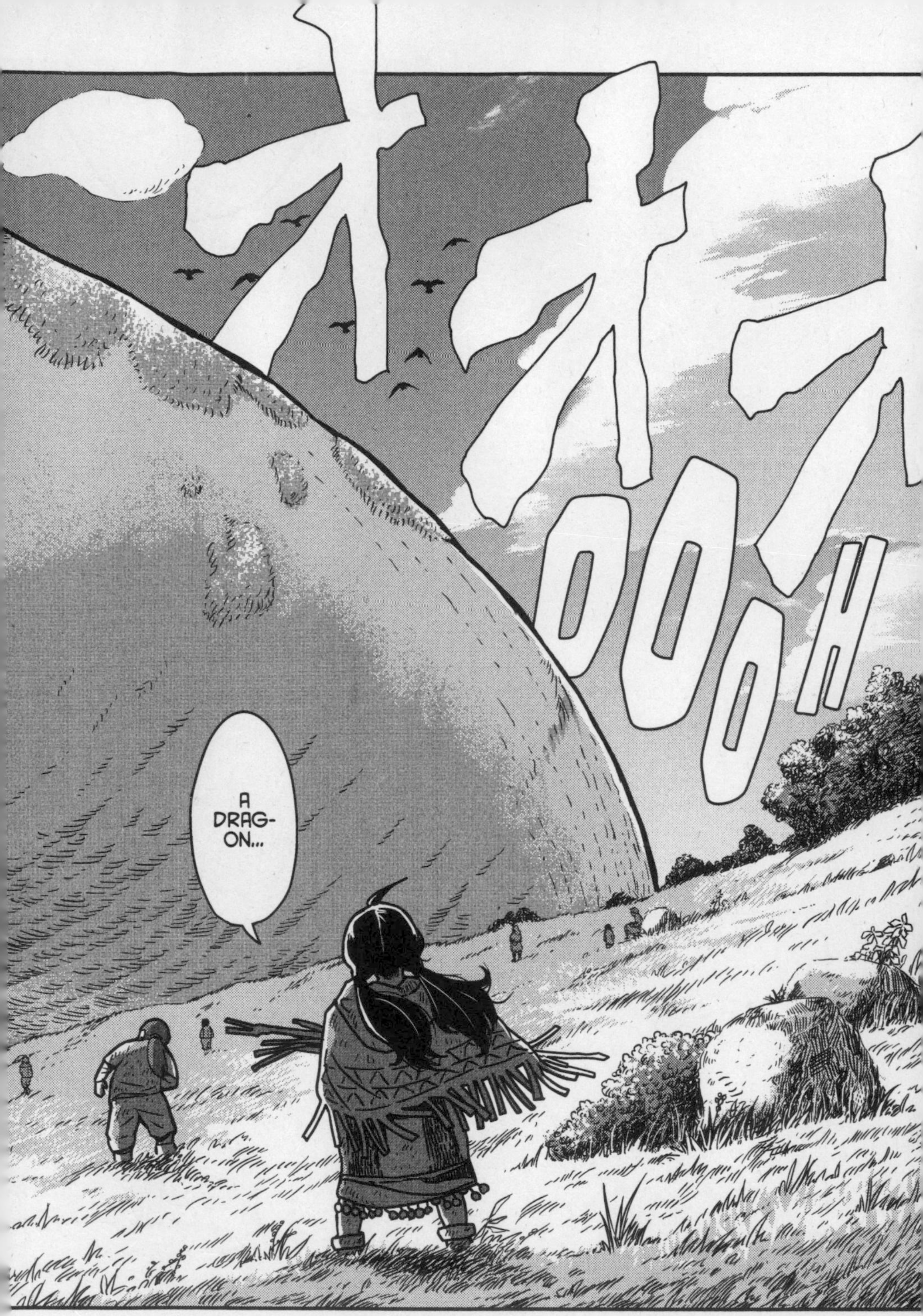
OOOOH
A DRAG-ON...

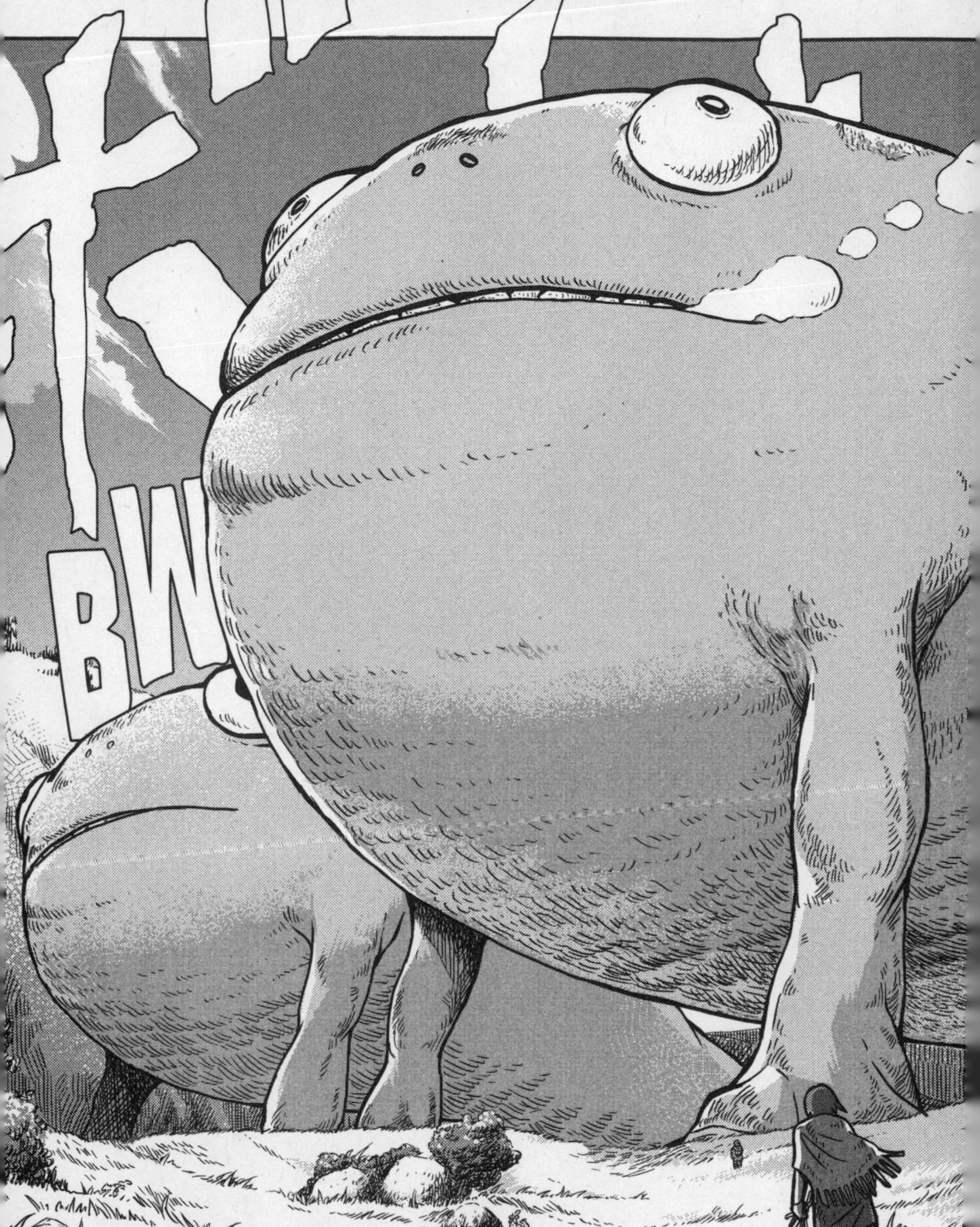
BW

No.1 | Nikola the Assistant

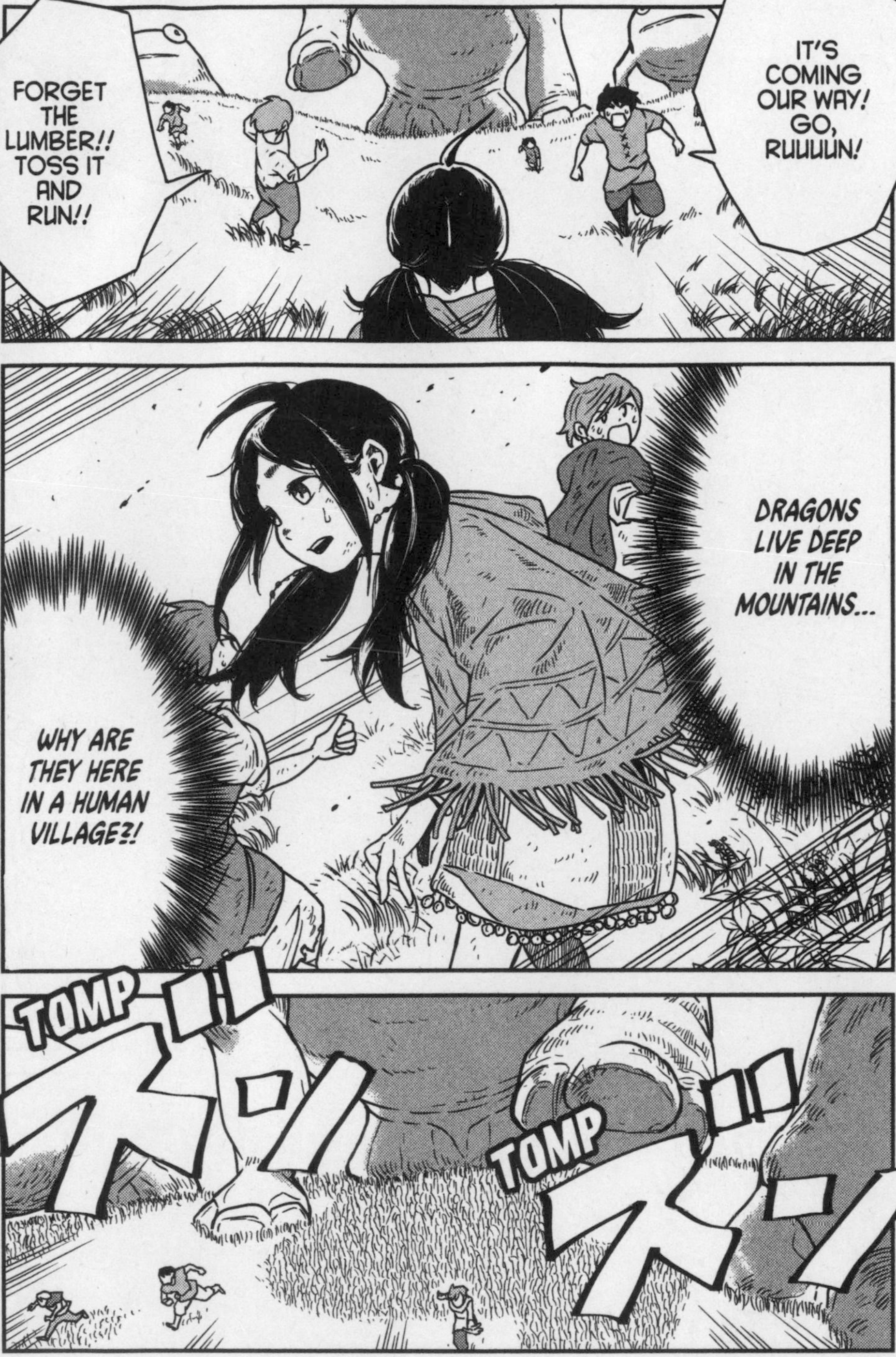
IT'S COMING OUR WAY! GO, RUUUUN!
FORGET THE LUMBER!! TOSS IT AND RUN!!
DRAGONS LIVE DEEP IN THE MOUNTAINS...
WHY ARE THEY HERE IN A HUMAN VILLAGE?!
TOMP
TOMP

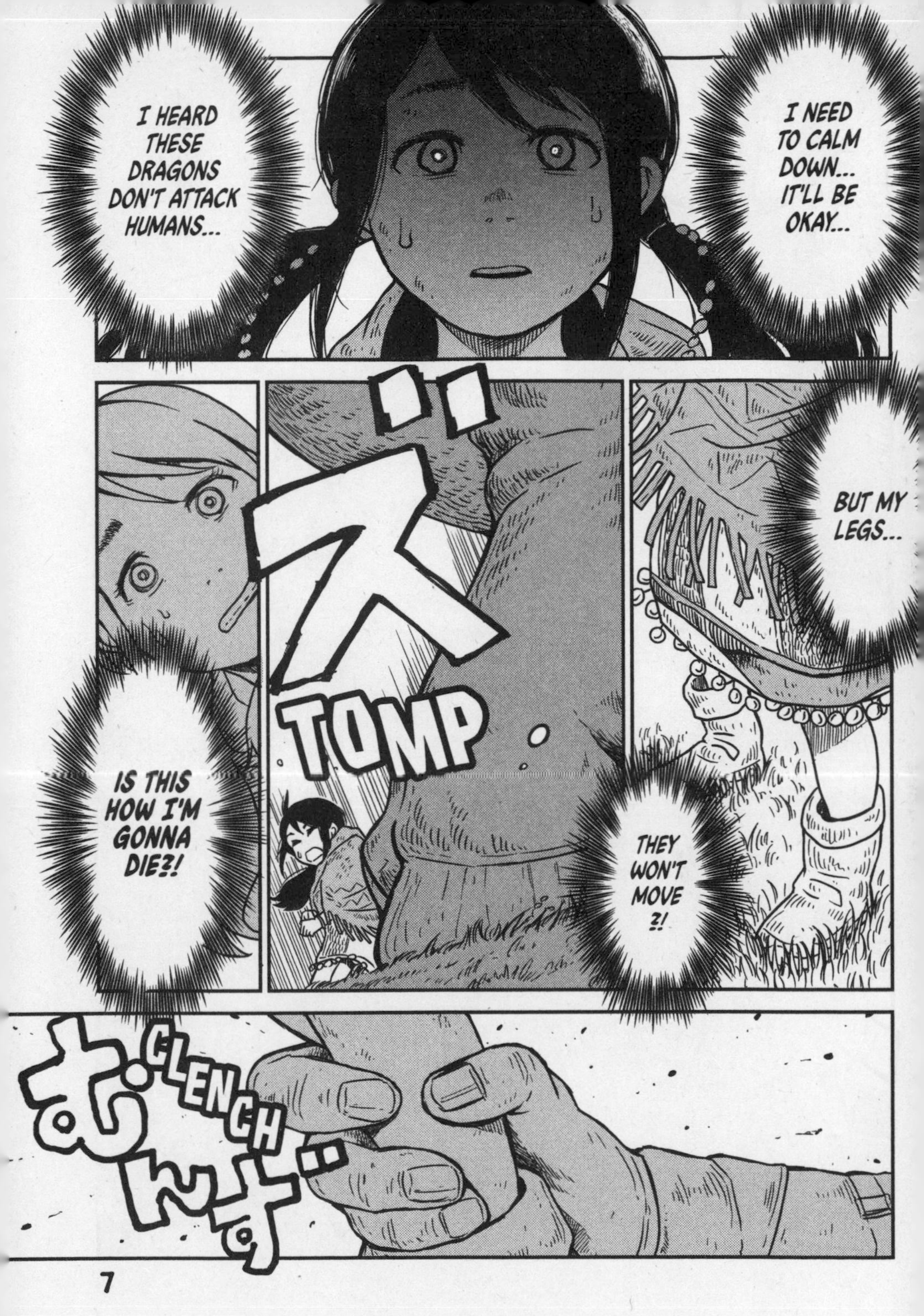
I NEED TO CALM DOWN... IT'LL BE OKAY...
I HEARD THESE DRAGONS DON'T ATTACK HUMANS...
BUT MY LEGS...
THEY WON'T MOVE?!
ズ
TOMP
IS THIS HOW I'M GONNA DIE?!
CLENCH

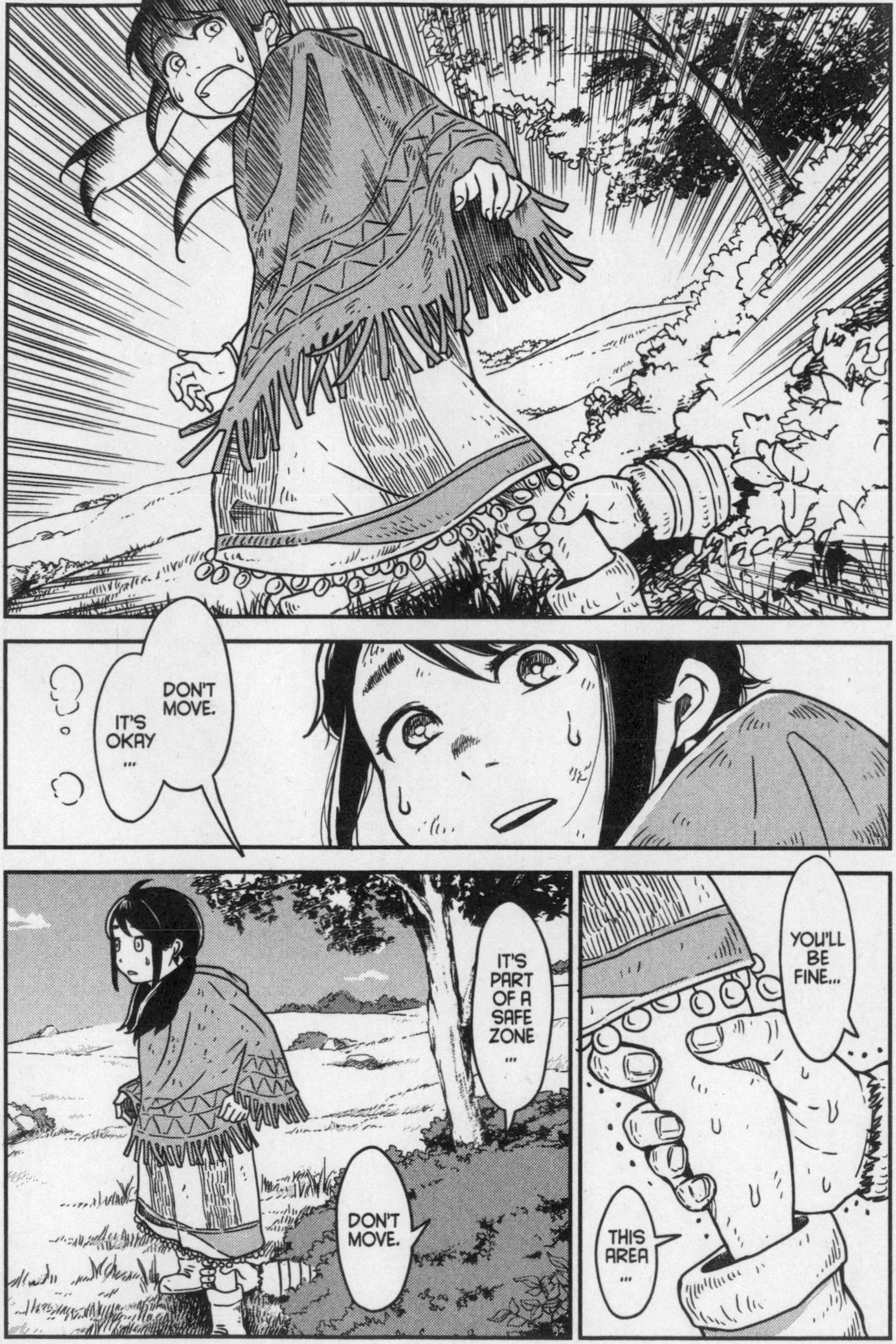
DON'T MOVE. IT'S OKAY ...
YOU'LL BE FINE...
THIS AREA ...
IT'S PART OF A SAFE ZONE ...
DON'T MOVE.

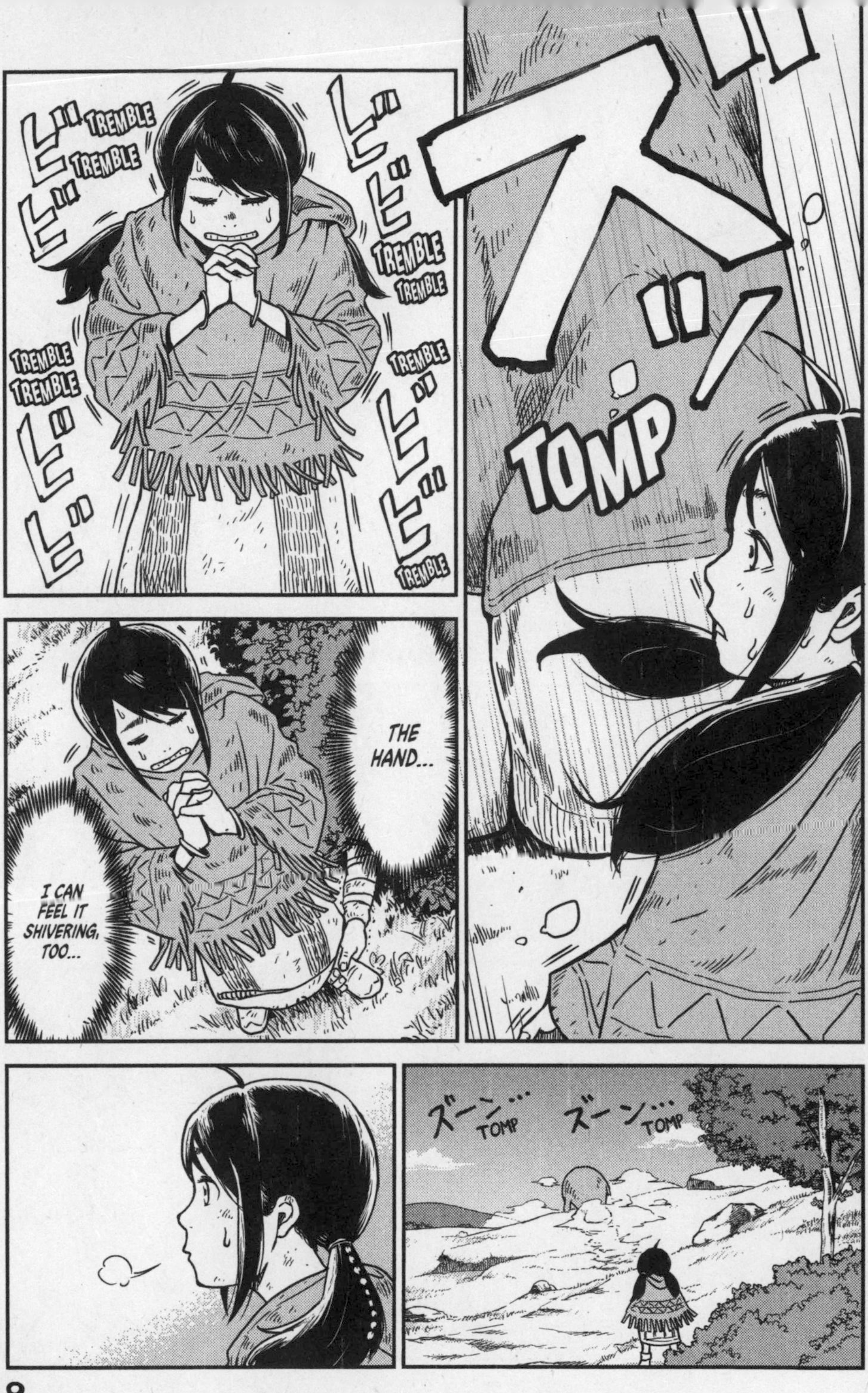
TOMP
TREMBLE TREMBLE
TREMBLE TREMBLE
TREMBLE
TREMBLE TREMBLE
TREMBLE
THE HAND...
I CAN FEEL IT SHIVERING, TOO...
ズーン… TOMP
ズーン… TOMP

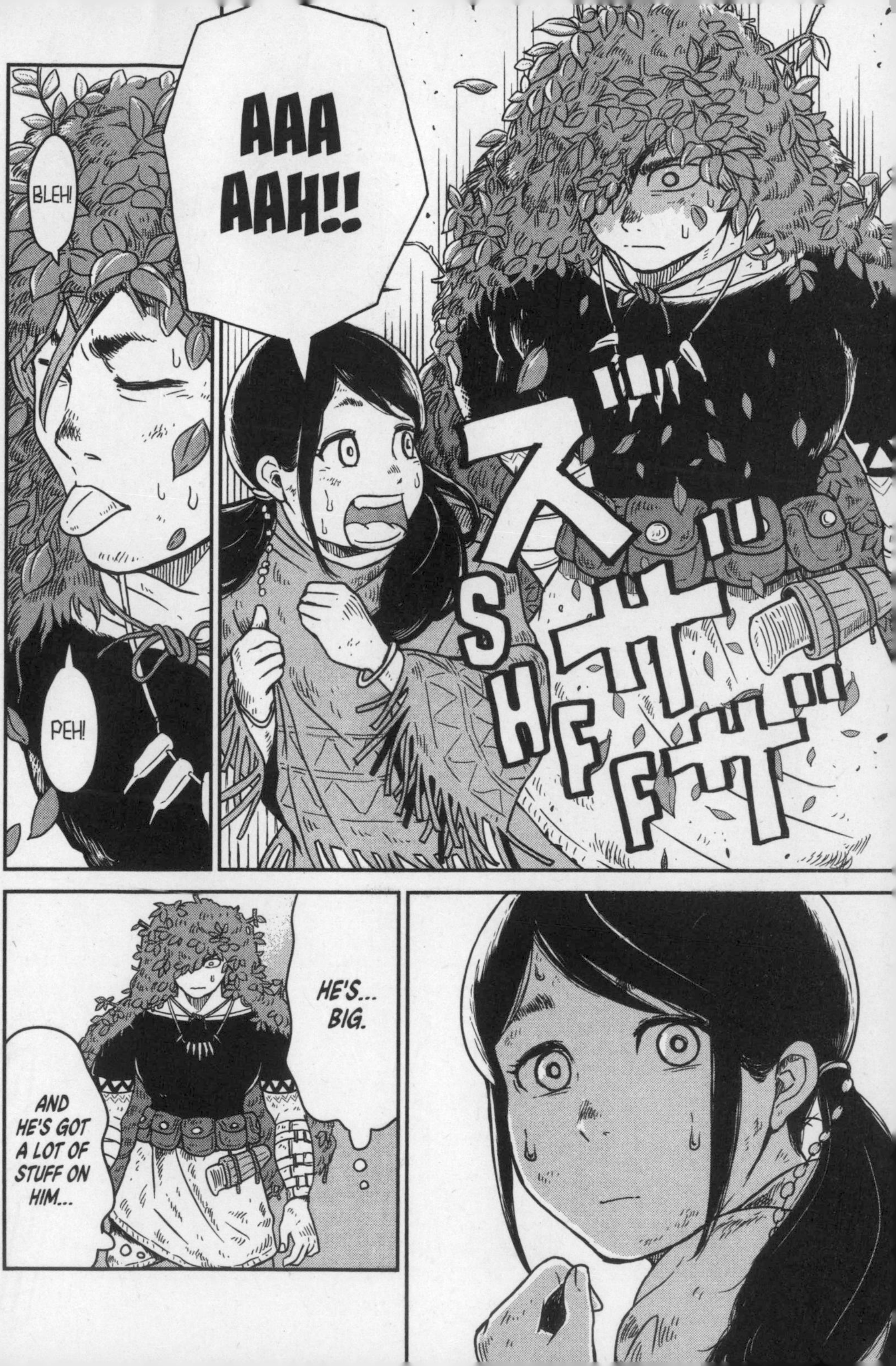
SHFF
AAA AAH!!
BLEH!
PEH!
HE'S... BIG.
AND HE'S GOT A LOT OF STUFF ON HIM...

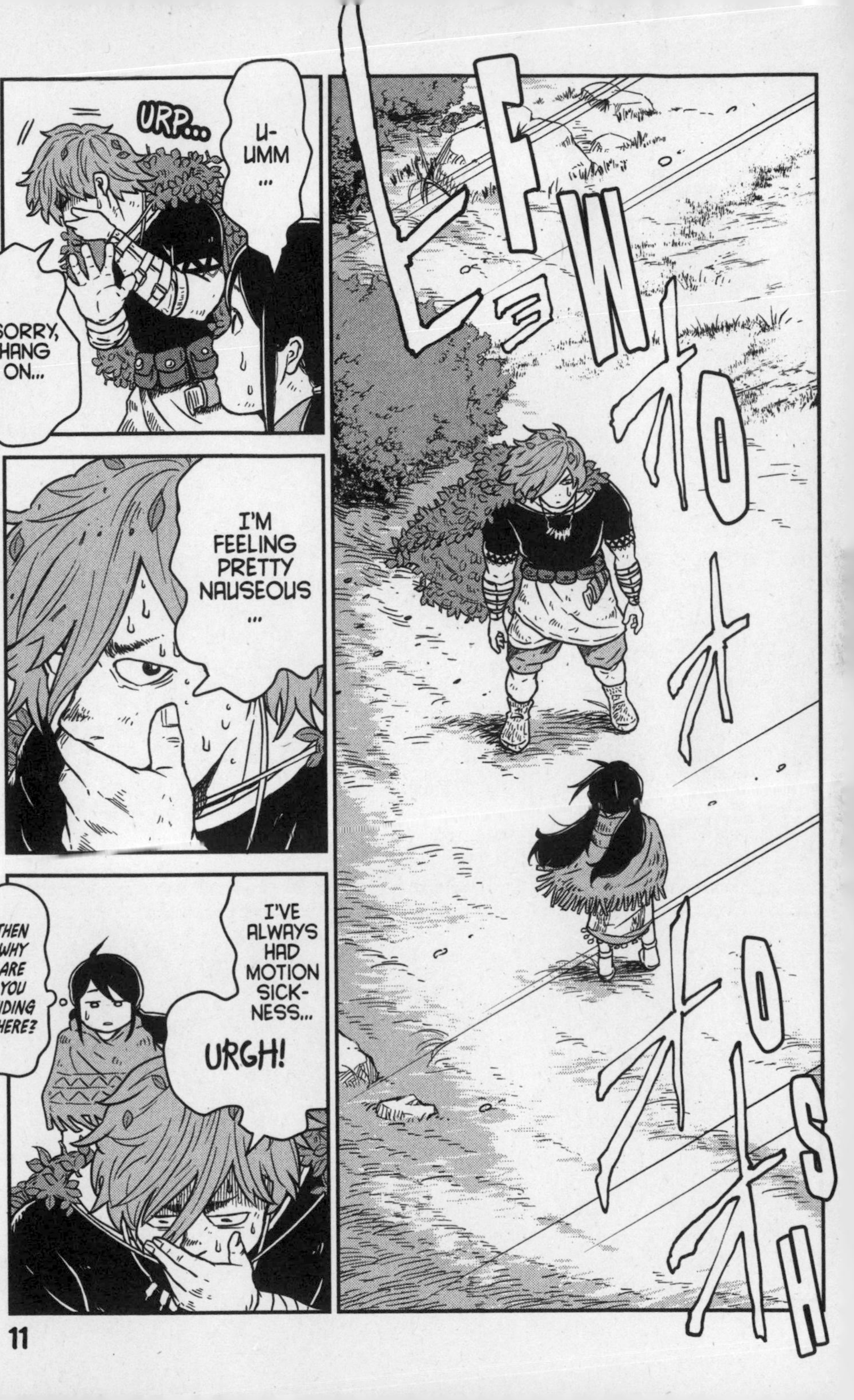
FWOOSH
U-UMM...
URP...
SORRY, HANG ON...
I'M FEELING PRETTY NAUSEOUS...
I'VE ALWAYS HAD MOTION SICKNESS...
URGH!
THEN WHY ARE YOU HIDING THERE?

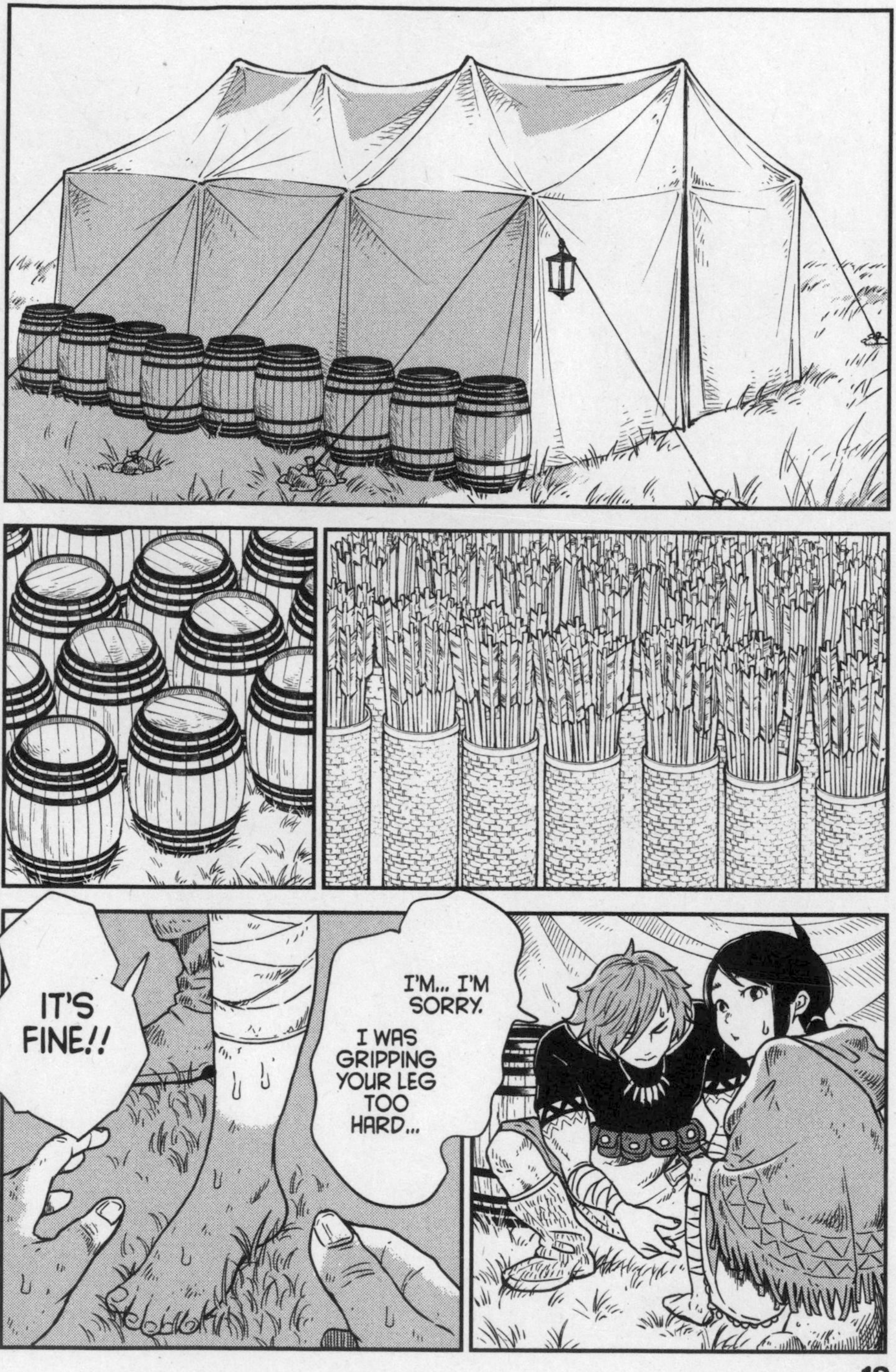
I'M... I'M SORRY.
I WAS GRIPPING YOUR LEG TOO HARD...
IT'S FINE!!

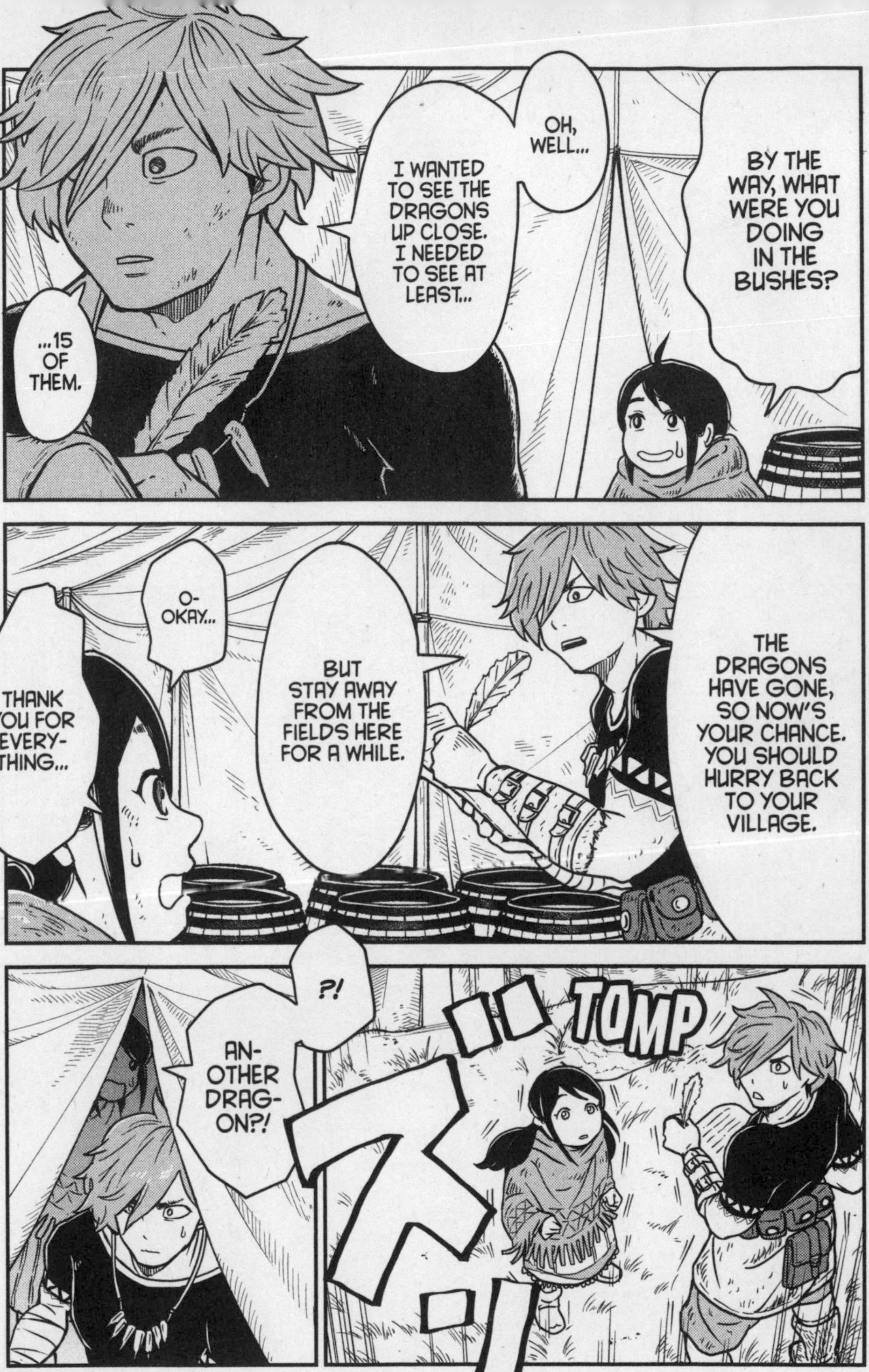

BY THE WAY, WHAT WERE YOU DOING IN THE BUSHES?
OH, WELL...
I WANTED TO SEE THE DRAGONS UP CLOSE. I NEEDED TO SEE AT LEAST...
...15 OF THEM.
THE DRAGONS HAVE GONE, SO NOW'S YOUR CHANCE. YOU SHOULD HURRY BACK TO YOUR VILLAGE.
BUT STAY AWAY FROM THE FIELDS HERE FOR A WHILE.
O-OKAY...
THANK YOU FOR EVERYTHING...
TOMP
?!
AN-OTHER DRAGON?!

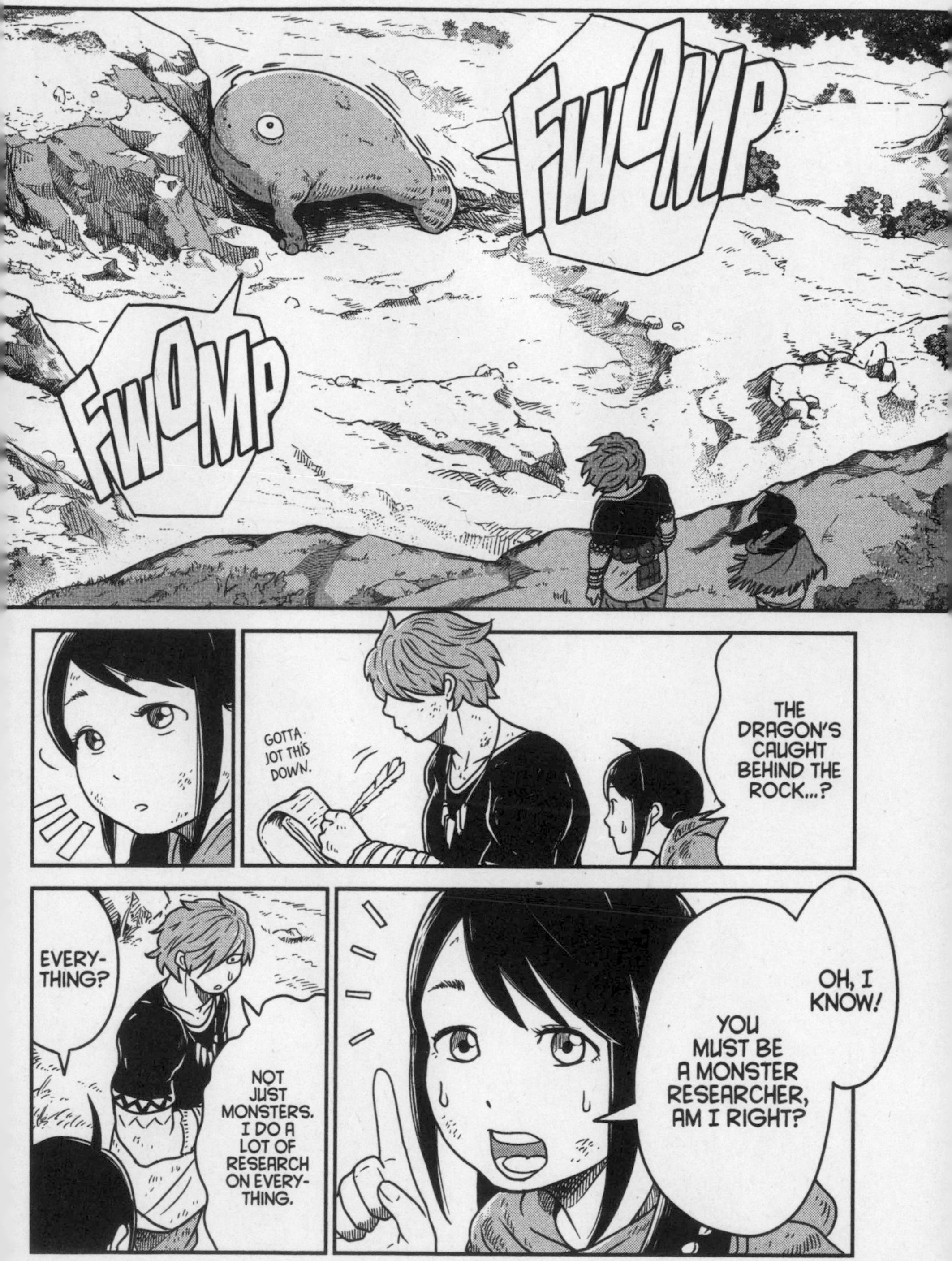
FWOMP
FWOMP
THE DRAGON'S CAUGHT BEHIND THE ROCK...?
GOTTA JOT THIS DOWN.
OH, I KNOW!
YOU MUST BE A MONSTER RESEARCHER, AM I RIGHT?
NOT JUST MONSTERS. I DO A LOT OF RESEARCH ON EVERY-THING.
EVERY-THING?

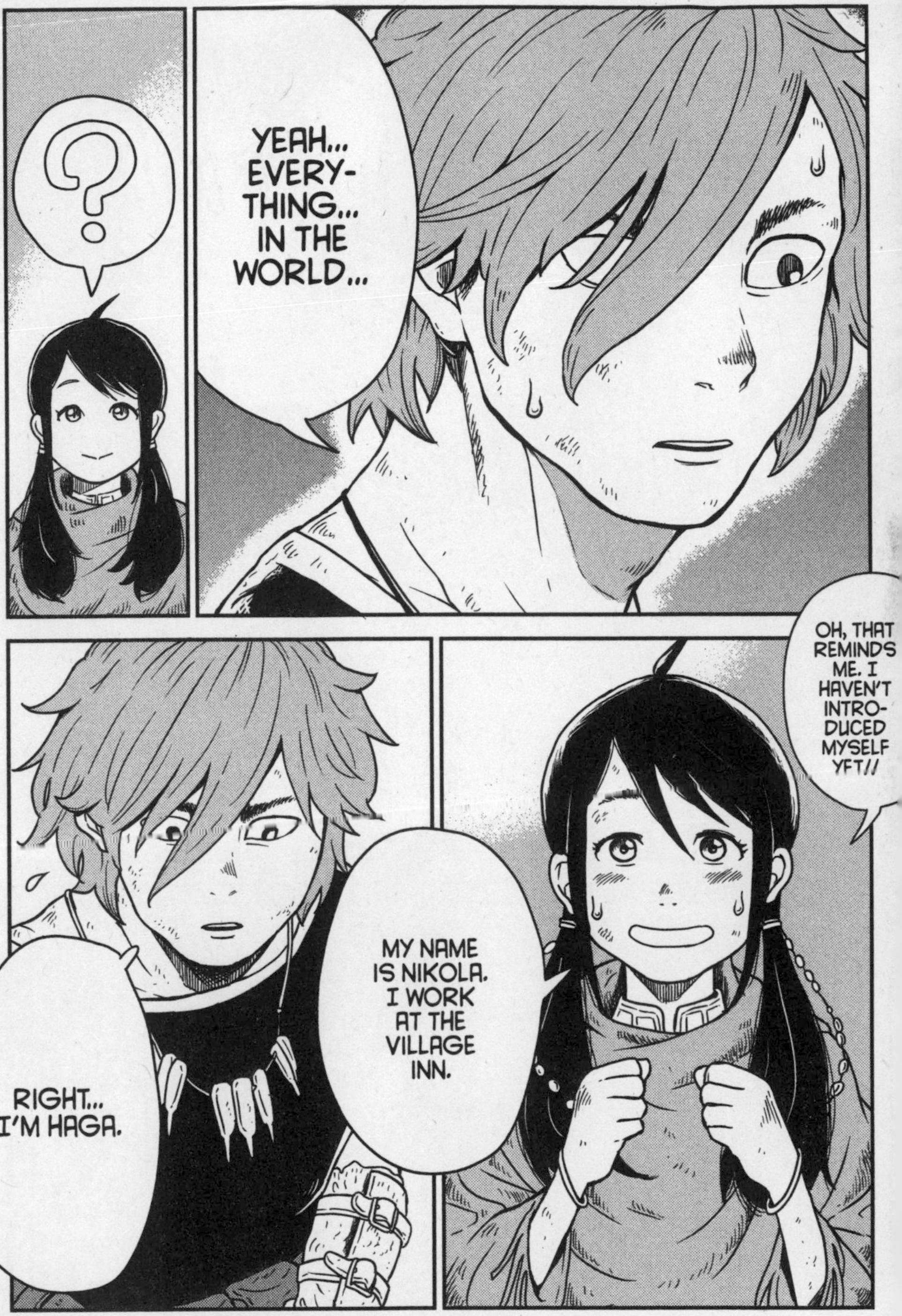
YEAH... EVERY-THING... IN THE WORLD...
?
OH, THAT REMINDS ME. I HAVEN'T INTRO-DUCED MYSELF YET!!
MY NAME IS NIKOLA. I WORK AT THE VILLAGE INN.
RIGHT... I'M HAGA.

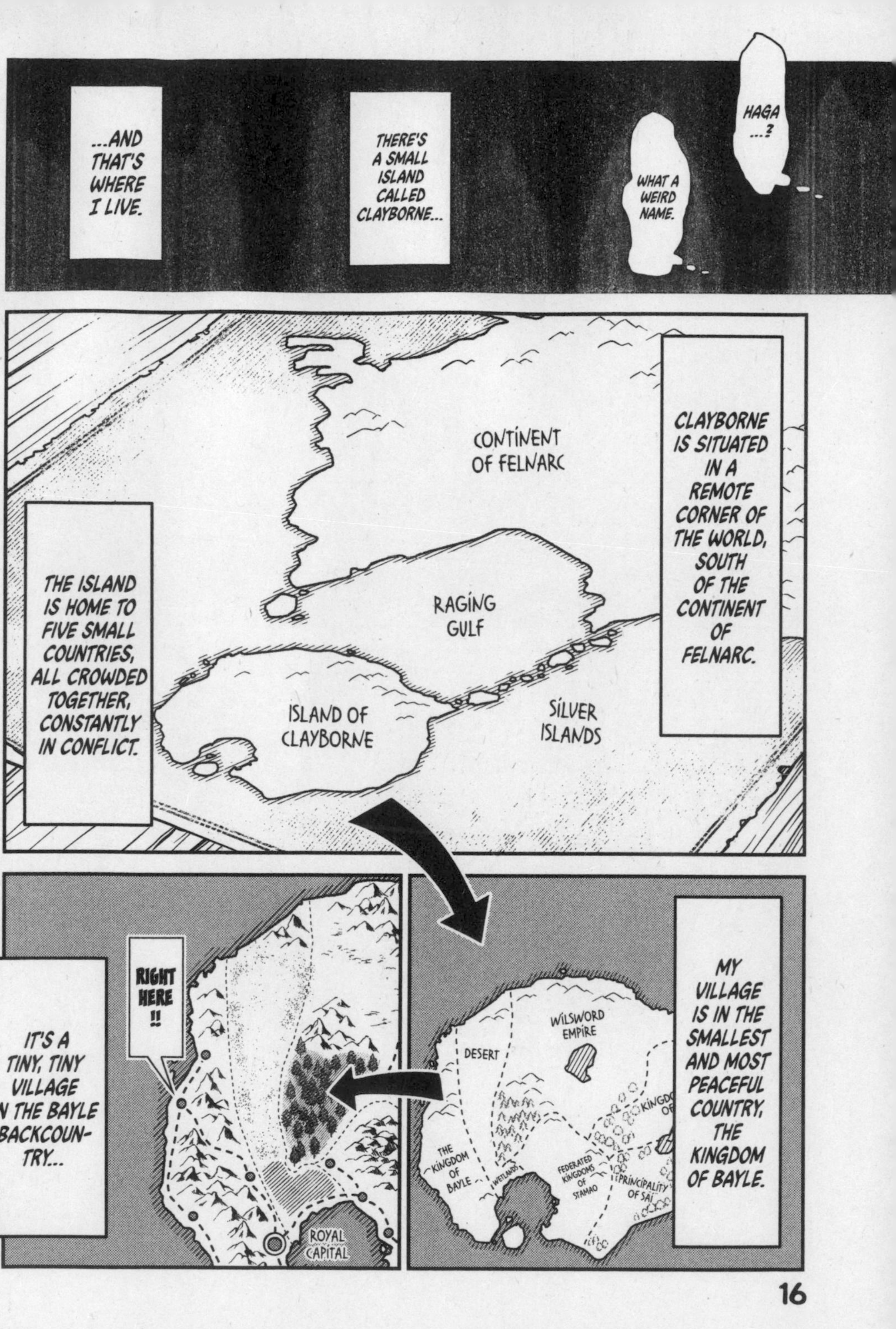
HAGA ...?
WHAT A WEIRD NAME.
THERE'S A SMALL ISLAND CALLED CLAYBORNE...
...AND THAT'S WHERE I LIVE.
CLAYBORNE IS SITUATED IN A REMOTE CORNER OF THE WORLD, SOUTH OF THE CONTINENT OF FELNARC.
CONTINENT OF FELNARC
RAGING GULF
SILVER ISLANDS
ISLAND OF CLAYBORNE
THE ISLAND IS HOME TO FIVE SMALL COUNTRIES, ALL CROWDED TOGETHER, CONSTANTLY IN CONFLICT.
MY VILLAGE IS IN THE SMALLEST AND MOST PEACEFUL COUNTRY, THE KINGDOM OF BAYLE.
WILSWORD EMPIRE
DESERT
THE KINGDOM OF BAYLE
WETLANDS
FEDERATED KINGDOMS OF STAMAO
PRINCIPALITY OF SAI
RIGHT HERE !!
ROYAL CAPITAL
IT'S A TINY, TINY VILLAGE IN THE BAYLE BACKCOUNTRY...

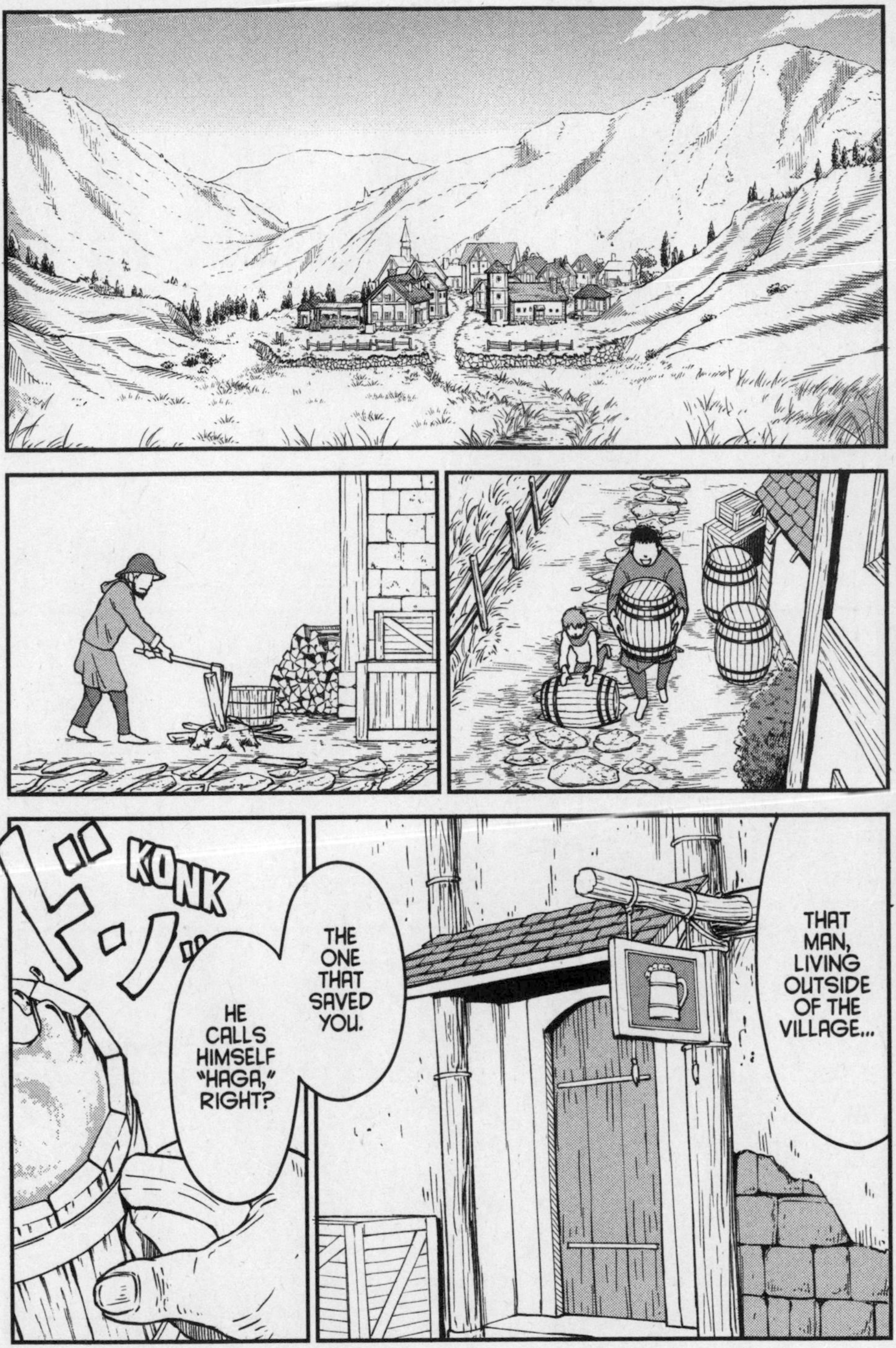
THAT MAN, LIVING OUTSIDE OF THE VILLAGE...
THE ONE THAT SAVED YOU.
HE CALLS HIMSELF "HAGA," RIGHT?
KONK

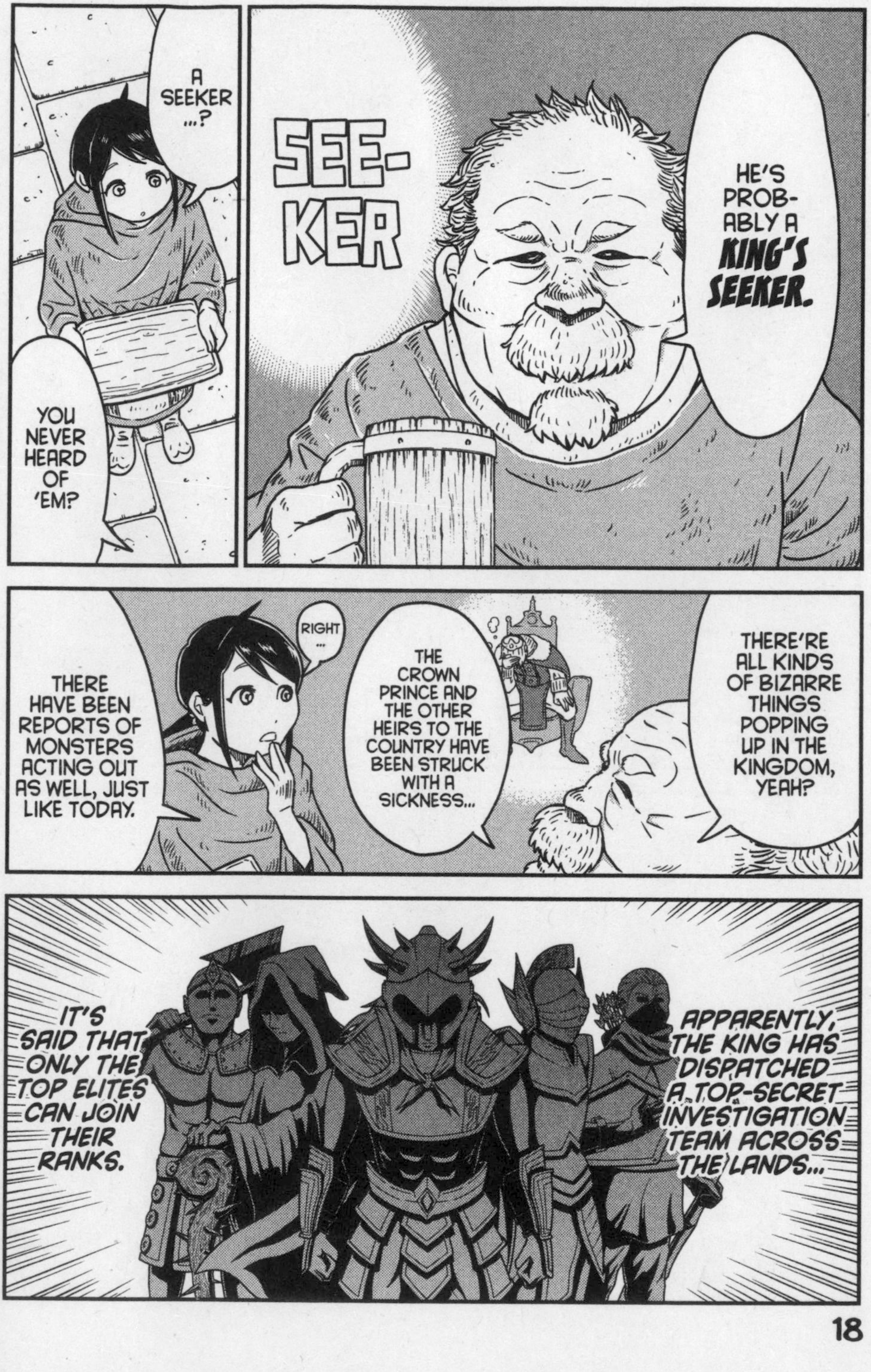
HE'S PROBABLY A KING'S SEEKER.
SEE-KER
A SEEKER ...?
YOU NEVER HEARD OF 'EM?
THERE'RE ALL KINDS OF BIZARRE THINGS POPPING UP IN THE KINGDOM, YEAH?
THE CROWN PRINCE AND THE OTHER HEIRS TO THE COUNTRY HAVE BEEN STRUCK WITH A SICKNESS...
RIGHT ...
THERE HAVE BEEN REPORTS OF MONSTERS ACTING OUT AS WELL, JUST LIKE TODAY.
APPARENTLY, THE KING HAS DISPATCHED A TOP-SECRET INVESTIGATION TEAM ACROSS THE LANDS...
IT'S SAID THAT ONLY THE TOP ELITES CAN JOIN THEIR RANKS.

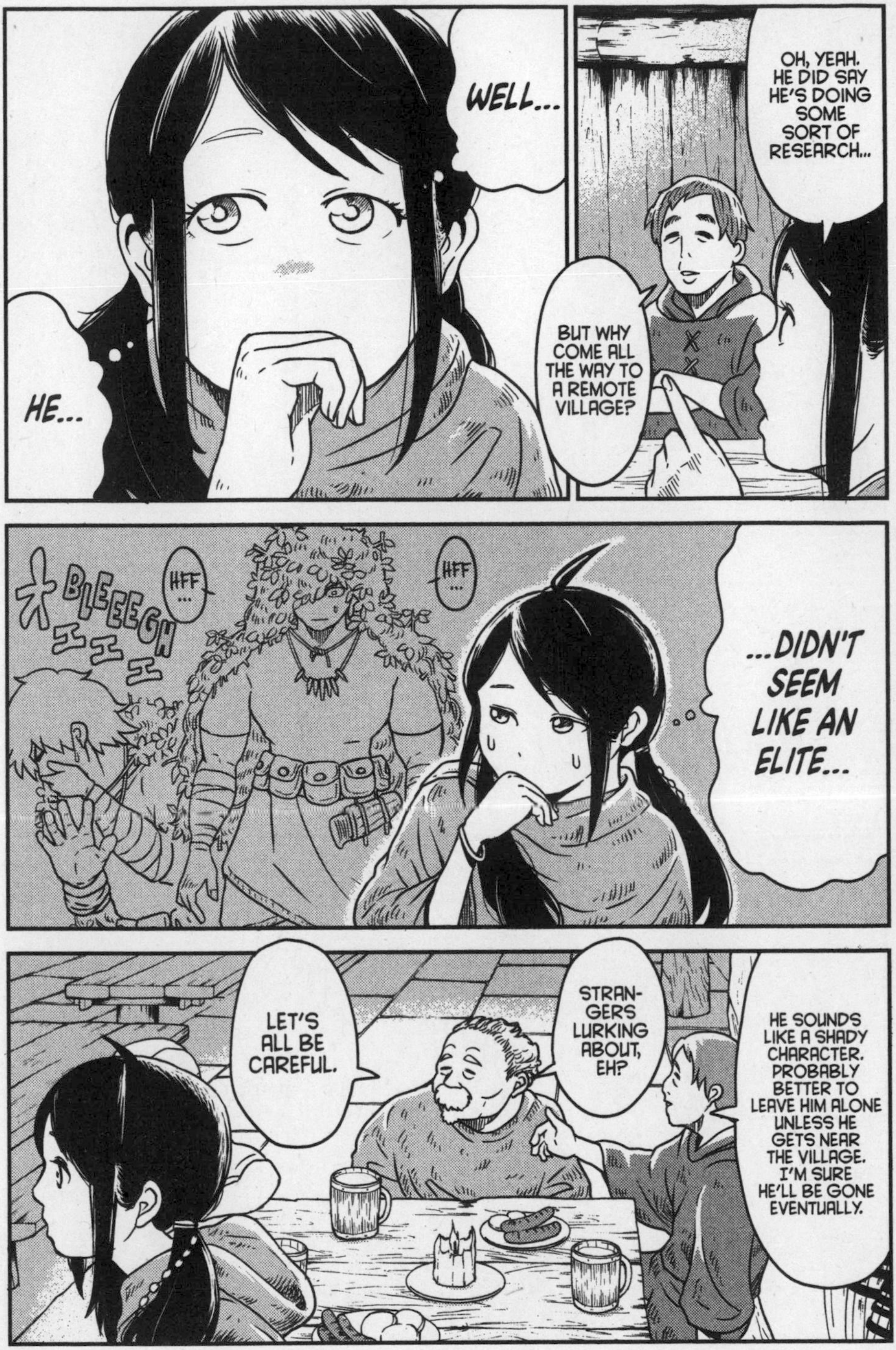
OH, YEAH. HE DID SAY HE'S DOING SOME SORT OF RESEARCH...
BUT WHY COME ALL THE WAY TO A REMOTE VILLAGE?
WELL...
HE...
...DIDN'T SEEM LIKE AN ELITE...
HFF...
HFF...
BLEEEGH
HE SOUNDS LIKE A SHADY CHARACTER. PROBABLY BETTER TO LEAVE HIM ALONE UNLESS HE GETS NEAR THE VILLAGE. I'M SURE HE'LL BE GONE EVENTUALLY.
STRAN-GERS LURKING ABOUT, EH?
LET'S ALL BE CAREFUL.

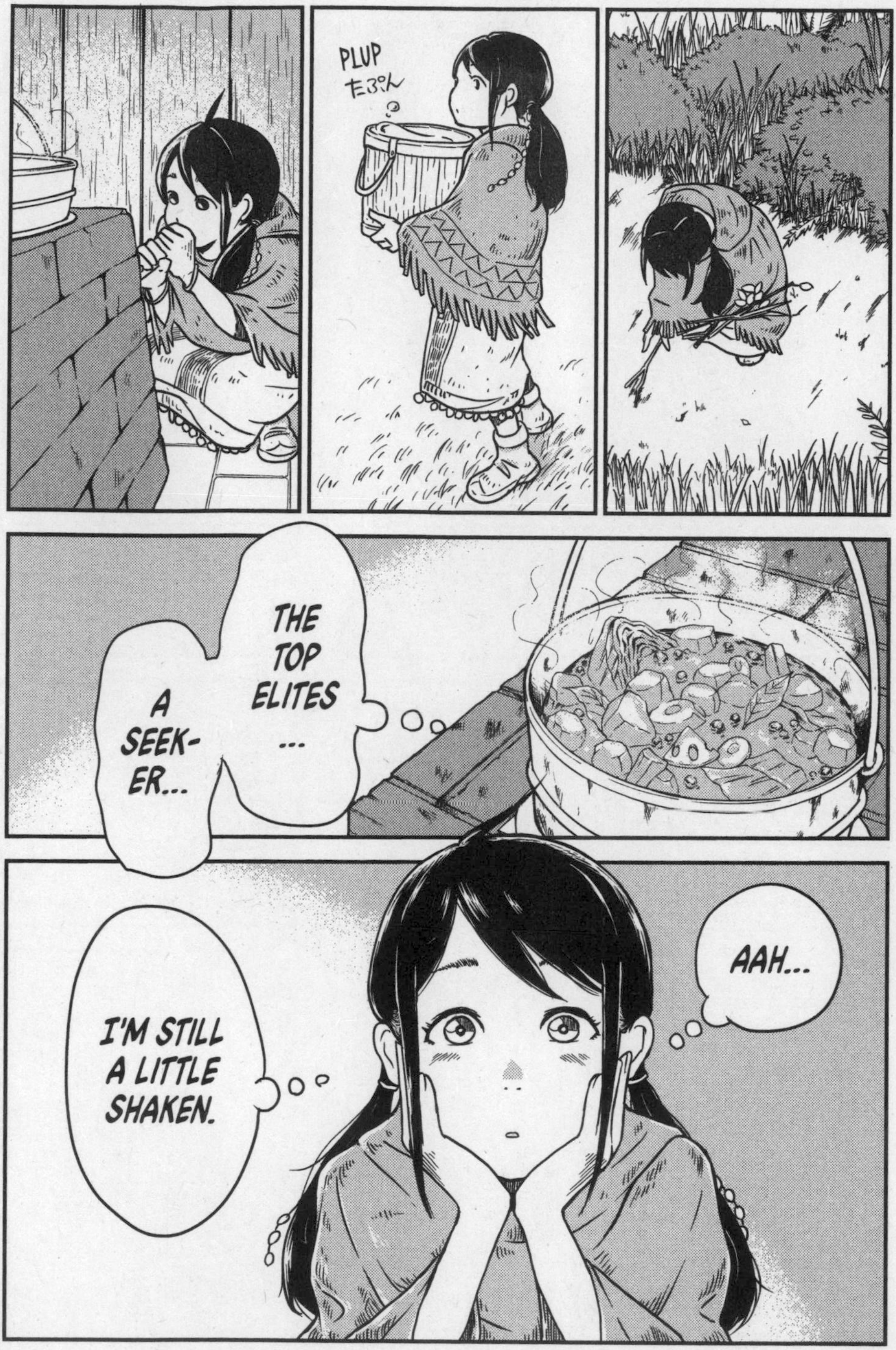
PLUP
たぷん
THE TOP ELITES ...
A SEEK-ER...
AAH...
I'M STILL A LITTLE SHAKEN.

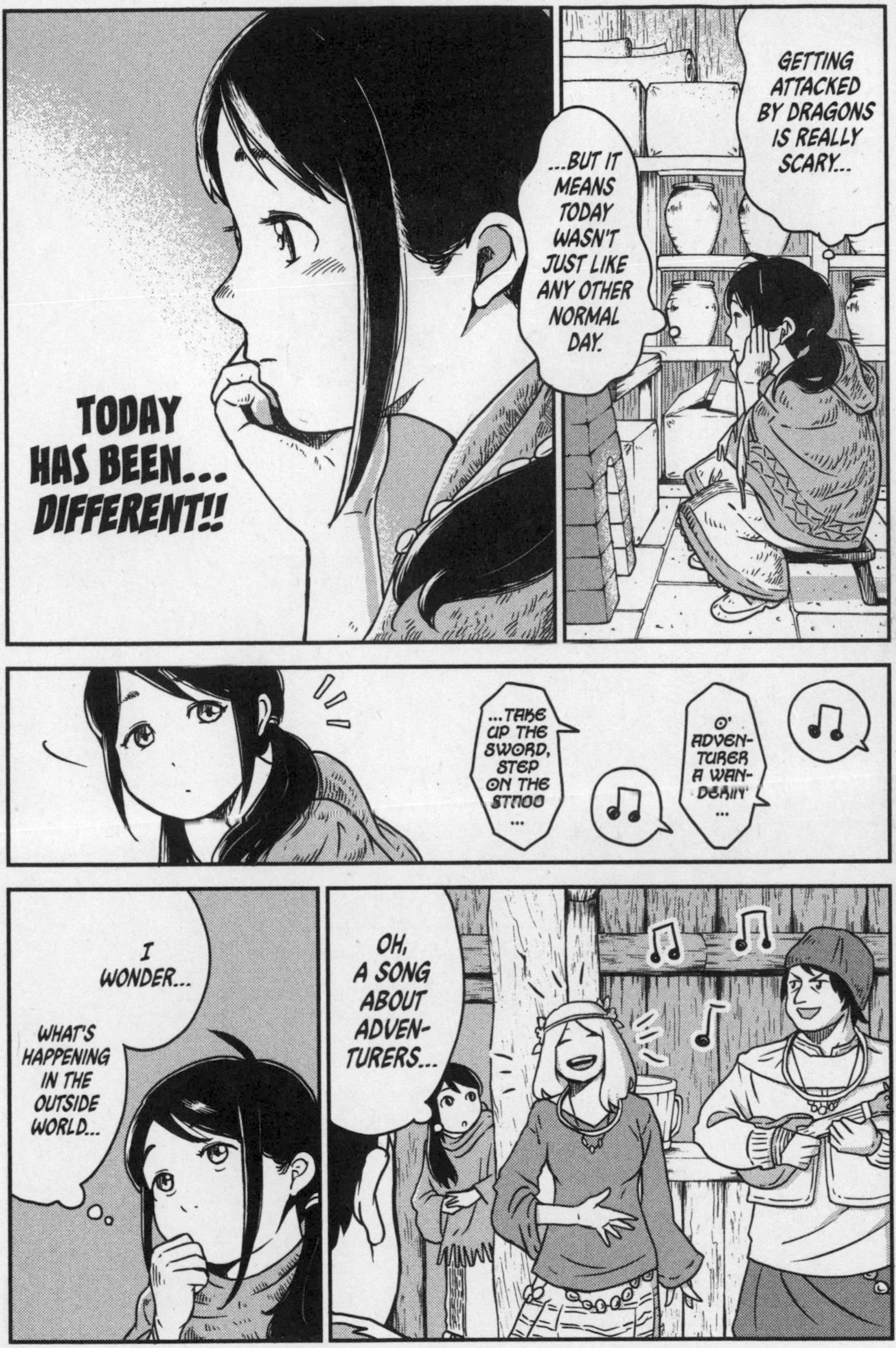
GETTING ATTACKED BY DRAGONS IS REALLY SCARY...
...BUT IT MEANS TODAY WASN'T JUST LIKE ANY OTHER NORMAL DAY.
TODAY HAS BEEN... DIFFERENT!!
O' ADVENTURER A WAN- ...
...TAKE UP THE SWORD, STEP ON THE ...
OH, A SONG ABOUT ADVENTURERS...
I WONDER...
WHAT'S HAPPENING IN THE OUTSIDE WORLD...

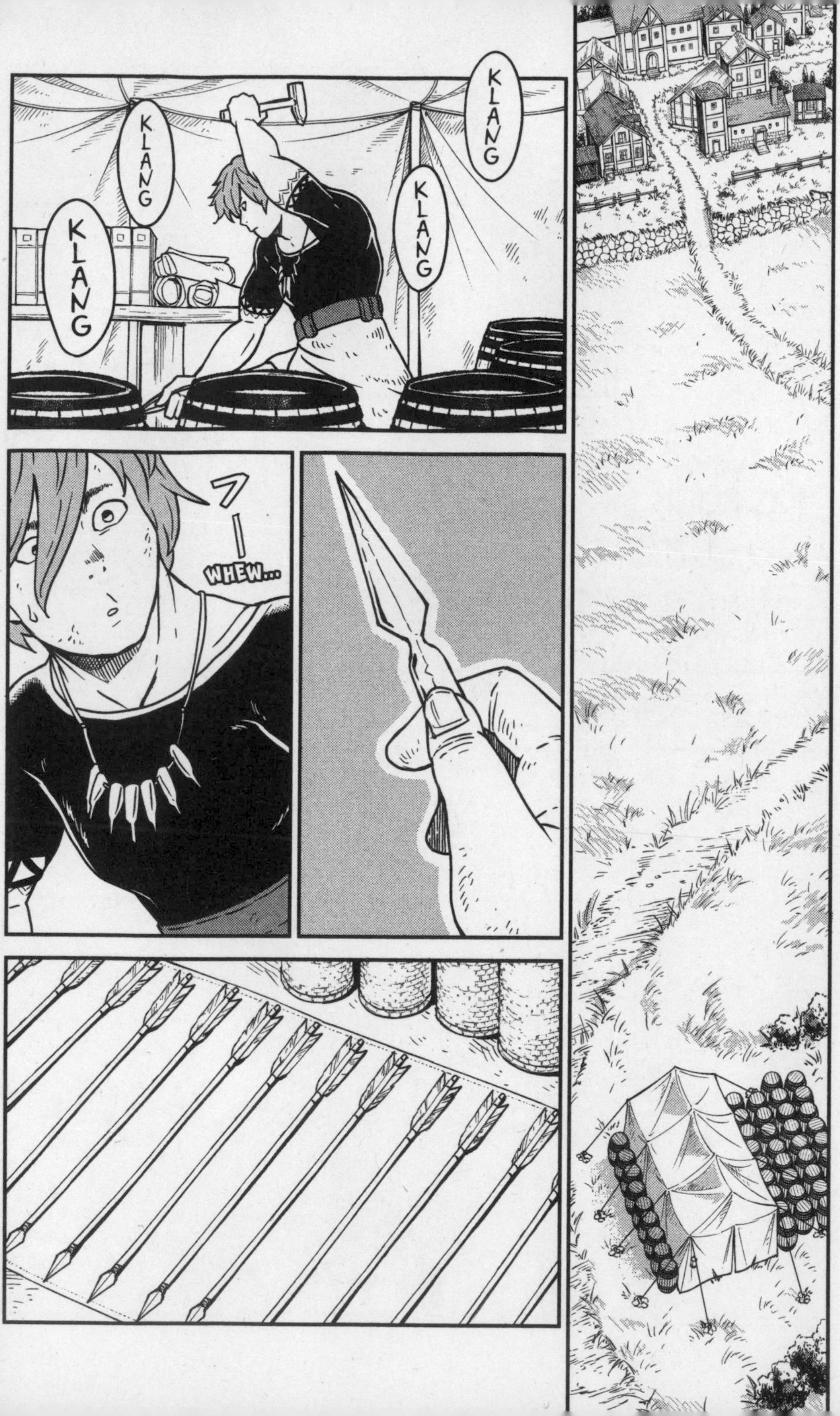
KLANG
KLANG
KLANG
KLANG
フー
WHEW...

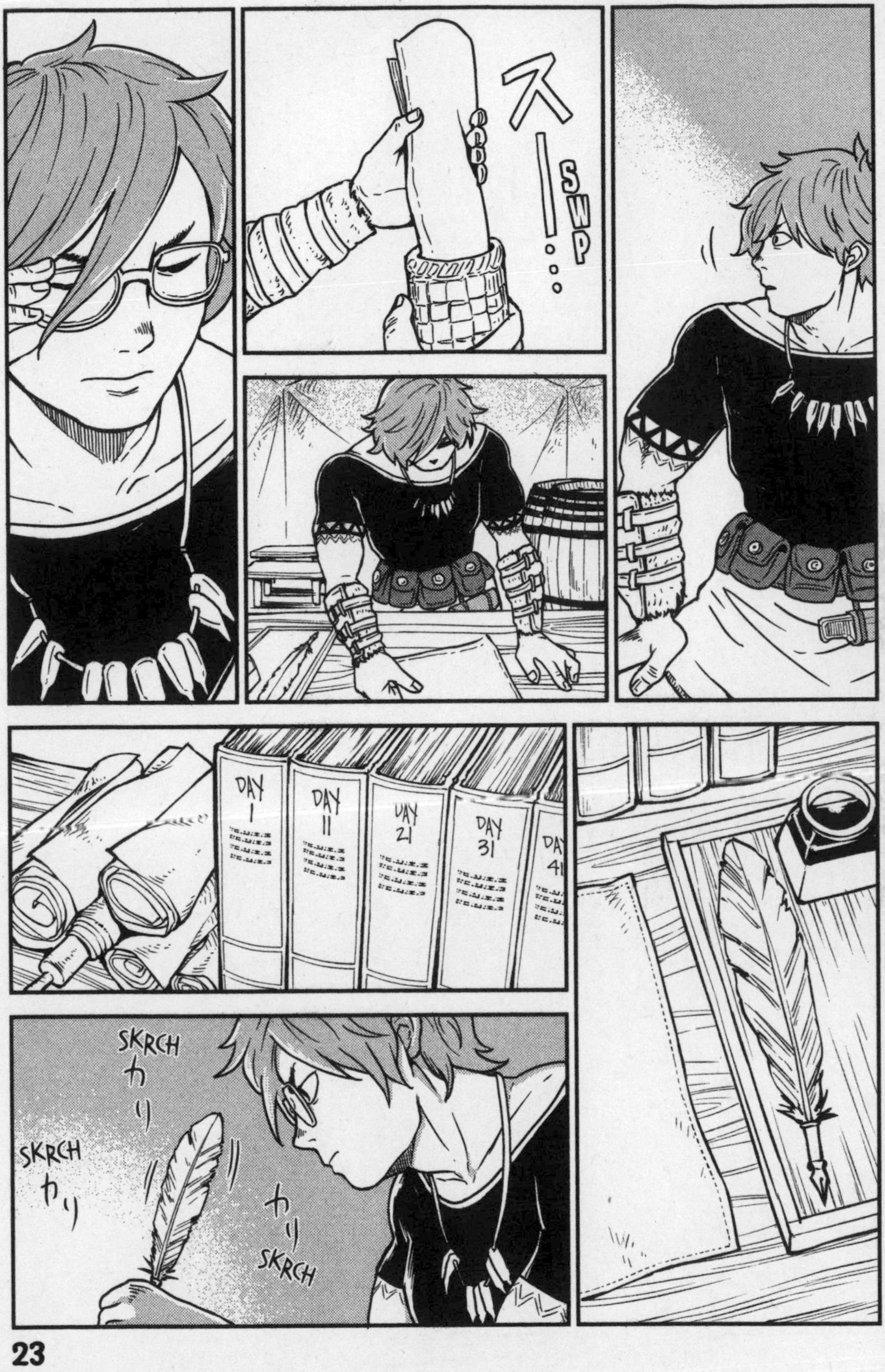
スー…
SWP
DAY 1
DAY 11
DAY 21
DAY 31
DAY 41
SKRCH
カリ
SKRCH
カリ
カリ
SKRCH

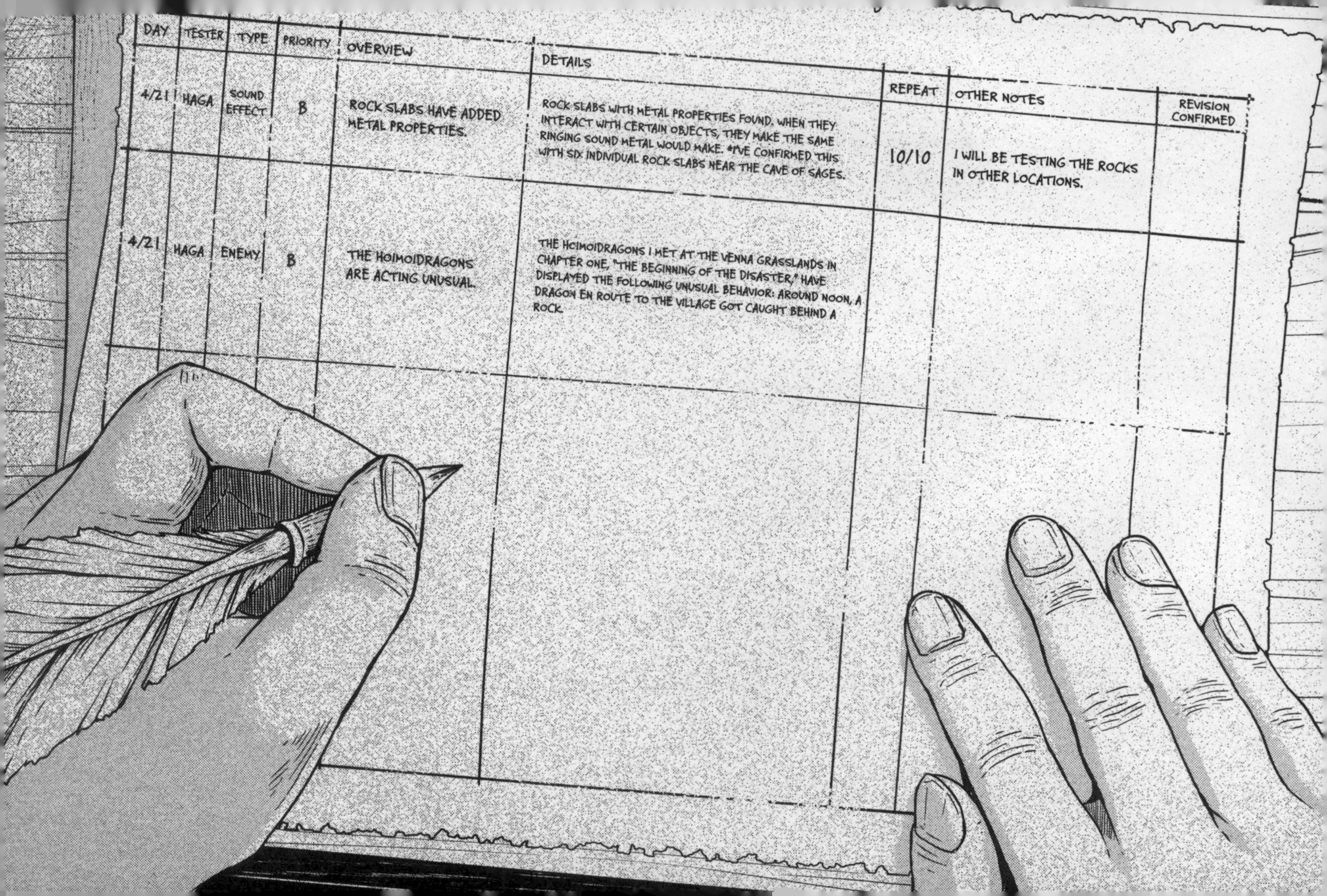
DAY
TESTER
TYPE
PRIORITY
OVERVIEW
DETAILS
REPEAT
OTHER NOTES
REVISION CONFIRMED
4/21
HAGA
SOUND EFFECT
B
ROCK SLABS HAVE ADDED METAL PROPERTIES.
ROCK SLABS WITH METAL PROPERTIES FOUND. WHEN THEY INTERACT WITH CERTAIN OBJECTS, THEY MAKE THE SAME RINGING SOUND METAL WOULD MAKE. *I'VE CONFIRMED THIS WITH SIX INDIVIDUAL ROCK SLABS NEAR THE CAVE OF SAGES.
10/10
I WILL BE TESTING THE ROCKS IN OTHER LOCATIONS.
4/21
HAGA
ENEMY
B
THE HOIMOIDRAGONS ARE ACTING UNUSUAL.
THE HOIMOIDRAGONS I MET AT THE VENNA GRASSLANDS IN CHAPTER ONE, "THE BEGINNING OF THE DISASTER," HAVE DISPLAYED THE FOLLOWING UNUSUAL BEHAVIOR: AROUND NOON, A DRAGON EN ROUTE TO THE VILLAGE GOT CAUGHT BEHIND A ROCK.

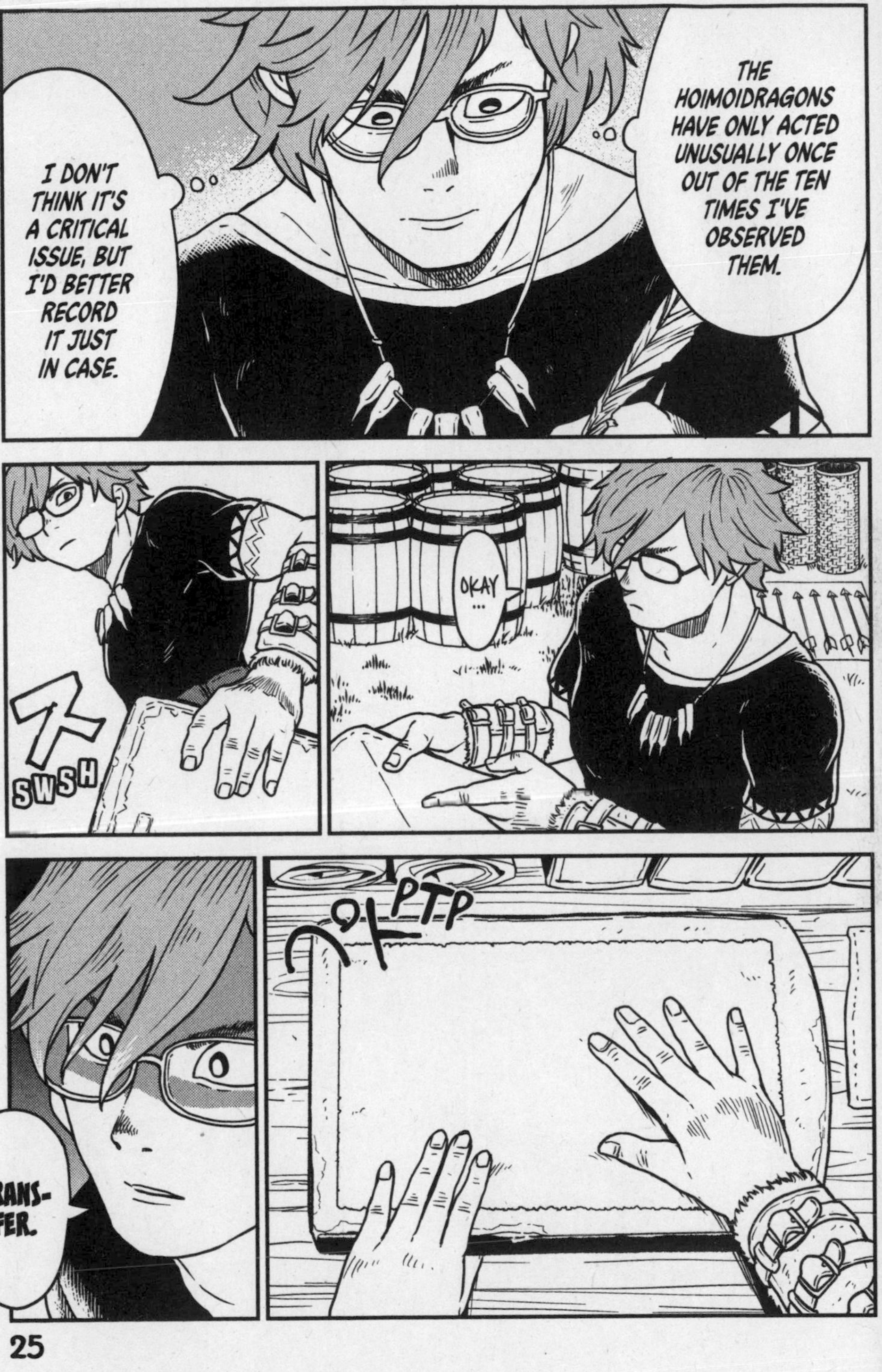
THE HOIMOIDRAGONS HAVE ONLY ACTED UNUSUALLY ONCE OUT OF THE TEN TIMES I'VE OBSERVED THEM.
I DON'T THINK IT'S A CRITICAL ISSUE, BUT I'D BETTER RECORD IT JUST IN CASE.
OKAY...
SWSH
PTP
TRANS-FER.

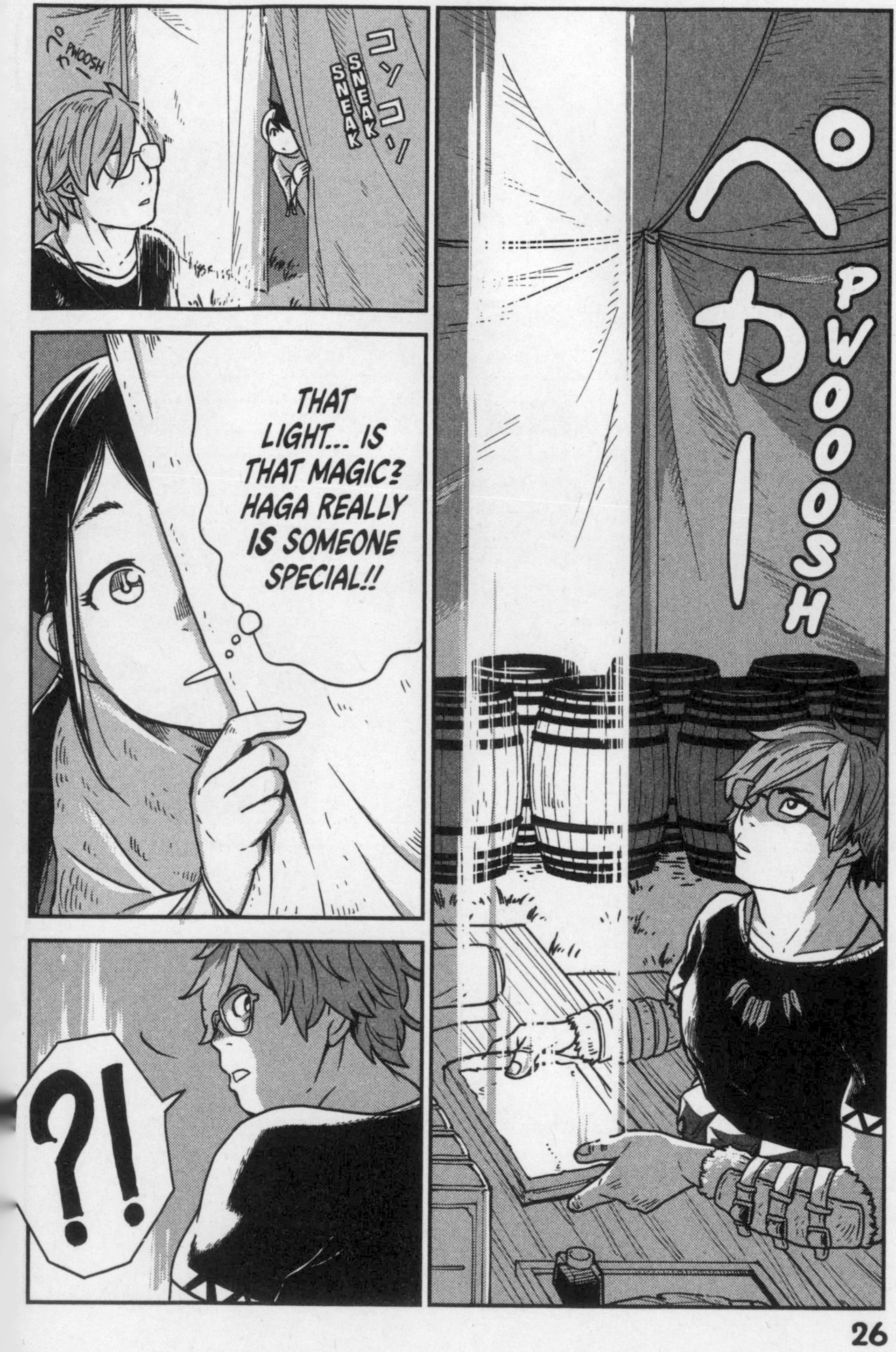
ぺわー
PWOOOOSH
ぱー
PWOOSH
コソコソ
SNEAK SNEAK
THAT LIGHT... IS THAT MAGIC? HAGA REALLY IS SOMEONE SPECIAL!!
?!

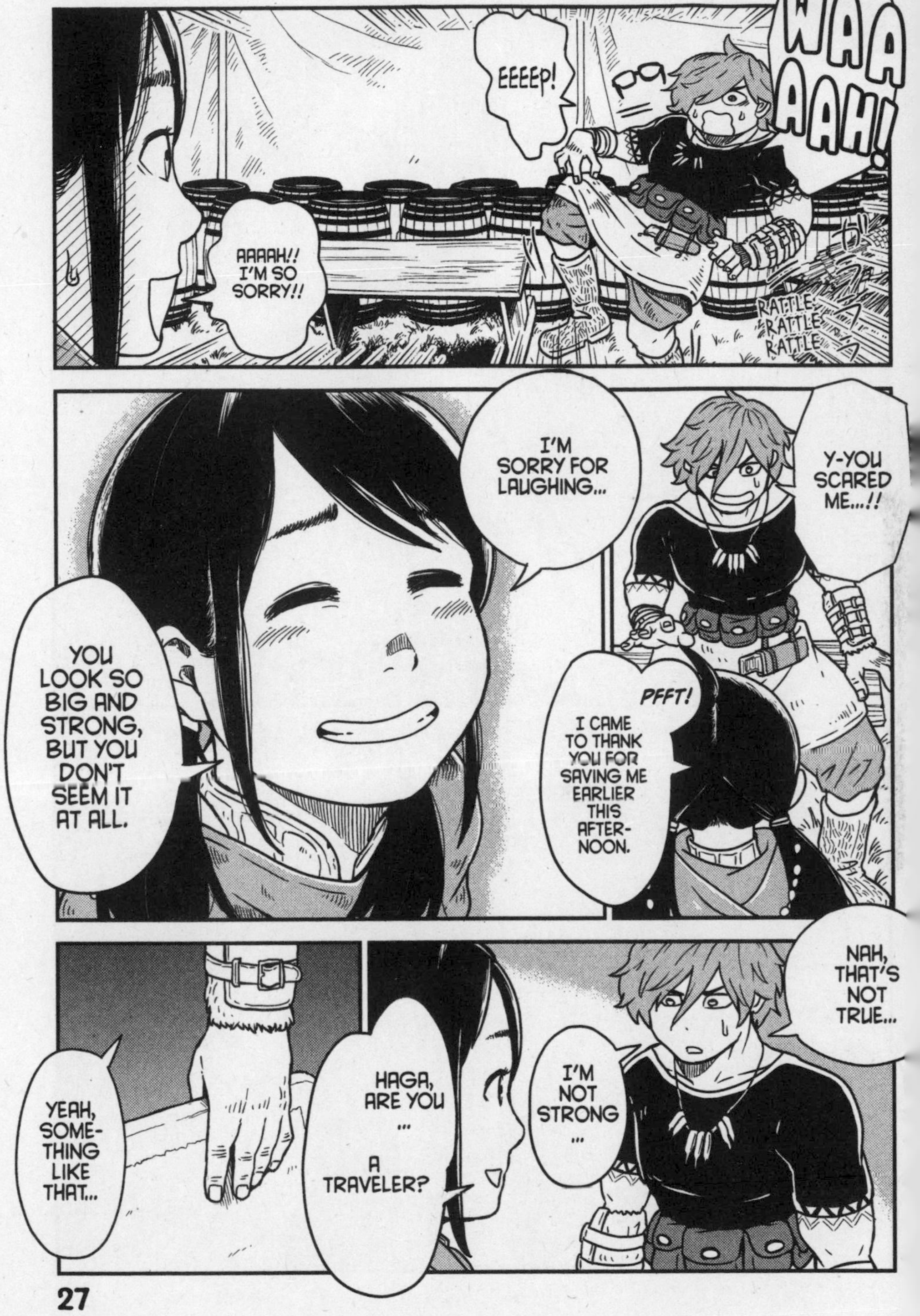
WAAAAH!
EEEEP!
RATTLE RATTLE RATTLE
AAAAH!! I'M SO SORRY!!
Y-YOU SCARED ME...!!
PFFT!
I CAME TO THANK YOU FOR SAVING ME EARLIER THIS AFTER-NOON.
I'M SORRY FOR LAUGHING...
YOU LOOK SO BIG AND STRONG, BUT YOU DON'T SEEM IT AT ALL.
NAH, THAT'S NOT TRUE...
I'M NOT STRONG ...
HAGA, ARE YOU ... A TRAVELER?
YEAH, SOME-THING LIKE THAT...

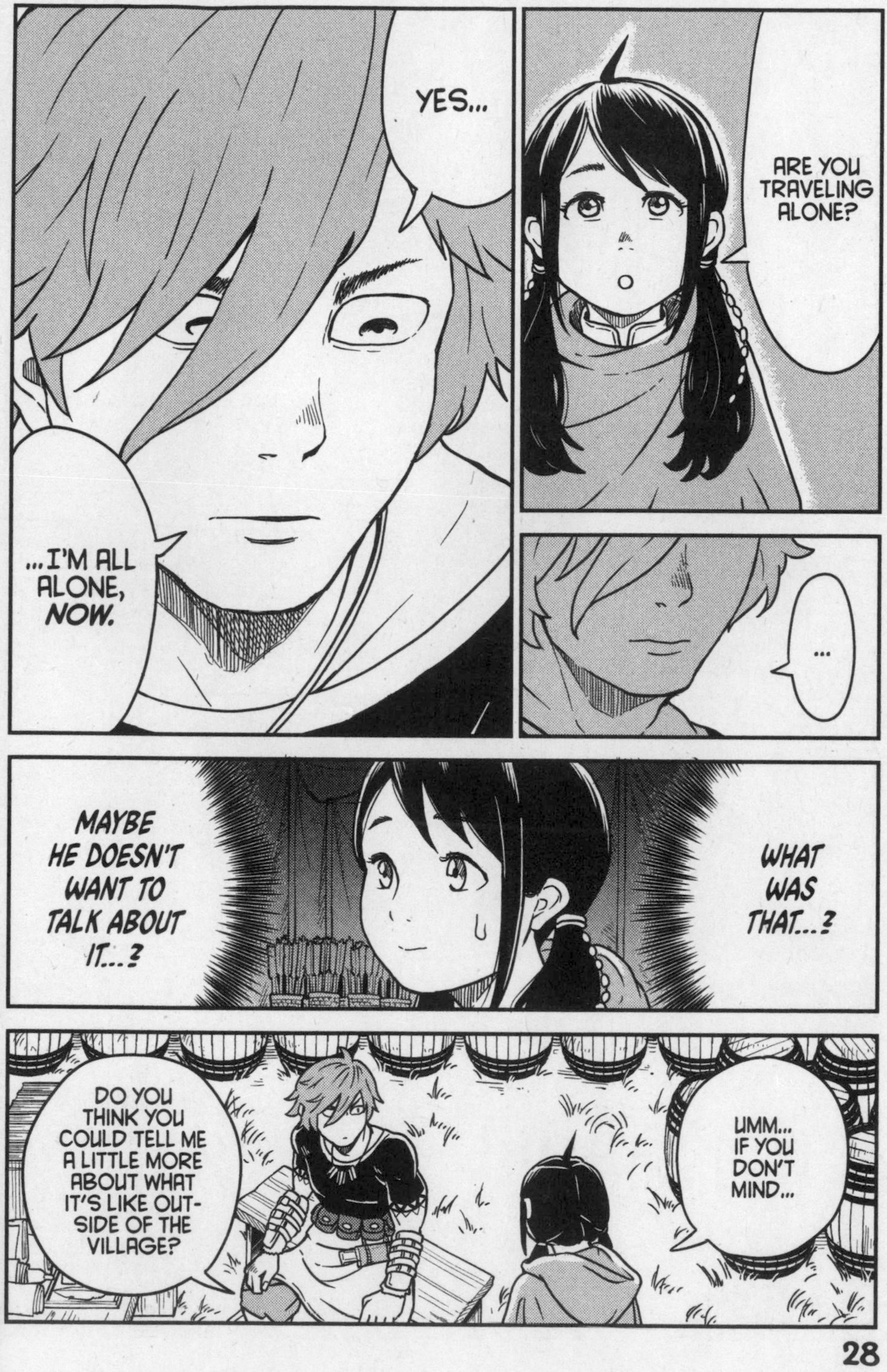
ARE YOU TRAVELING ALONE?
...
YES...
...I'M ALL ALONE, *NOW.*
WHAT WAS THAT...?
MAYBE HE DOESN'T WANT TO TALK ABOUT IT...?
UMM... IF YOU DON'T MIND...
DO YOU THINK YOU COULD TELL ME A LITTLE MORE ABOUT WHAT IT'S LIKE OUT-SIDE OF THE VILLAGE?

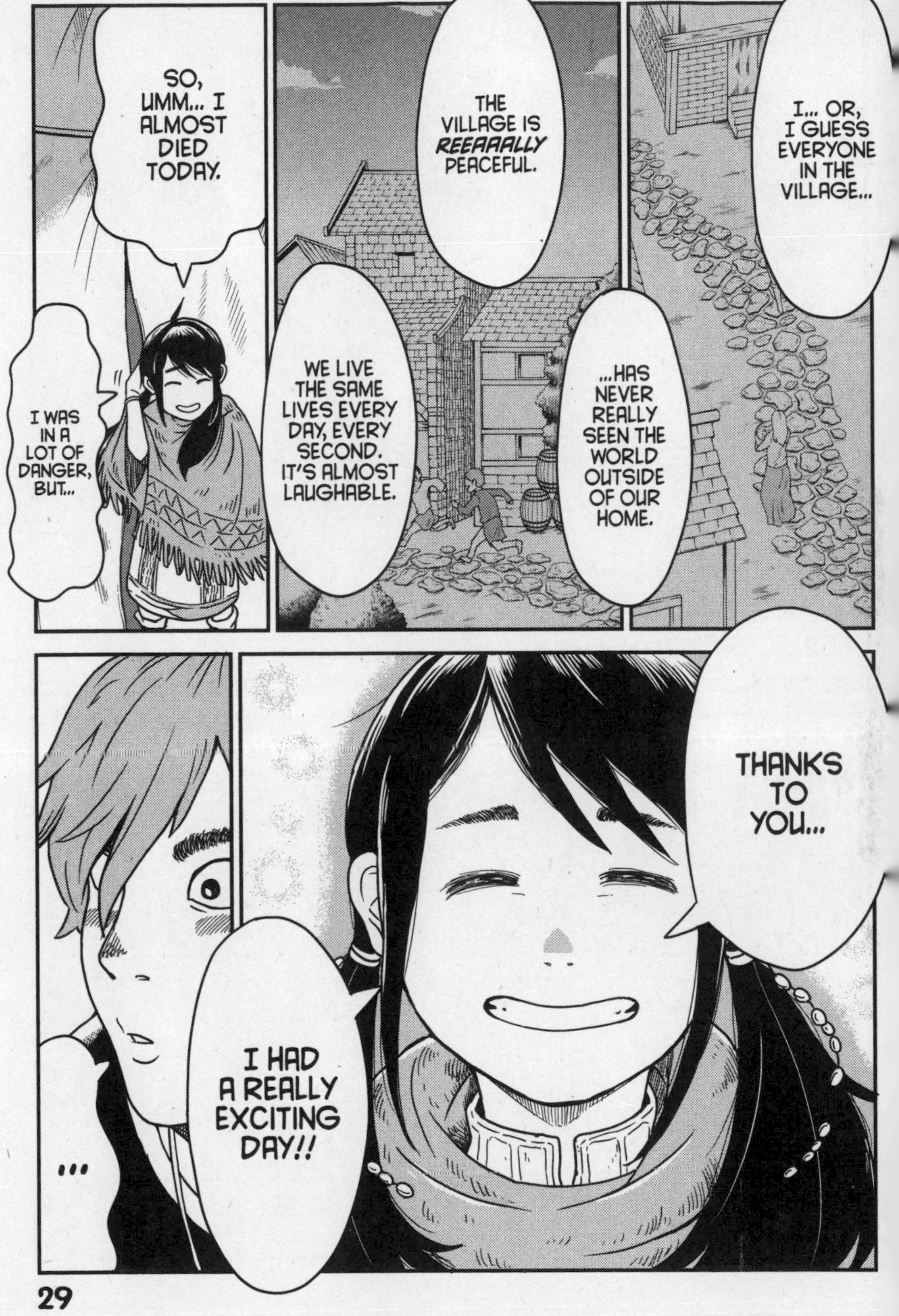
I... OR, I GUESS EVERYONE IN THE VILLAGE...
...HAS NEVER REALLY SEEN THE WORLD OUTSIDE OF OUR HOME.
THE VILLAGE IS *REEAAALLY* PEACEFUL.
WE LIVE THE SAME LIVES EVERY DAY, EVERY SECOND. IT'S ALMOST LAUGHABLE.
SO, UMM... I ALMOST DIED TODAY.
I WAS IN A LOT OF DANGER, BUT...
THANKS TO YOU...
I HAD A REALLY EXCITING DAY!!
...

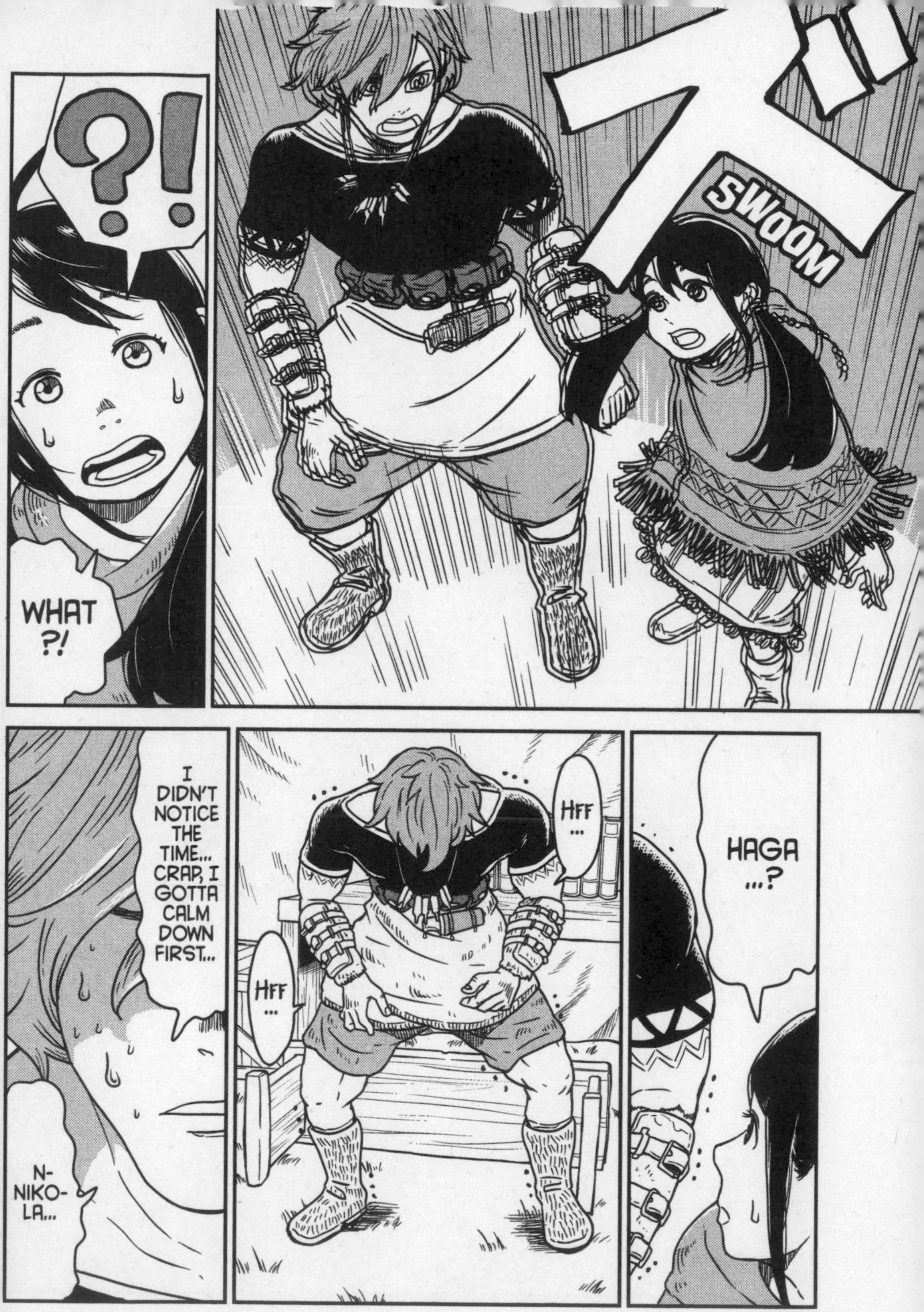
SWOOM
?!
WHAT ?!
HAGA ...?
Hff ...
Hff ...
I DIDN'T NOTICE THE TIME... CRAP, I GOTTA CALM DOWN FIRST...
N-NIKOLA...

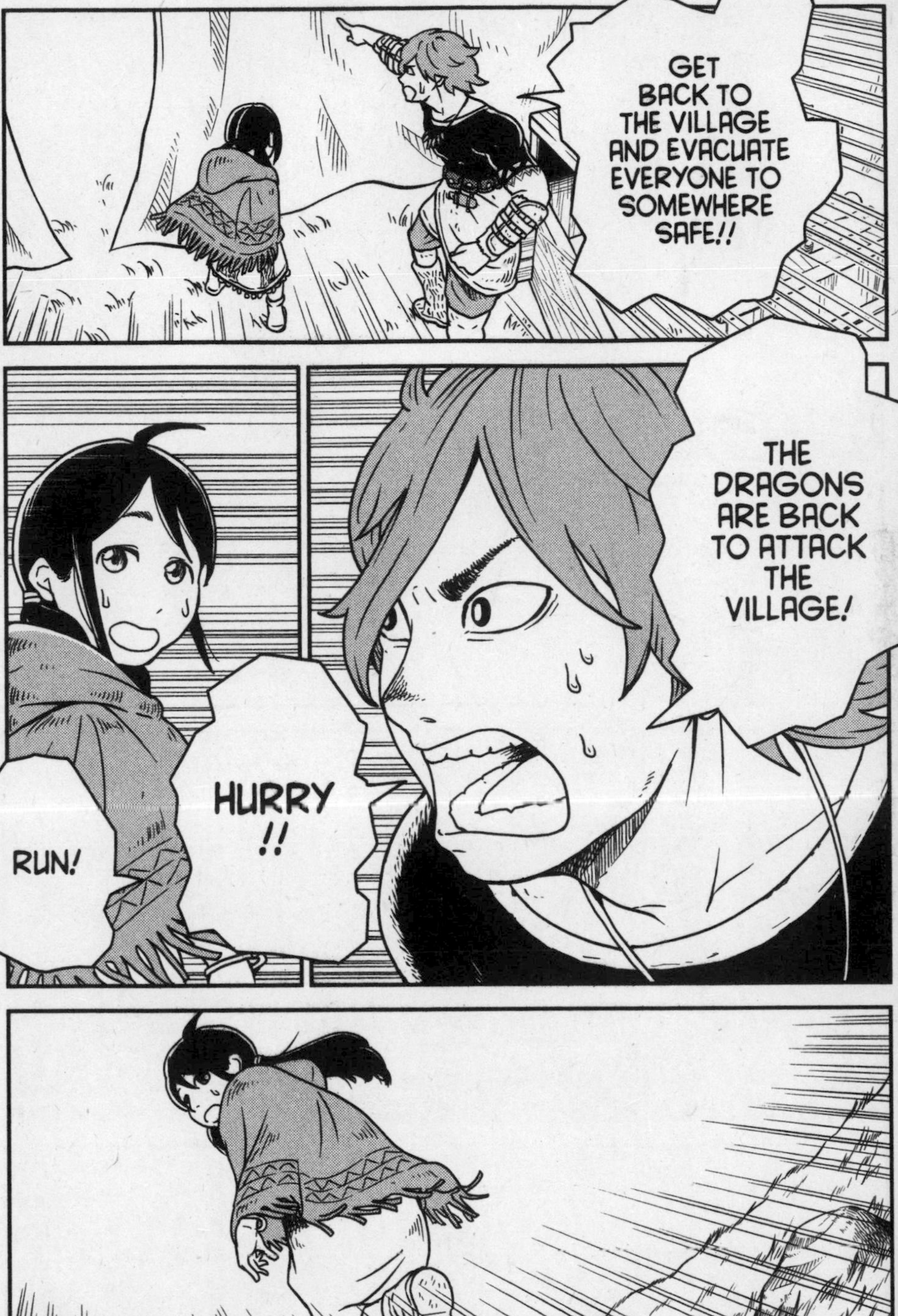
GET BACK TO THE VILLAGE AND EVACUATE EVERYONE TO SOMEWHERE SAFE!!
THE DRAGONS ARE BACK TO ATTACK THE VILLAGE!
HURRY!!
RUN!

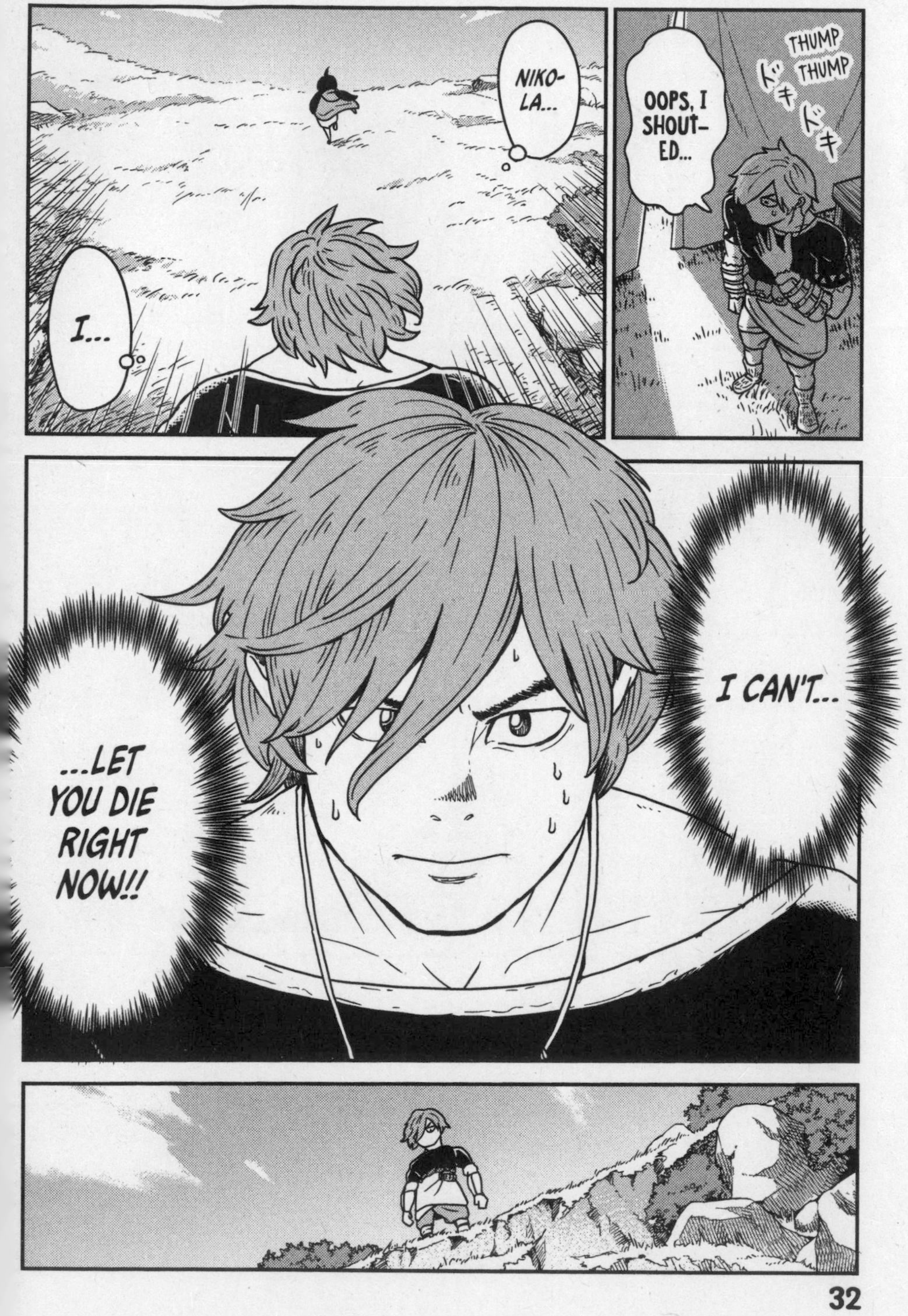
THUMP THUMP
ドキドキ
OOPS, I SHOUT-ED...
NIKO-LA...
I...
I CAN'T...
...LET YOU DIE RIGHT NOW!!

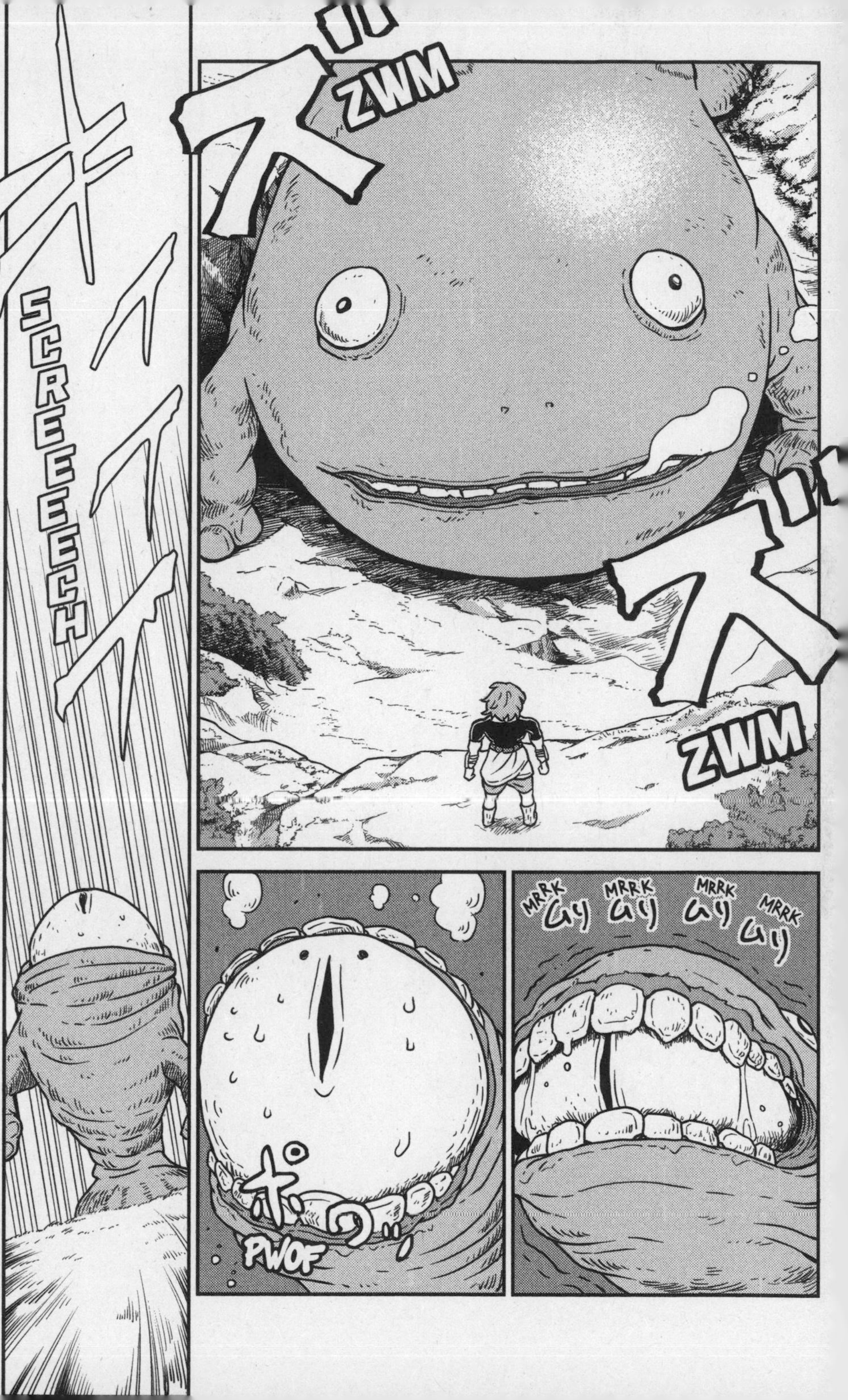
ZWM
ZWM
MRRK
MRRK
MRRK
MRRK
PWOF
SCREEEECH

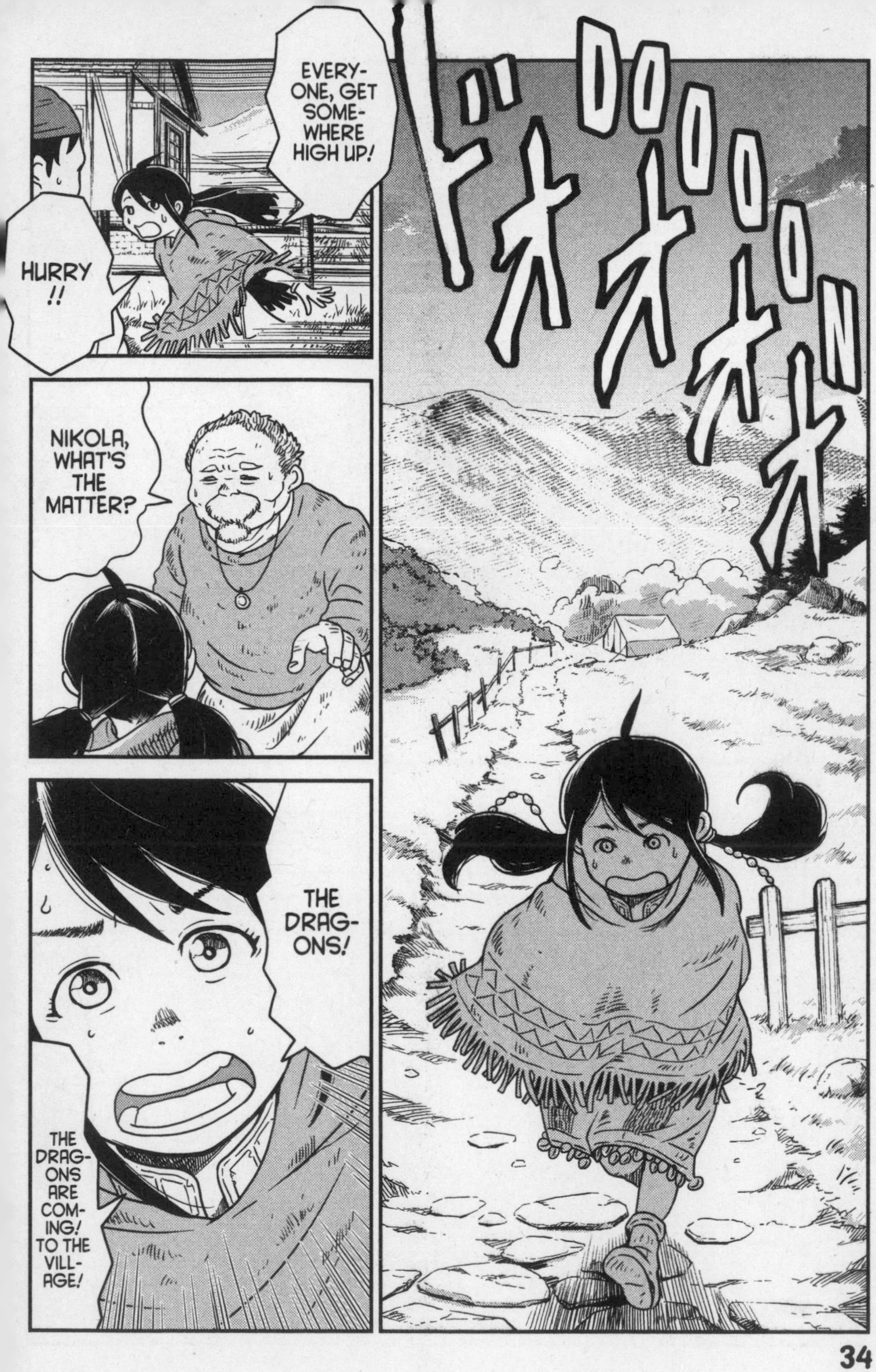
DOOOOOOON
EVERY-ONE, GET SOME-WHERE HIGH UP!
HURRY!!
NIKOLA, WHAT'S THE MATTER?
THE DRAG-ONS!
THE DRAG-ONS ARE COM-ING! TO THE VILL-AGE!

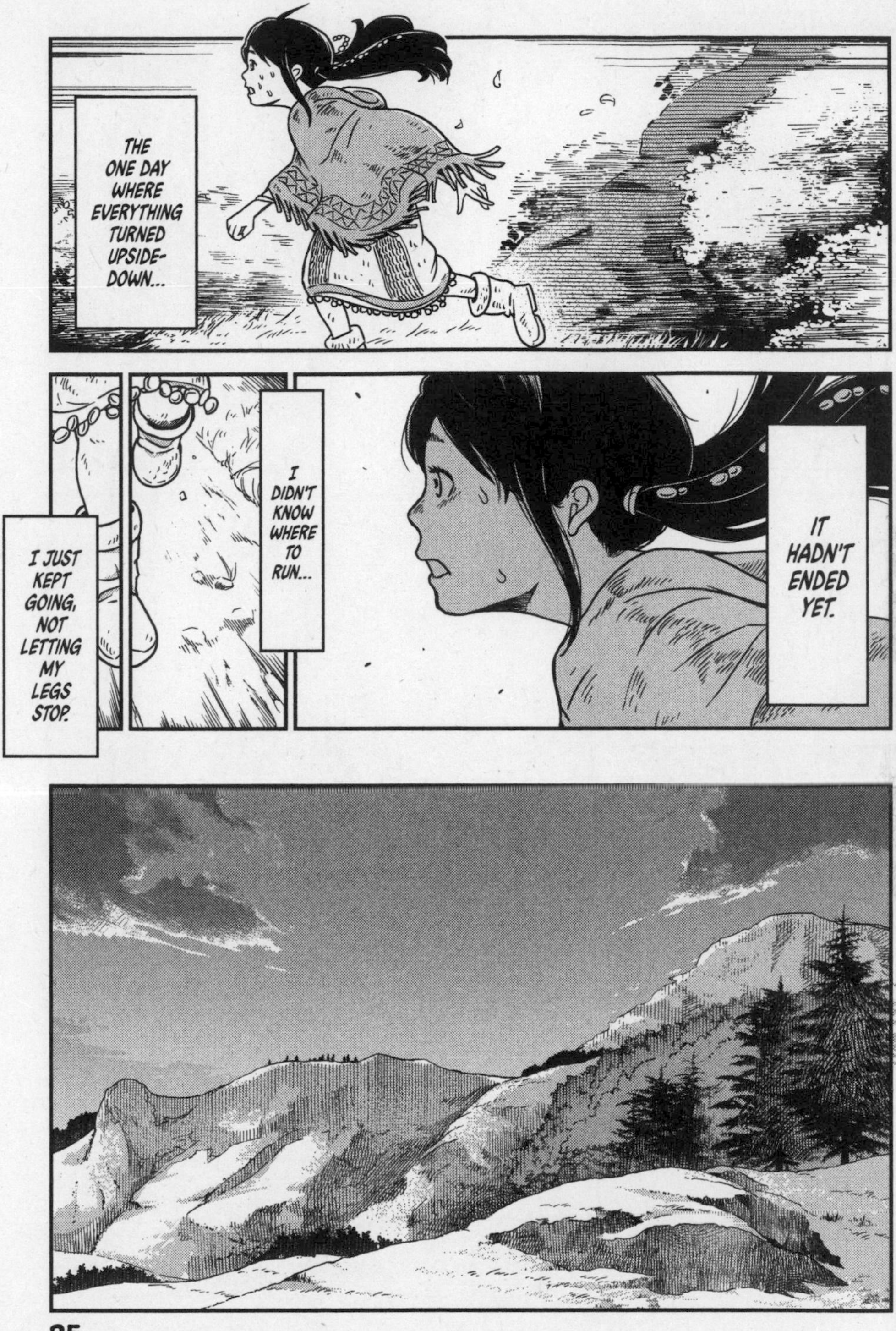
THE ONE DAY WHERE EVERYTHING TURNED UPSIDE-DOWN...
IT HADN'T ENDED YET.
I DIDN'T KNOW WHERE TO RUN...
I JUST KEPT GOING, NOT LETTING MY LEGS STOP.

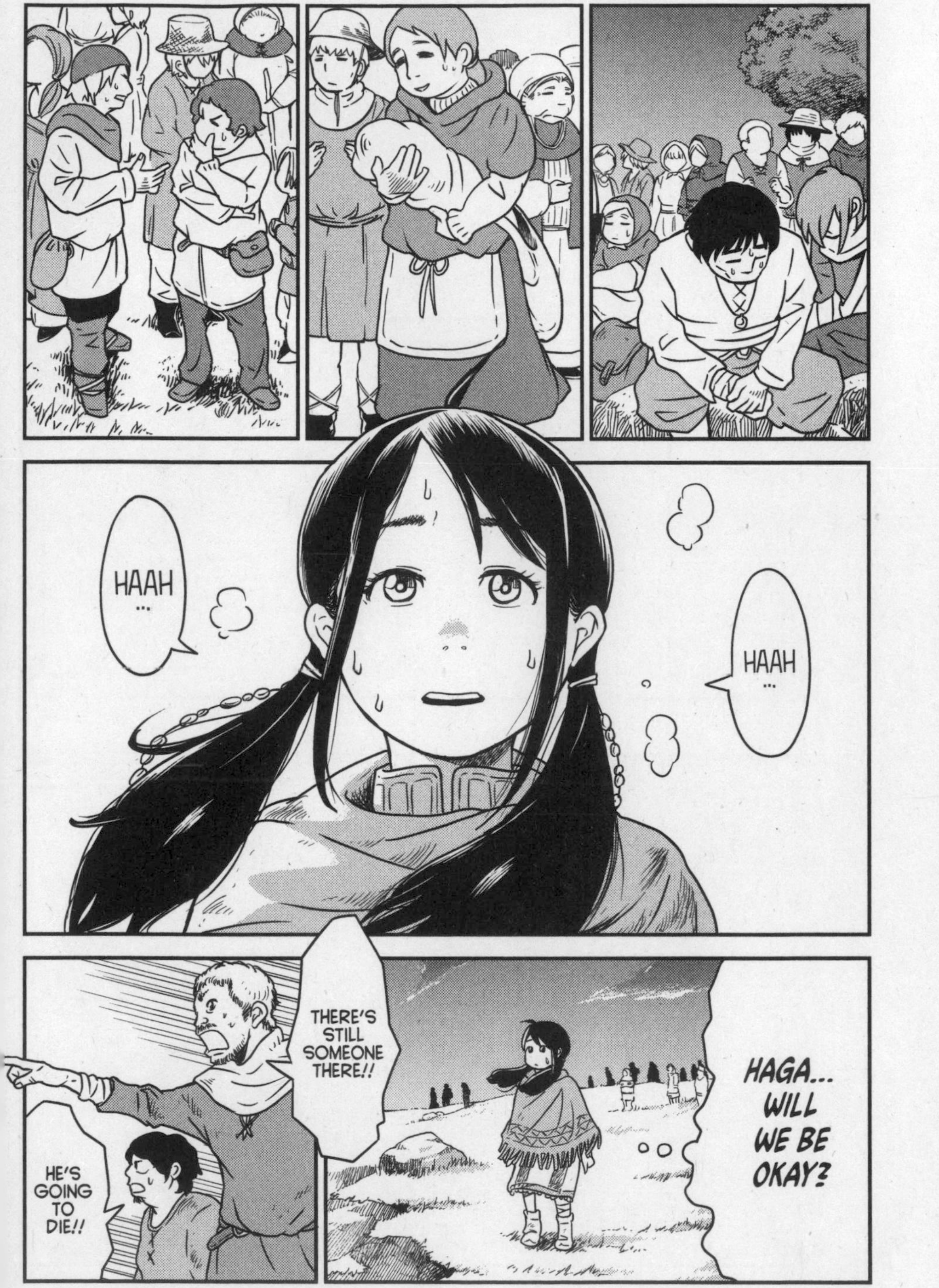
HAAH ...
HAAH ...
HAGA... WILL WE BE OKAY?
THERE'S STILL SOMEONE THERE!!
HE'S GOING TO DIE!!

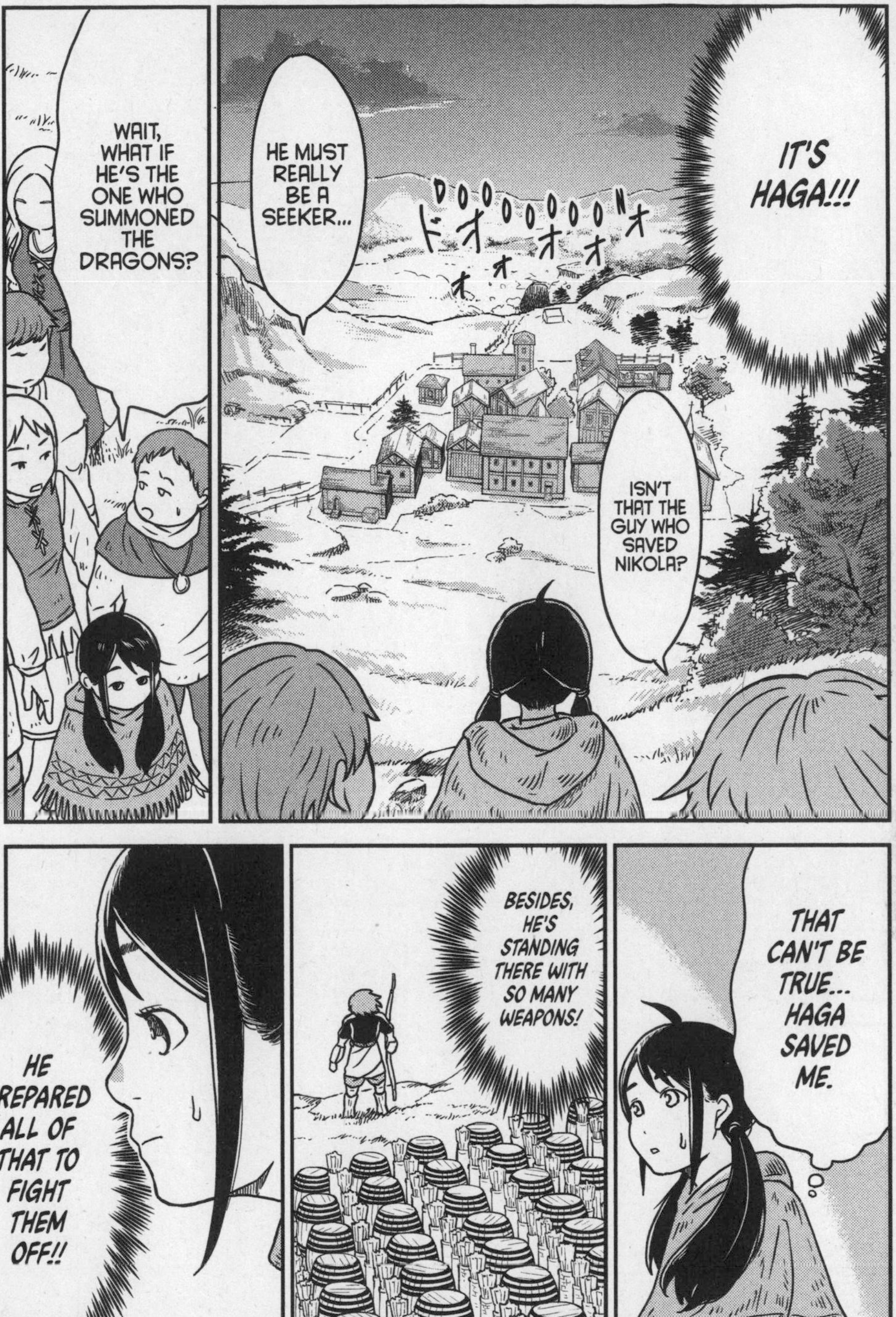
IT'S HAGA!!!
HE MUST REALLY BE A SEEKER...
DOOOOOOOON
ISN'T THAT THE GUY WHO SAVED NIKOLA?
WAIT, WHAT IF HE'S THE ONE WHO SUMMONED THE DRAGONS?
THAT CAN'T BE TRUE... HAGA SAVED ME.
BESIDES, HE'S STANDING THERE WITH SO MANY WEAPONS!
HE PREPARED ALL OF THAT TO FIGHT THEM OFF!!

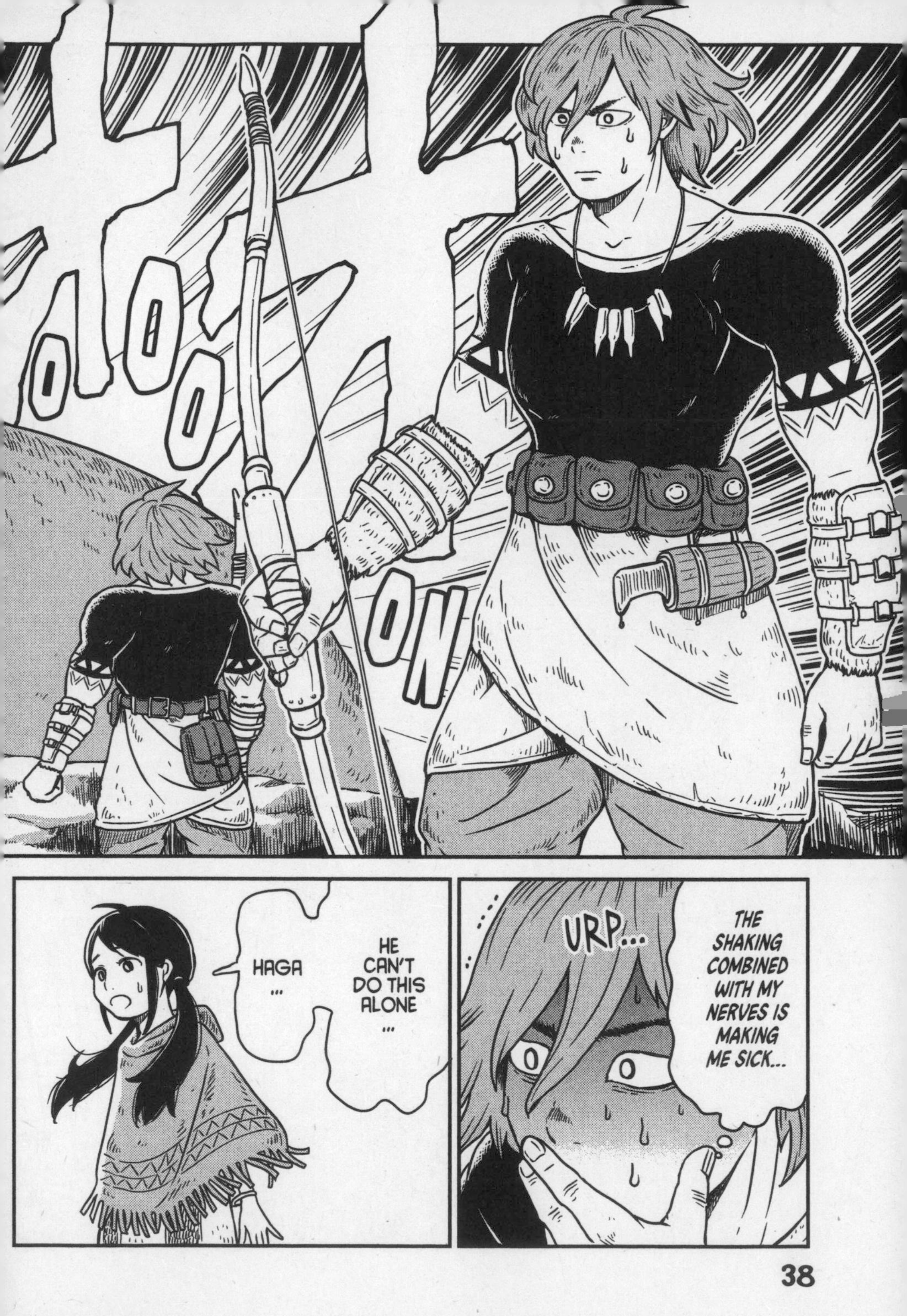
OOO
ON
URP...
THE SHAKING COMBINED WITH MY NERVES IS MAKING ME SICK...
HAGA ...
HE CAN'T DO THIS ALONE ...

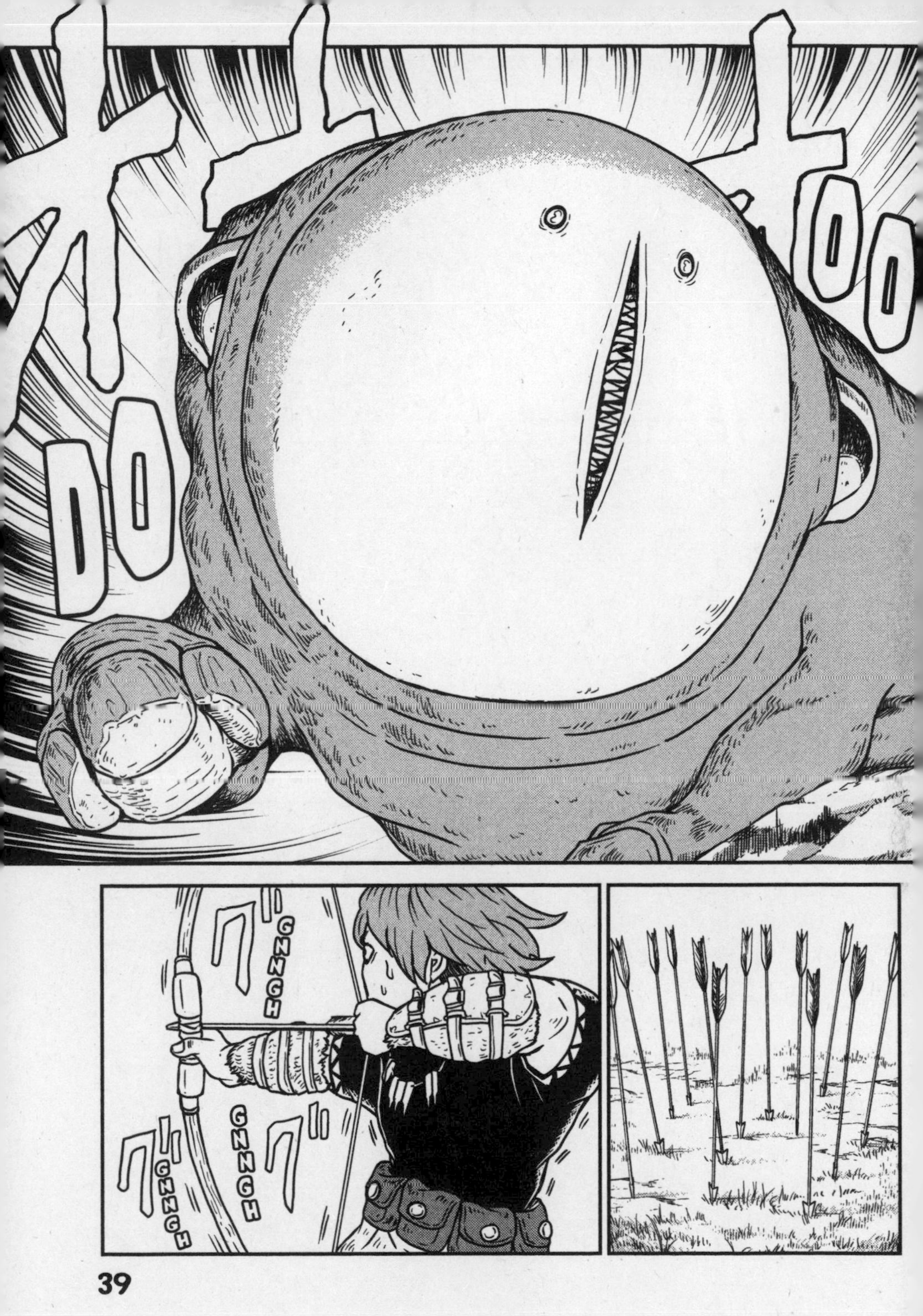
DOO
DO
GNNGH
GNNGH
GNNGH

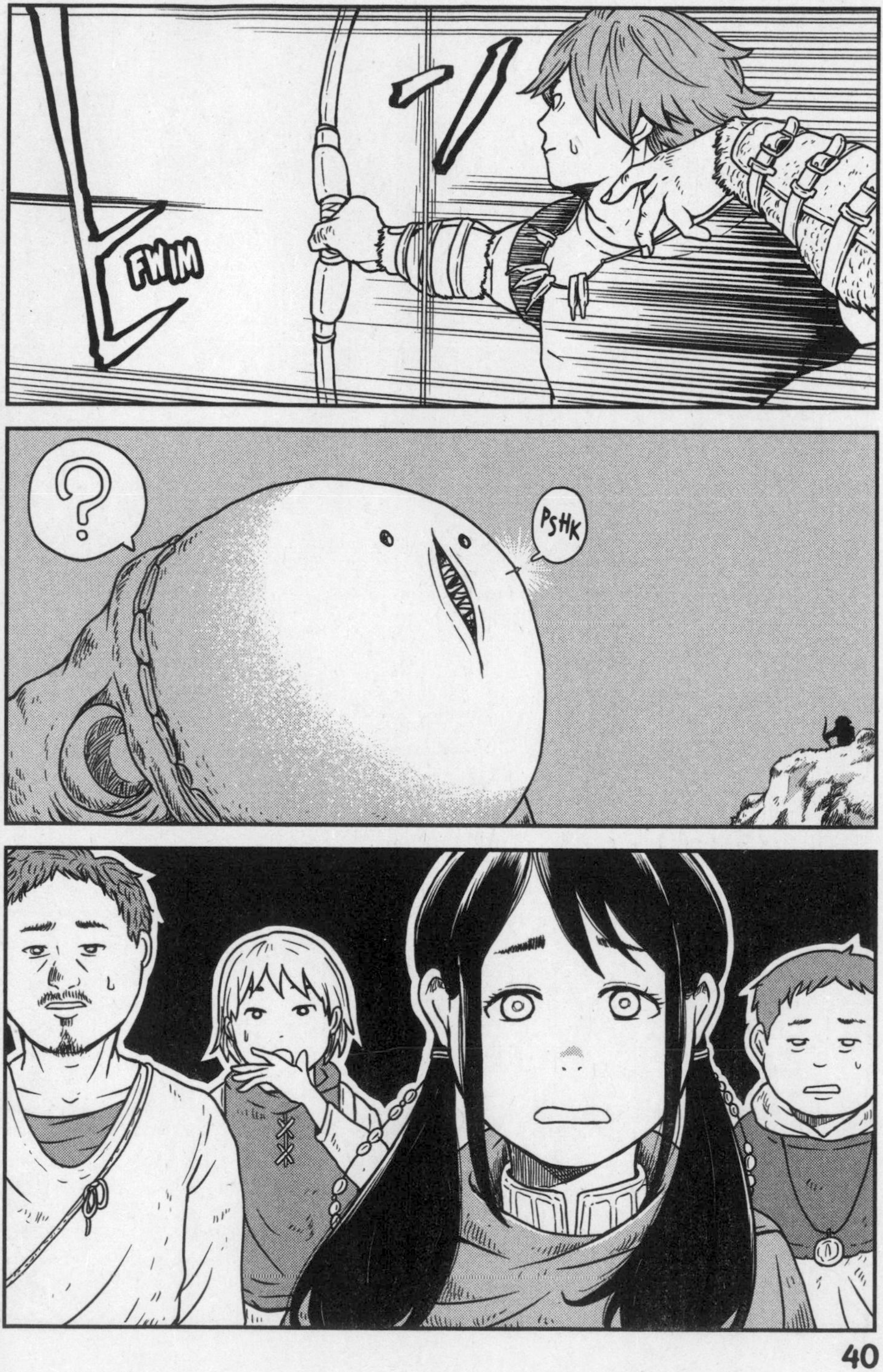
FWIM
?
PSHK

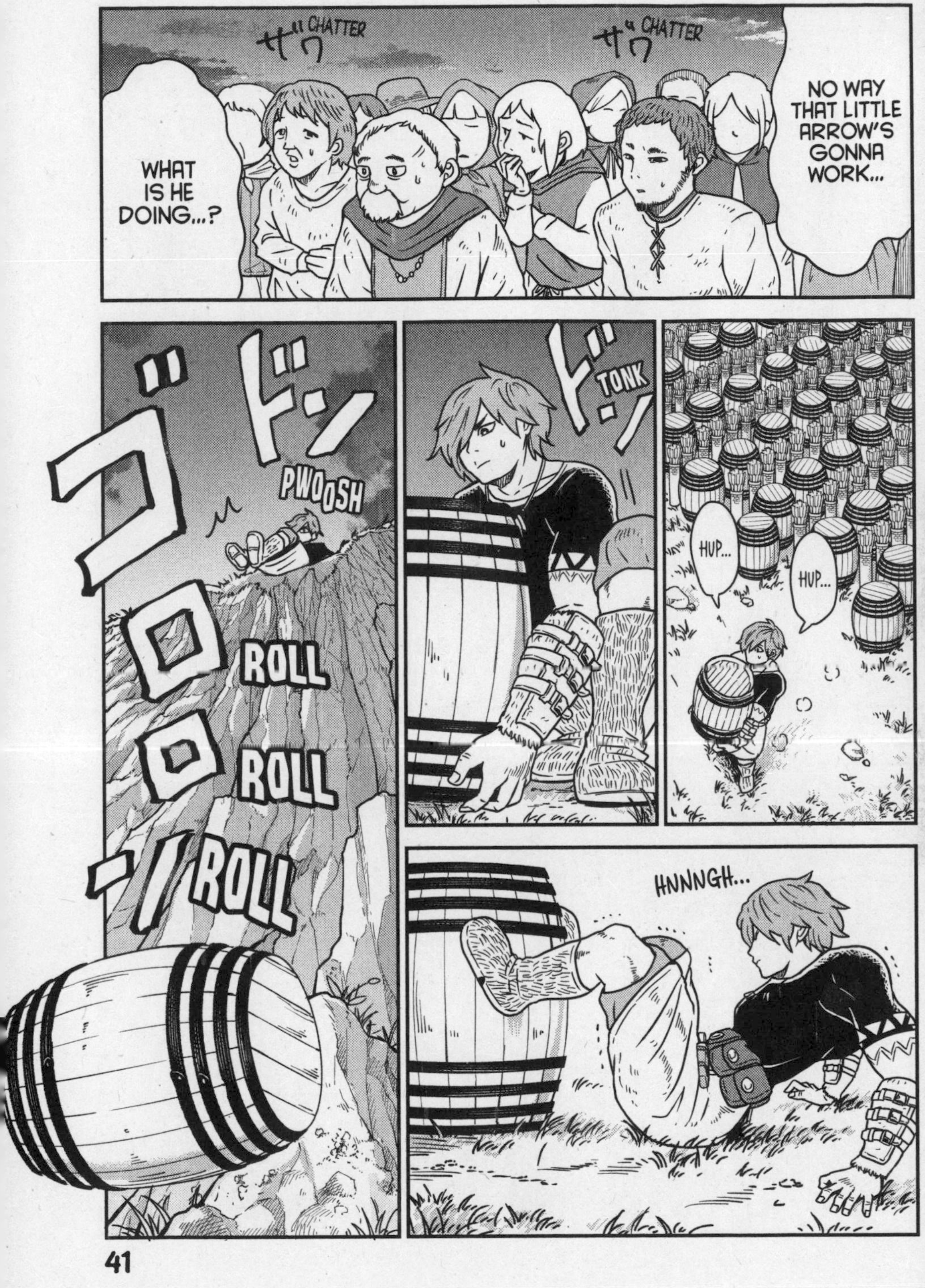
NO WAY THAT LITTLE ARROW'S GONNA WORK...
ザワ CHATTER
ザワ CHATTER
WHAT IS HE DOING...?
HUP...
HUP...
ドン TONK
HNNNGH...
ドン
PWOOSH
ゴロロー
ROLL
ROLL
ROLL

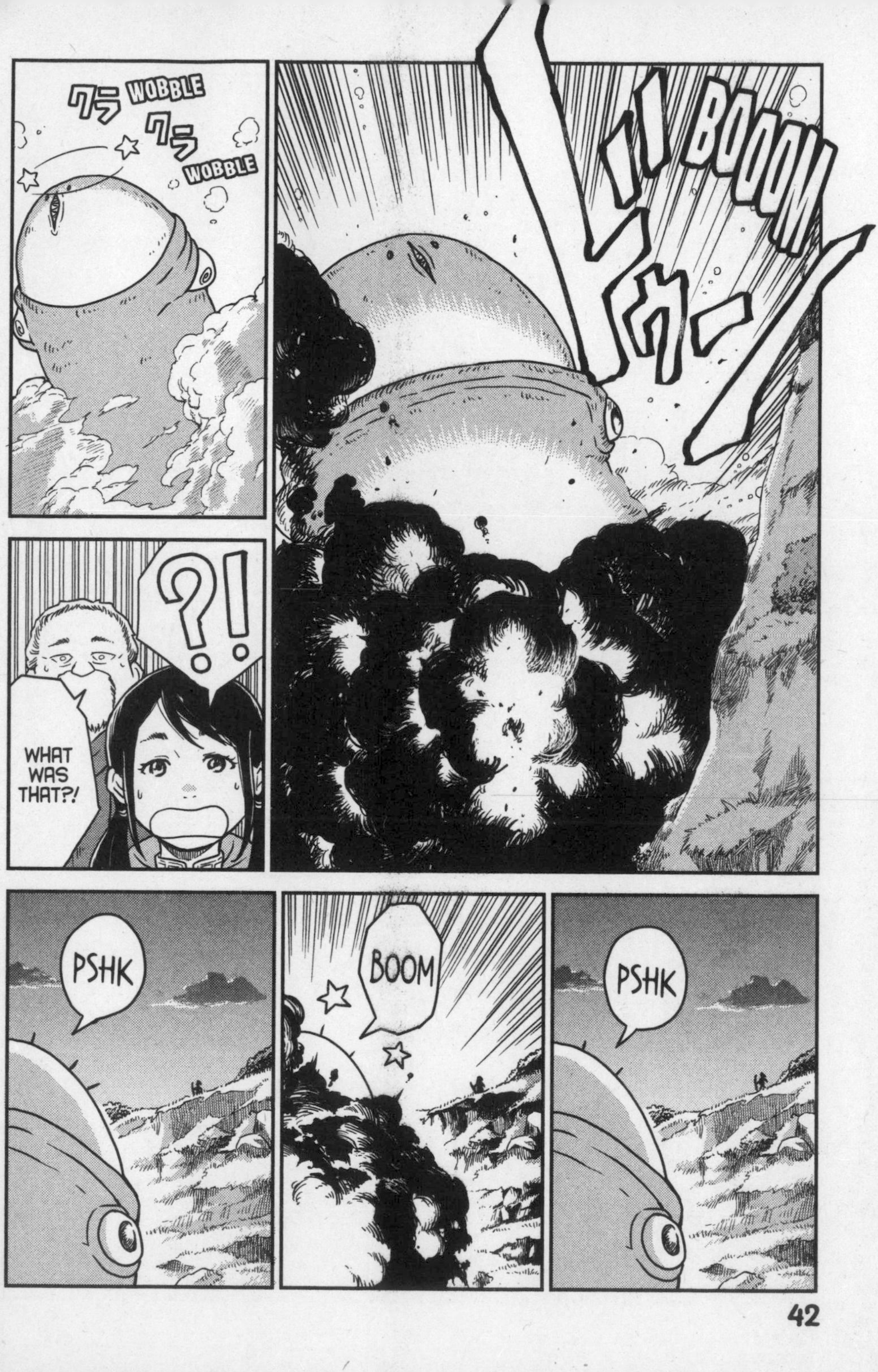

BOOOM
クラ WOBBLE
クラ WOBBLE
?!
WHAT WAS THAT?!
PSHK
BOOM
PSHK

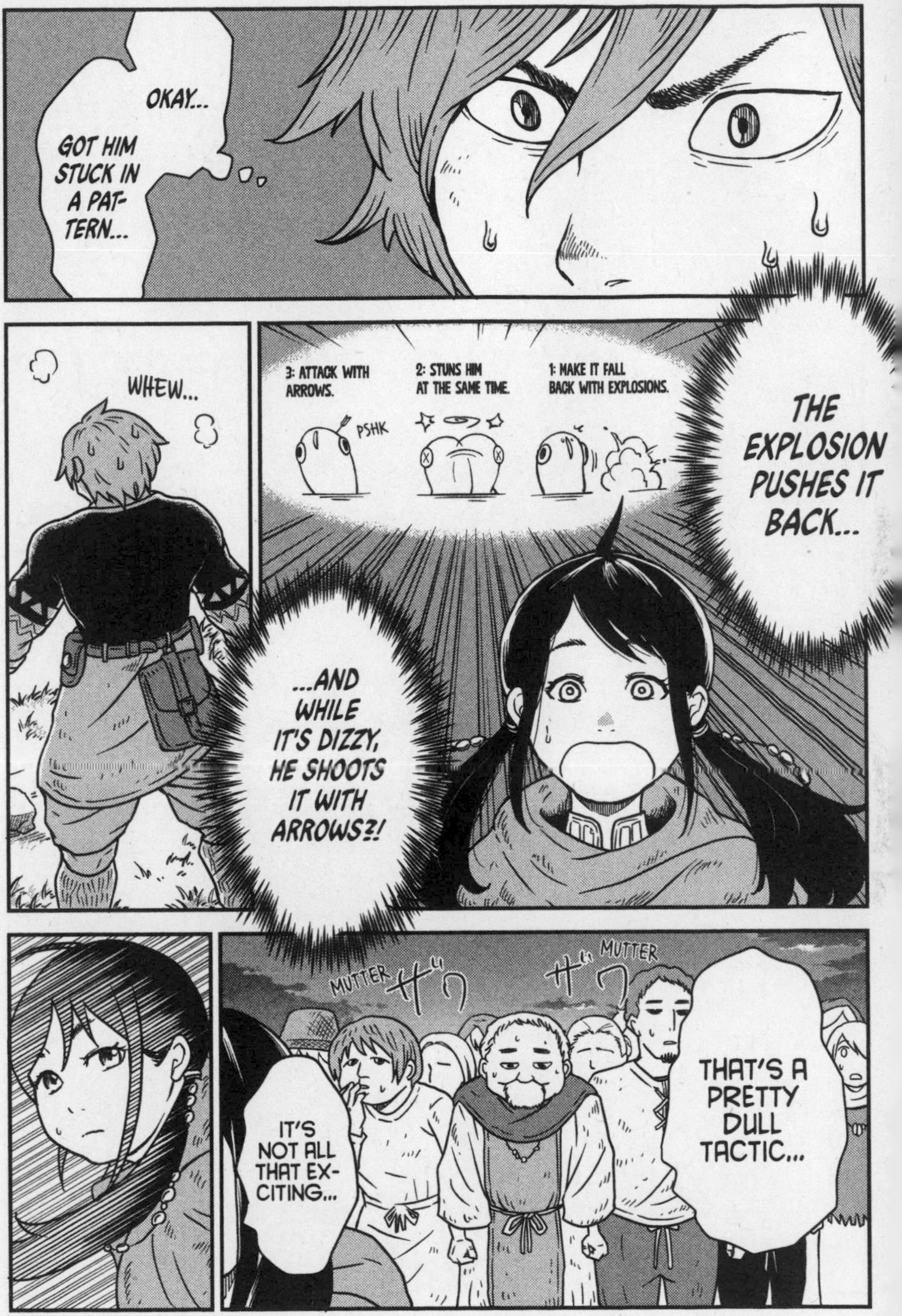
OKAY...
GOT HIM STUCK IN A PAT-TERN...
THE EXPLOSION PUSHES IT BACK...
1: MAKE IT FALL BACK WITH EXPLOSIONS.
2: STUNS HIM AT THE SAME TIME.
3: ATTACK WITH ARROWS.
PSHK
...AND WHILE IT'S DIZZY, HE SHOOTS IT WITH ARROWS?!
WHEW...
MUTTER
ザワ
MUTTER
ザワ
THAT'S A PRETTY DULL TACTIC...
IT'S NOT ALL THAT EX-CITING...

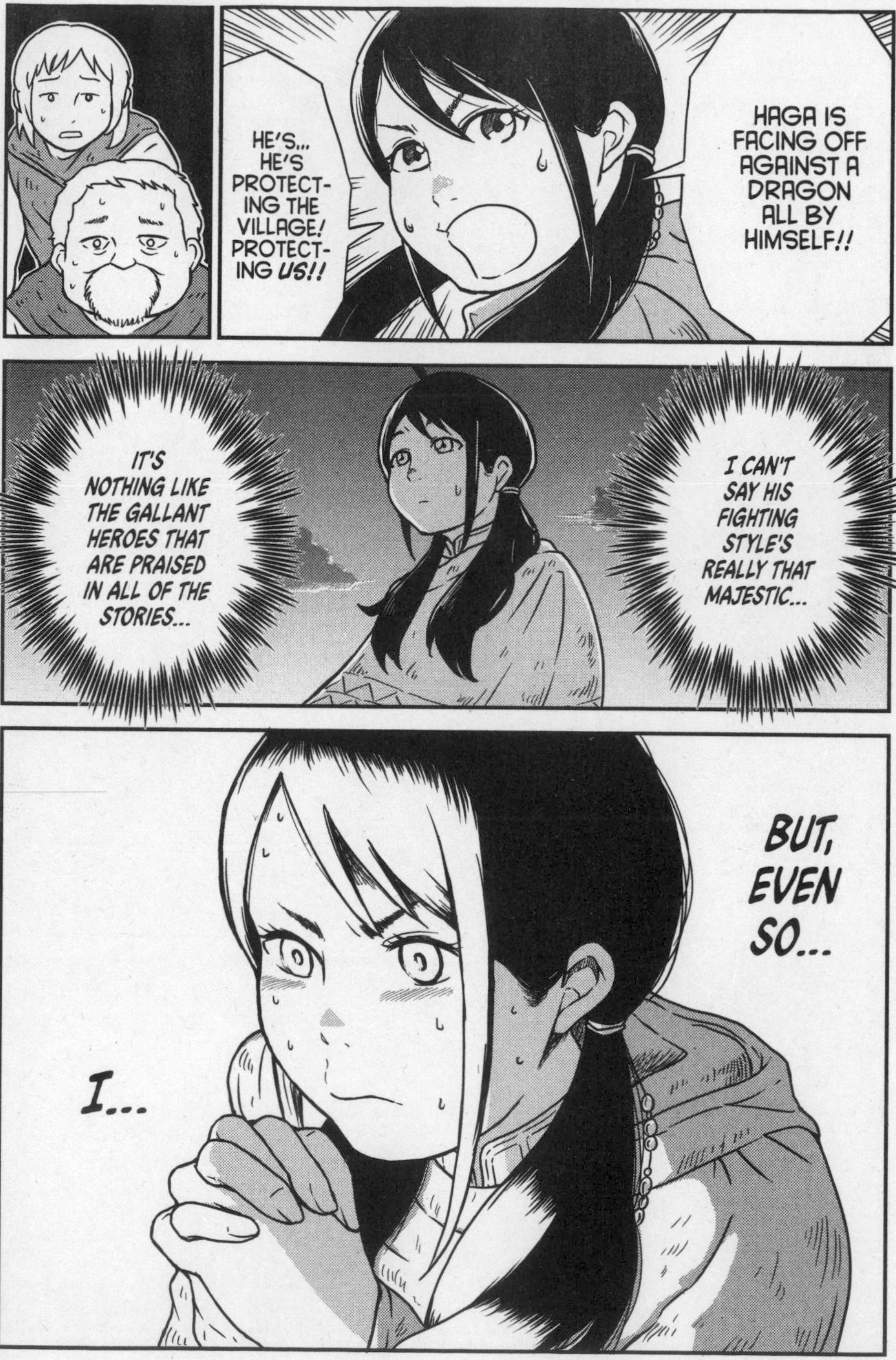
HAGA IS FACING OFF AGAINST A DRAGON ALL BY HIMSELF!!
HE'S... HE'S PROTECTING THE VILLAGE! PROTECTING *US!!*
I CAN'T SAY HIS FIGHTING STYLE'S REALLY THAT MAJESTIC...
IT'S NOTHING LIKE THE GALLANT HEROES THAT ARE PRAISED IN ALL OF THE STORIES...
BUT, EVEN SO...
I...

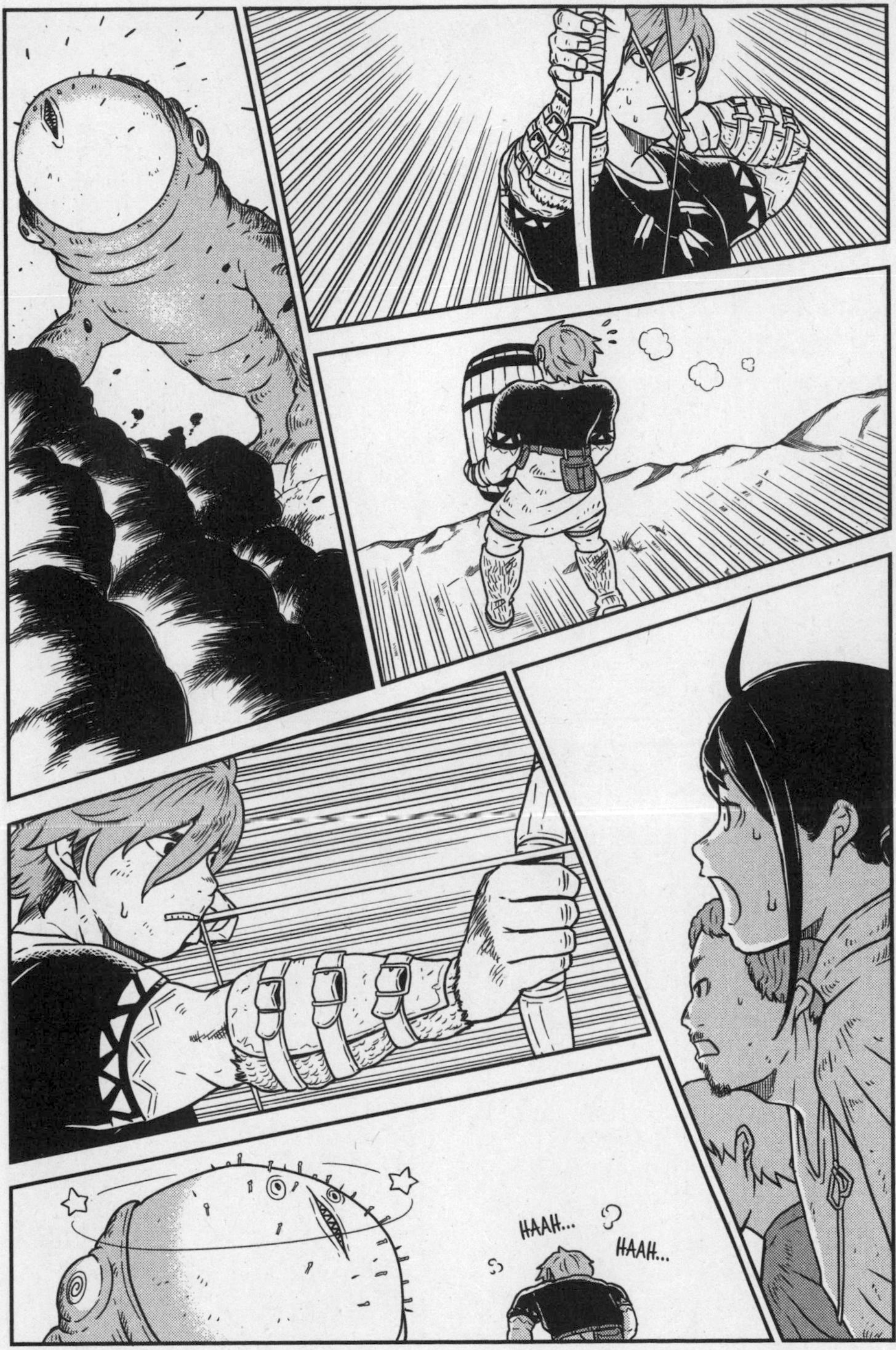
HAAH...
HAAH...

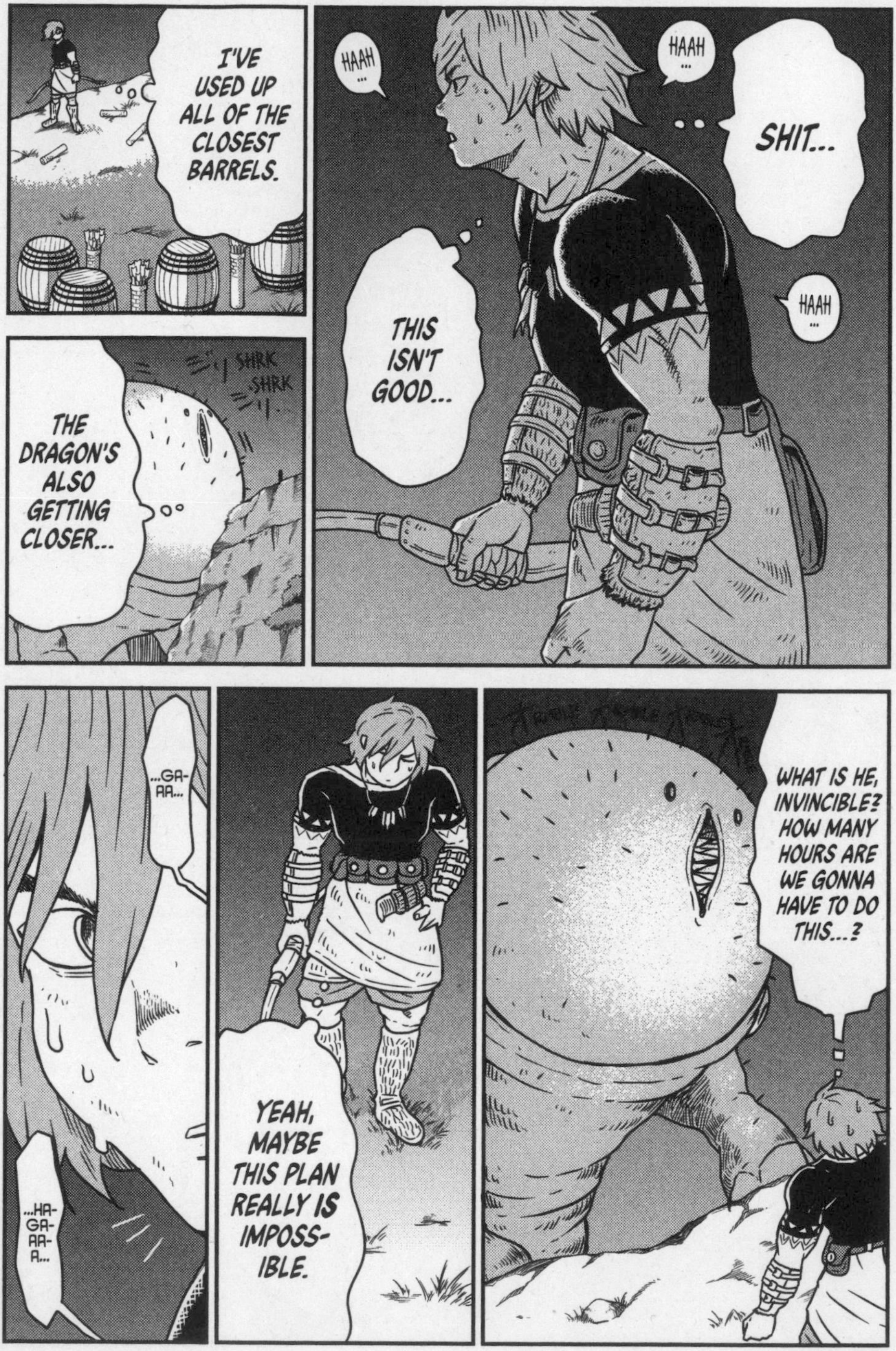
HAAH ...
SHIT...
HAAH ...
THIS ISN'T GOOD...
HAAH ...
I'VE USED UP ALL OF THE CLOSEST BARRELS.
SHRK SHRK
THE DRAGON'S ALSO GETTING CLOSER...
WHAT IS HE, INVINCIBLE? HOW MANY HOURS ARE WE GONNA HAVE TO DO THIS...?
YEAH, MAYBE THIS PLAN REALLY IS IMPOSS-IBLE.
...GA-AA...
...HA-GA-AA-A...

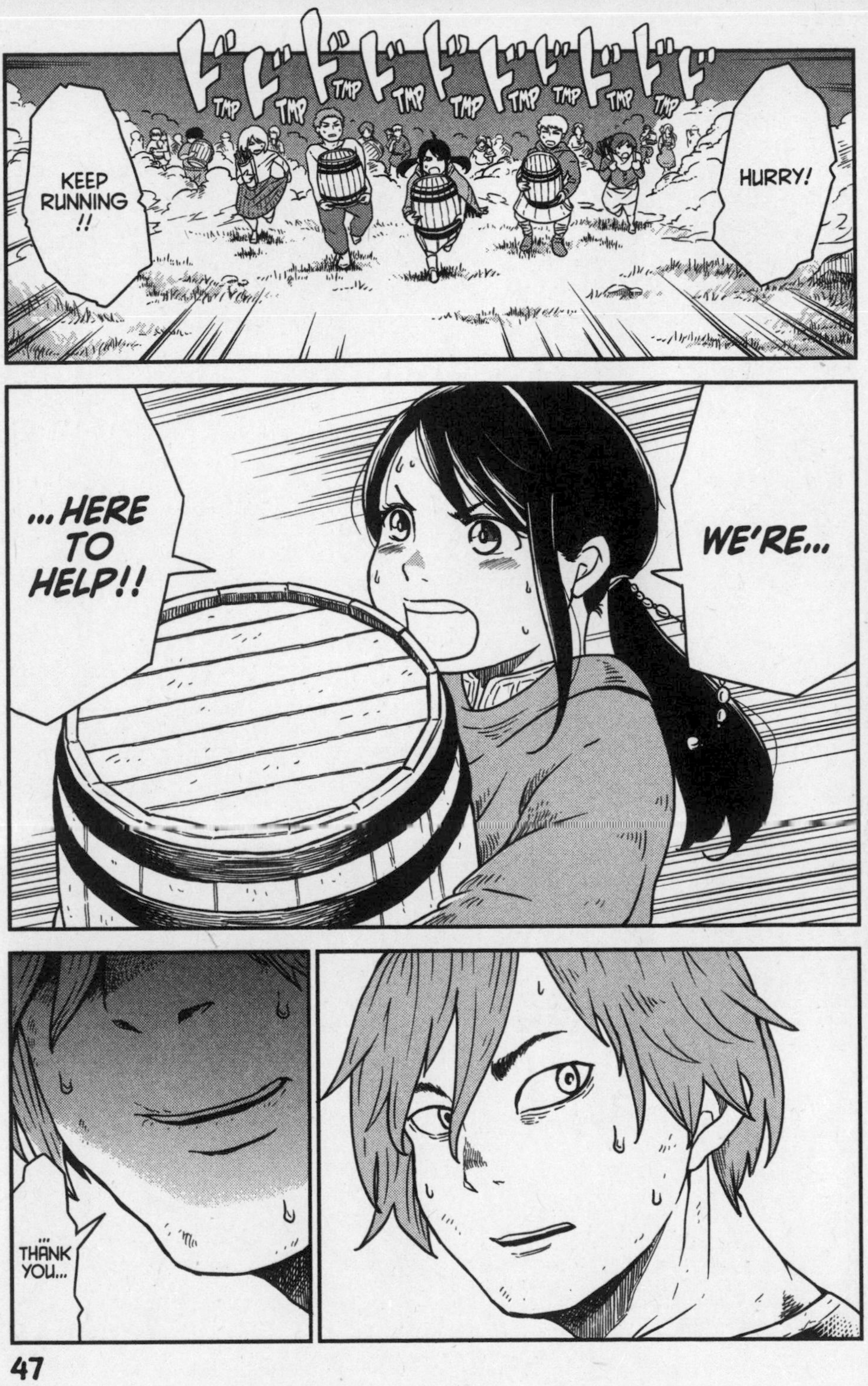
TMP TMP TMP TMP TMP TMP TMP TMP TMP TMP
HURRY!
KEEP RUNNING !!
WE'RE...
...HERE TO HELP!!
... THANK YOU...

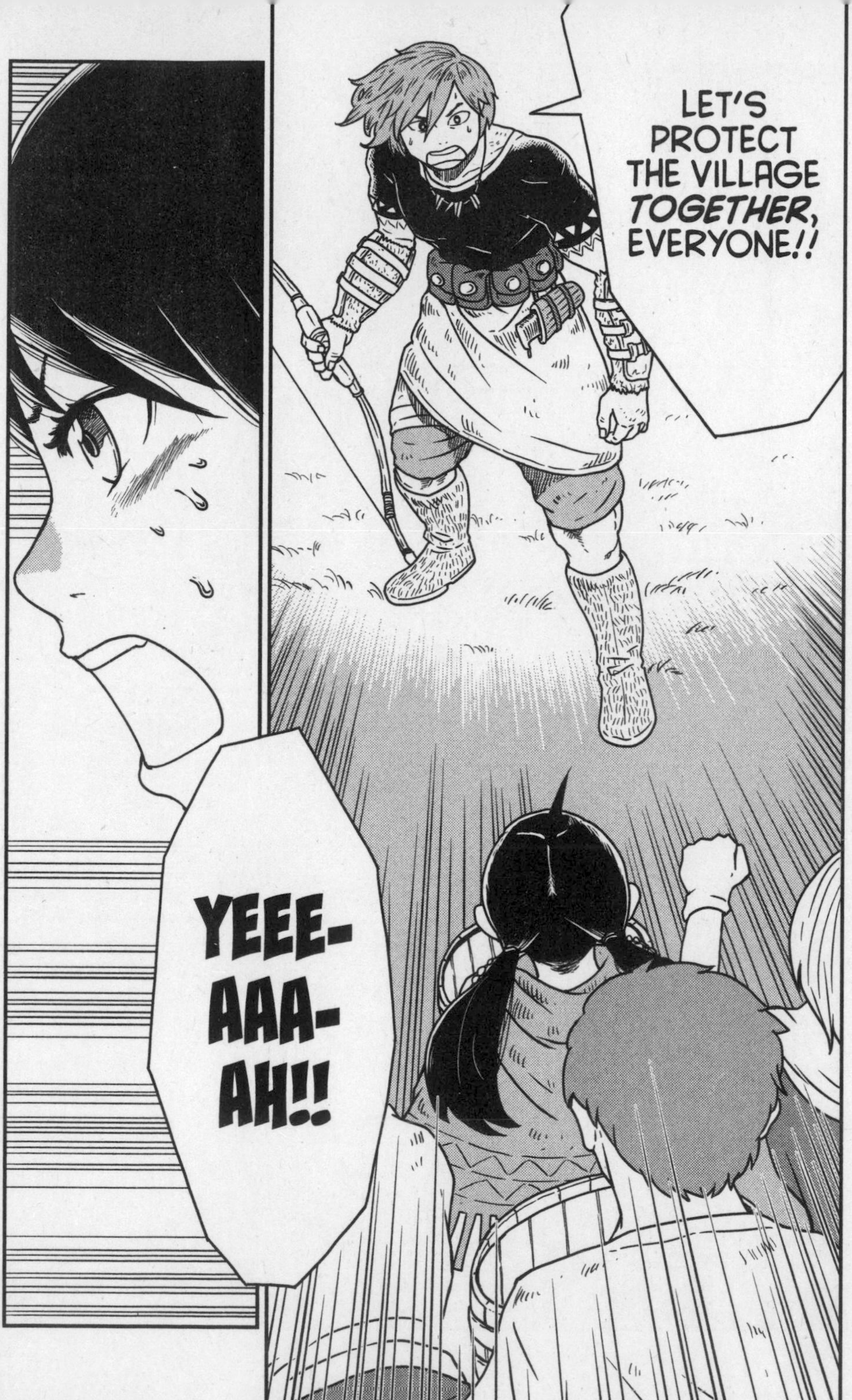
LET'S PROTECT THE VILLAGE *TOGETHER*, EVERYONE!!
YEEE-AAAA-AH!!

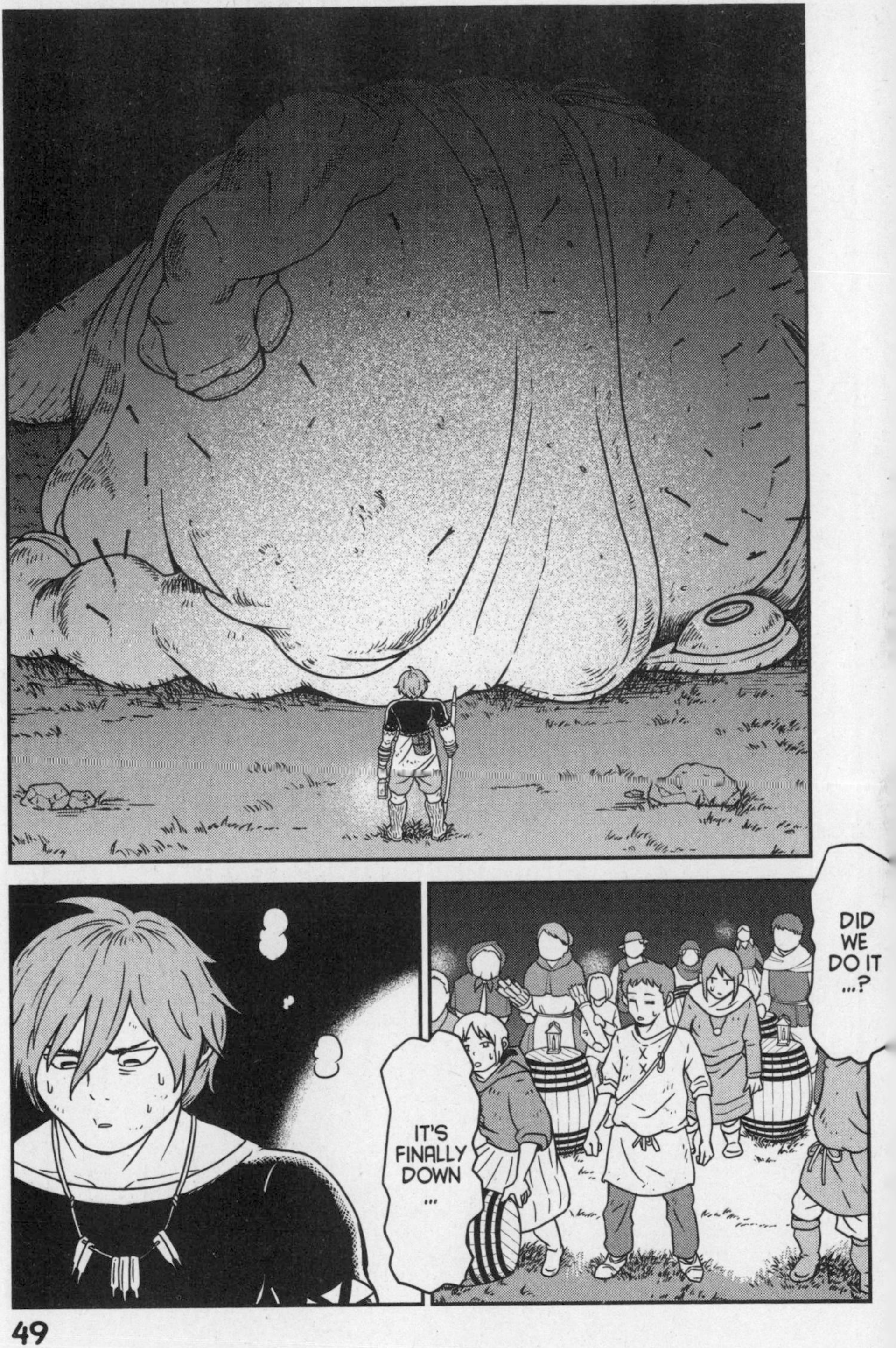
DID WE DO IT ...?
IT'S FINALLY DOWN ...

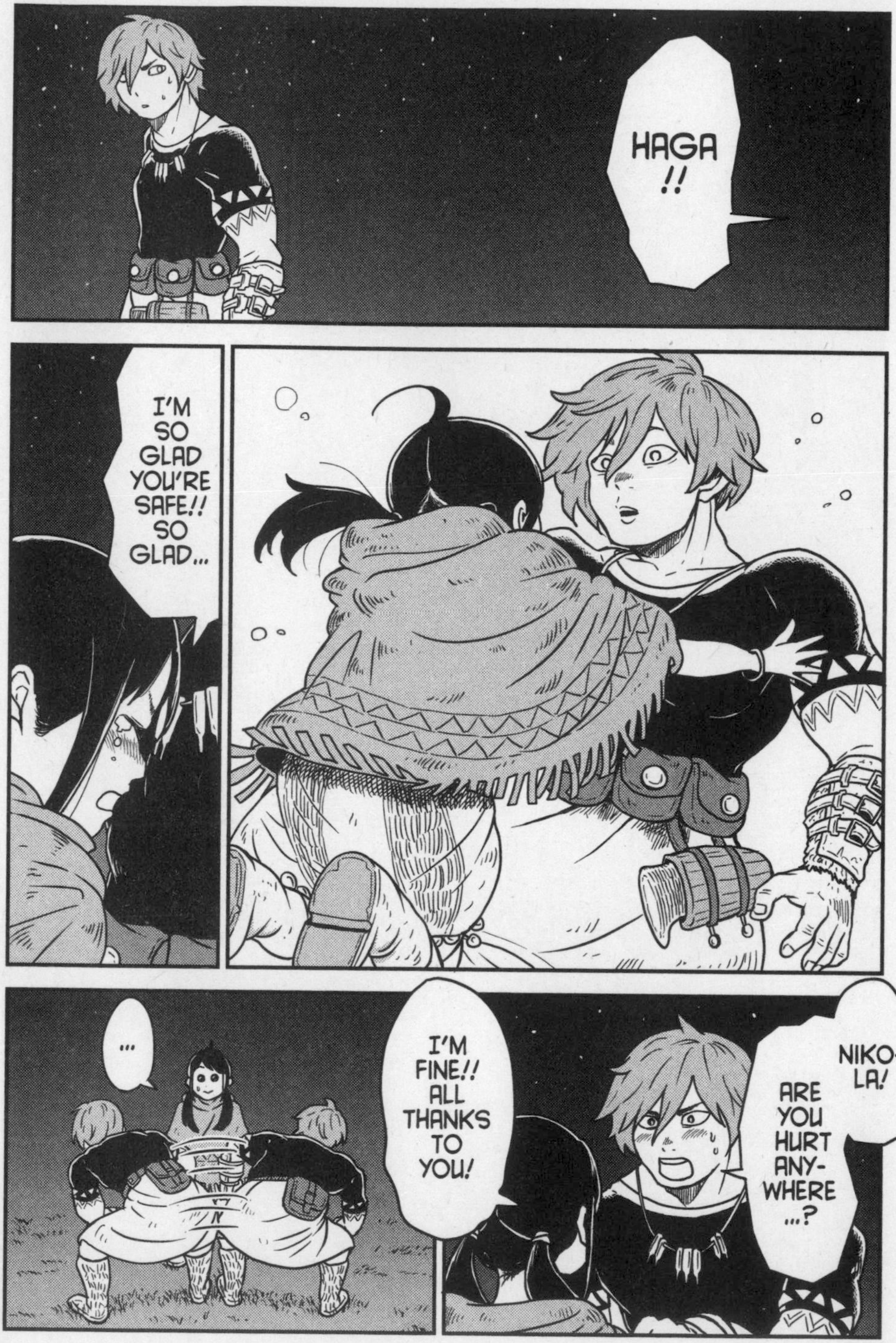
HAGA!!
I'M SO GLAD YOU'RE SAFE!! SO GLAD...
NIKO-LA!
ARE YOU HURT ANY-WHERE ...?
I'M FINE!! ALL THANKS TO YOU!
...

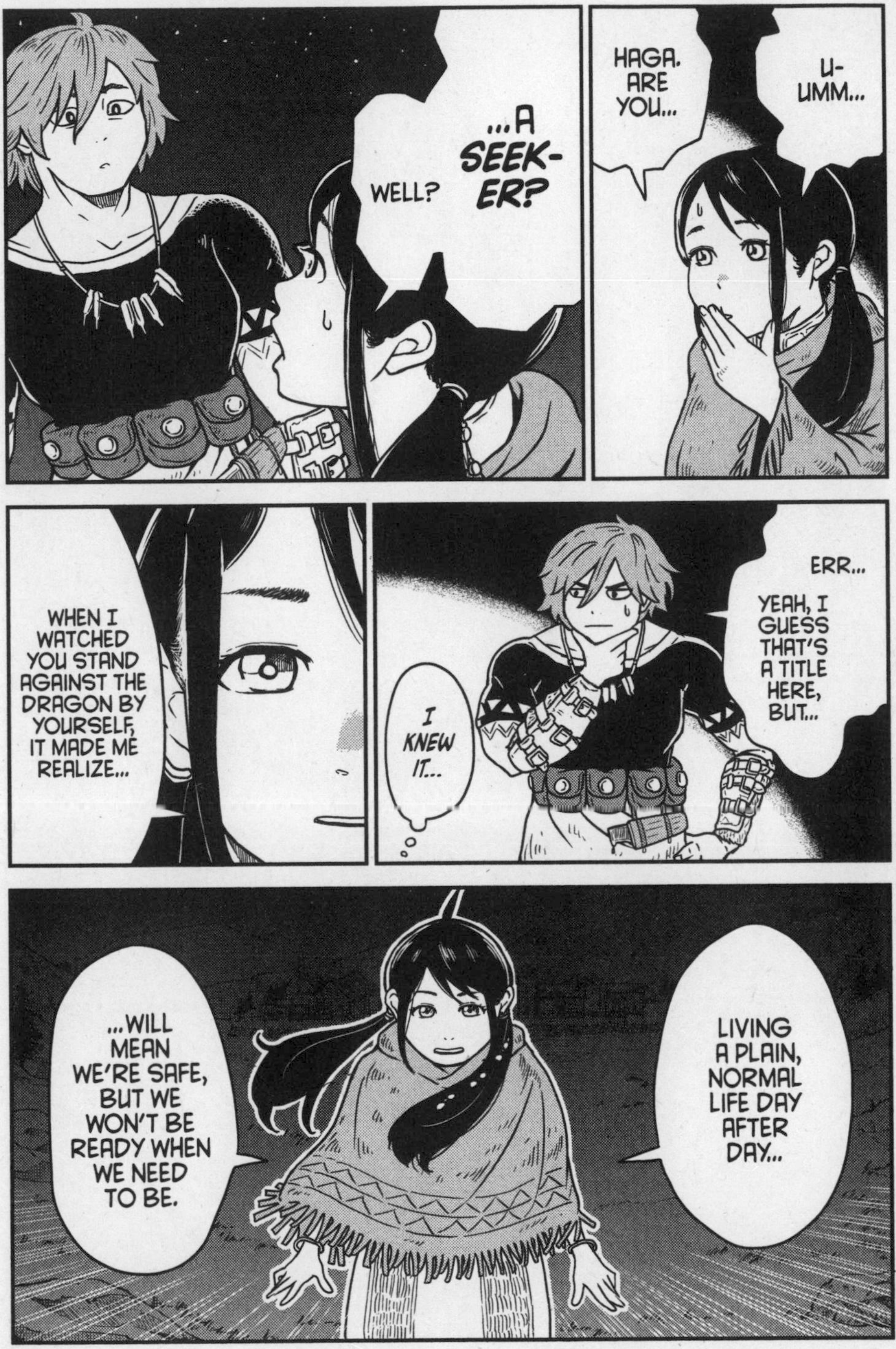
U-UMM...
HAGA. ARE YOU...
...A SEEKER?
WELL?
ERR...
YEAH, I GUESS THAT'S A TITLE HERE, BUT...
I KNEW IT...
WHEN I WATCHED YOU STAND AGAINST THE DRAGON BY YOURSELF, IT MADE ME REALIZE...
LIVING A PLAIN, NORMAL LIFE DAY AFTER DAY...
...WILL MEAN WE'RE SAFE, BUT WE WON'T BE READY WHEN WE NEED TO BE.

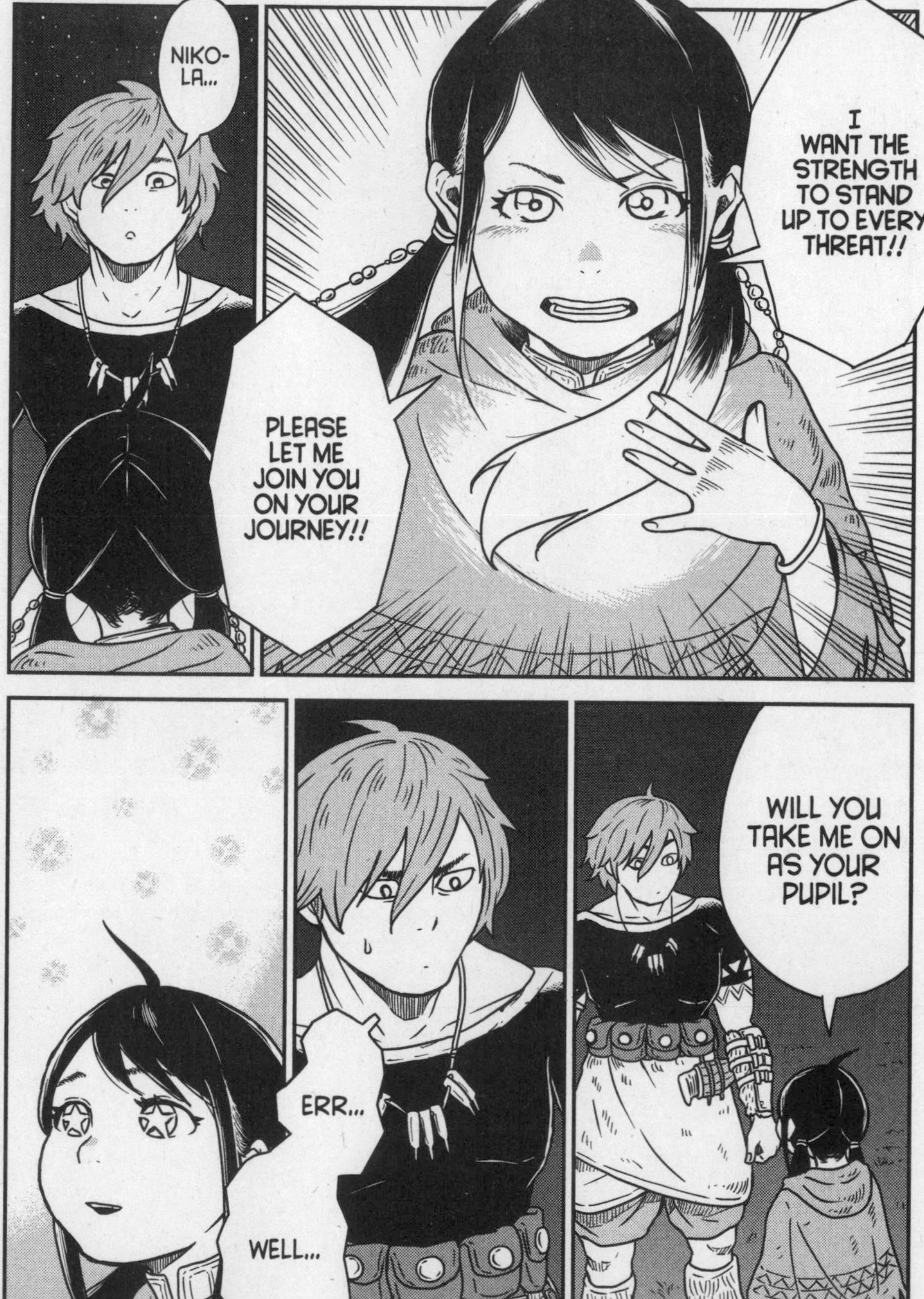
I WANT THE STRENGTH TO STAND UP TO EVERY THREAT!!
PLEASE LET ME JOIN YOU ON YOUR JOURNEY!!
NIKO-LA...
WILL YOU TAKE ME ON AS YOUR PUPIL?
ERR...
WELL...

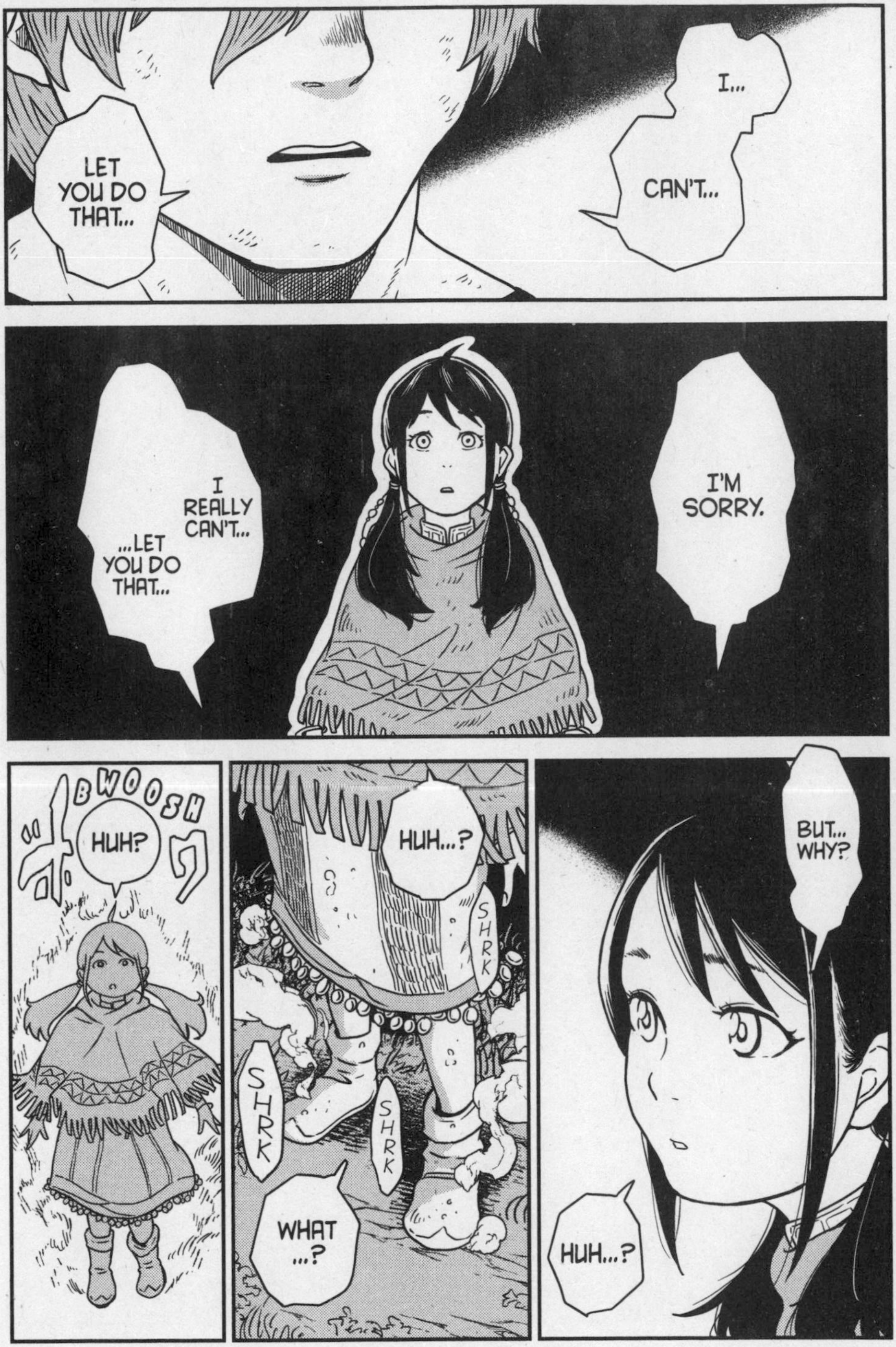
I...
CAN'T...
LET YOU DO THAT...
I'M SORRY.
I REALLY CAN'T...
...LET YOU DO THAT...
BUT... WHY?
HUH...?
HUH...?
SHRK
SHRK
SHRK
WHAT ...?
BWOOSH
HUH?

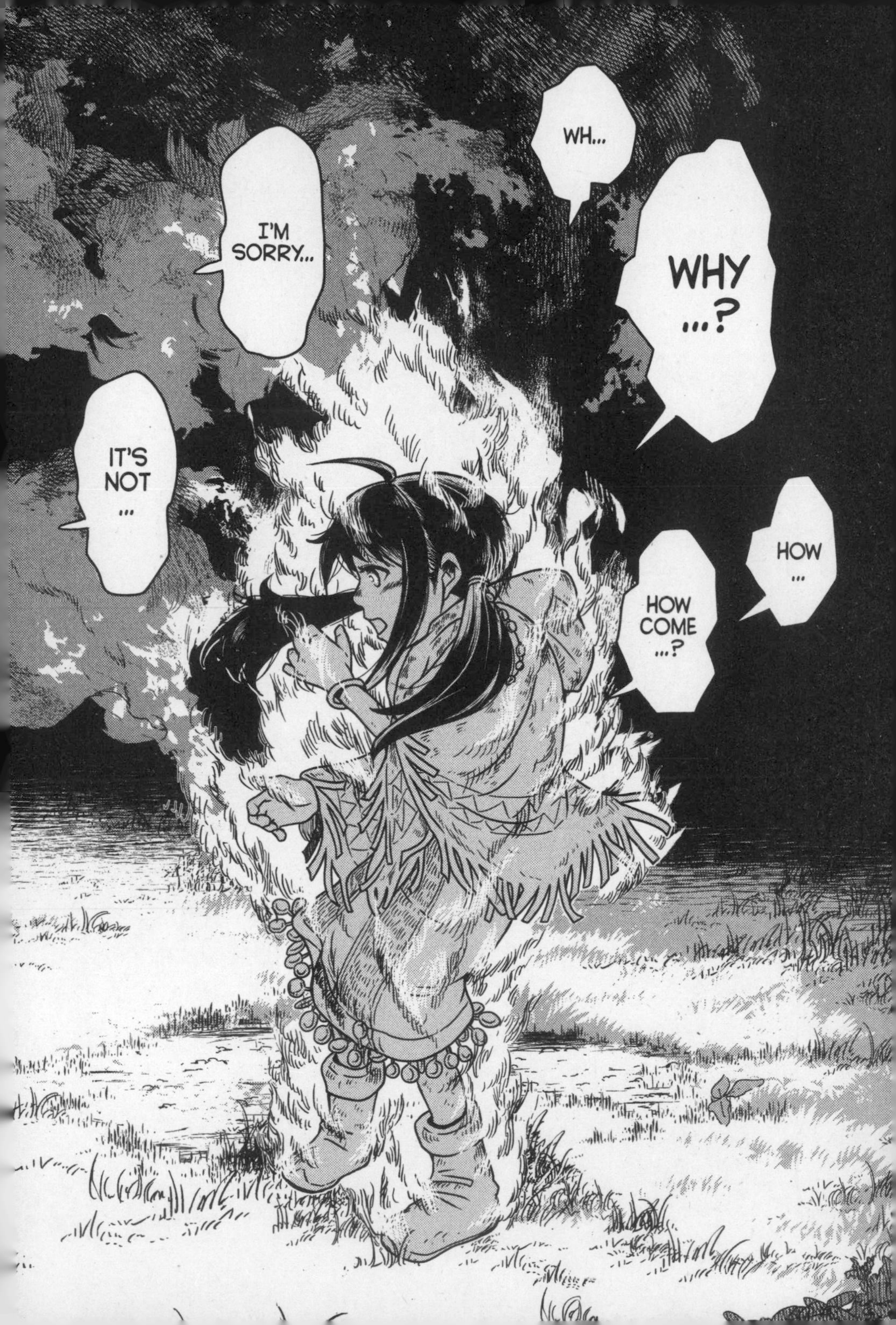
WH...
WHY ...?
I'M SORRY...
HOW ...
HOW COME ...?
IT'S NOT ...

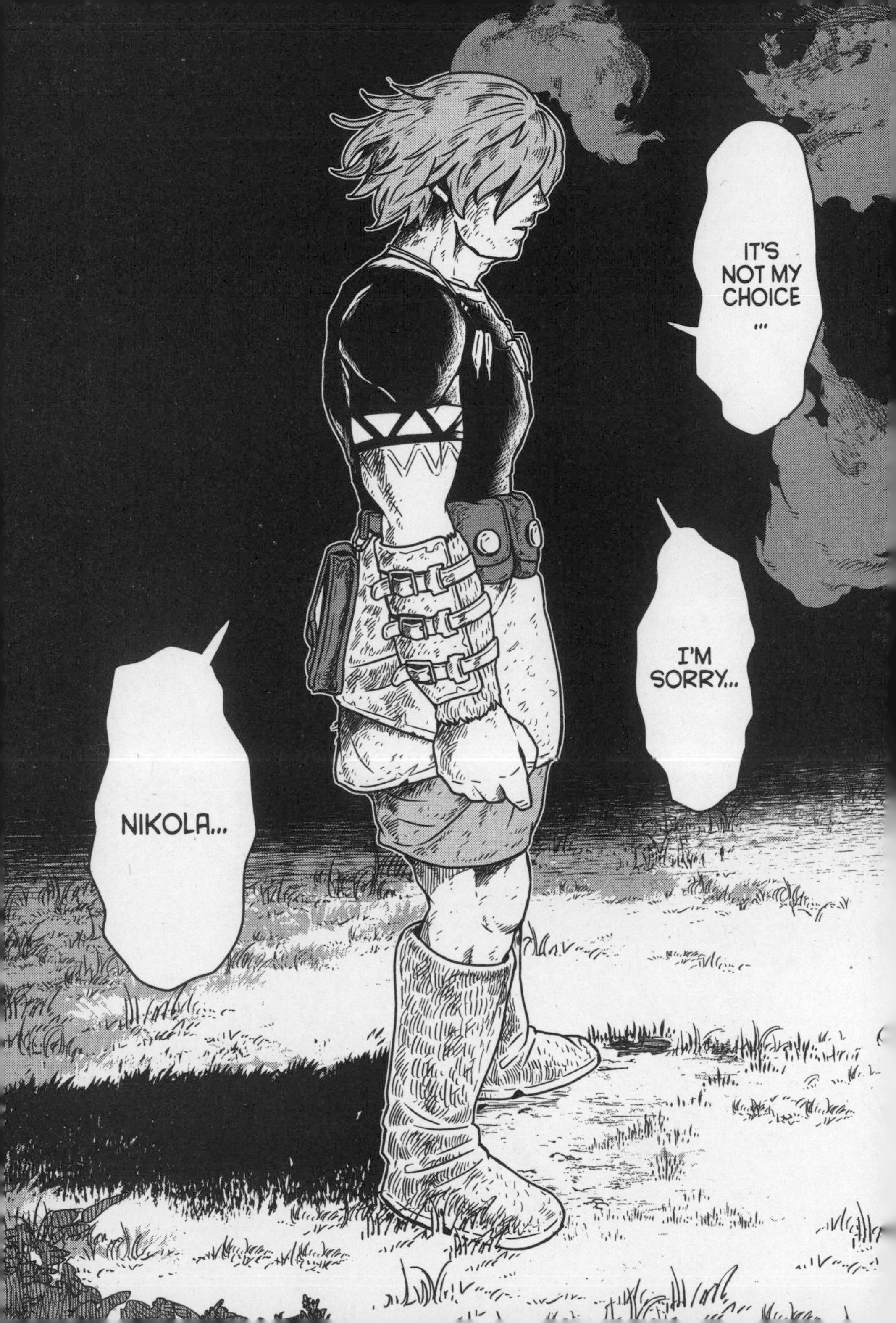
IT'S NOT MY CHOICE ...
I'M SORRY...
NIKOLA...

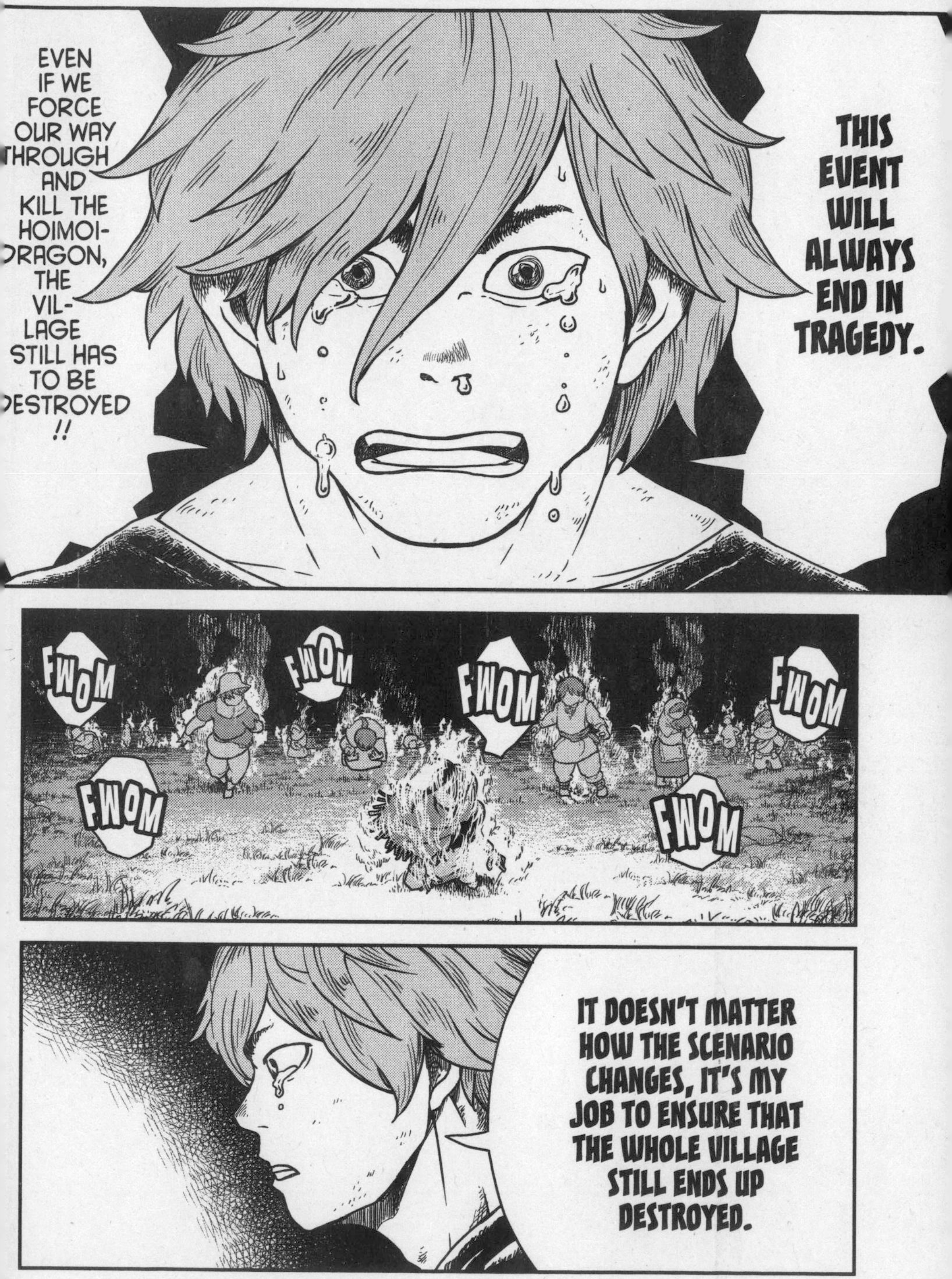
THIS EVENT WILL ALWAYS END IN TRAGEDY.
EVEN IF WE FORCE OUR WAY THROUGH AND KILL THE HOIMOI-DRAGON, THE VIL-LAGE STILL HAS TO BE DESTROYED!!
FWOM
FWOM
FWOM
FWOM
FWOM
FWOM
IT DOESN'T MATTER HOW THE SCENARIO CHANGES, IT'S MY JOB TO ENSURE THAT THE WHOLE VILLAGE STILL ENDS UP DESTROYED.

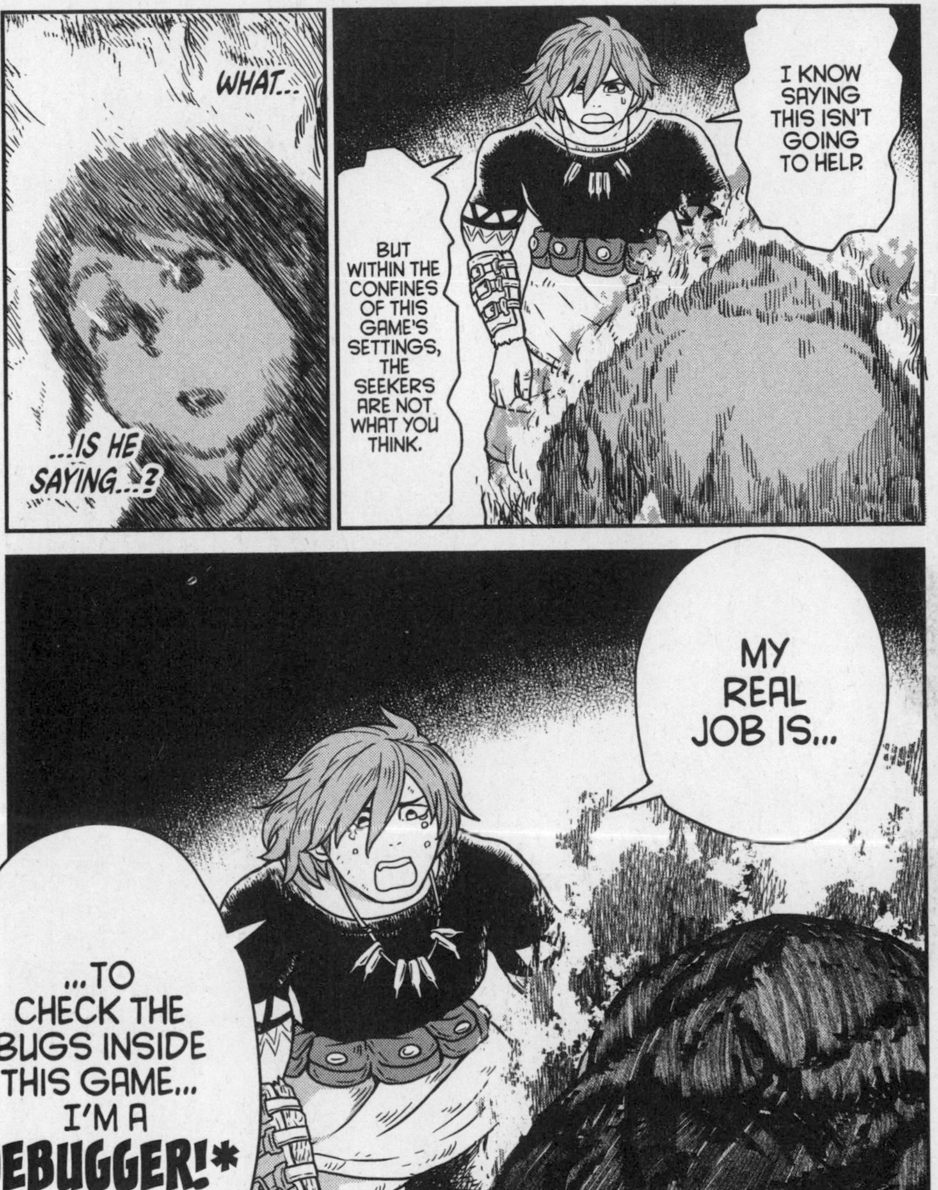
I KNOW SAYING THIS ISN'T GOING TO HELP.
BUT WITHIN THE CONFINES OF THIS GAME'S SETTINGS, THE SEEKERS ARE NOT WHAT YOU THINK.
WHAT...
...IS HE SAYING...?
MY REAL JOB IS...
...TO CHECK THE BUGS INSIDE THIS GAME... I'M A DEBUGGER!*

*Debuggers are called QA (Quality Assurance) or Testers.

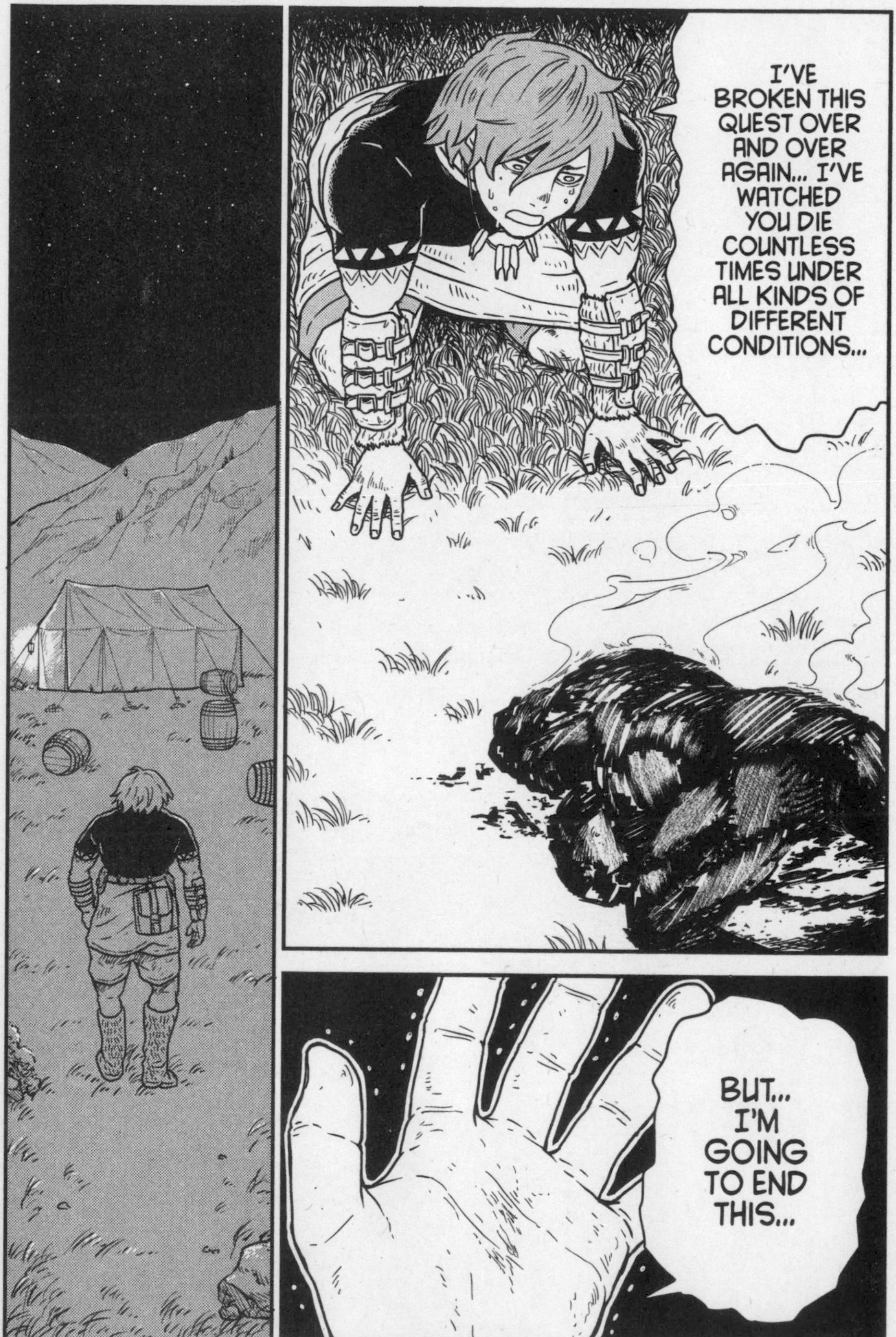
I'VE BROKEN THIS QUEST OVER AND OVER AGAIN... I'VE WATCHED YOU DIE COUNTLESS TIMES UNDER ALL KINDS OF DIFFERENT CONDITIONS...
BUT... I'M GOING TO END THIS...

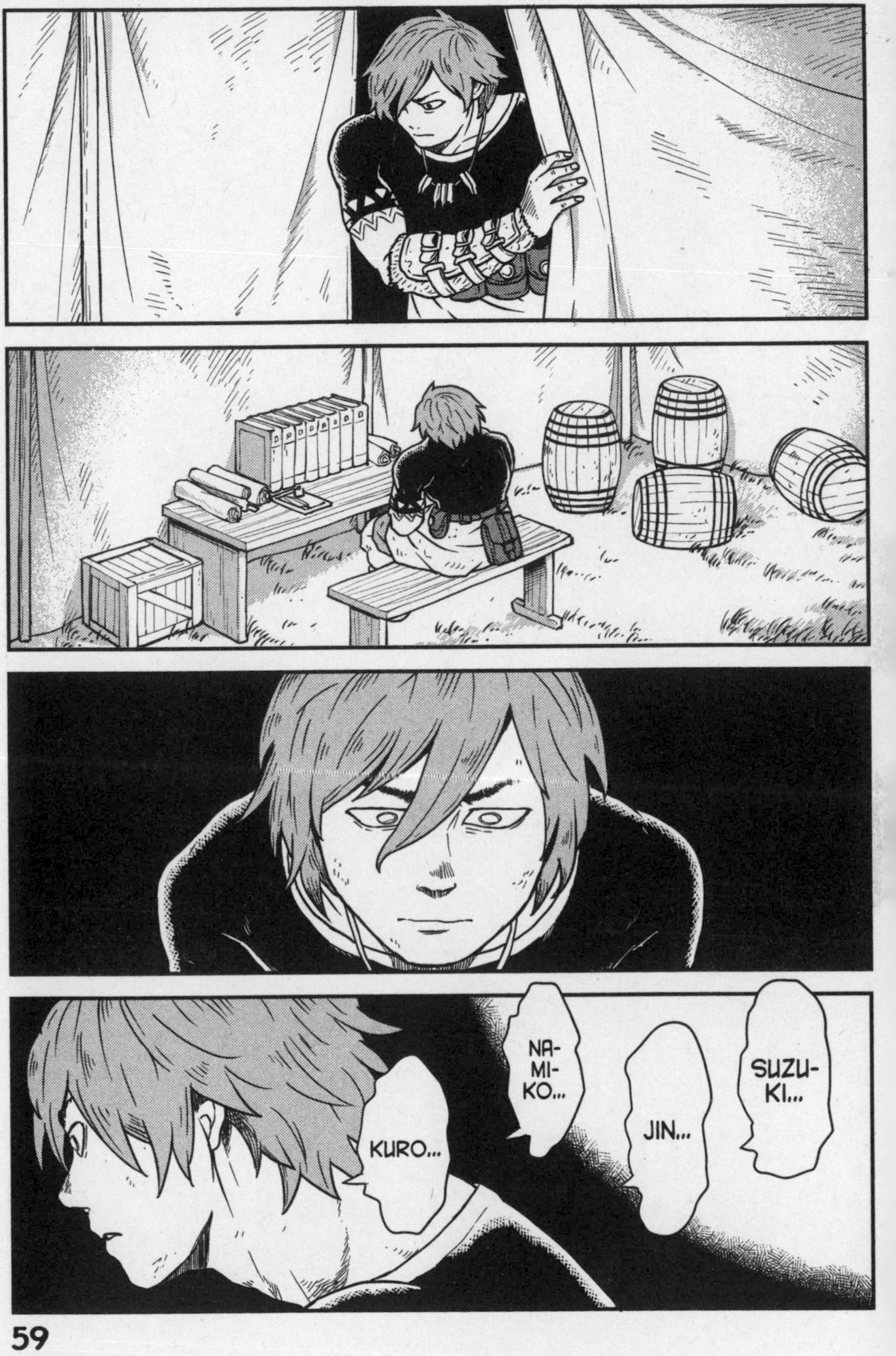
SUZUKI...
JIN...
NAMIKO...
KURO...

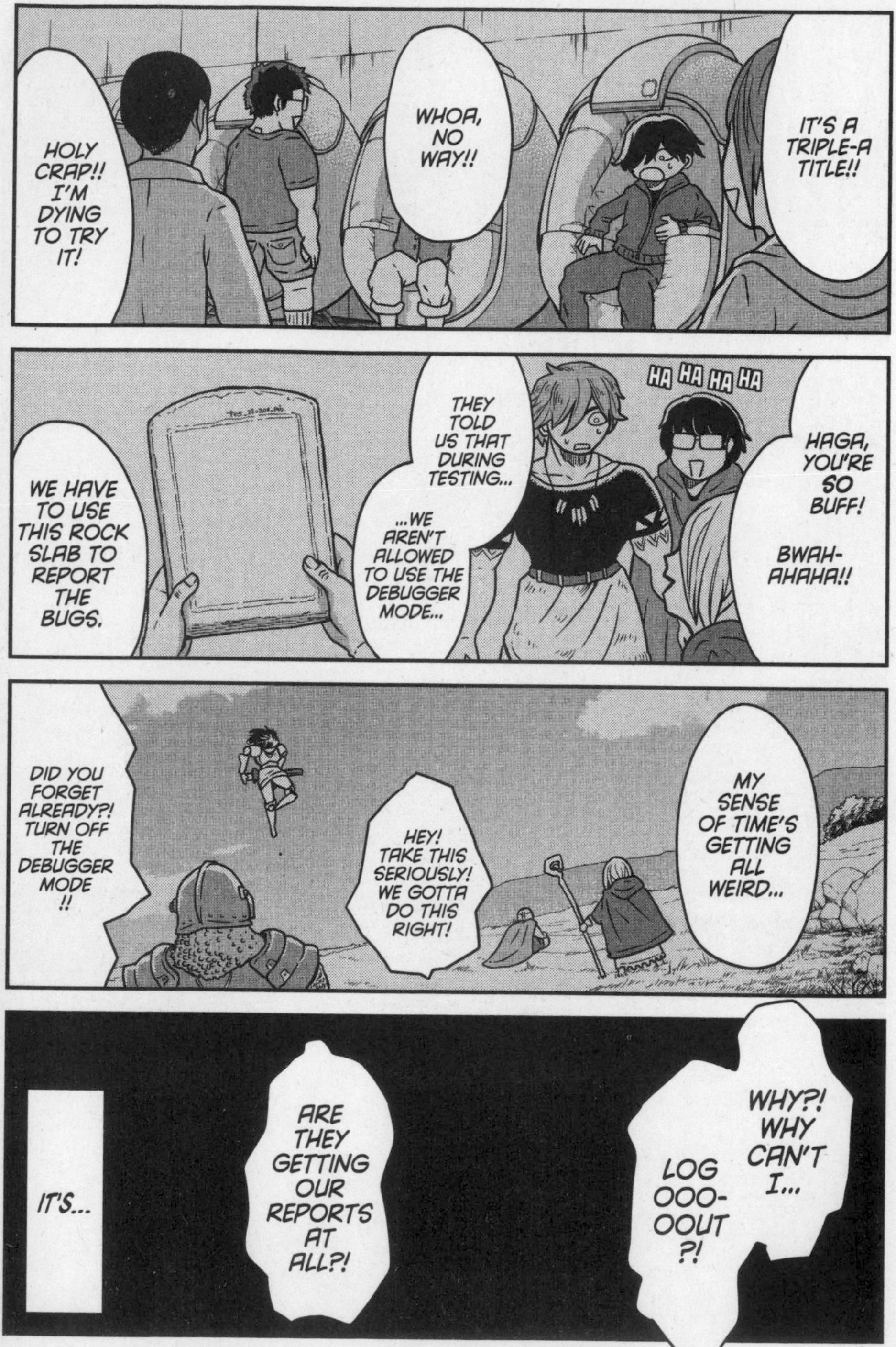
IT'S A TRIPLE-A TITLE!!
WHOA, NO WAY!!
HOLY CRAP!! I'M DYING TO TRY IT!
HA HA HA HA
HAGA, YOU'RE SO BUFF!
BWAH-AHAHA!!
THEY TOLD US THAT DURING TESTING...
...WE AREN'T ALLOWED TO USE THE DEBUGGER MODE...
WE HAVE TO USE THIS ROCK SLAB TO REPORT THE BUGS.
MY SENSE OF TIME'S GETTING ALL WEIRD...
HEY! TAKE THIS SERIOUSLY! WE GOTTA DO THIS RIGHT!
DID YOU FORGET ALREADY?! TURN OFF THE DEBUGGER MODE!!
WHY?! WHY CAN'T I...
LOG OOO-OOUT?!
ARE THEY GETTING OUR REPORTS AT ALL?!
IT'S...

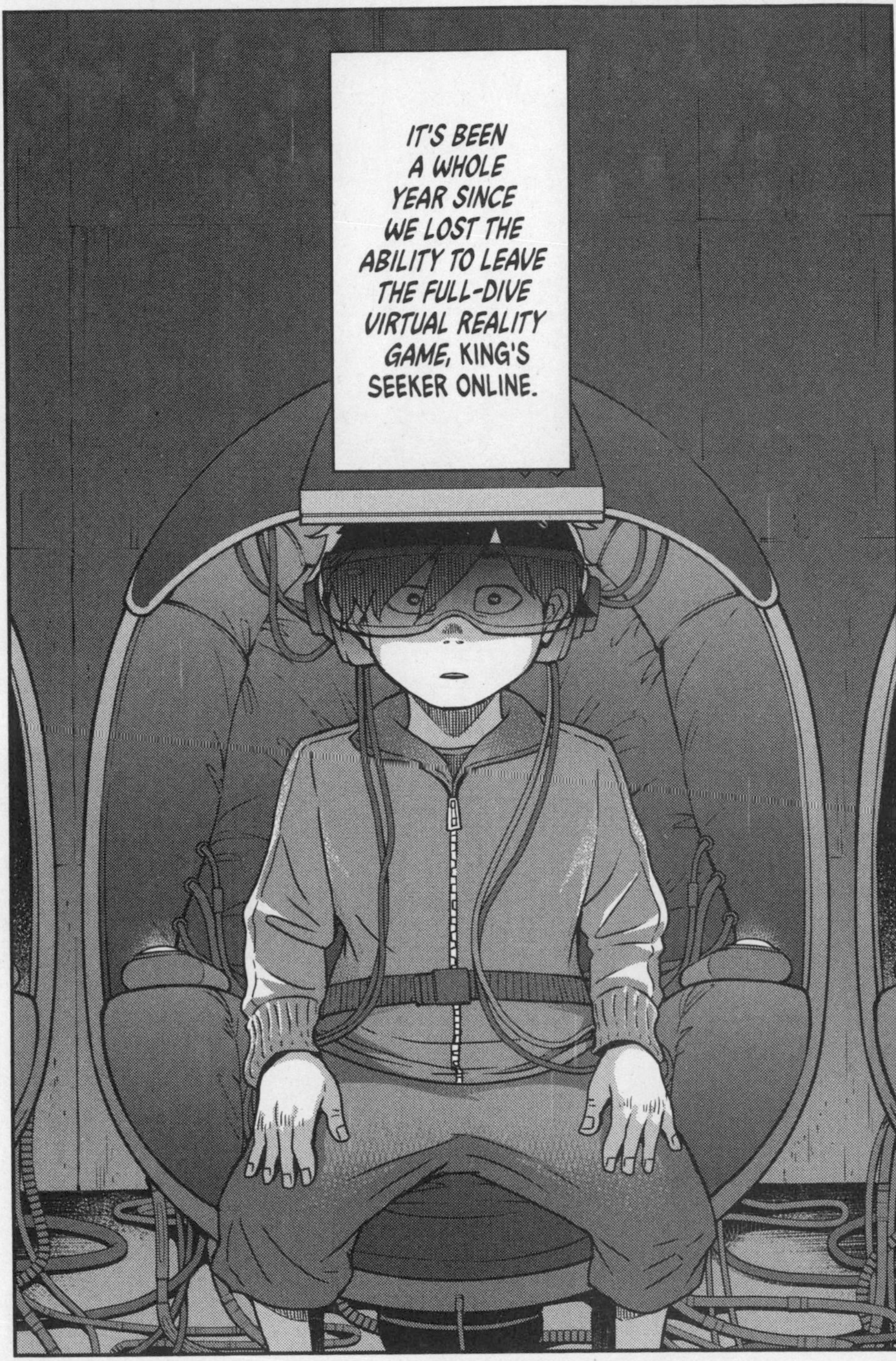
IT'S BEEN A WHOLE YEAR SINCE WE LOST THE ABILITY TO LEAVE THE FULL-DIVE VIRTUAL REALITY GAME, KING'S SEEKER ONLINE.

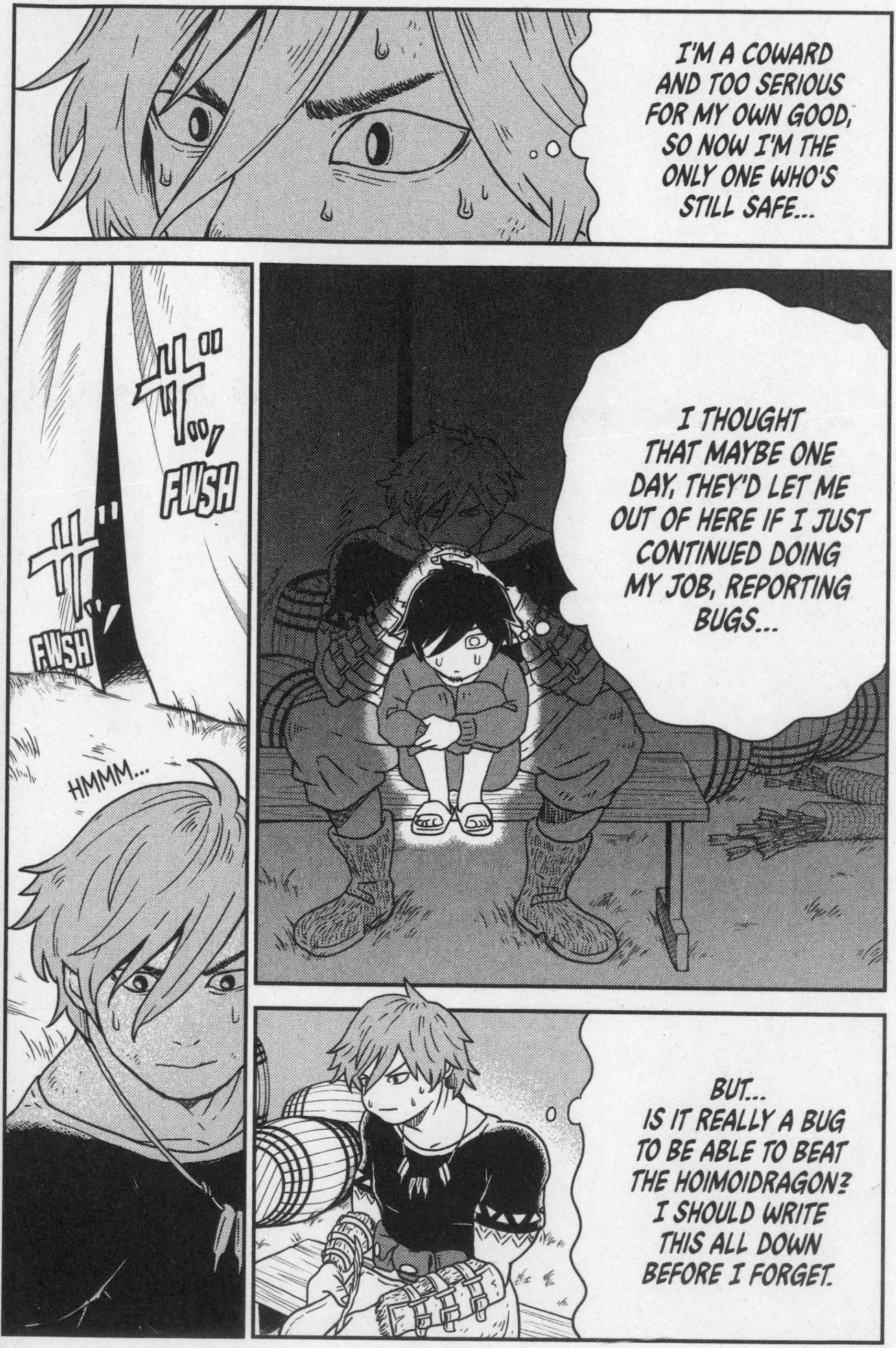
I'M A COWARD AND TOO SERIOUS FOR MY OWN GOOD, SO NOW I'M THE ONLY ONE WHO'S STILL SAFE...
I THOUGHT THAT MAYBE ONE DAY, THEY'D LET ME OUT OF HERE IF I JUST CONTINUED DOING MY JOB, REPORTING BUGS...
BUT... IS IT REALLY A BUG TO BE ABLE TO BEAT THE HOIMOIDRAGON? I SHOULD WRITE THIS ALL DOWN BEFORE I FORGET.
FWSH
FWSH
HMMM...

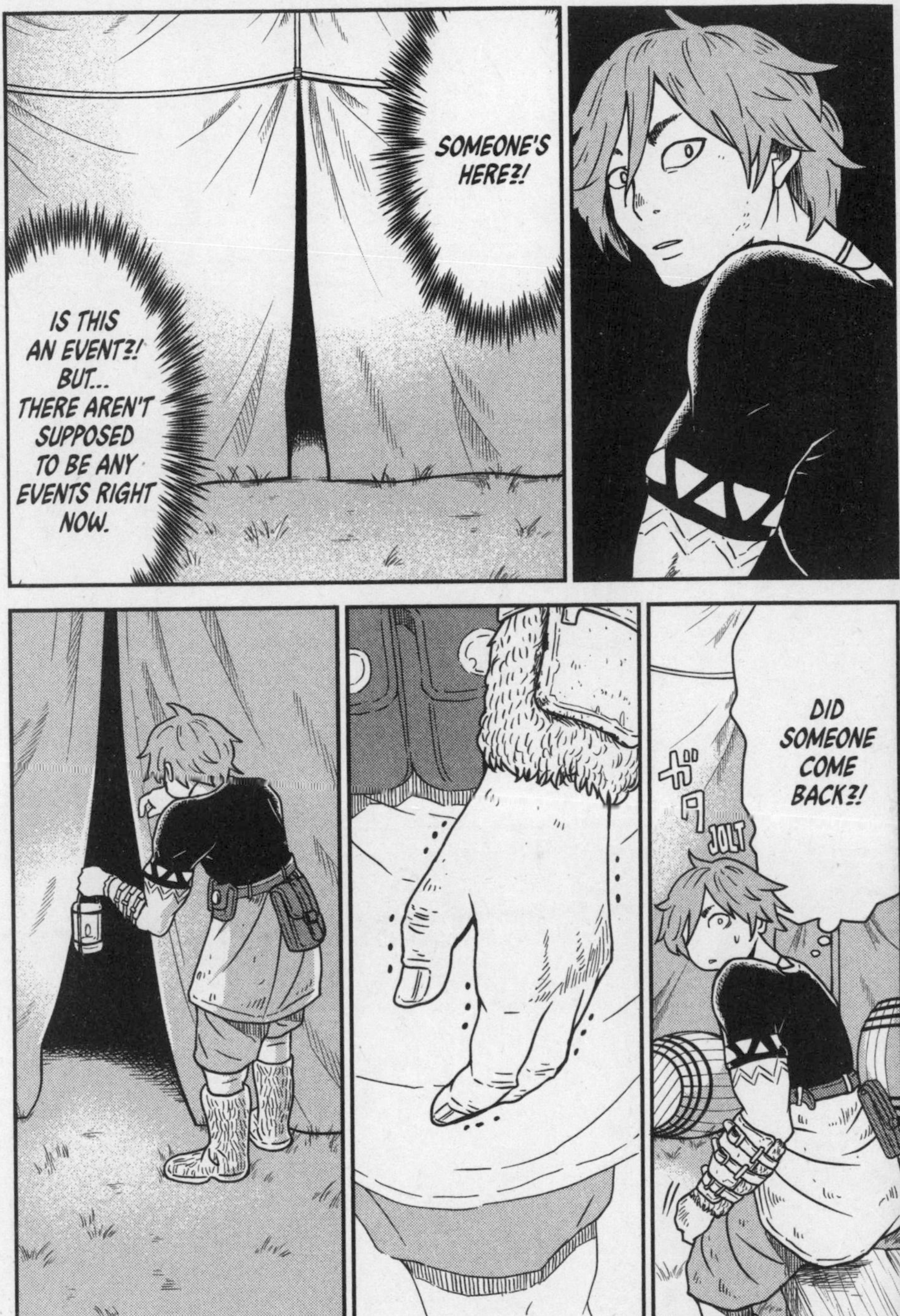
SOMEONE'S HERE?!
IS THIS AN EVENT?! BUT... THERE AREN'T SUPPOSED TO BE ANY EVENTS RIGHT NOW.
ガタ
JOLT
DID SOMEONE COME BACK?!

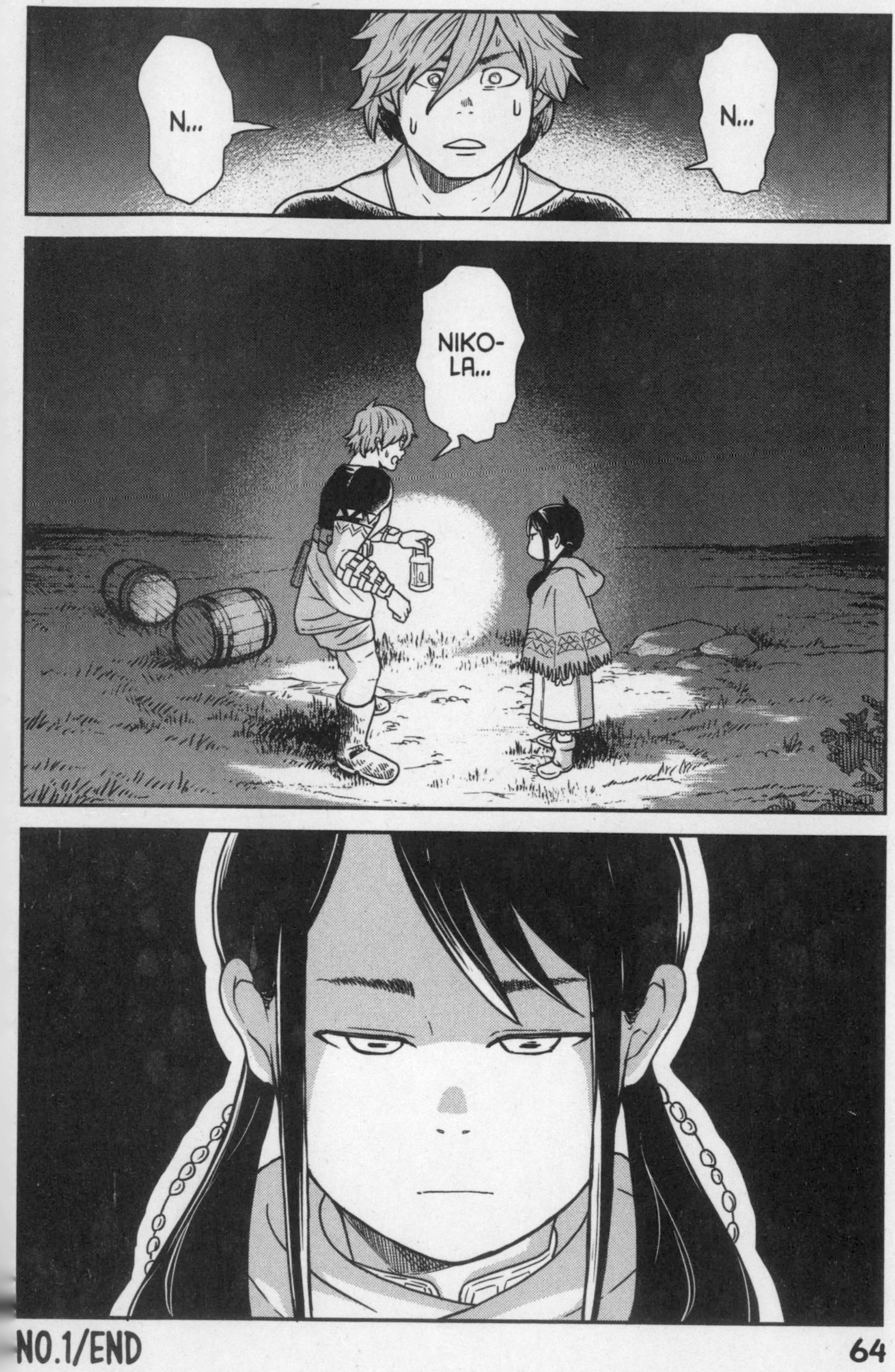
N...
N...
NIKO-LA...

NO.1/END

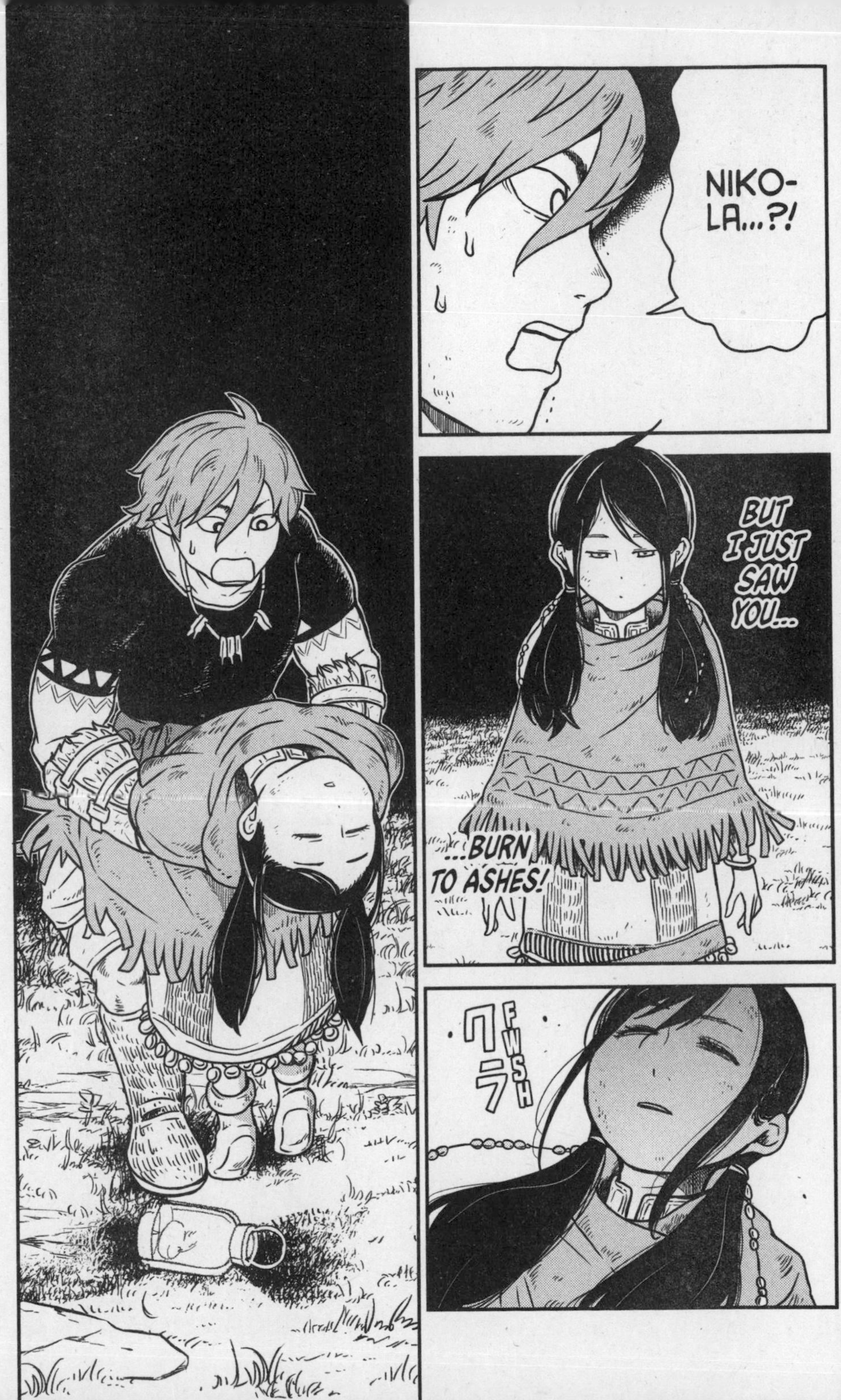
NIKO-LA...?!
BUT I JUST SAW YOU...
...BURN TO ASHES!
FWSH

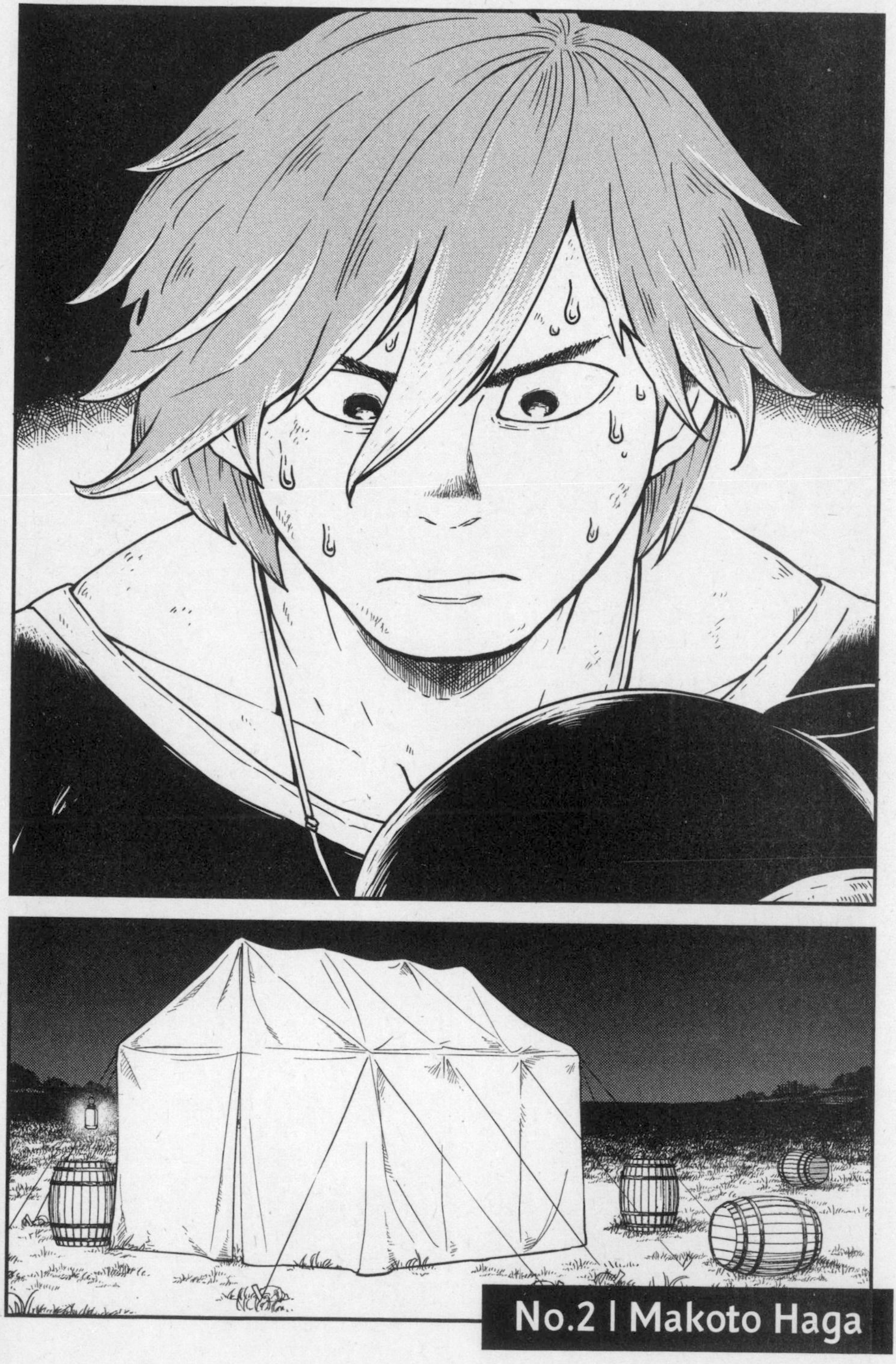
No.2 | Makoto Haga

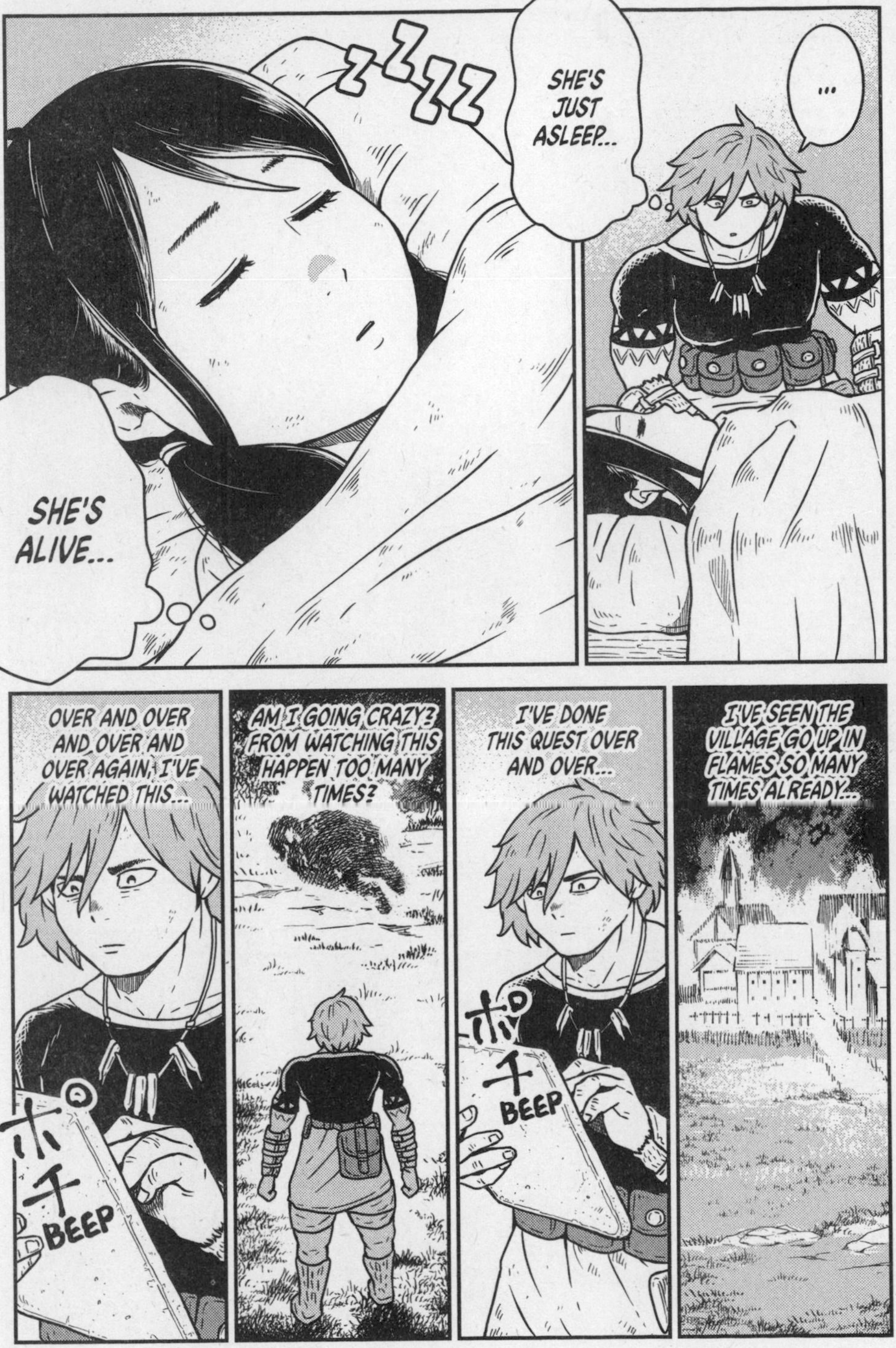
...
SHE'S JUST ASLEEP...
ZZZZ
SHE'S ALIVE...
I'VE SEEN THE VILLAGE GO UP IN FLAMES SO MANY TIMES ALREADY...
I'VE DONE THIS QUEST OVER AND OVER...
ポチ
BEEP
AM I GOING CRAZY? FROM WATCHING THIS HAPPEN TOO MANY TIMES?
OVER AND OVER AND OVER AND OVER AGAIN, I'VE WATCHED THIS...
ポチ
BEEP

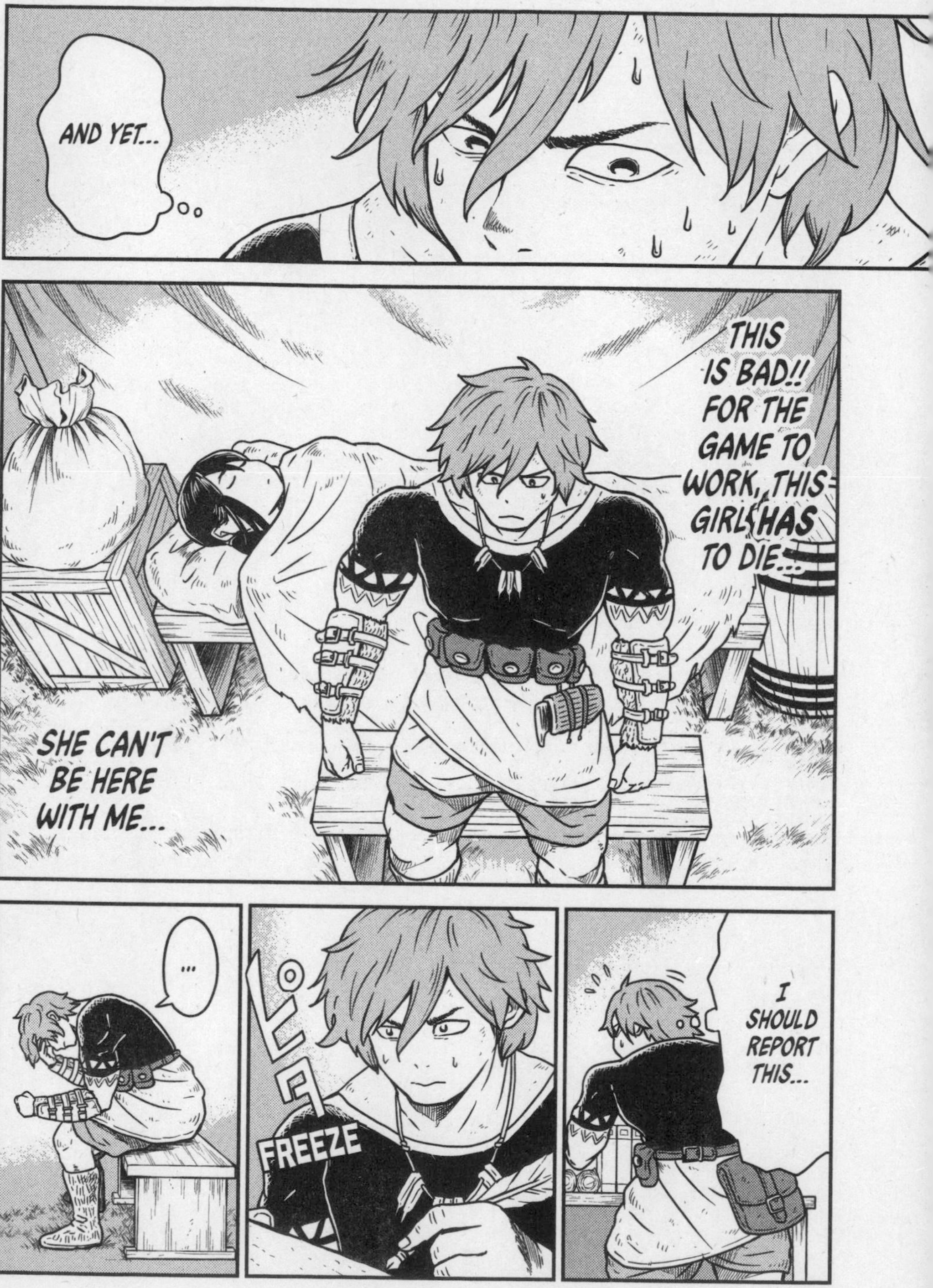
AND YET...
THIS IS BAD!! FOR THE GAME TO WORK, THIS GIRL HAS TO DIE...
SHE CAN'T BE HERE WITH ME...
I SHOULD REPORT THIS...
ピク
FREEZE
...

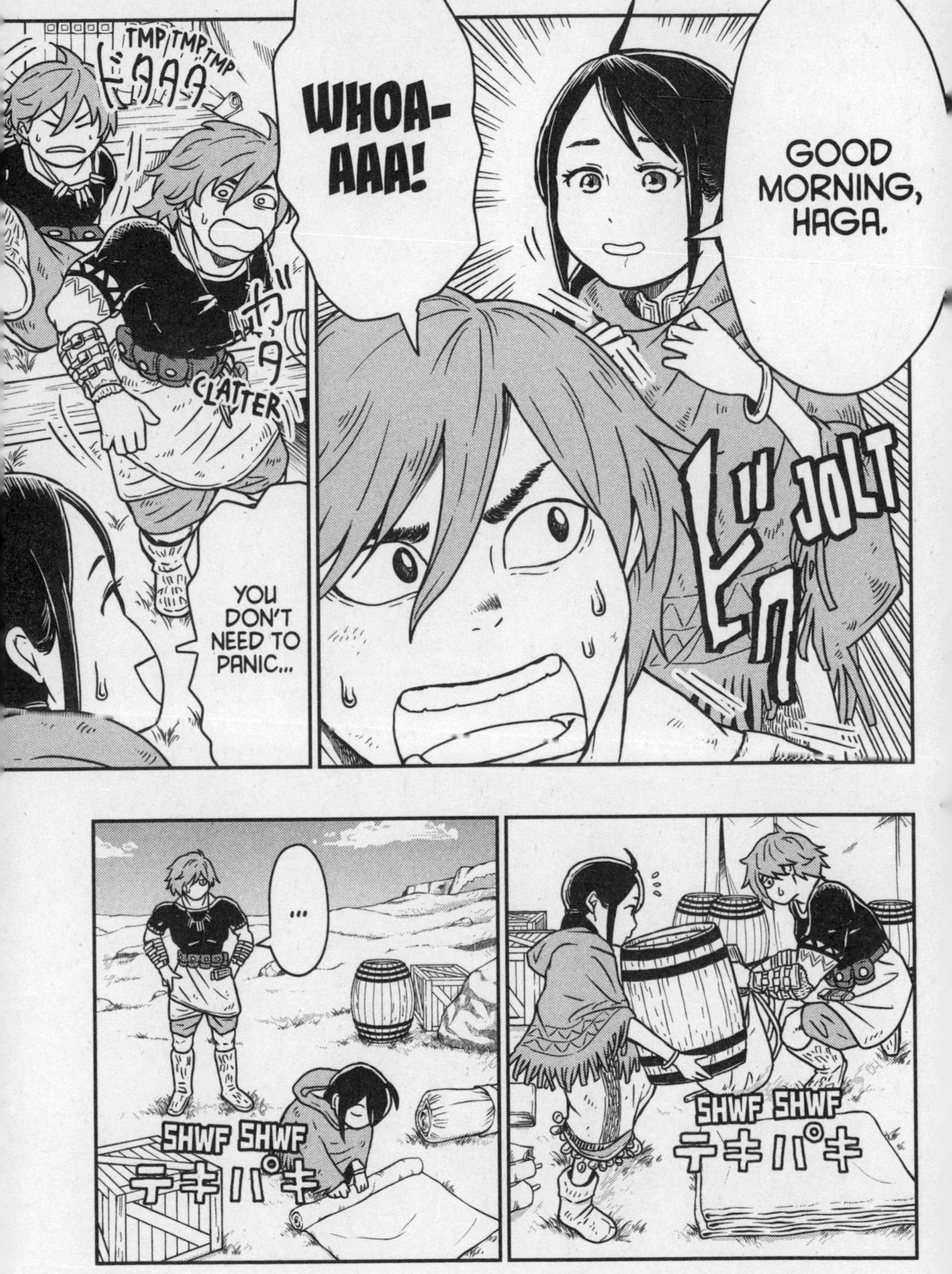
GOOD MORNING, HAGA.
ビクッ
JOLT
WHOA-AAA!
ドタタタ
TMP TMP TMP
ガタ
CLATTER
YOU DON'T NEED TO PANIC...
SHWF SHWF
テキパキ
...
SHWF SHWF
テキパキ

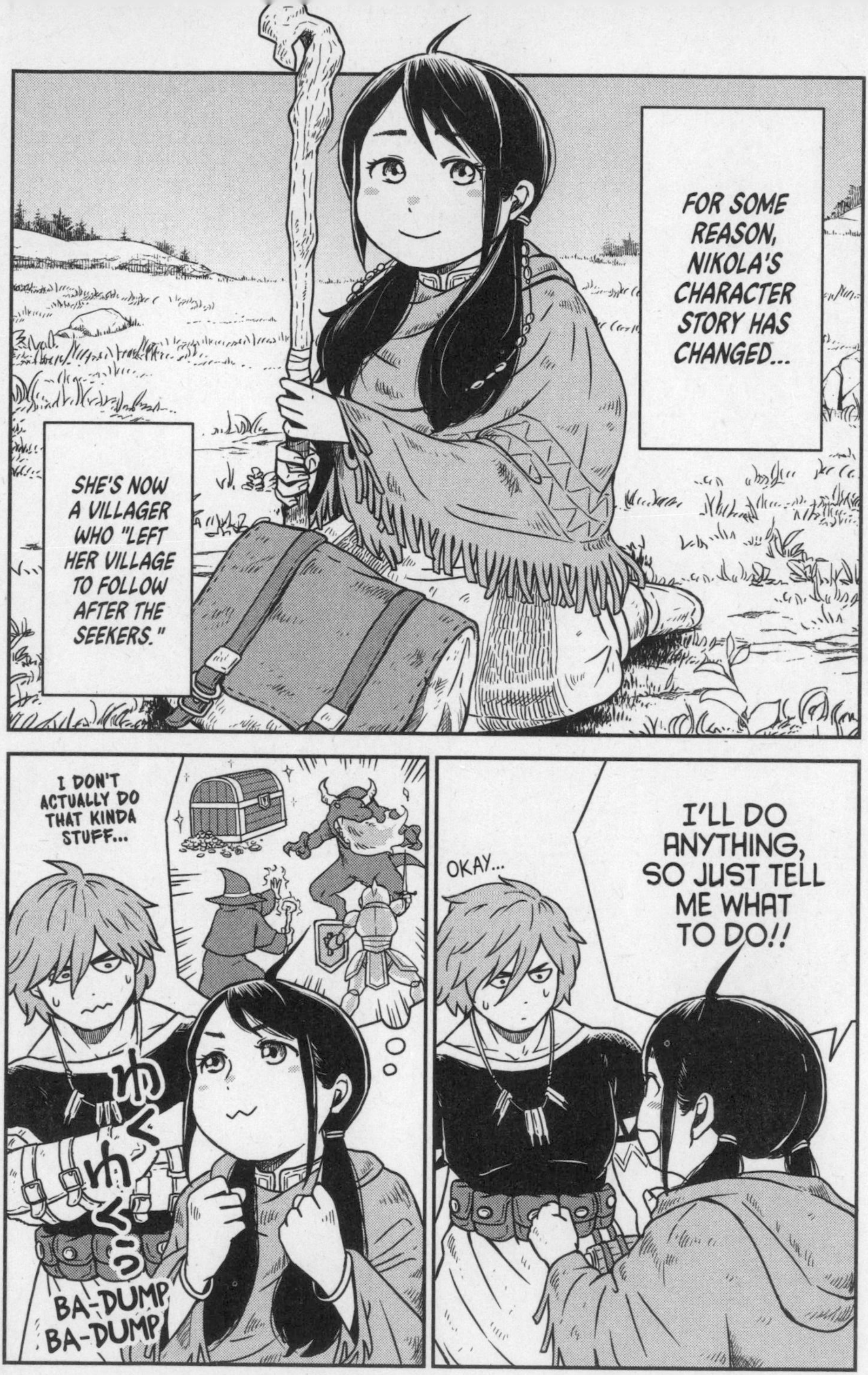

FOR SOME REASON, NIKOLA'S CHARACTER STORY HAS CHANGED...
SHE'S NOW A VILLAGER WHO "LEFT HER VILLAGE TO FOLLOW AFTER THE SEEKERS."
I'LL DO ANYTHING, SO JUST TELL ME WHAT TO DO!!
OKAY...
I DON'T ACTUALLY DO THAT KINDA STUFF...
わくわく
BA-DUMP BA-DUMP

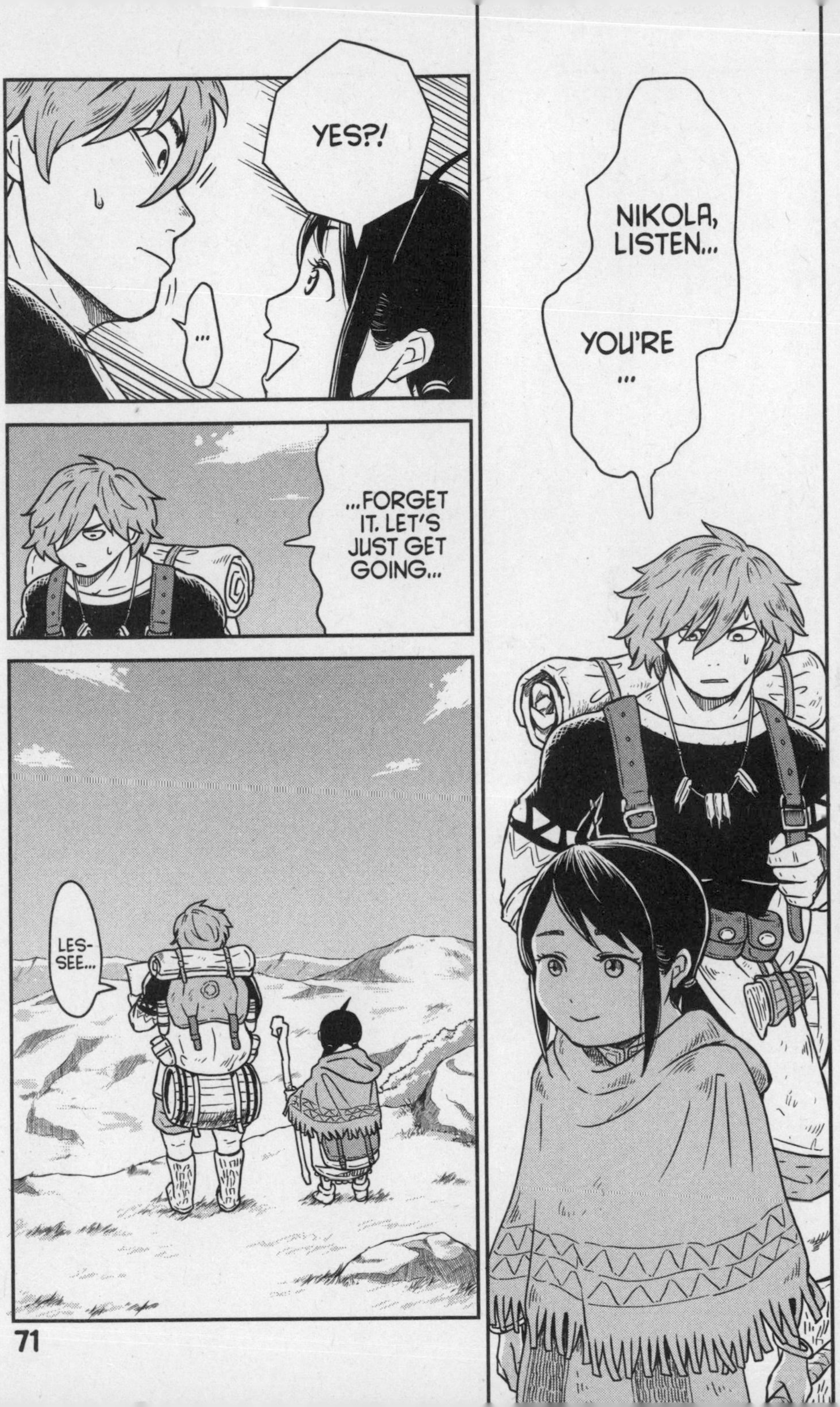
NIKOLA, LISTEN...
YOU'RE ...
YES?!
...
...FORGET IT. LET'S JUST GET GOING...
LES-SEE...

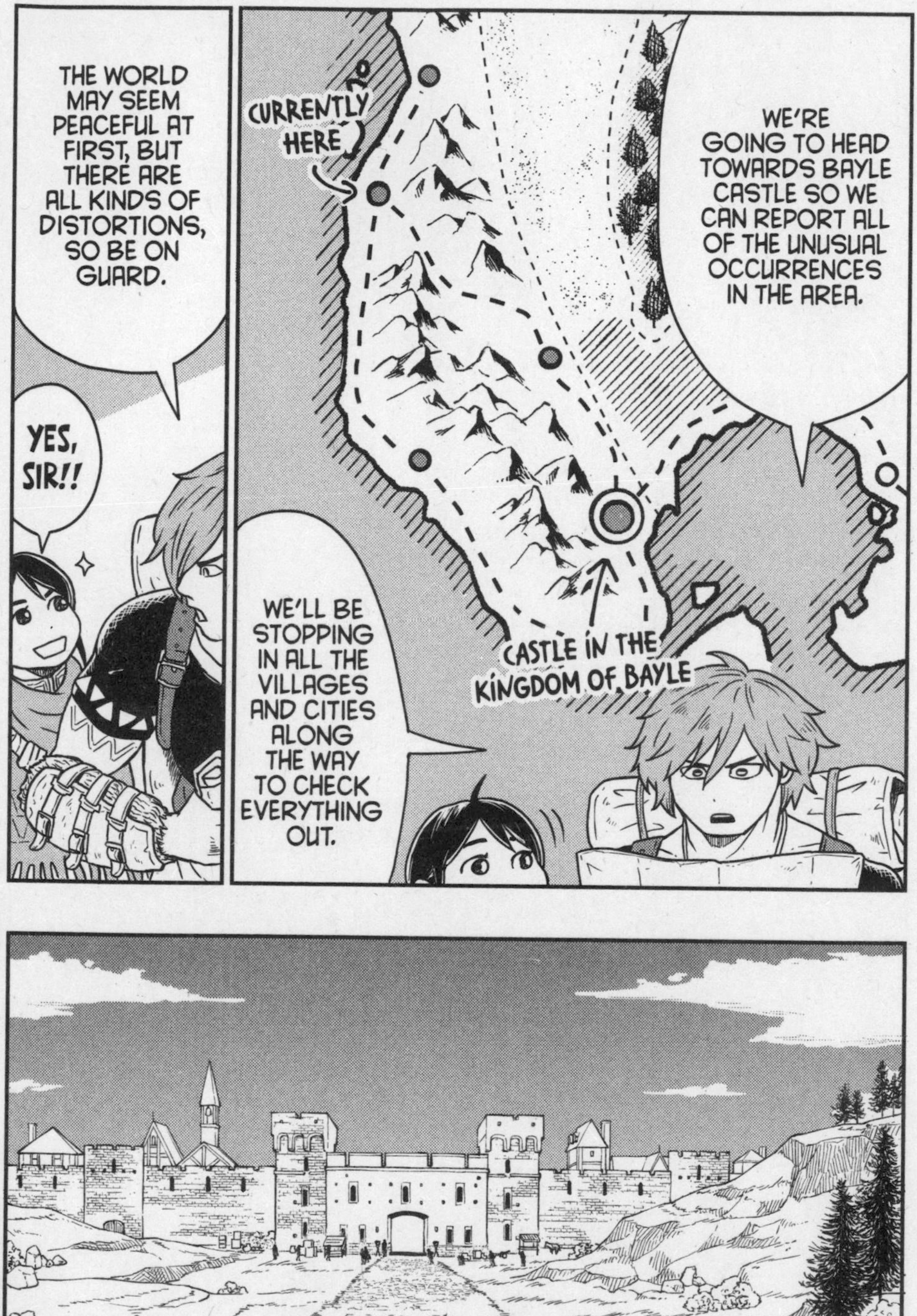
WE'RE GOING TO HEAD TOWARDS BAYLE CASTLE SO WE CAN REPORT ALL OF THE UNUSUAL OCCURRENCES IN THE AREA.
CURRENTLY HERE
CASTLE IN THE KINGDOM OF BAYLE
WE'LL BE STOPPING IN ALL THE VILLAGES AND CITIES ALONG THE WAY TO CHECK EVERYTHING OUT.
THE WORLD MAY SEEM PEACEFUL AT FIRST, BUT THERE ARE ALL KINDS OF DISTORTIONS, SO BE ON GUARD.
YES, SIR!!

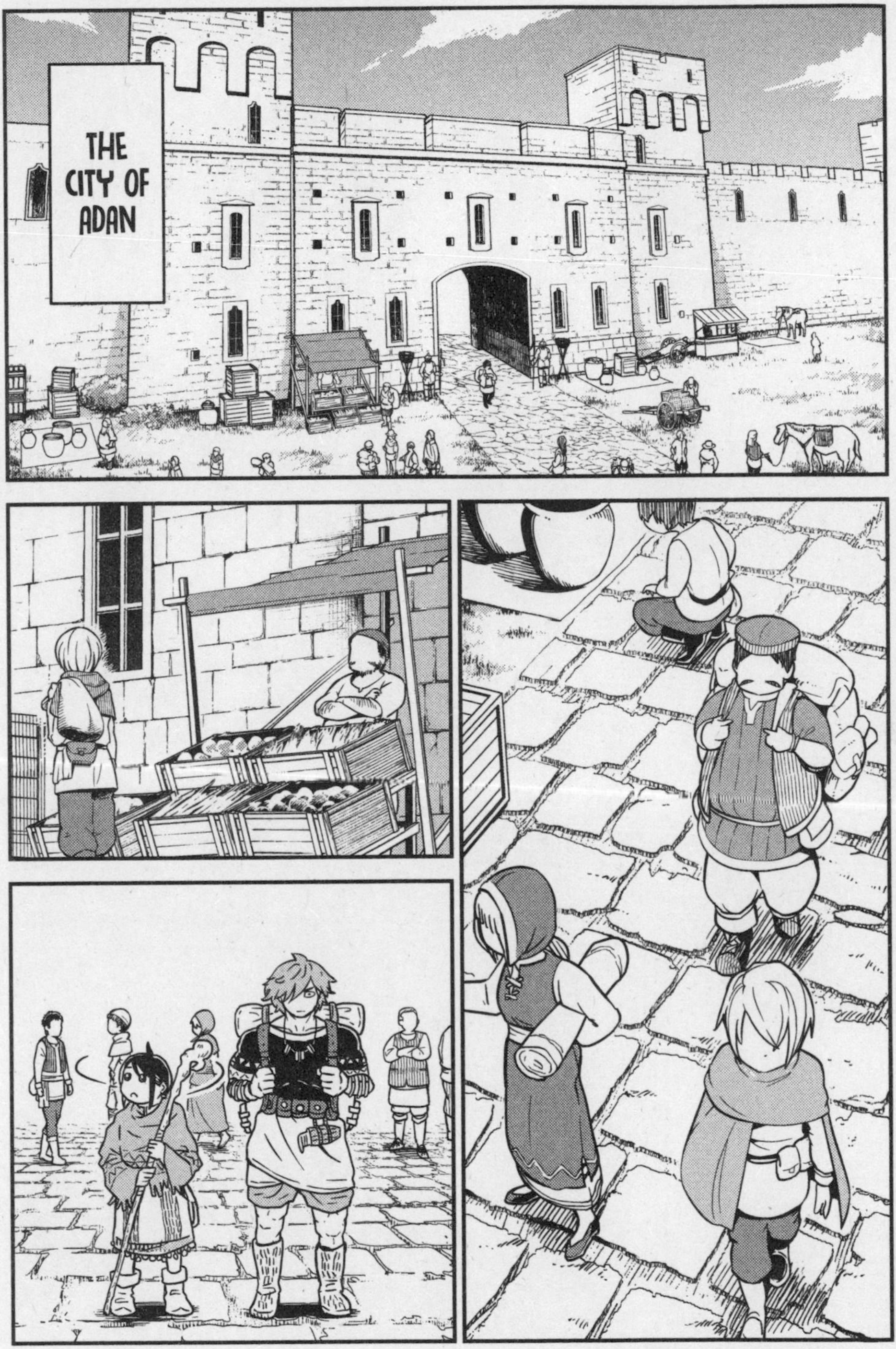
THE CITY OF ADAN

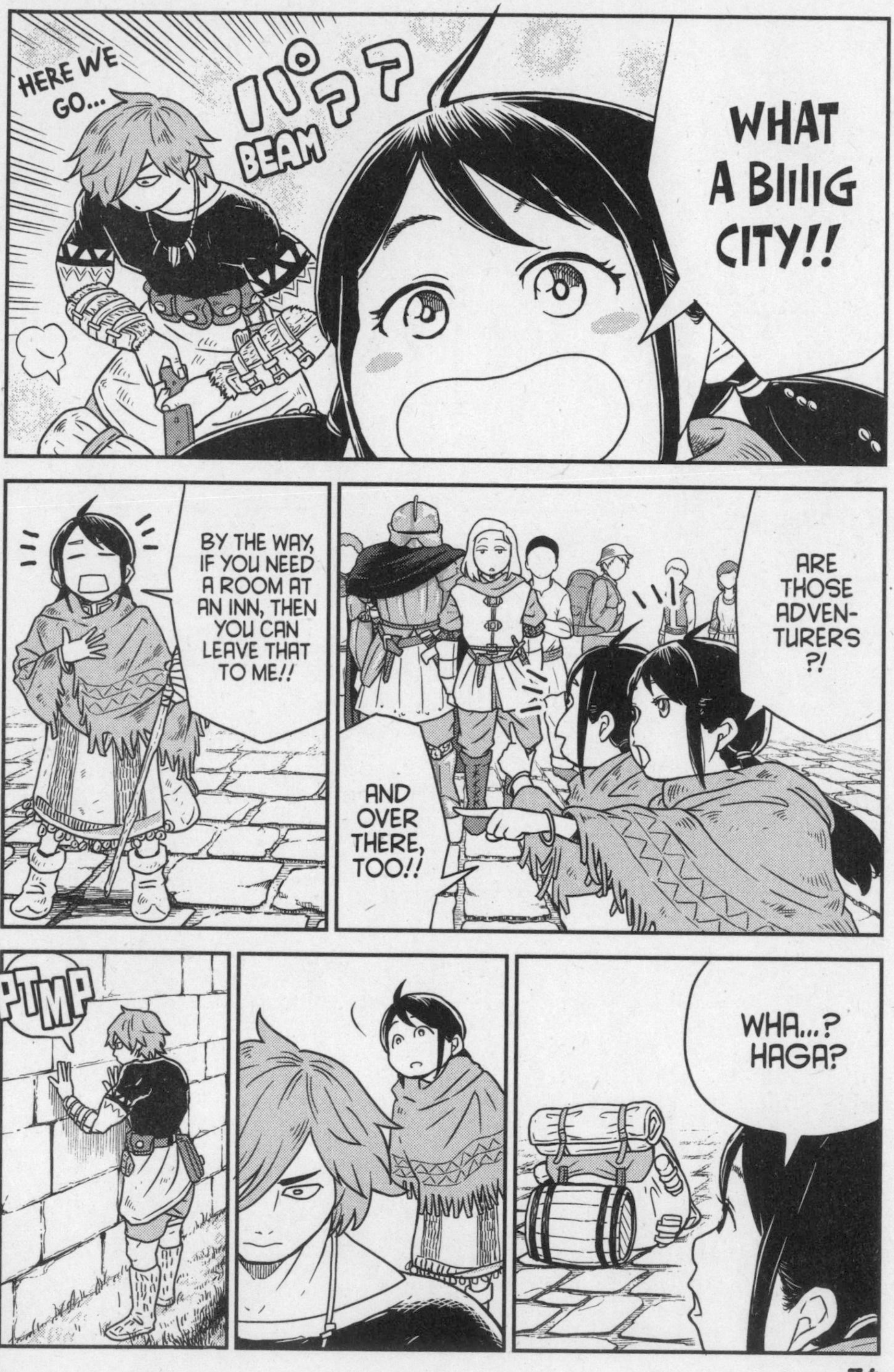
WHAT A BIIIG CITY!!
パァァ BEAM
HERE WE GO...
ARE THOSE ADVEN-TURERS?!
AND OVER THERE, TOO!!
BY THE WAY, IF YOU NEED A ROOM AT AN INN, THEN YOU CAN LEAVE THAT TO ME!!
WHA...? HAGA?
PTMP

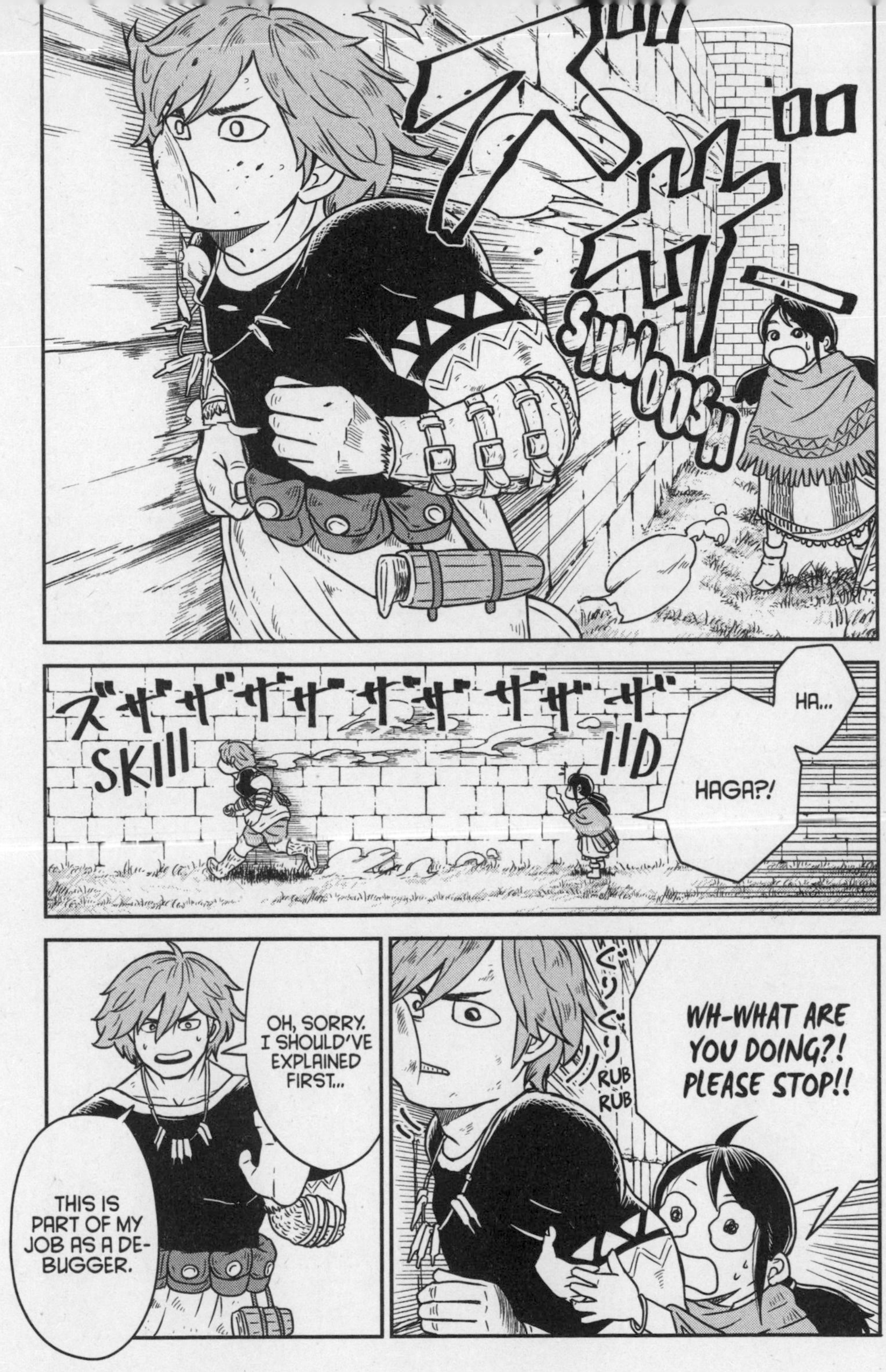
SHWOOSH
ズザザザザザザザザザ
SKIIIIID
HA...
HAGA?!
ぐりぐりぐり
RUB RUB
WH-WHAT ARE YOU DOING?! PLEASE STOP!!
OH, SORRY. I SHOULD'VE EXPLAINED FIRST...
THIS IS PART OF MY JOB AS A DE-BUGGER.

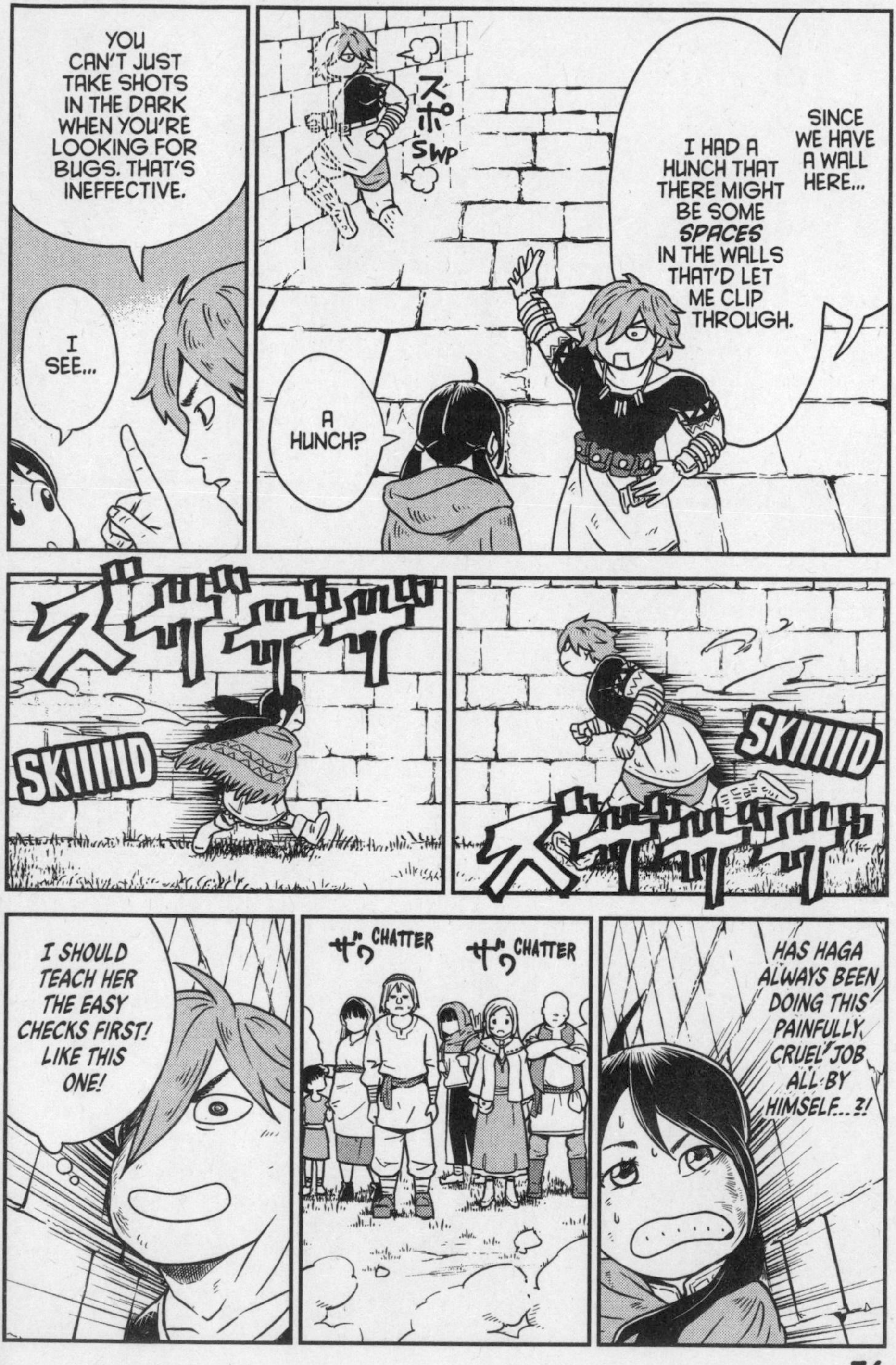
SINCE WE HAVE A WALL HERE...
I HAD A HUNCH THAT THERE MIGHT BE SOME *SPACES* IN THE WALLS THAT'D LET ME CLIP THROUGH.
ズポ SWP
A HUNCH?
YOU CAN'T JUST TAKE SHOTS IN THE DARK WHEN YOU'RE LOOKING FOR BUGS. THAT'S INEFFECTIVE.
I SEE...
SKIIIIID
SKIIIIID
HAS HAGA ALWAYS BEEN DOING THIS PAINFULLY CRUEL JOB ALL BY HIMSELF...?!
ザワ CHATTER
ザワ CHATTER
I SHOULD TEACH HER THE EASY CHECKS FIRST! LIKE THIS ONE!

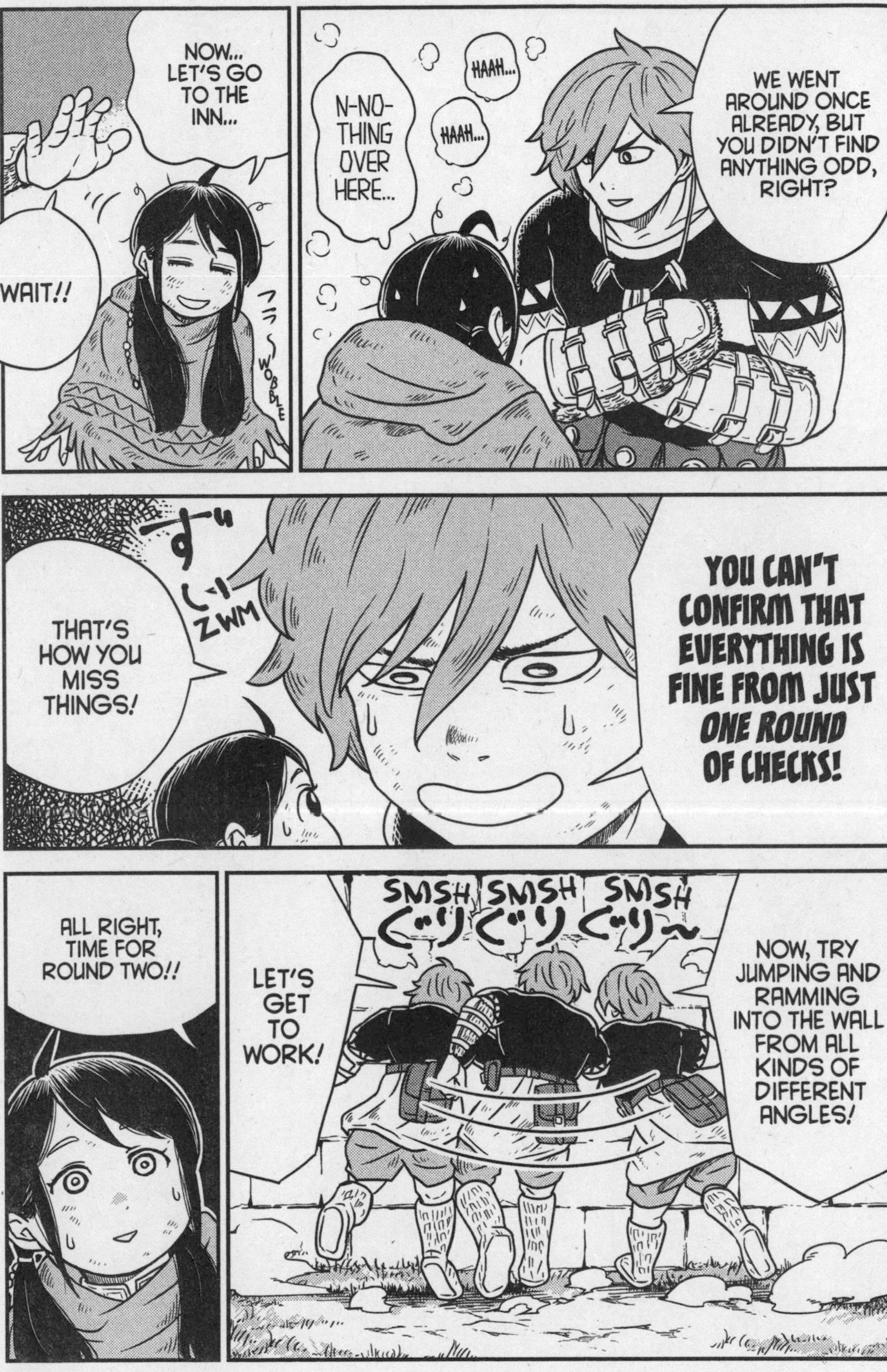
WE WENT AROUND ONCE ALREADY, BUT YOU DIDN'T FIND ANYTHING ODD, RIGHT?
HAAH...
N-NO-THING OVER HERE...
HAAH...
NOW... LET'S GO TO THE INN...
WAIT!!
フラ
WOBBLE
YOU CAN'T CONFIRM THAT EVERYTHING IS FINE FROM JUST *ONE ROUND* OF CHECKS!
ずい
ZWM
THAT'S HOW YOU MISS THINGS!
SMSH SMSH SMSH
ぐり ぐり ぐり〜
NOW, TRY JUMPING AND RAMMING INTO THE WALL FROM ALL KINDS OF DIFFERENT ANGLES!
LET'S GET TO WORK!
ALL RIGHT, TIME FOR ROUND TWO!!

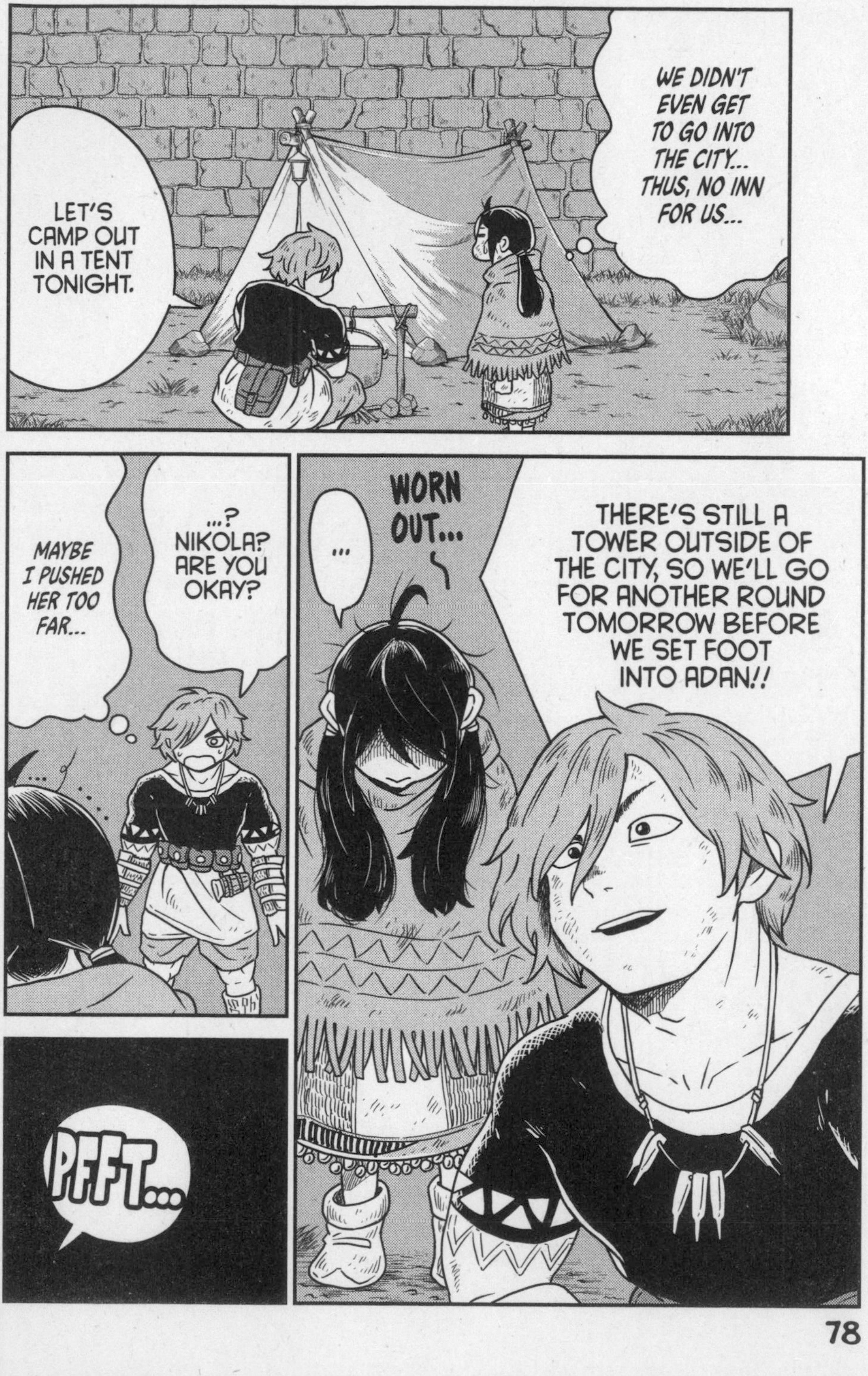
WE DIDN'T EVEN GET TO GO INTO THE CITY... THUS, NO INN FOR US...
LET'S CAMP OUT IN A TENT TONIGHT.
THERE'S STILL A TOWER OUTSIDE OF THE CITY, SO WE'LL GO FOR ANOTHER ROUND TOMORROW BEFORE WE SET FOOT INTO ADAN!!
WORN OUT...
...
...? NIKOLA? ARE YOU OKAY?
MAYBE I PUSHED HER TOO FAR...
...
PFFT...

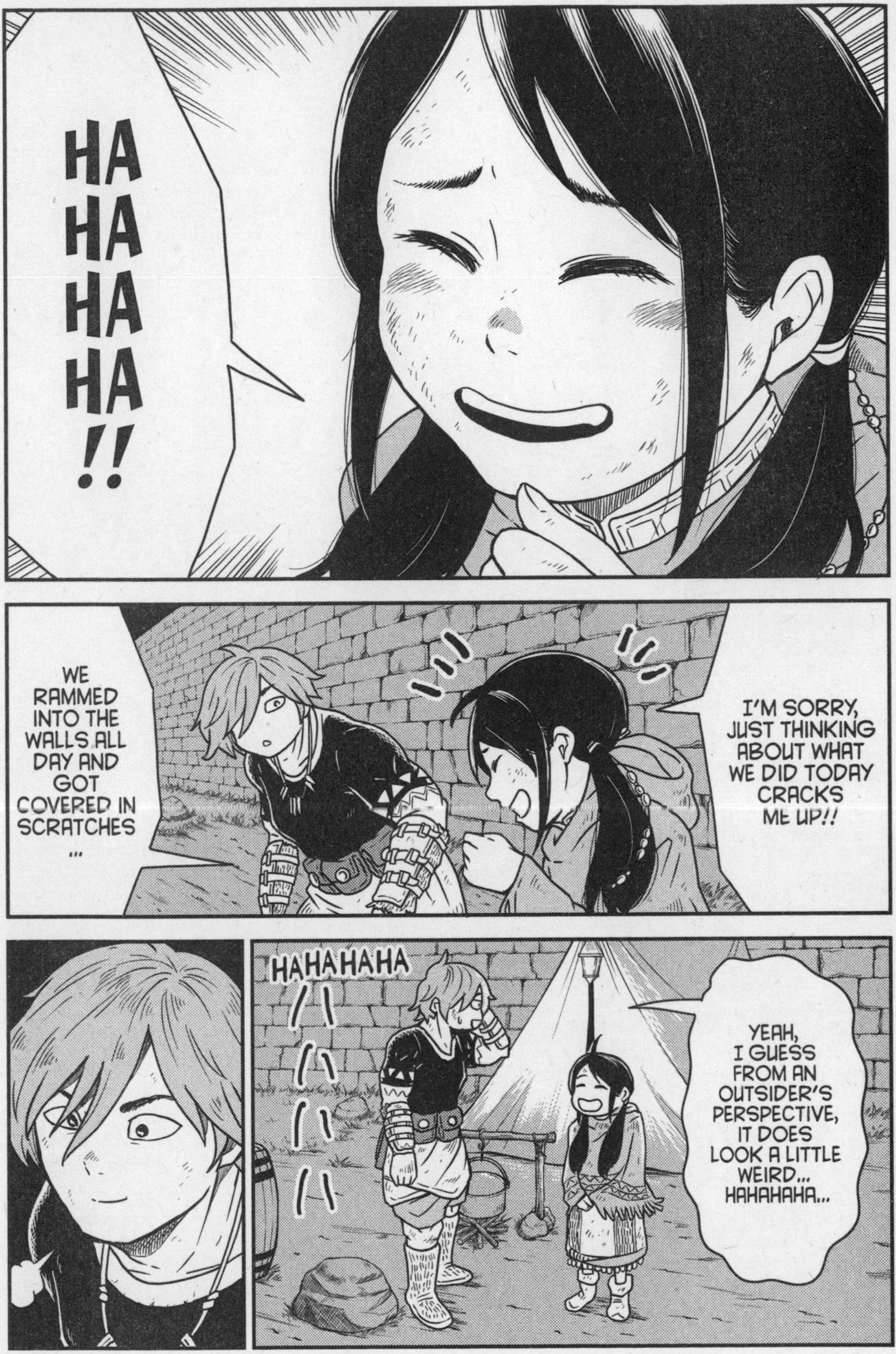
HA HA HA HA!!
I'M SORRY, JUST THINKING ABOUT WHAT WE DID TODAY CRACKS ME UP!!
WE RAMMED INTO THE WALLS ALL DAY AND GOT COVERED IN SCRATCHES ...
YEAH, I GUESS FROM AN OUTSIDER'S PERSPECTIVE, IT DOES LOOK A LITTLE WEIRD... HAHAHAHA...
HAHAHAHA

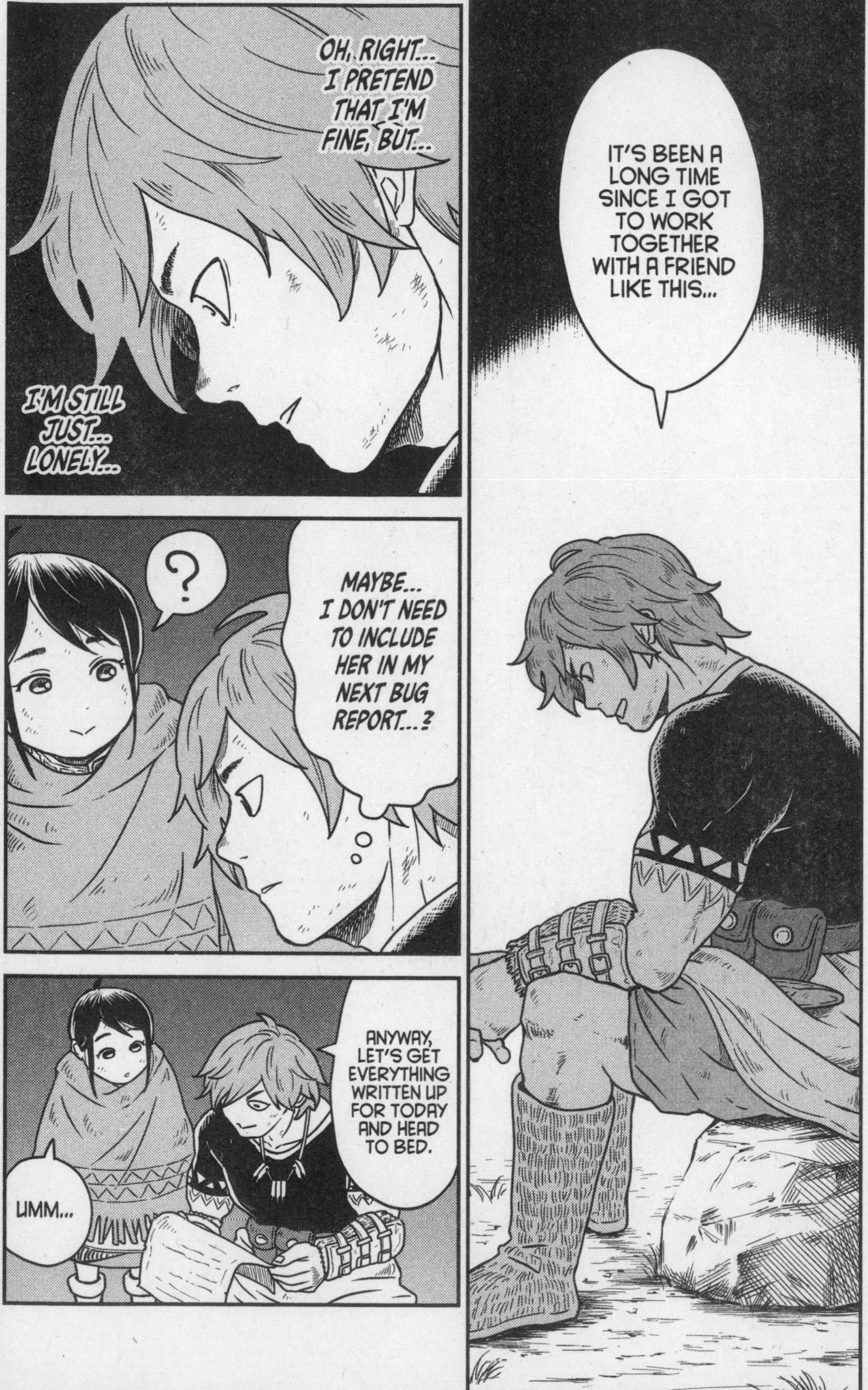
IT'S BEEN A LONG TIME SINCE I GOT TO WORK TOGETHER WITH A FRIEND LIKE THIS...
OH, RIGHT... I PRETEND THAT I'M FINE, BUT...
I'M STILL JUST... LONELY...
MAYBE... I DON'T NEED TO INCLUDE HER IN MY NEXT BUG REPORT...?
?
ANYWAY, LET'S GET EVERYTHING WRITTEN UP FOR TODAY AND HEAD TO BED.
UMM...

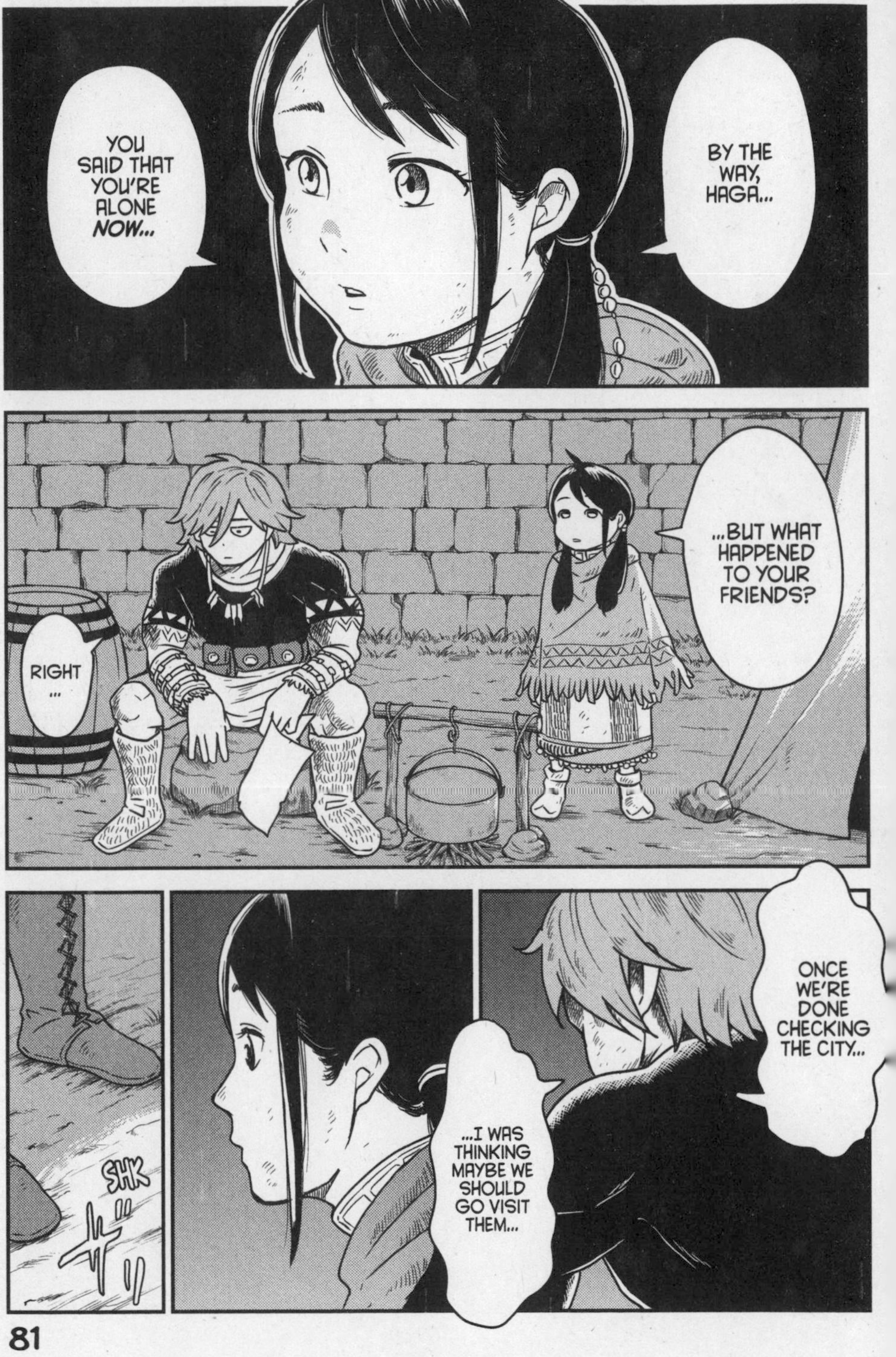
BY THE WAY, HAGA...
YOU SAID THAT YOU'RE ALONE *NOW*...
...BUT WHAT HAPPENED TO YOUR FRIENDS?
RIGHT ...
ONCE WE'RE DONE CHECKING THE CITY...
...I WAS THINKING MAYBE WE SHOULD GO VISIT THEM...
SHK
ザッ

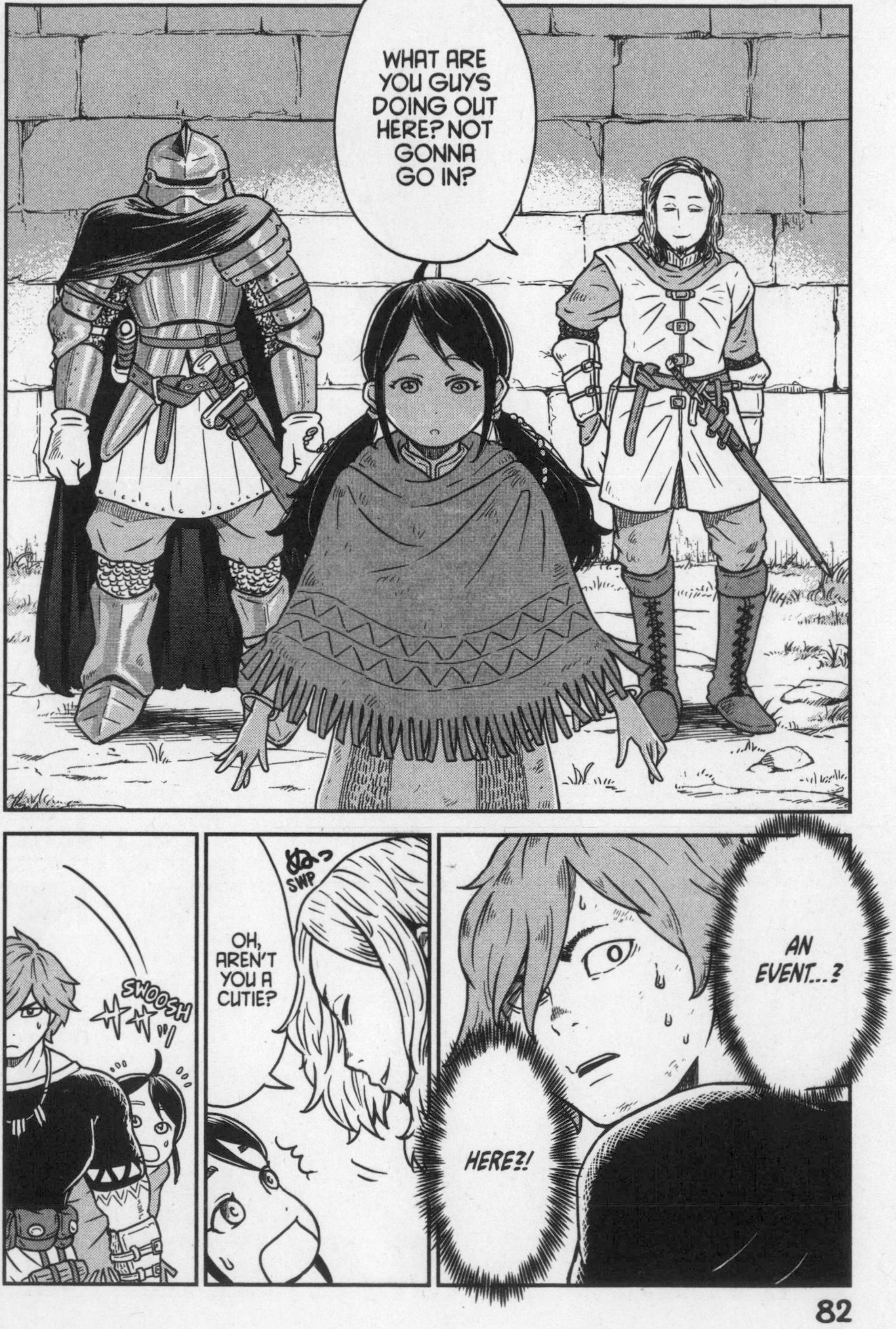
WHAT ARE YOU GUYS DOING OUT HERE? NOT GONNA GO IN?
AN EVENT...?
HERE?!
SWP
OH, AREN'T YOU A CUTIE?
SWOOSH

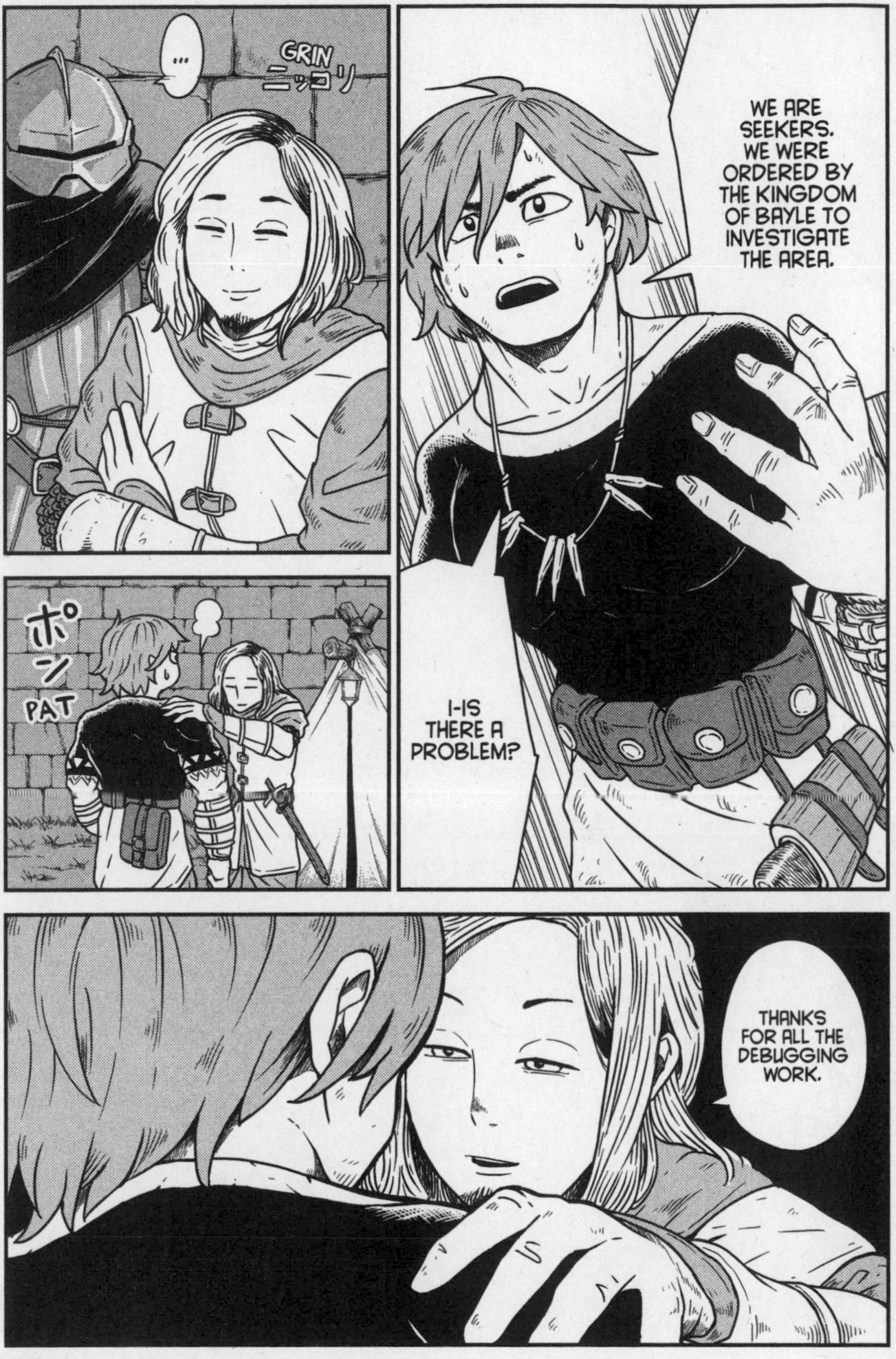
WE ARE SEEKERS. WE WERE ORDERED BY THE KINGDOM OF BAYLE TO INVESTIGATE THE AREA.
I-IS THERE A PROBLEM?
GRIN
ニッコリ
...
ポン
PAT
THANKS FOR ALL THE DEBUGGING WORK.

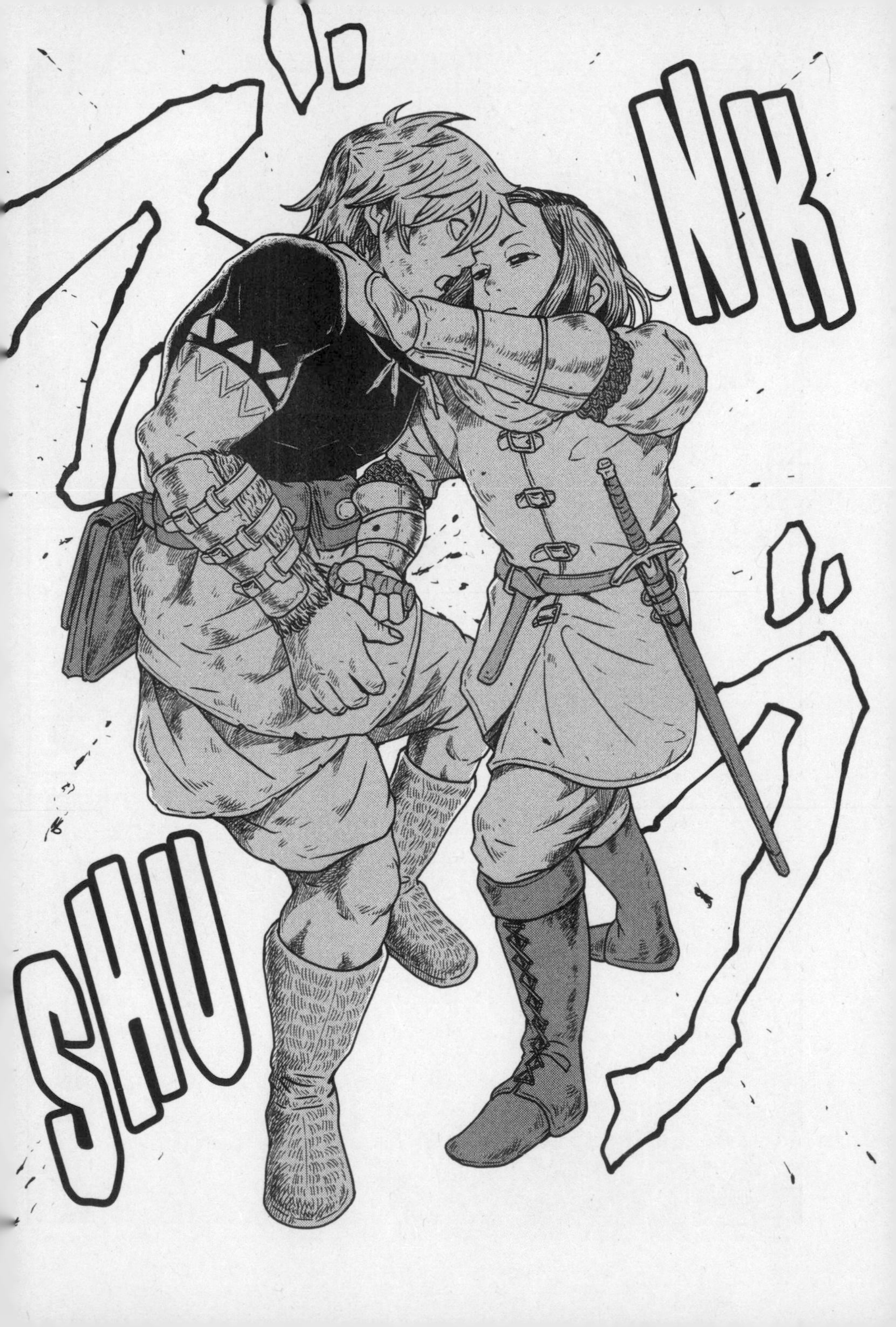
SHU
NK

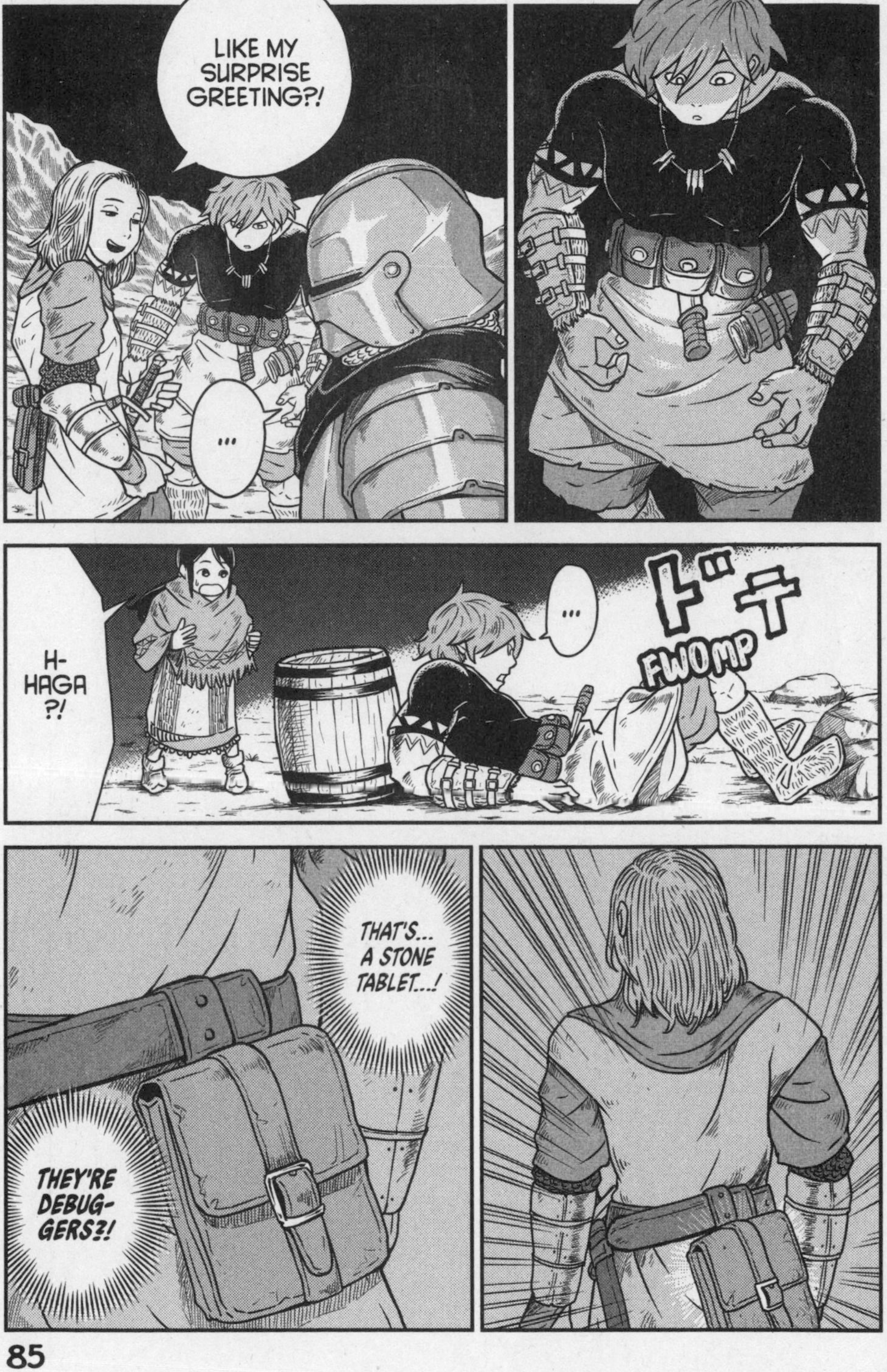
LIKE MY SURPRISE GREETING?!
...
ドテ
FWOMP
...
H-HAGA?!
THAT'S... A STONE TABLET...!
THEY'RE DEBUG-GERS?!

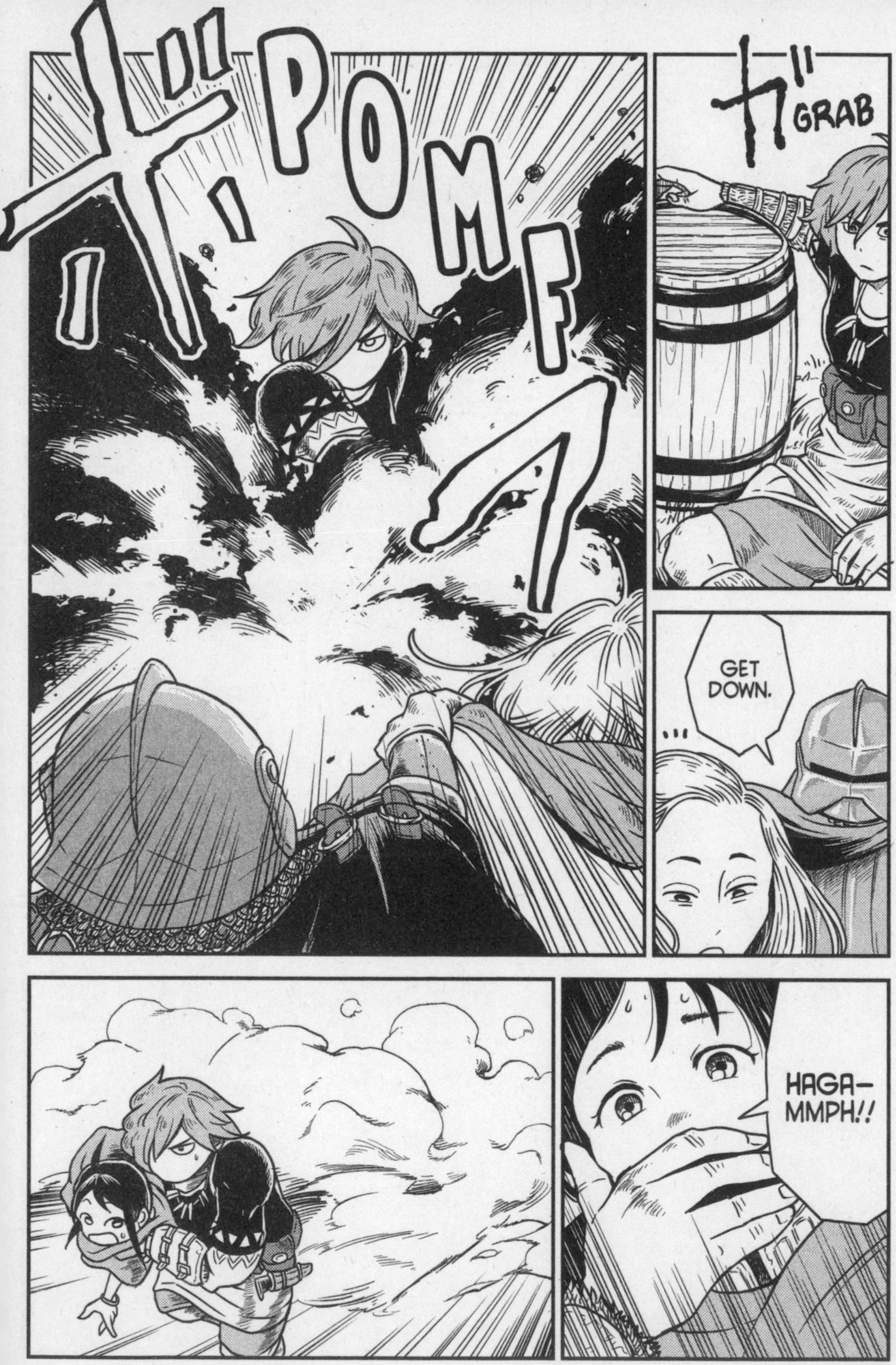
GRAB
GET DOWN.
...
POMF
HAGA-MMPH!!

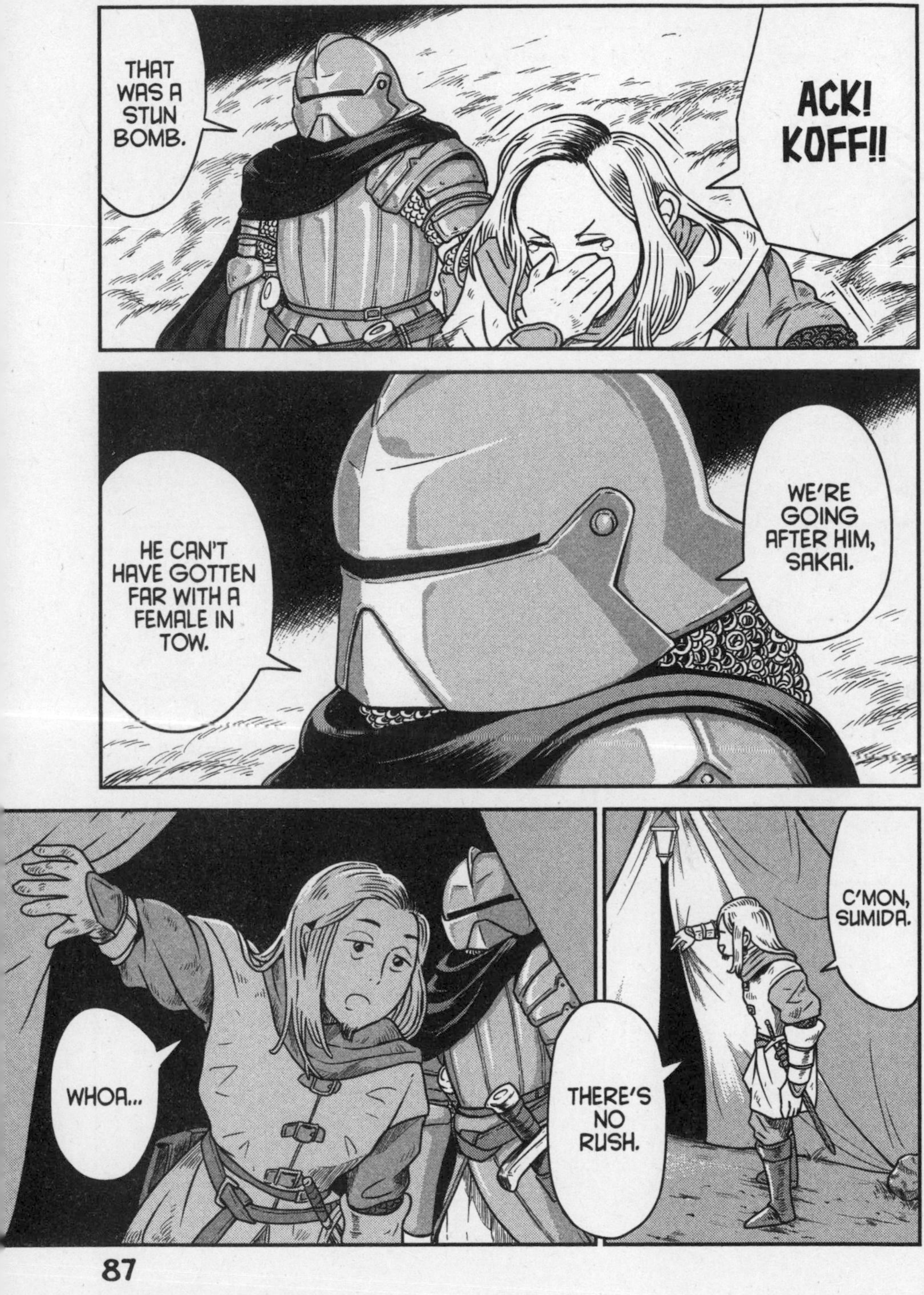
ACK! KOFF!!
THAT WAS A STUN BOMB.
WE'RE GOING AFTER HIM, SAKAI.
HE CAN'T HAVE GOTTEN FAR WITH A FEMALE IN TOW.
C'MON, SUMIDA.
THERE'S NO RUSH.
WHOA...

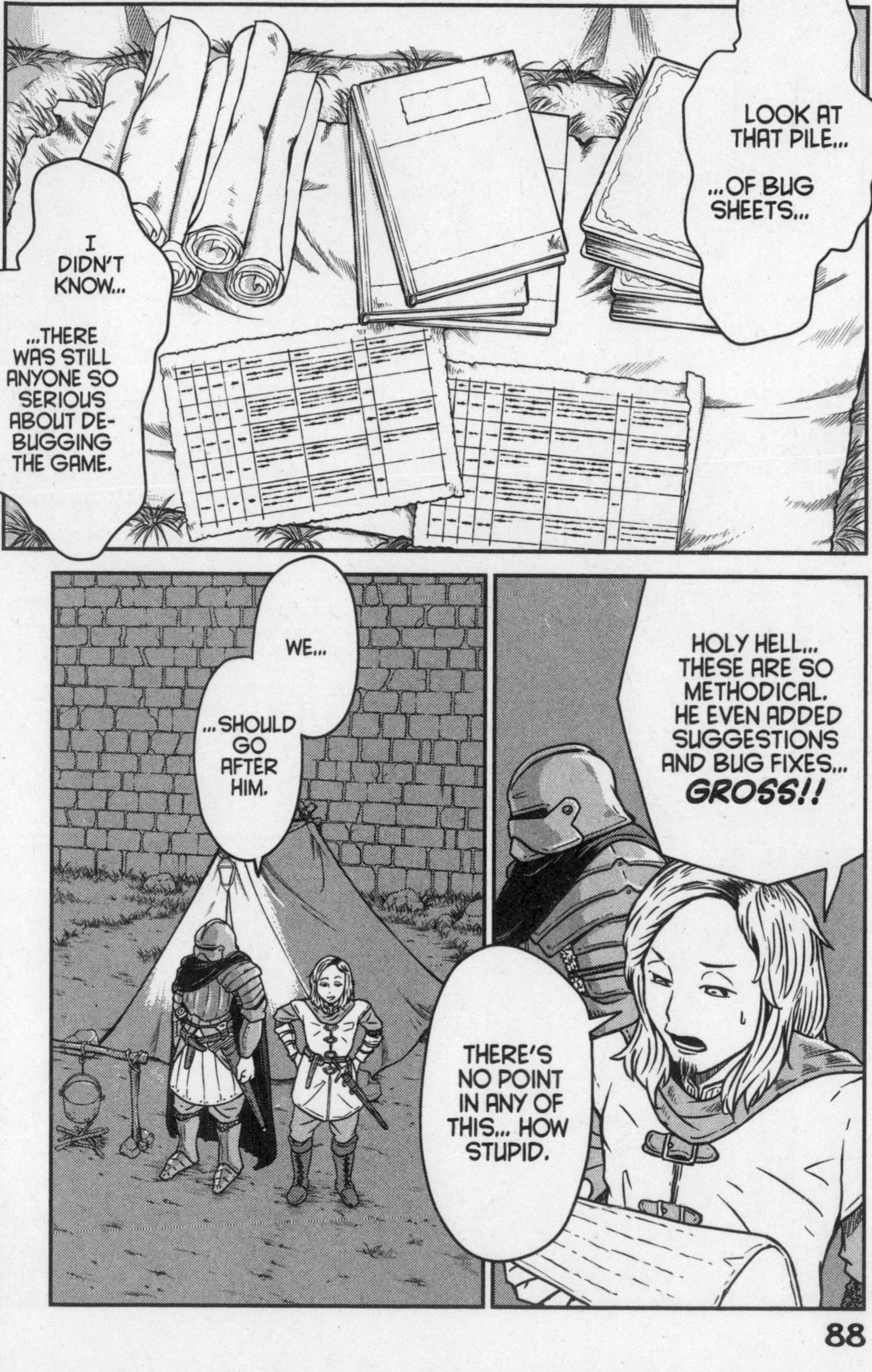
LOOK AT THAT PILE...
...OF BUG SHEETS...
I DIDN'T KNOW...
...THERE WAS STILL ANYONE SO SERIOUS ABOUT DE-BUGGING THE GAME.
HOLY HELL... THESE ARE SO METHODICAL. HE EVEN ADDED SUGGESTIONS AND BUG FIXES... GROSS!!
THERE'S NO POINT IN ANY OF THIS... HOW STUPID.
WE...
...SHOULD GO AFTER HIM.

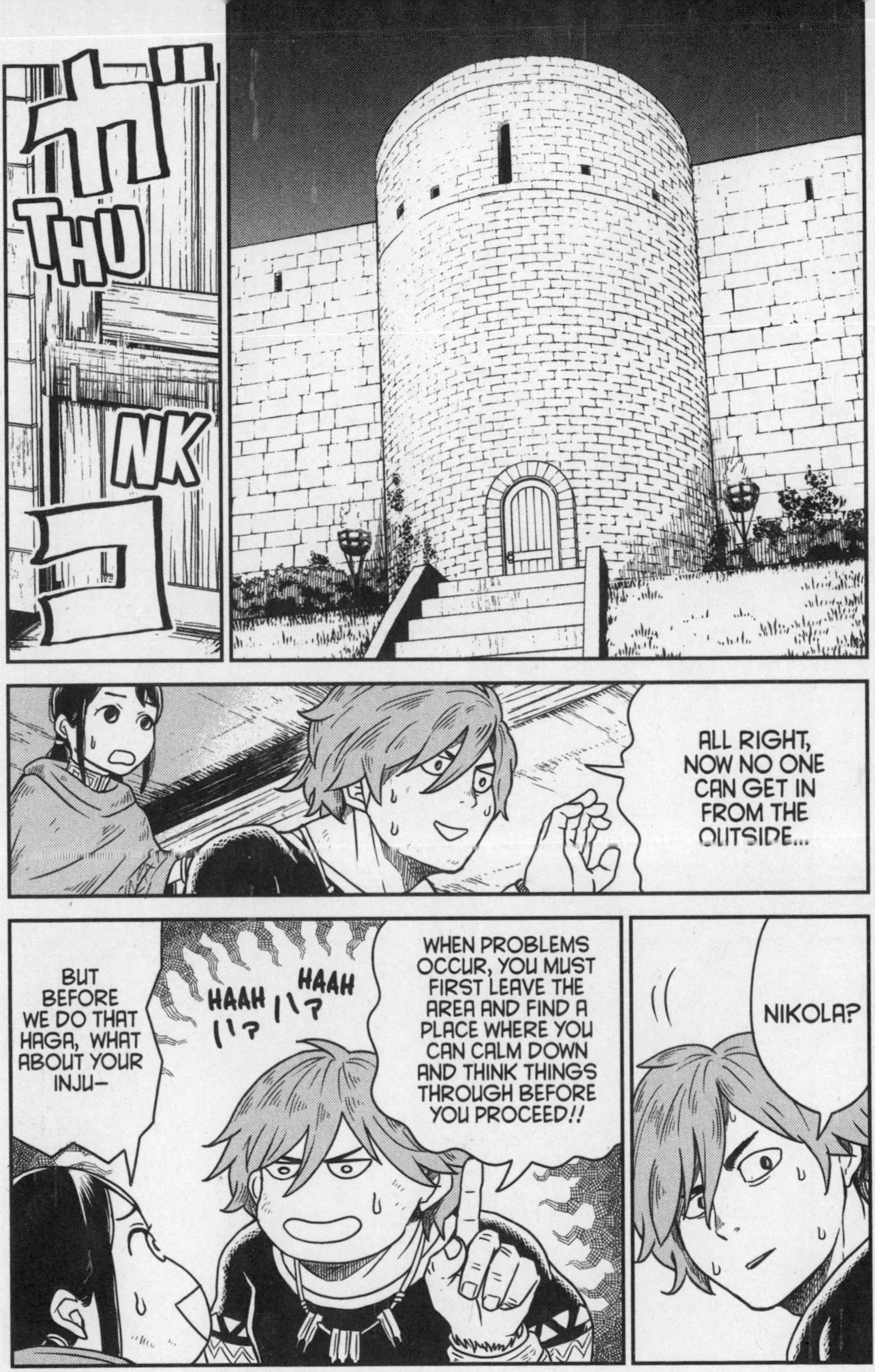
THU
NK
ALL RIGHT, NOW NO ONE CAN GET IN FROM THE OUTSIDE...
NIKOLA?
WHEN PROBLEMS OCCUR, YOU MUST FIRST LEAVE THE AREA AND FIND A PLACE WHERE YOU CAN CALM DOWN AND THINK THINGS THROUGH BEFORE YOU PROCEED!!
HAAH
HAAH
BUT BEFORE WE DO THAT HAGA, WHAT ABOUT YOUR INJU–

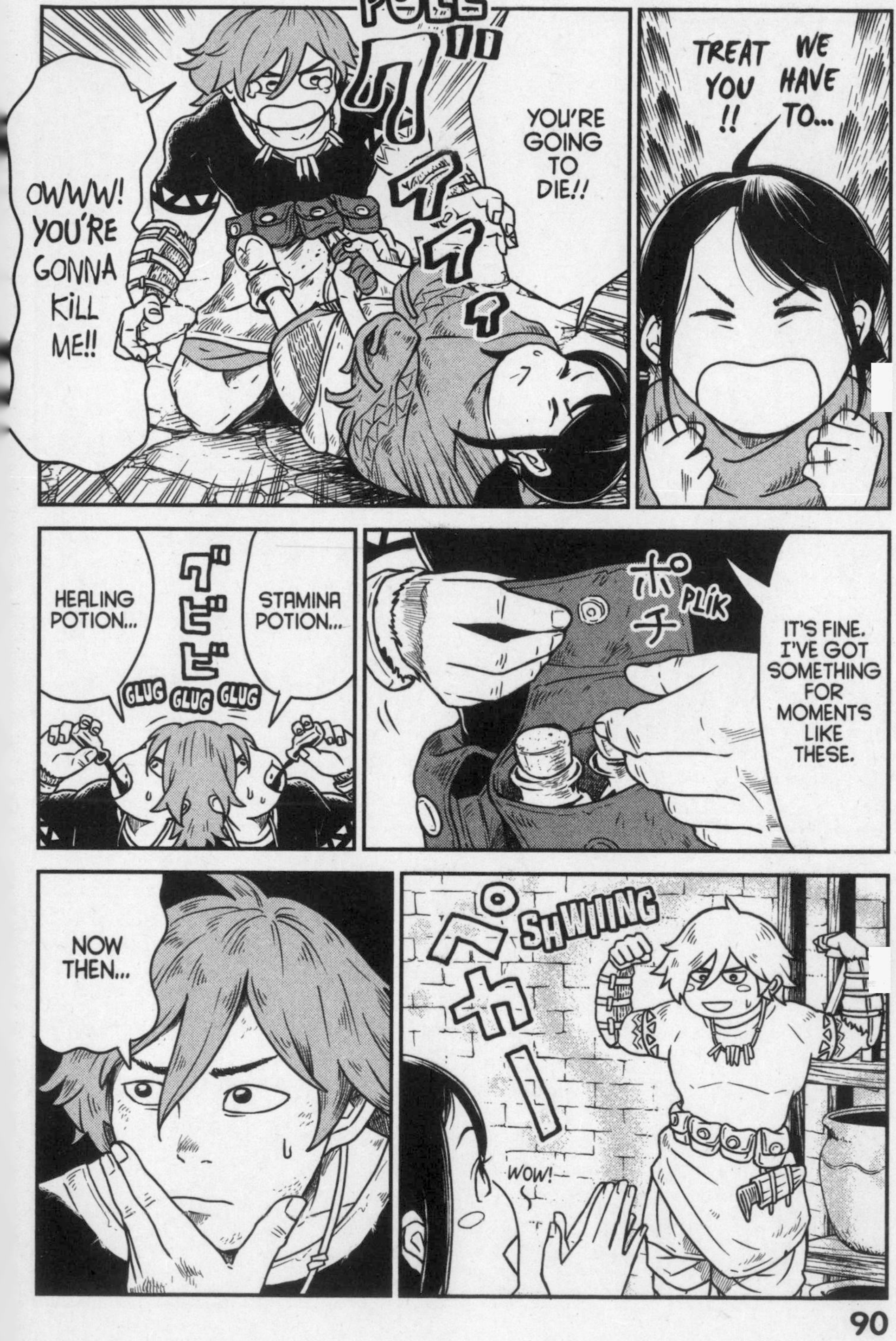

WE HAVE TO... TREAT YOU!!
PULL
YOU'RE GOING TO DIE!!
OWWW! YOU'RE GONNA KILL ME!!
IT'S FINE. I'VE GOT SOMETHING FOR MOMENTS LIKE THESE.
ポチ
PLIK
STAMINA POTION...
グビビ
HEALING POTION...
GLUG GLUG GLUG
ペカー
SHWIIING
WOW!
NOW THEN...

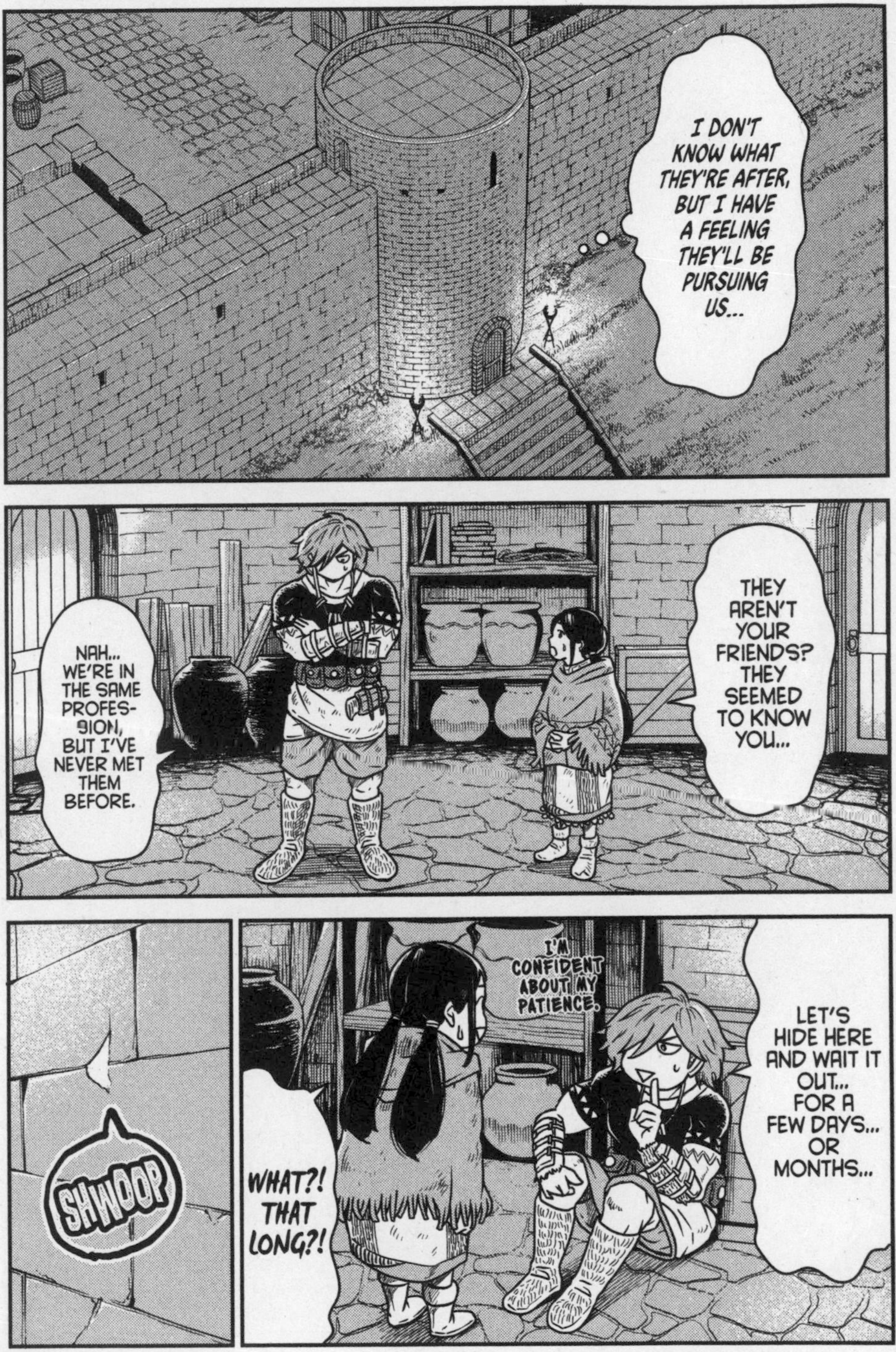
I DON'T KNOW WHAT THEY'RE AFTER, BUT I HAVE A FEELING THEY'LL BE PURSUING US...
THEY AREN'T YOUR FRIENDS? THEY SEEMED TO KNOW YOU...
NAH... WE'RE IN THE SAME PROFES-SION, BUT I'VE NEVER MET THEM BEFORE.
LET'S HIDE HERE AND WAIT IT OUT... FOR A FEW DAYS... OR MONTHS...
I'M CONFIDENT ABOUT MY PATIENCE.
WHAT?! THAT LONG?!
SHWOOP

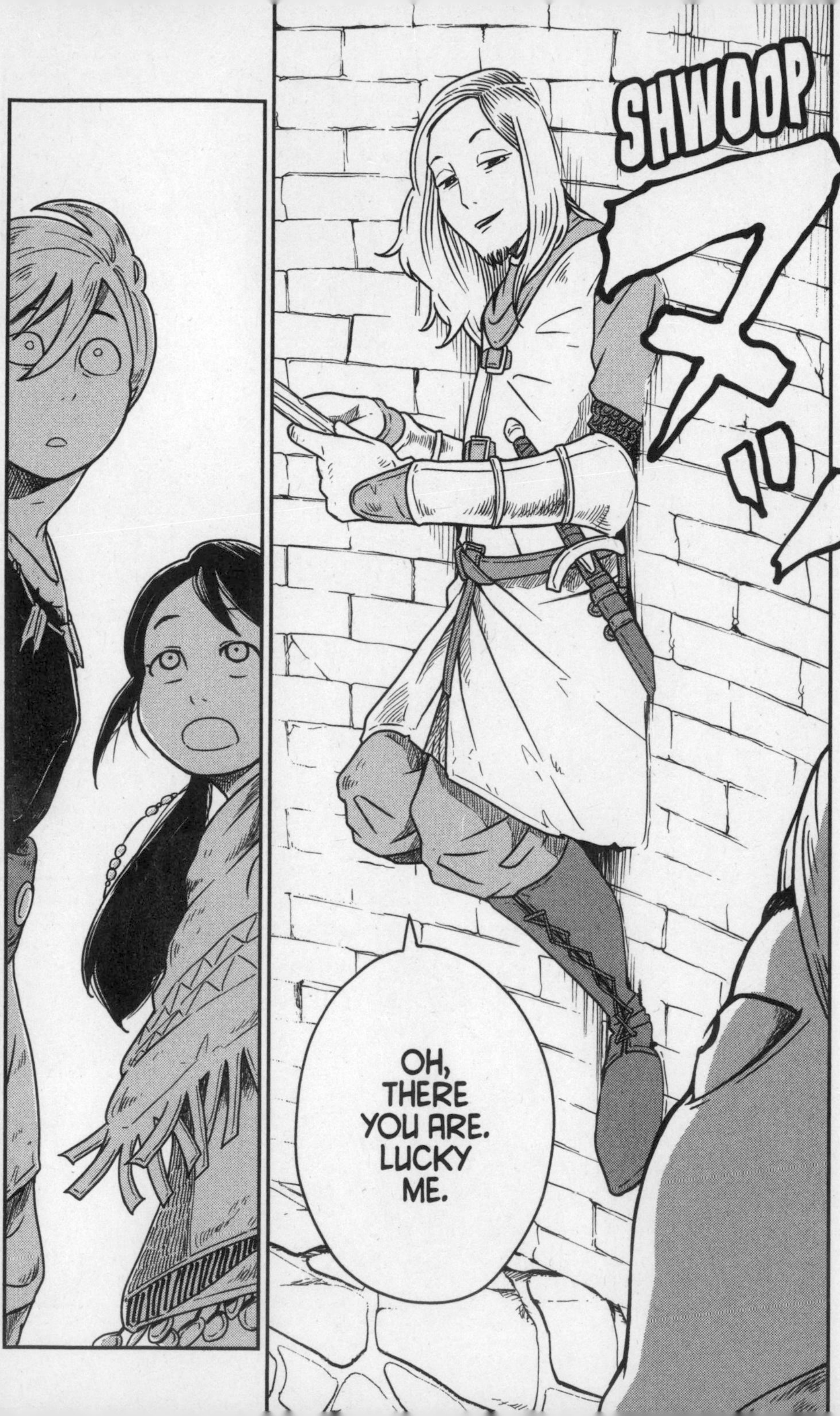
SHWOOP
OH, THERE YOU ARE. LUCKY ME.

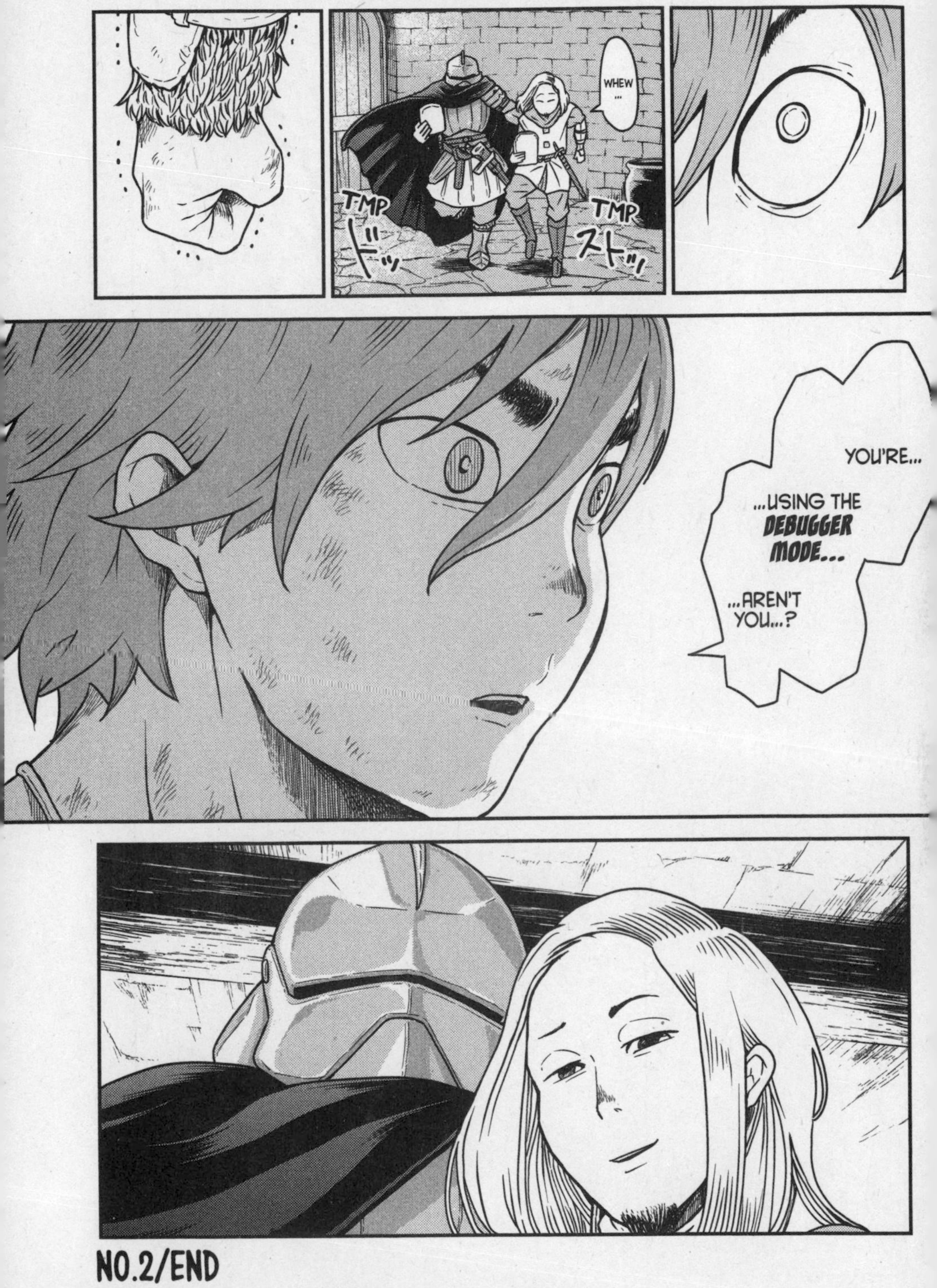
WHEW...
TMP ストッ
TMP ドッ
YOU'RE...
...USING THE DEBUGGER MODE...
...AREN'T YOU...?

NO.2/END

King's Seekers

The kings of Clayborne have gathered adventurers from across the island to create an exploration unit called the King's Seekers to travel and investigate the land.

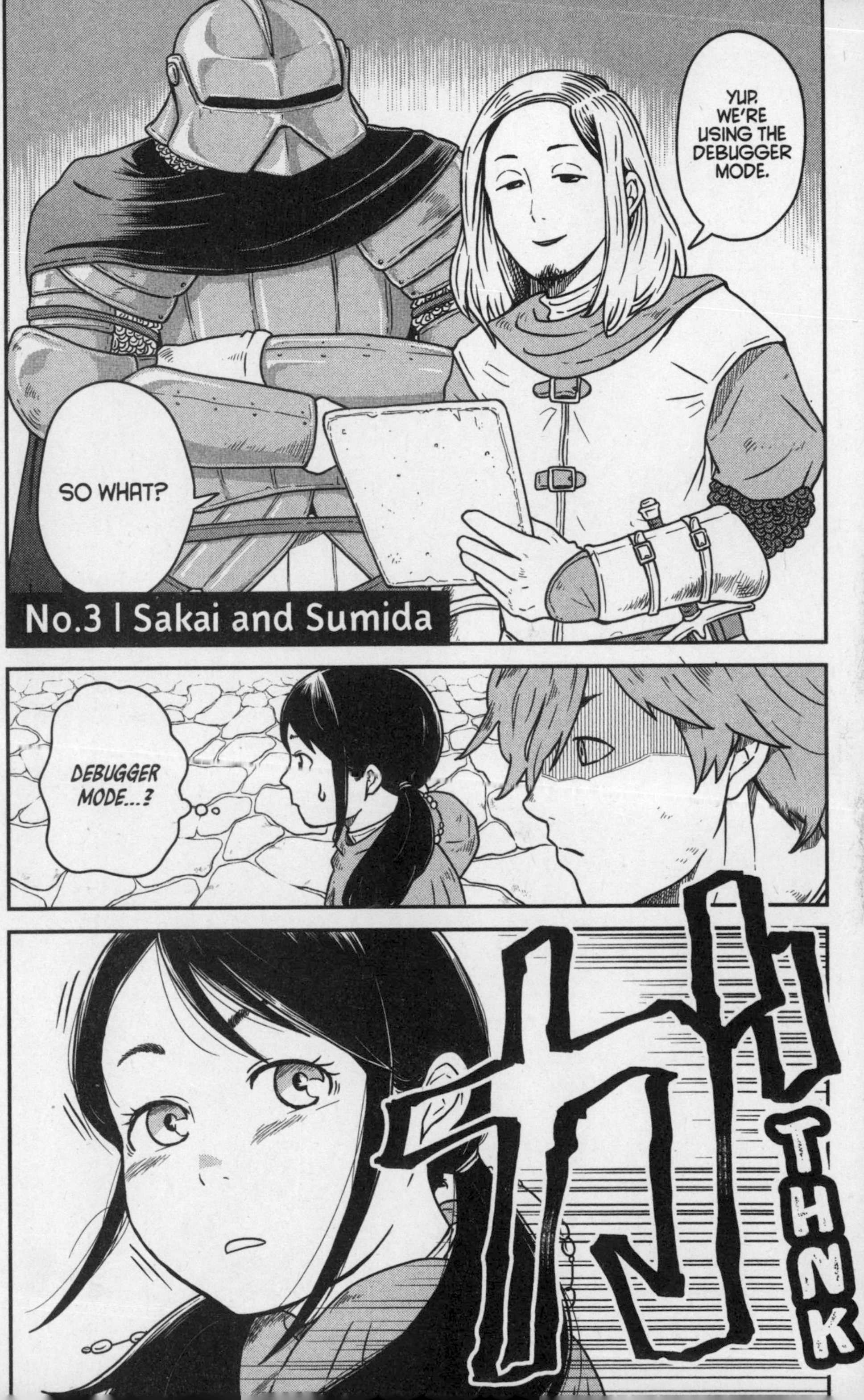
YUP. WE'RE USING THE DEBUGGER MODE.
SO WHAT?
No.3 | Sakai and Sumida
DEBUGGER MODE...?
THNK

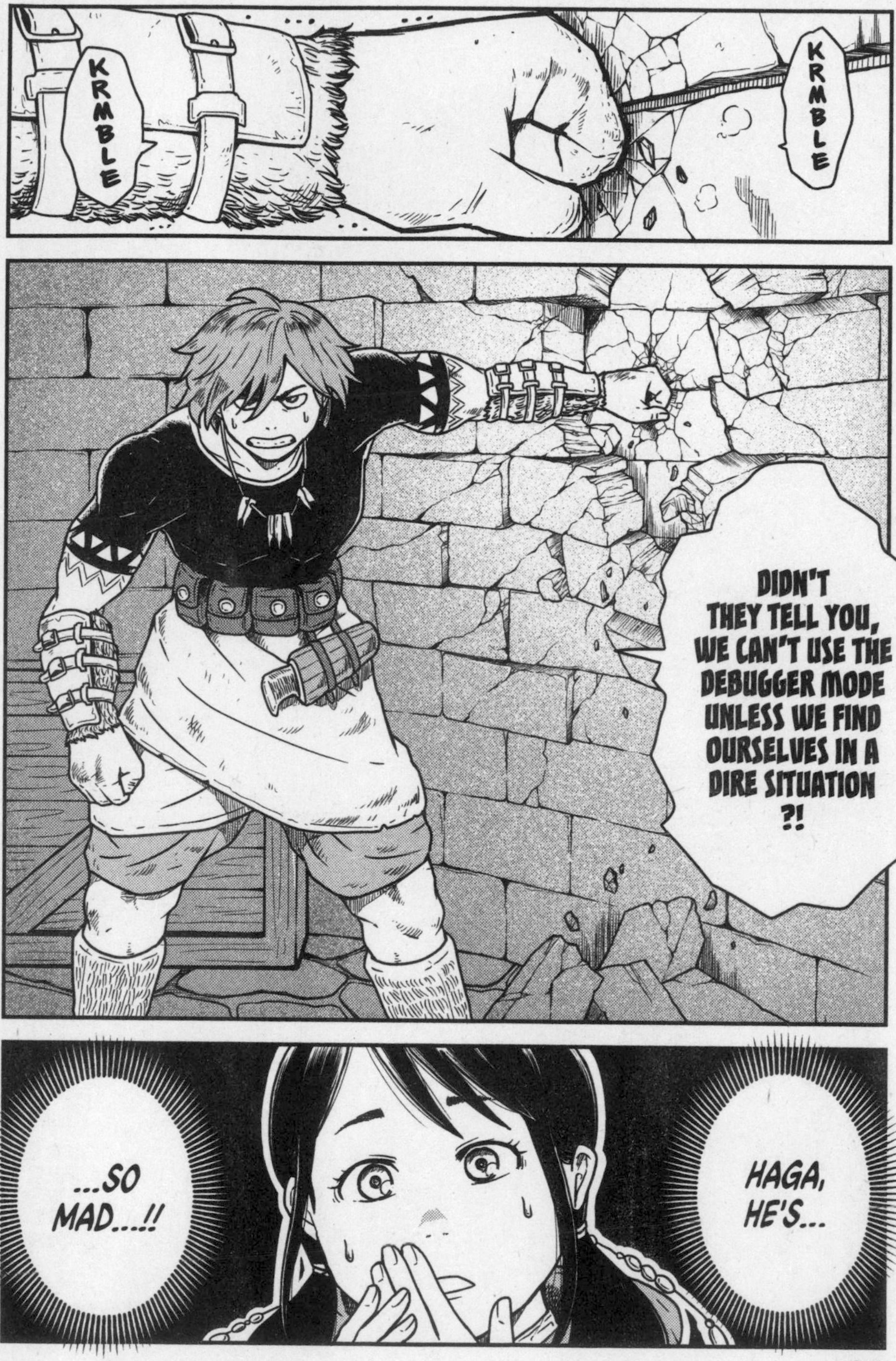
KRMBLE
KRMBLE
DIDN'T THEY TELL YOU, WE CAN'T USE THE DEBUGGER MODE UNLESS WE FIND OURSELVES IN A DIRE SITUATION ?!
HAGA, HE'S...
...SO MAD...!!

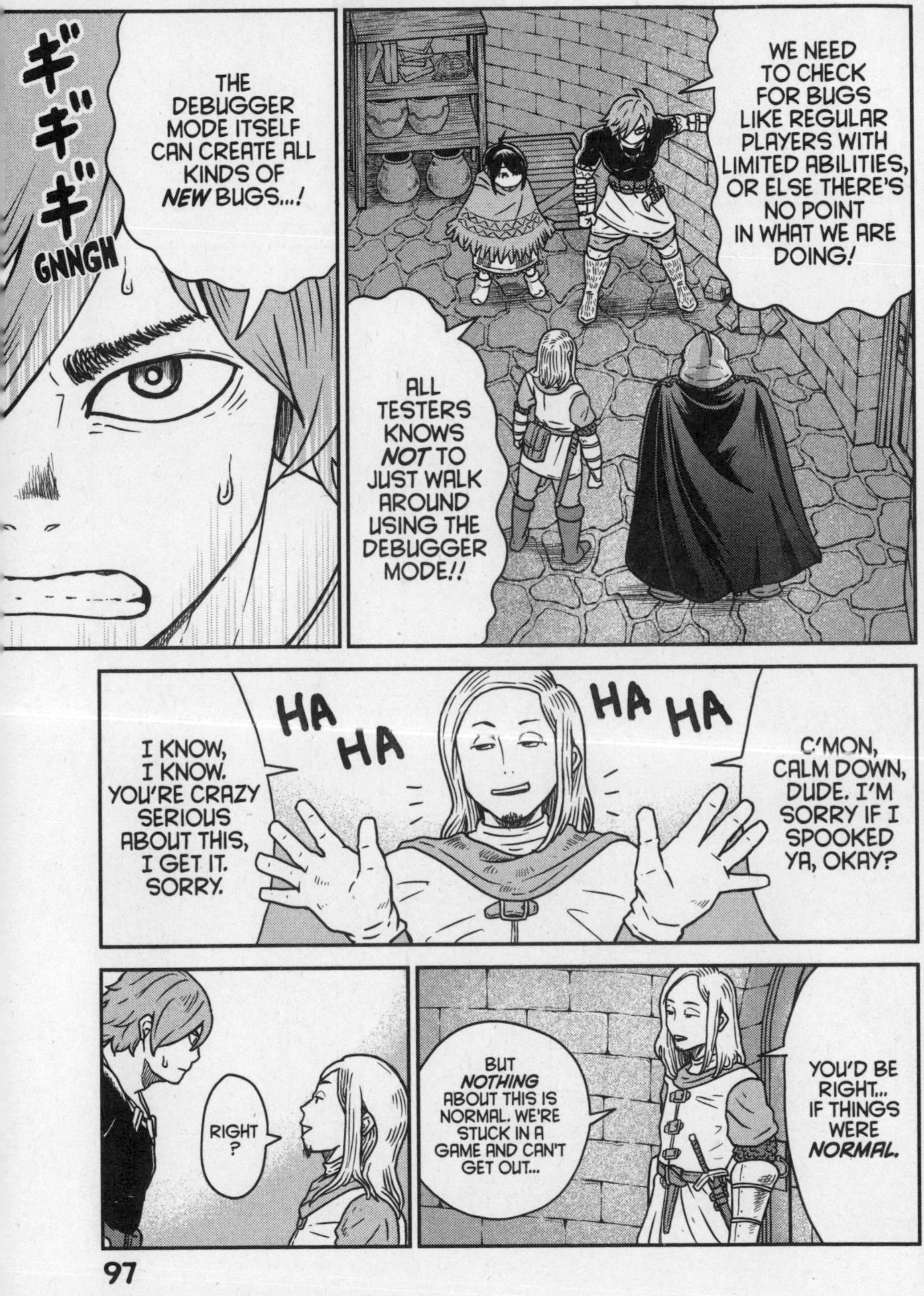
WE NEED TO CHECK FOR BUGS LIKE REGULAR PLAYERS WITH LIMITED ABILITIES, OR ELSE THERE'S NO POINT IN WHAT WE ARE DOING!
ALL TESTERS KNOWS *NOT* TO JUST WALK AROUND USING THE DEBUGGER MODE!!
ギギギ
GNNGH
THE DEBUGGER MODE ITSELF CAN CREATE ALL KINDS OF *NEW* BUGS...!
HA HA
C'MON, CALM DOWN, DUDE. I'M SORRY IF I SPOOKED YA, OKAY?
HA HA
I KNOW, I KNOW. YOU'RE CRAZY SERIOUS ABOUT THIS, I GET IT. SORRY.
YOU'D BE RIGHT... IF THINGS WERE *NORMAL.*
BUT *NOTHING* ABOUT THIS IS NORMAL. WE'RE STUCK IN A GAME AND CAN'T GET OUT...
RIGHT?

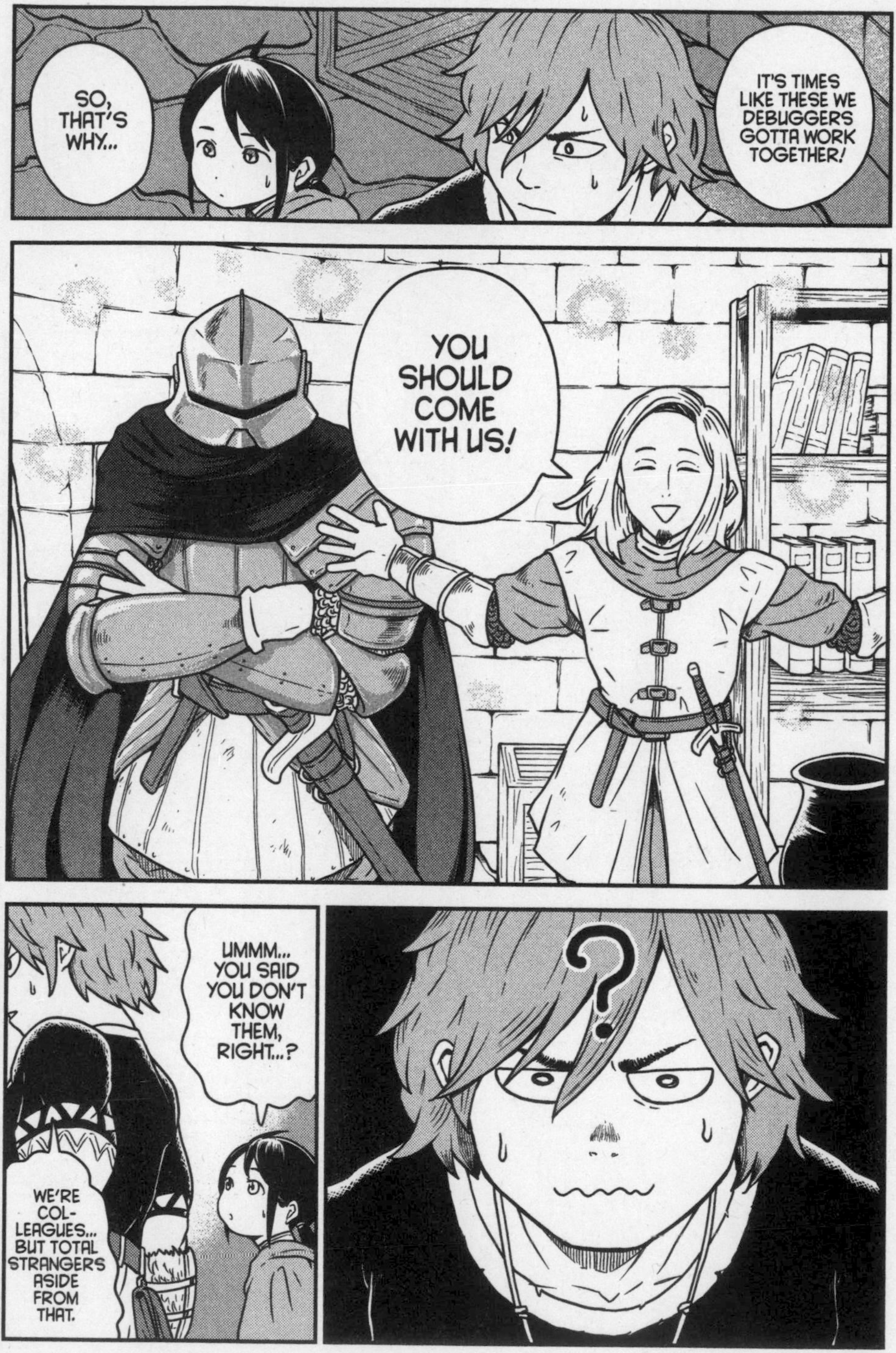
IT'S TIMES LIKE THESE WE DEBUGGERS GOTTA WORK TOGETHER!
SO, THAT'S WHY...
YOU SHOULD COME WITH US!
?
UMMM... YOU SAID YOU DON'T KNOW THEM, RIGHT...?
WE'RE COL-LEAGUES... BUT TOTAL STRANGERS ASIDE FROM THAT.

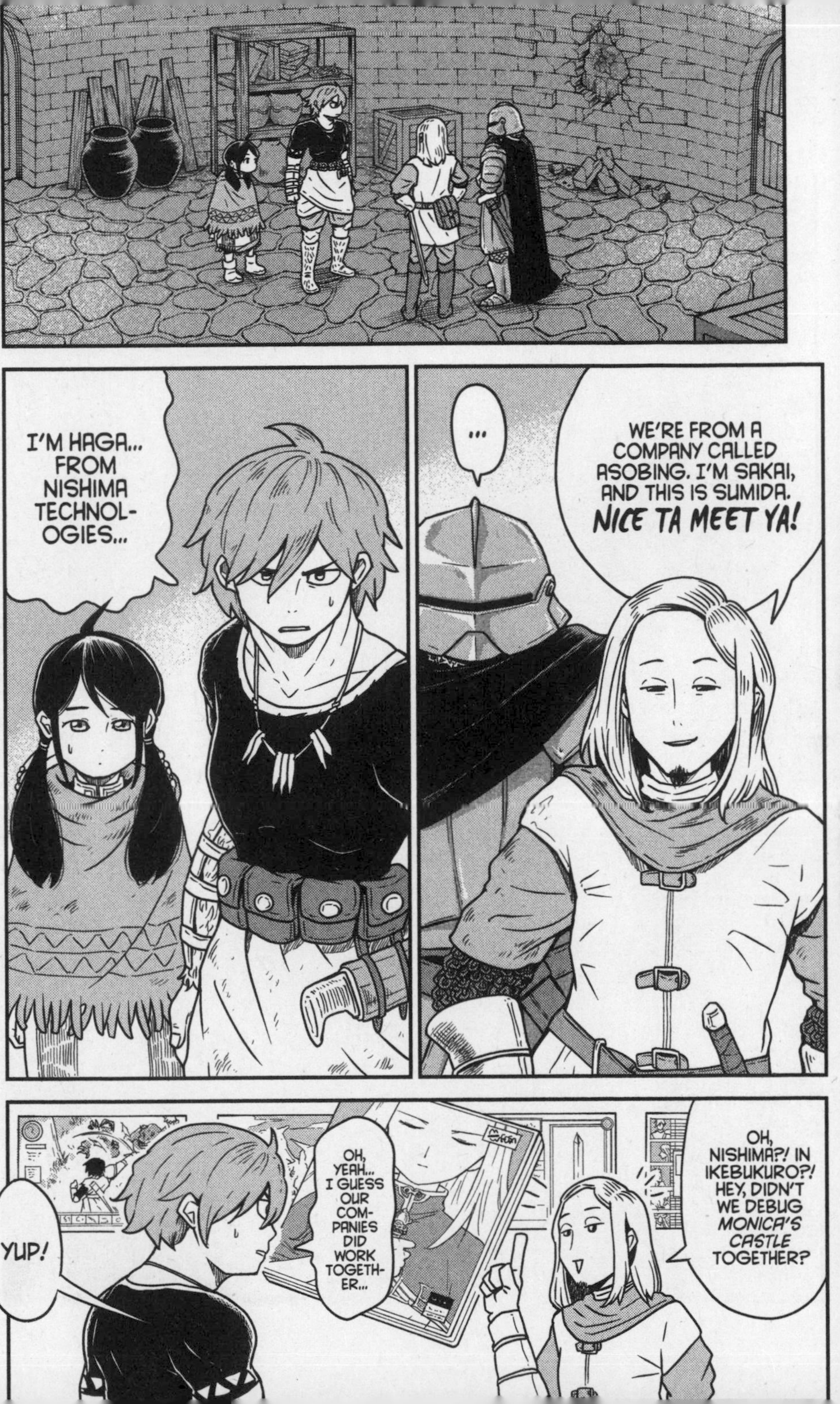
WE'RE FROM A COMPANY CALLED ASOBING. I'M SAKAI, AND THIS IS SUMIDA. NICE TA MEET YA!
...
I'M HAGA... FROM NISHIMA TECHNOLOGIES...
OH, NISHIMA?! IN IKEBUKURO?! HEY, DIDN'T WE DEBUG MONICA'S CASTLE TOGETHER?
OH, YEAH... I GUESS OUR COMPANIES DID WORK TOGETHER...
YUP!

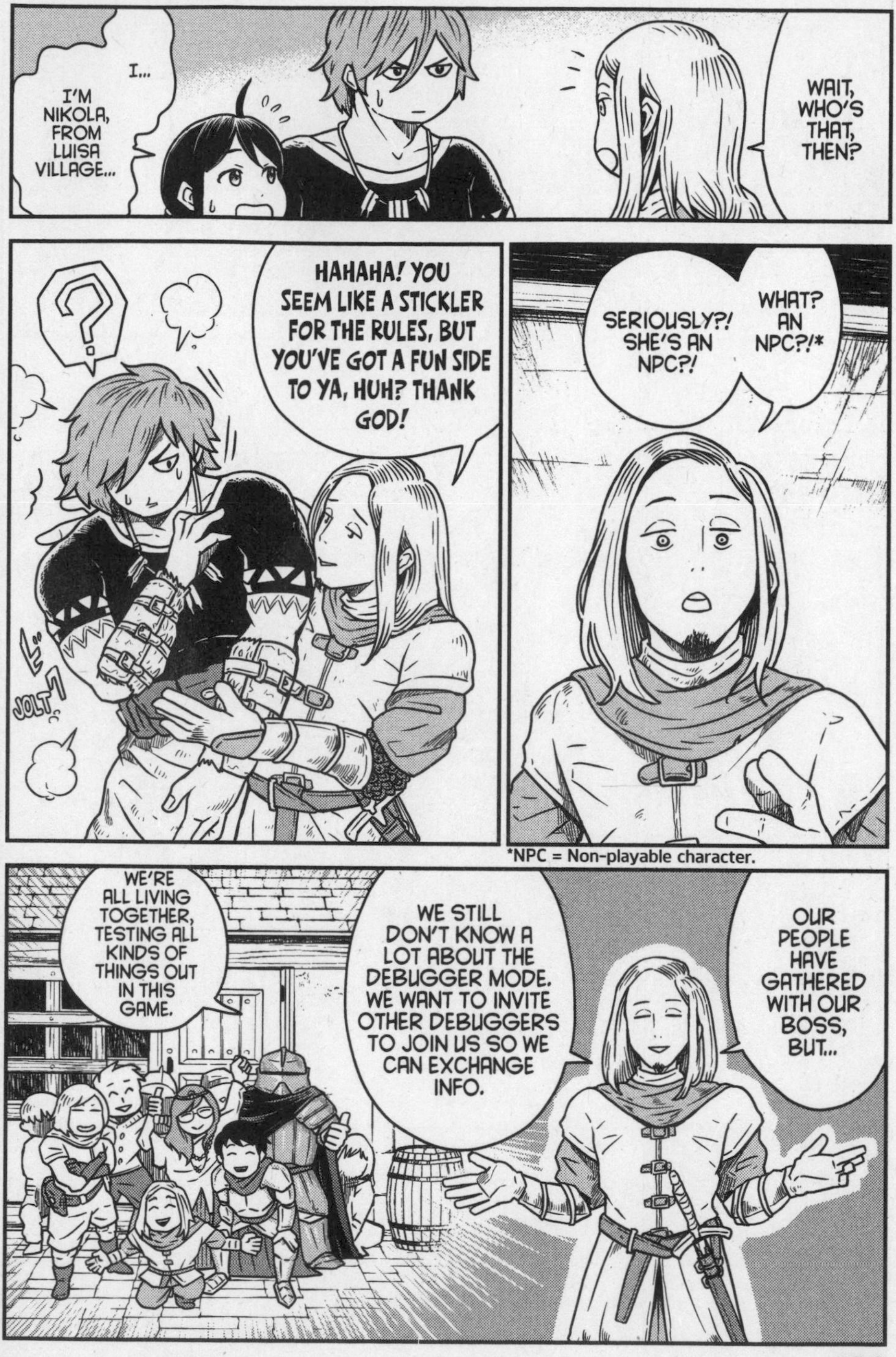
WAIT, WHO'S THAT, THEN?
I...
I'M NIKOLA, FROM LUISA VILLAGE...
WHAT? AN NPC?!*
SERIOUSLY?! SHE'S AN NPC?!
HAHAHA! YOU SEEM LIKE A STICKLER FOR THE RULES, BUT YOU'VE GOT A FUN SIDE TO YA, HUH? THANK GOD!
JOLT
OUR PEOPLE HAVE GATHERED WITH OUR BOSS, BUT...
WE STILL DON'T KNOW A LOT ABOUT THE DEBUGGER MODE. WE WANT TO INVITE OTHER DEBUGGERS TO JOIN US SO WE CAN EXCHANGE INFO.
WE'RE ALL LIVING TOGETHER, TESTING ALL KINDS OF THINGS OUT IN THIS GAME.

*NPC = Non-playable character.

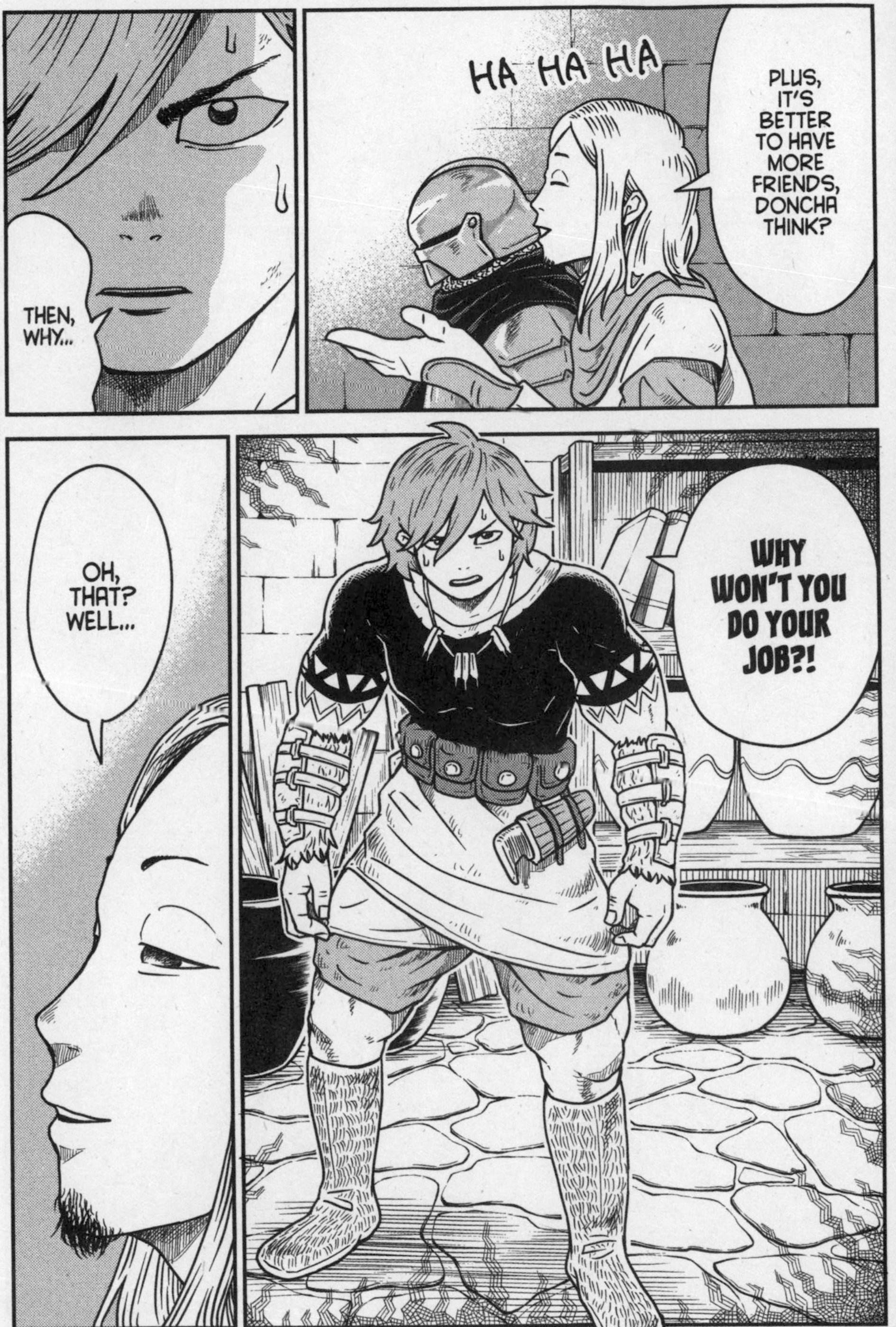
HA HA HA
PLUS, IT'S BETTER TO HAVE MORE FRIENDS, DONCHA THINK?
THEN, WHY...
WHY WON'T YOU DO YOUR JOB?!
OH, THAT? WELL...

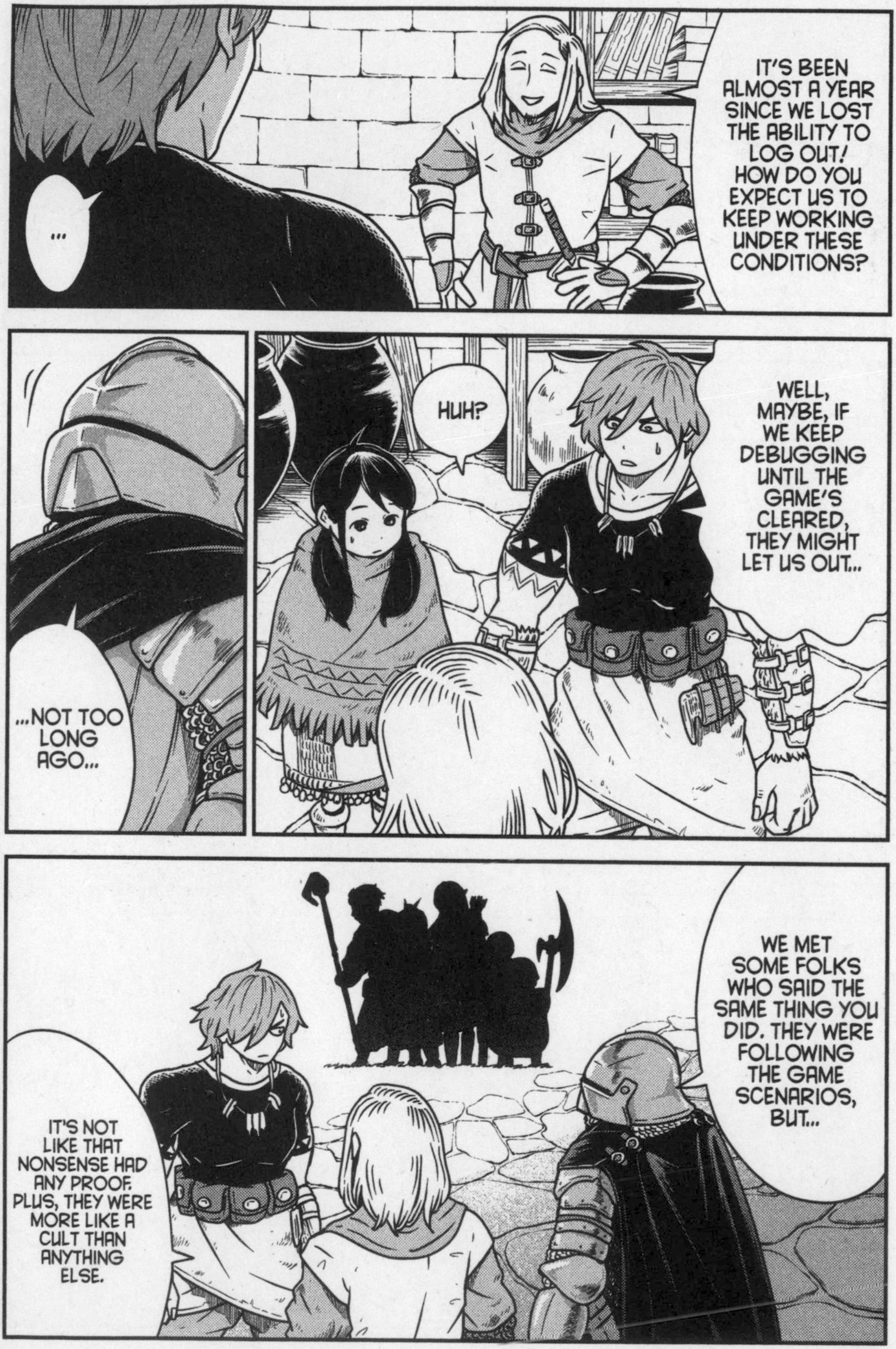
IT'S BEEN ALMOST A YEAR SINCE WE LOST THE ABILITY TO LOG OUT! HOW DO YOU EXPECT US TO KEEP WORKING UNDER THESE CONDITIONS?
...
WELL, MAYBE, IF WE KEEP DEBUGGING UNTIL THE GAME'S CLEARED, THEY MIGHT LET US OUT...
HUH?
...NOT TOO LONG AGO...
WE MET SOME FOLKS WHO SAID THE SAME THING YOU DID. THEY WERE FOLLOWING THE GAME SCENARIOS, BUT...
IT'S NOT LIKE THAT NONSENSE HAD ANY PROOF. PLUS, THEY WERE MORE LIKE A CULT THAN ANYTHING ELSE.

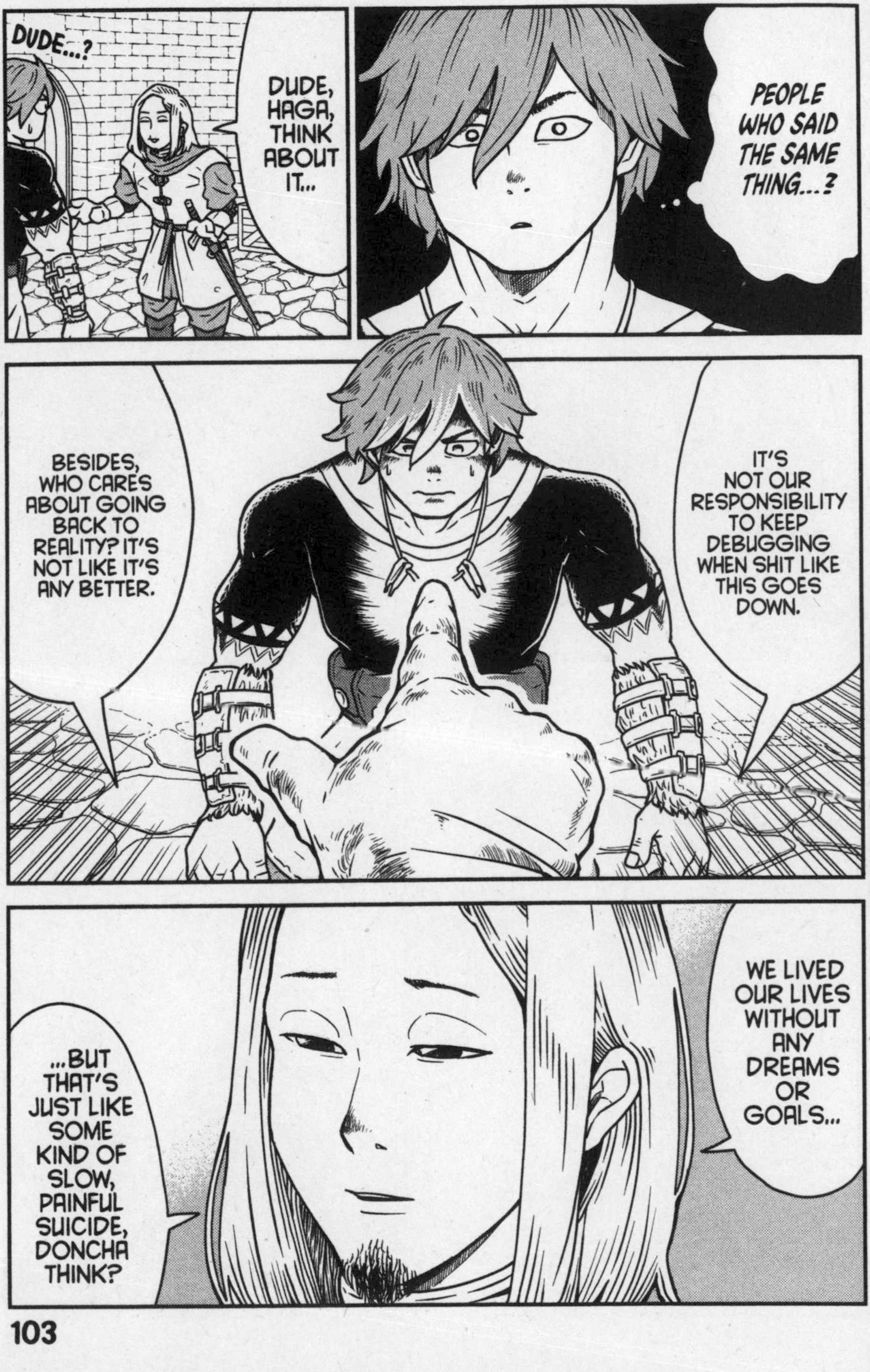
PEOPLE WHO SAID THE SAME THING...?
DUDE, HAGA, THINK ABOUT IT...
DUDE...?
IT'S NOT OUR RESPONSIBILITY TO KEEP DEBUGGING WHEN SHIT LIKE THIS GOES DOWN.
BESIDES, WHO CARES ABOUT GOING BACK TO REALITY? IT'S NOT LIKE IT'S ANY BETTER.
WE LIVED OUR LIVES WITHOUT ANY DREAMS OR GOALS...
...BUT THAT'S JUST LIKE SOME KIND OF SLOW, PAINFUL SUICIDE, DONCHA THINK?

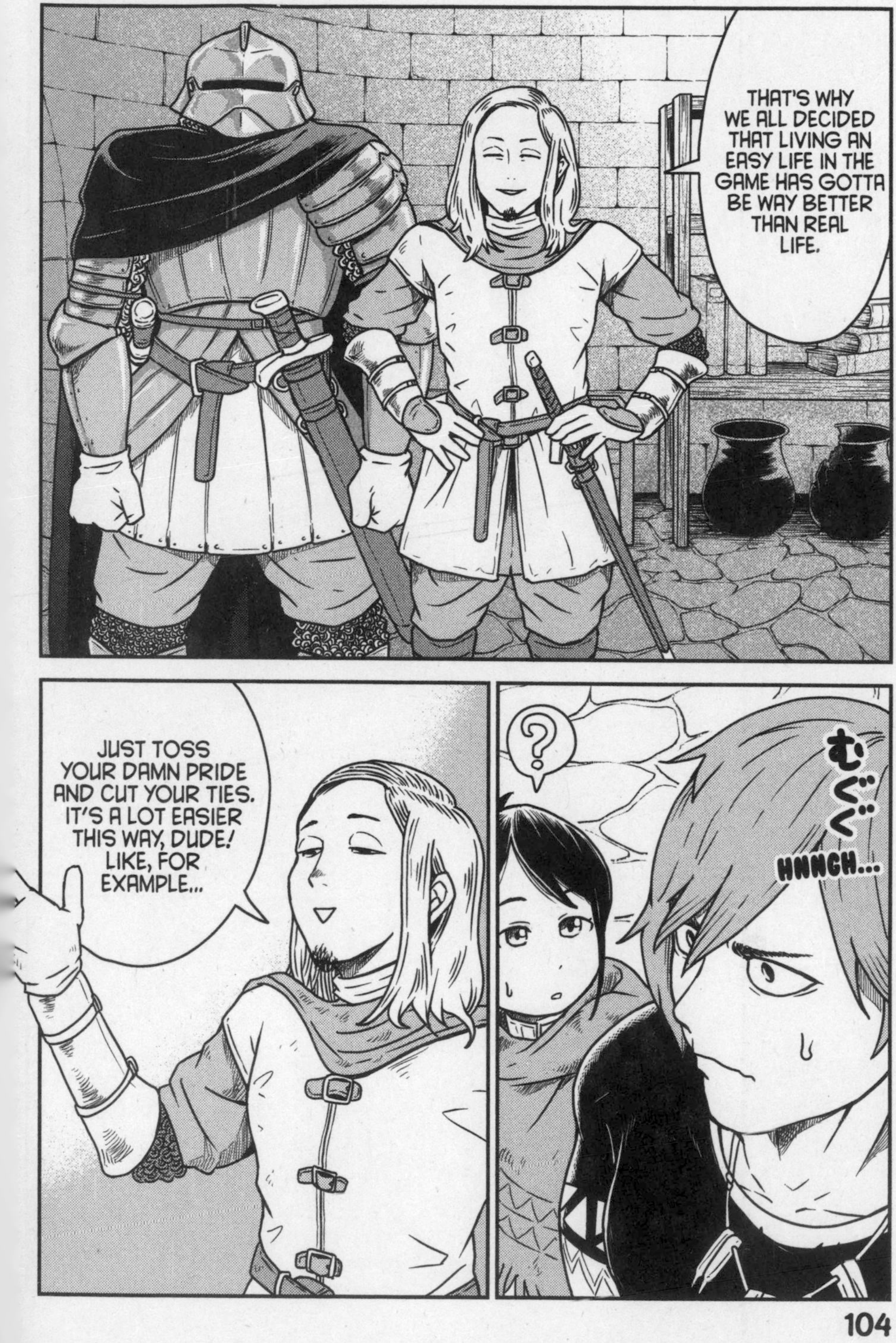
THAT'S WHY WE ALL DECIDED THAT LIVING AN EASY LIFE IN THE GAME HAS GOTTA BE WAY BETTER THAN REAL LIFE.
むぐぐ
HNNGH...
?
JUST TOSS YOUR DAMN PRIDE AND CUT YOUR TIES. IT'S A LOT EASIER THIS WAY, DUDE! LIKE, FOR EXAMPLE...

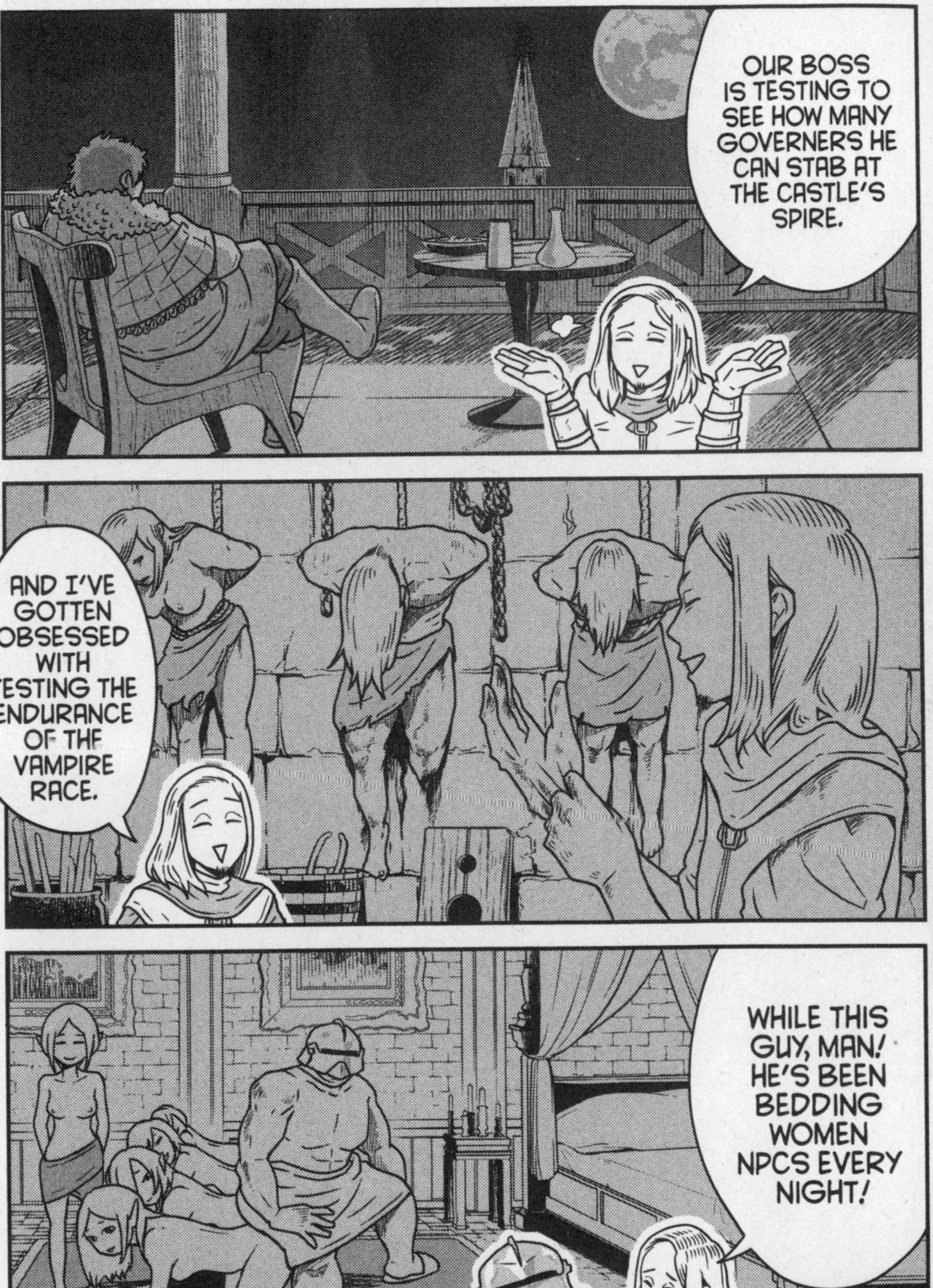
OUR BOSS IS TESTING TO SEE HOW MANY GOVERNERS HE CAN STAB AT THE CASTLE'S SPIRE.
AND I'VE GOTTEN OBSESSED WITH TESTING THE ENDURANCE OF THE VAMPIRE RACE.
WHILE THIS GUY, MAN! HE'S BEEN BEDDING WOMEN NPCS EVERY NIGHT!

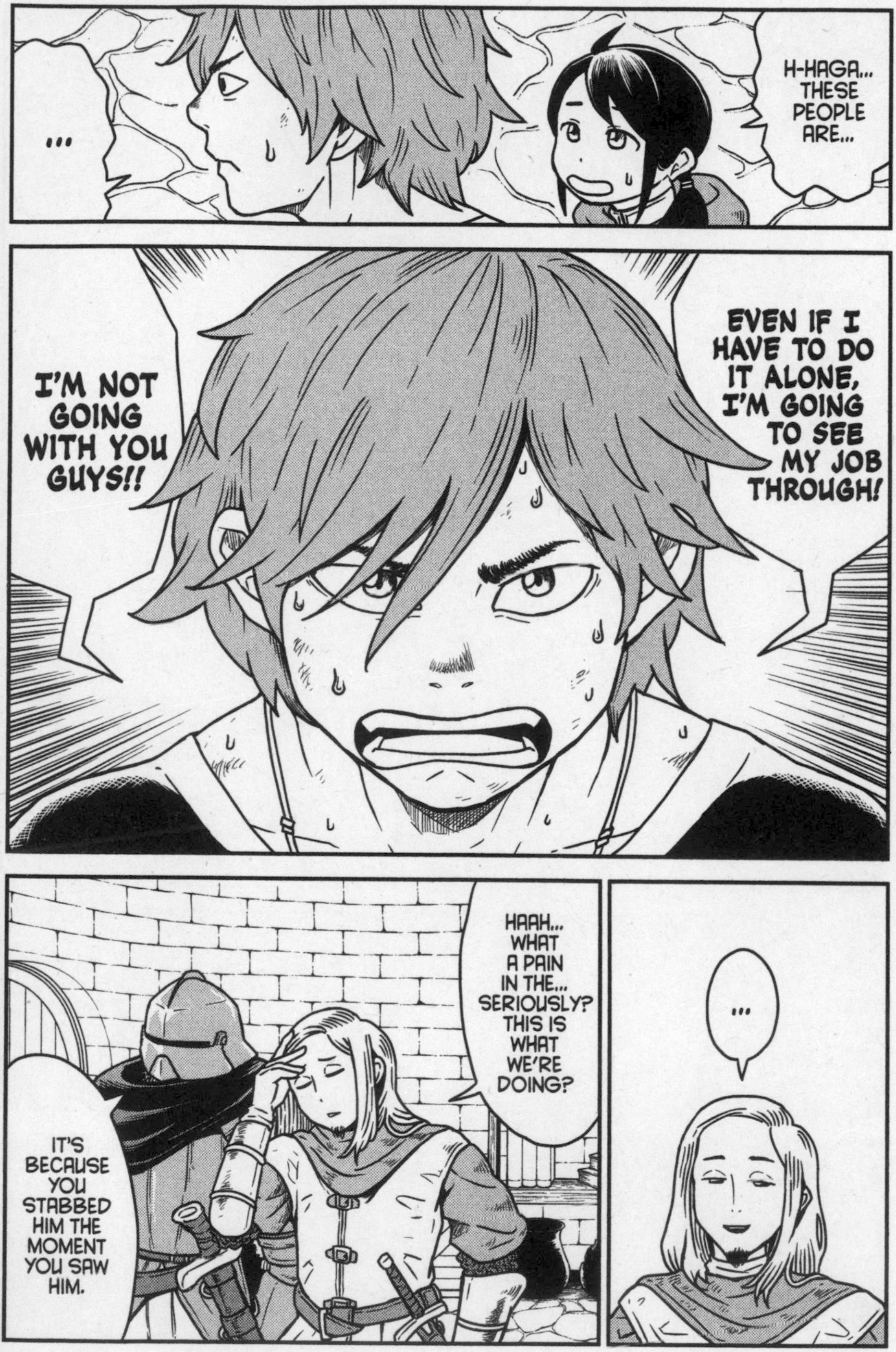
H-HAGA... THESE PEOPLE ARE...
...
EVEN IF I HAVE TO DO IT ALONE, I'M GOING TO SEE MY JOB THROUGH!
I'M NOT GOING WITH YOU GUYS!!
...
HAAH... WHAT A PAIN IN THE... SERIOUSLY? THIS IS WHAT WE'RE DOING?
IT'S BECAUSE YOU STABBED HIM THE MOMENT YOU SAW HIM.

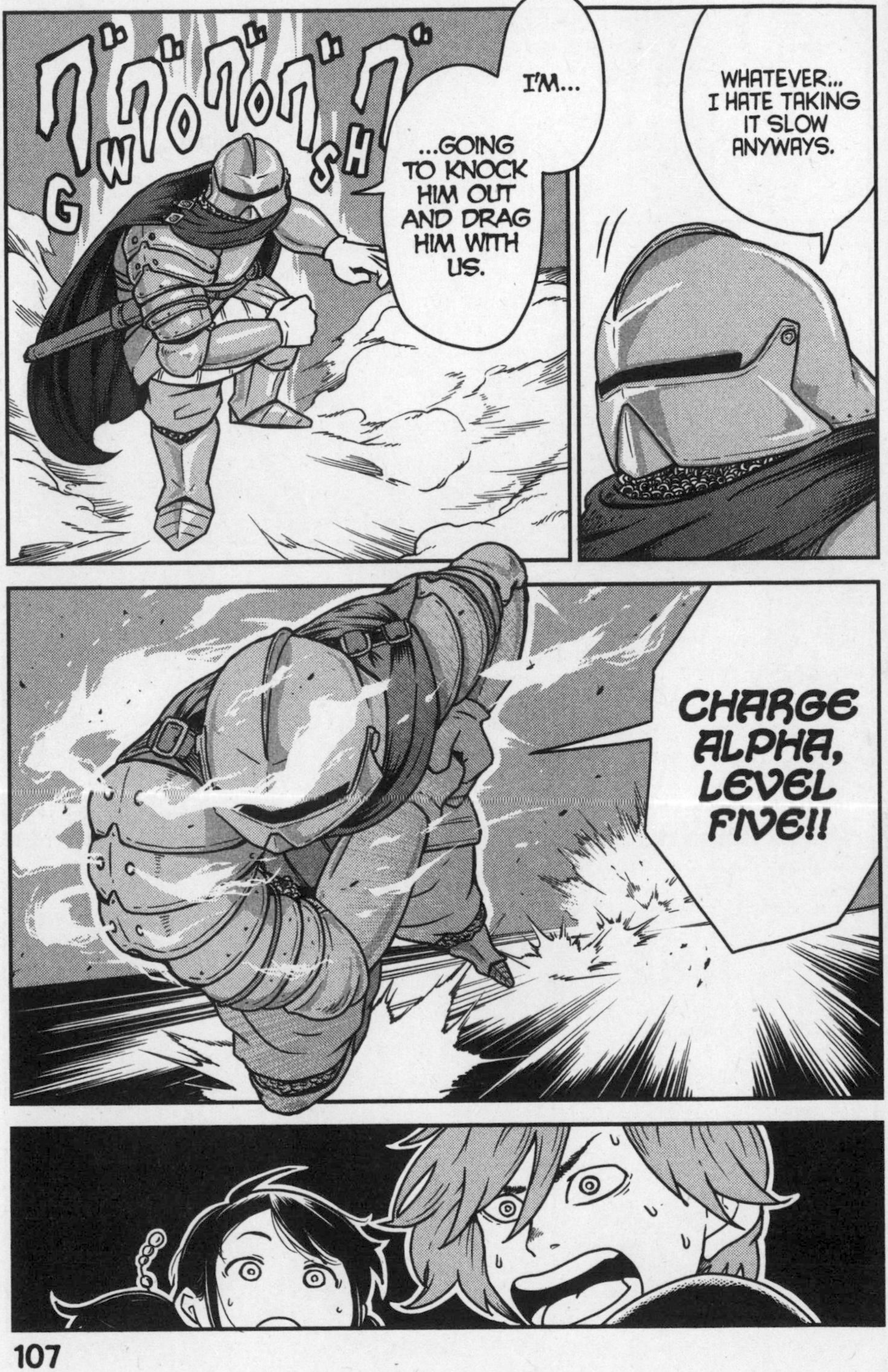
WHATEVER... I HATE TAKING IT SLOW ANYWAYS.
I'M...
...GOING TO KNOCK HIM OUT AND DRAG HIM WITH US.
GWOOSH
CHARGE ALPHA, LEVEL FIVE!!

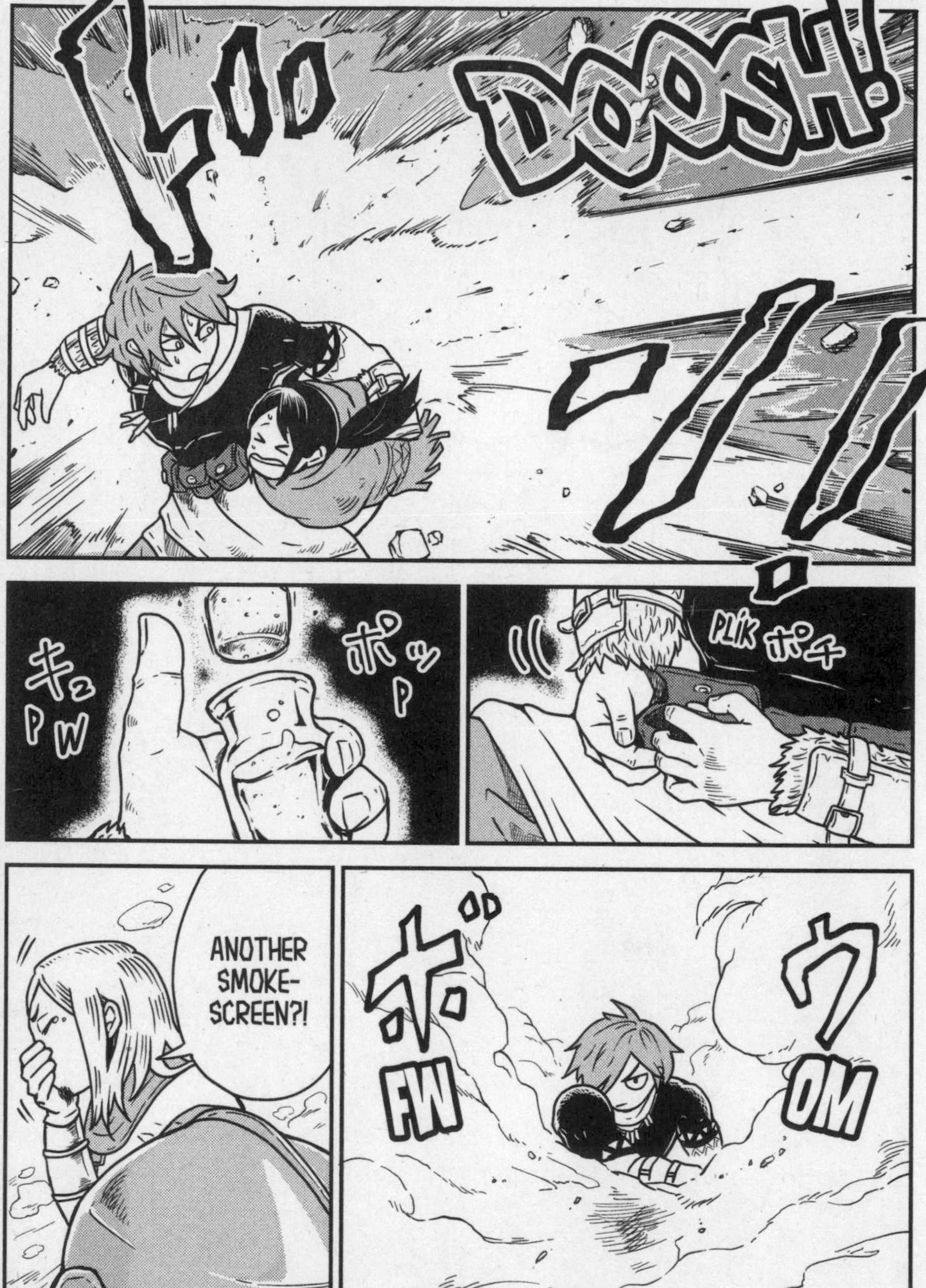
LOO
DOOSH!
PLIK
ポチ
ポッ
P
キュ
PW
ボ
FW
ウ
OM
ANOTHER SMOKE-SCREEN?!

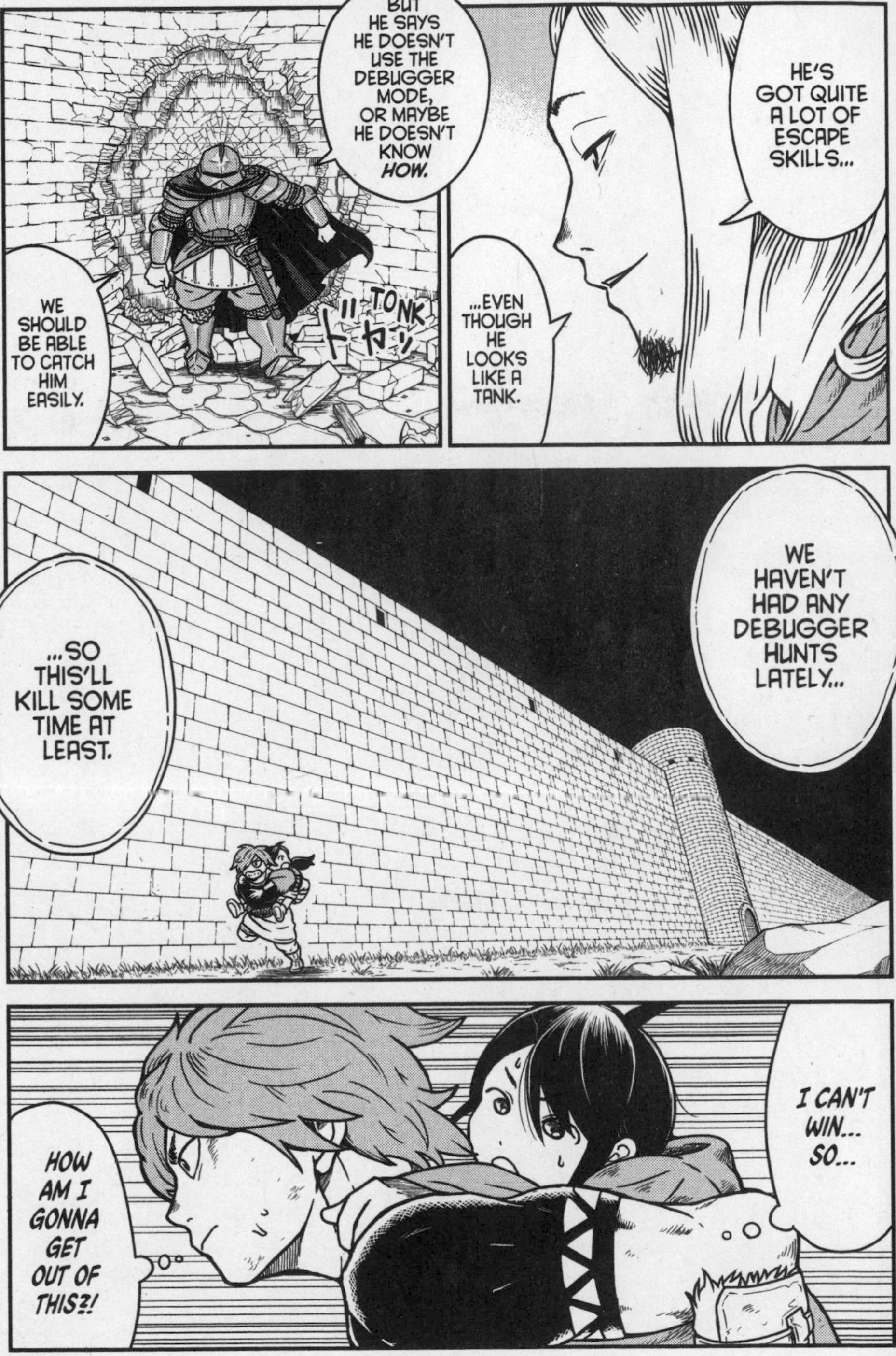
HE'S GOT QUITE A LOT OF ESCAPE SKILLS...
...EVEN THOUGH HE LOOKS LIKE A TANK.
BUT HE SAYS HE DOESN'T USE THE DEBUGGER MODE, OR MAYBE HE DOESN'T KNOW *HOW.*
TONK
WE SHOULD BE ABLE TO CATCH HIM EASILY.
WE HAVEN'T HAD ANY DEBUGGER HUNTS LATELY...
...SO THIS'LL KILL SOME TIME AT LEAST.
I CAN'T WIN... SO...
HOW AM I GONNA GET OUT OF THIS?!

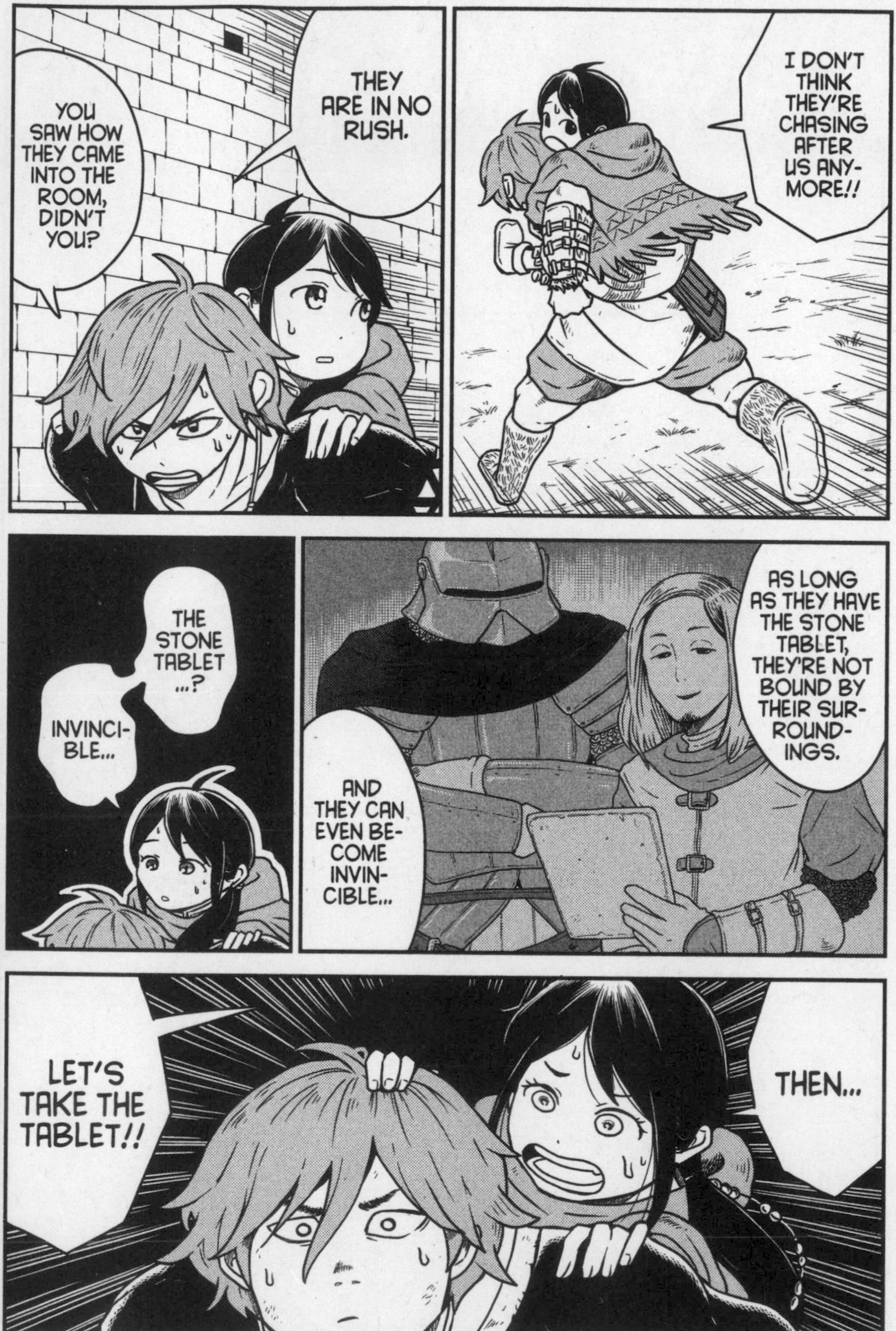
I DON'T THINK THEY'RE CHASING AFTER US ANY-MORE!!
THEY ARE IN NO RUSH.
YOU SAW HOW THEY CAME INTO THE ROOM, DIDN'T YOU?
AS LONG AS THEY HAVE THE STONE TABLET, THEY'RE NOT BOUND BY THEIR SUR-ROUND-INGS.
AND THEY CAN EVEN BE-COME INVIN-CIBLE...
THE STONE TABLET ...?
INVINCI-BLE...
THEN...
LET'S TAKE THE TABLET!!

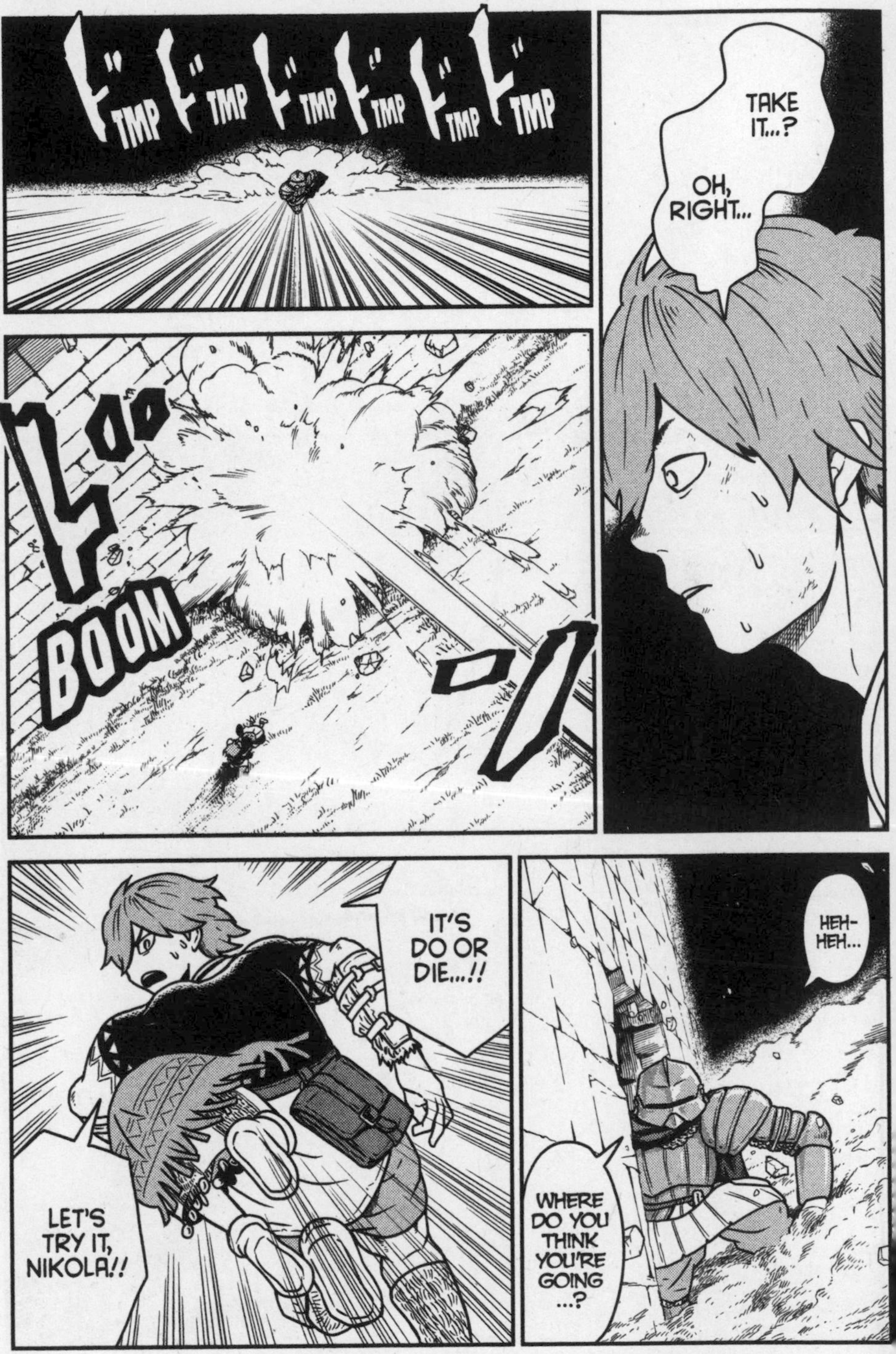
TAKE IT...?
OH, RIGHT...
TMP TMP TMP TMP TMP TMP
BOOM
HEH-HEH...
WHERE DO YOU THINK YOU'RE GOING ...?
IT'S DO OR DIE...!!
LET'S TRY IT, NIKOLA!!

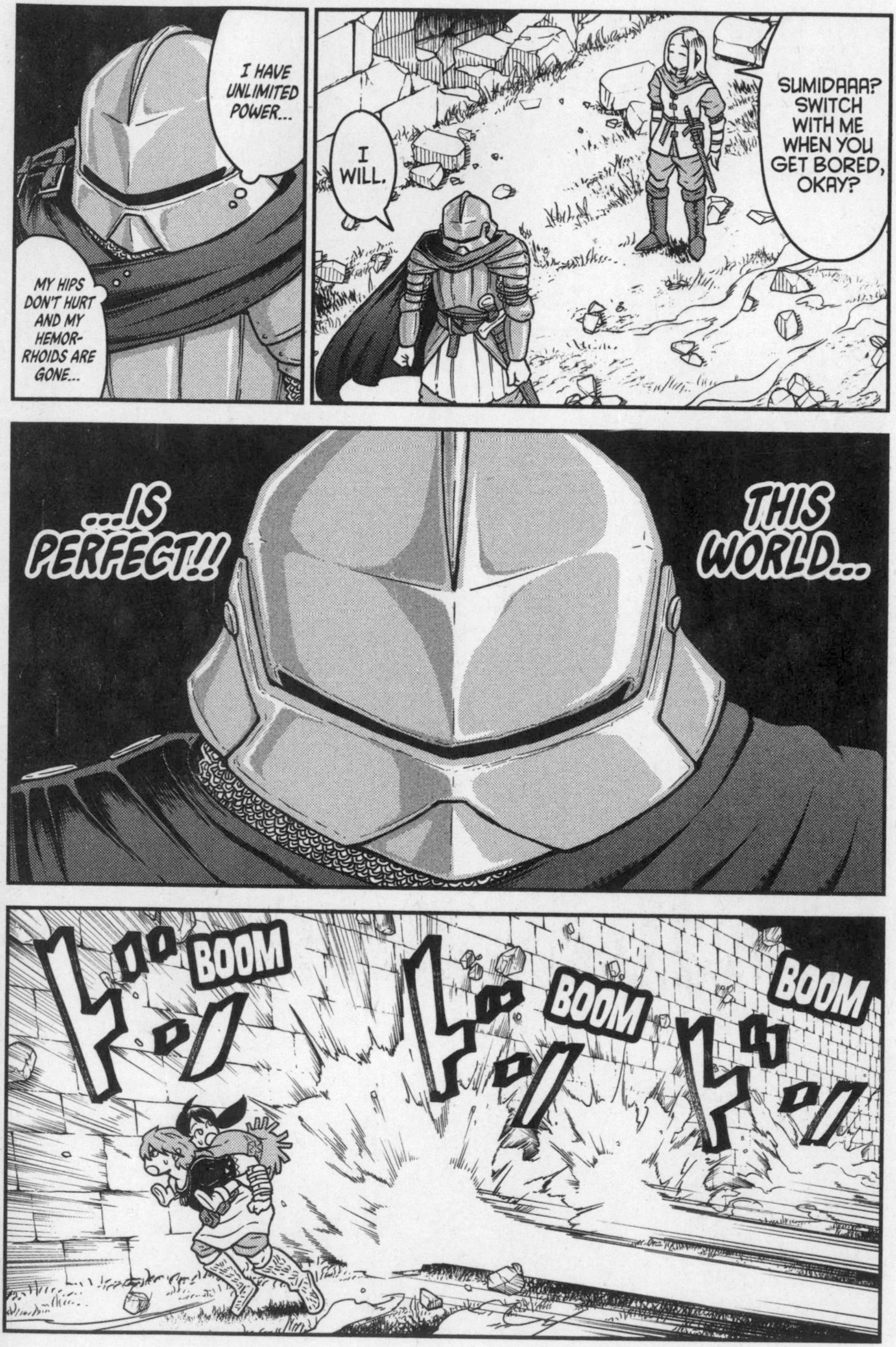
SUMIDAAA? SWITCH WITH ME WHEN YOU GET BORED, OKAY?
I WILL.
I HAVE UNLIMITED POWER...
MY HIPS DON'T HURT AND MY HEMOR-RHOIDS ARE GONE...
THIS WORLD...
...IS PERFECT!!
BOOM
BOOM
BOOM

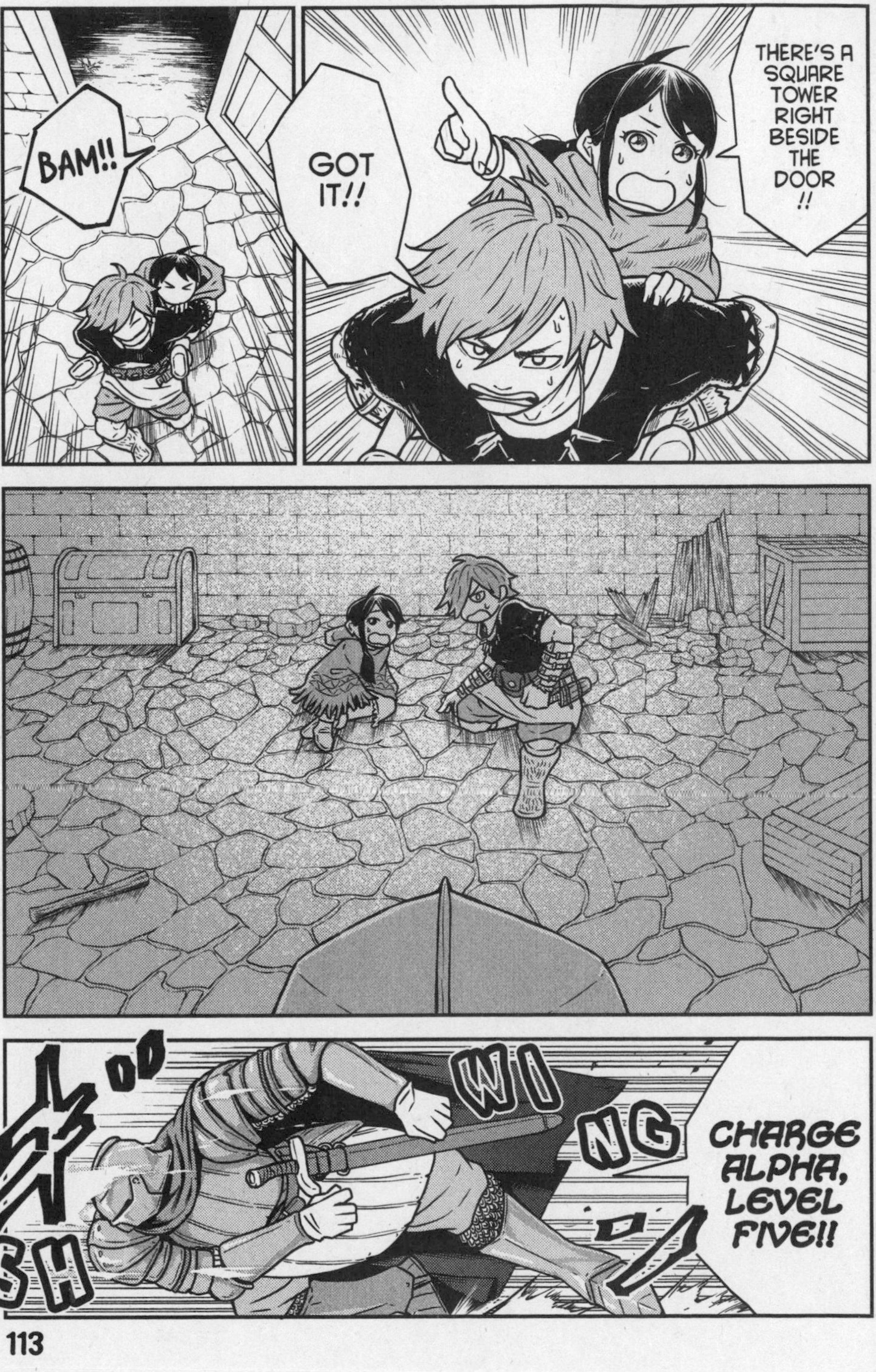
THERE'S A SQUARE TOWER RIGHT BESIDE THE DOOR!!
GOT IT!!
BAM!!
CHARGE ALPHA, LEVEL FIVE!!
SHWING

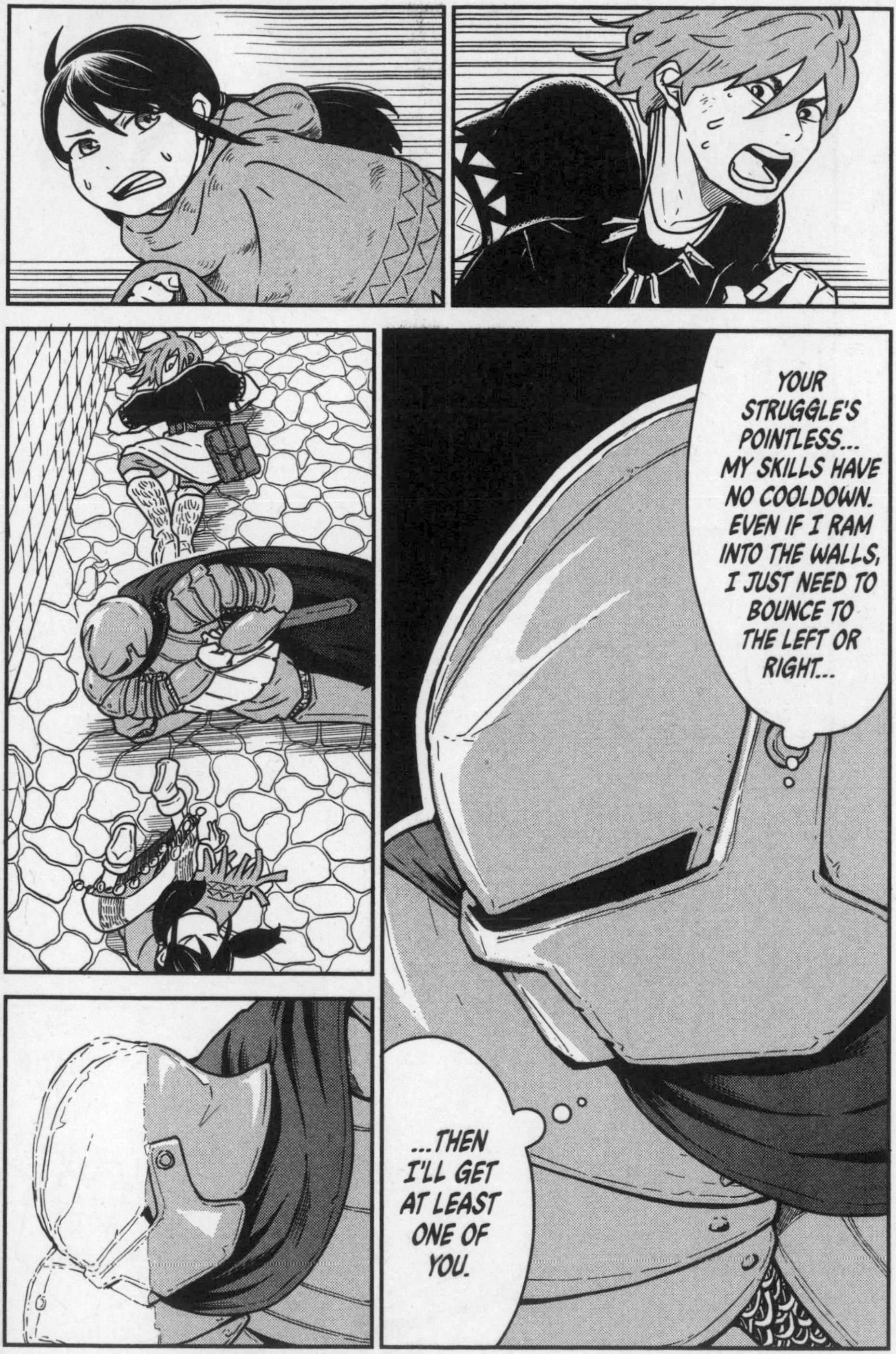
YOUR STRUGGLE'S POINTLESS... MY SKILLS HAVE NO COOLDOWN. EVEN IF I RAM INTO THE WALLS, I JUST NEED TO BOUNCE TO THE LEFT OR RIGHT...
...THEN I'LL GET AT LEAST ONE OF YOU.

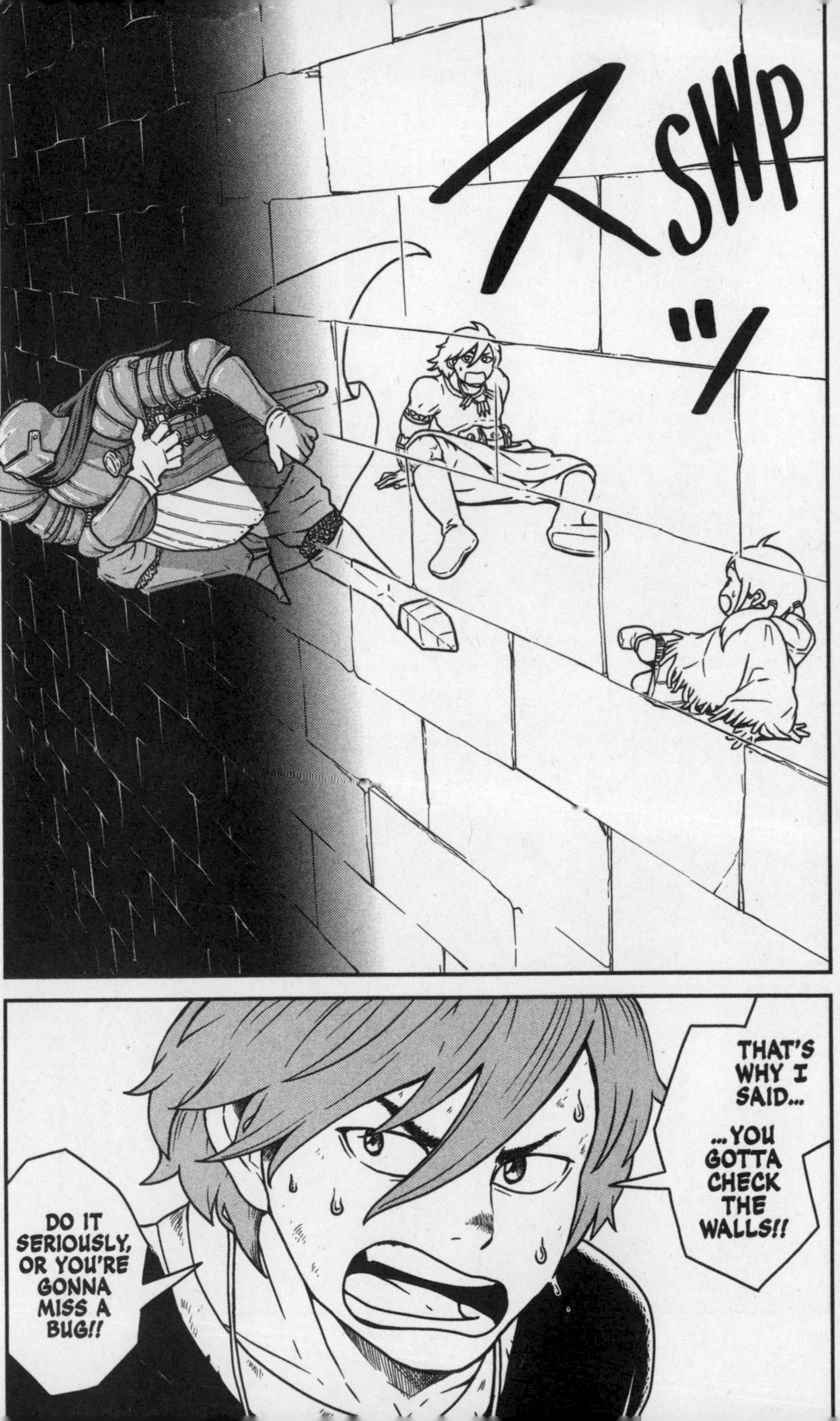
スッ
SWP
THAT'S WHY I SAID...
...YOU GOTTA CHECK THE WALLS!!
DO IT SERIOUSLY, OR YOU'RE GONNA MISS A BUG!!

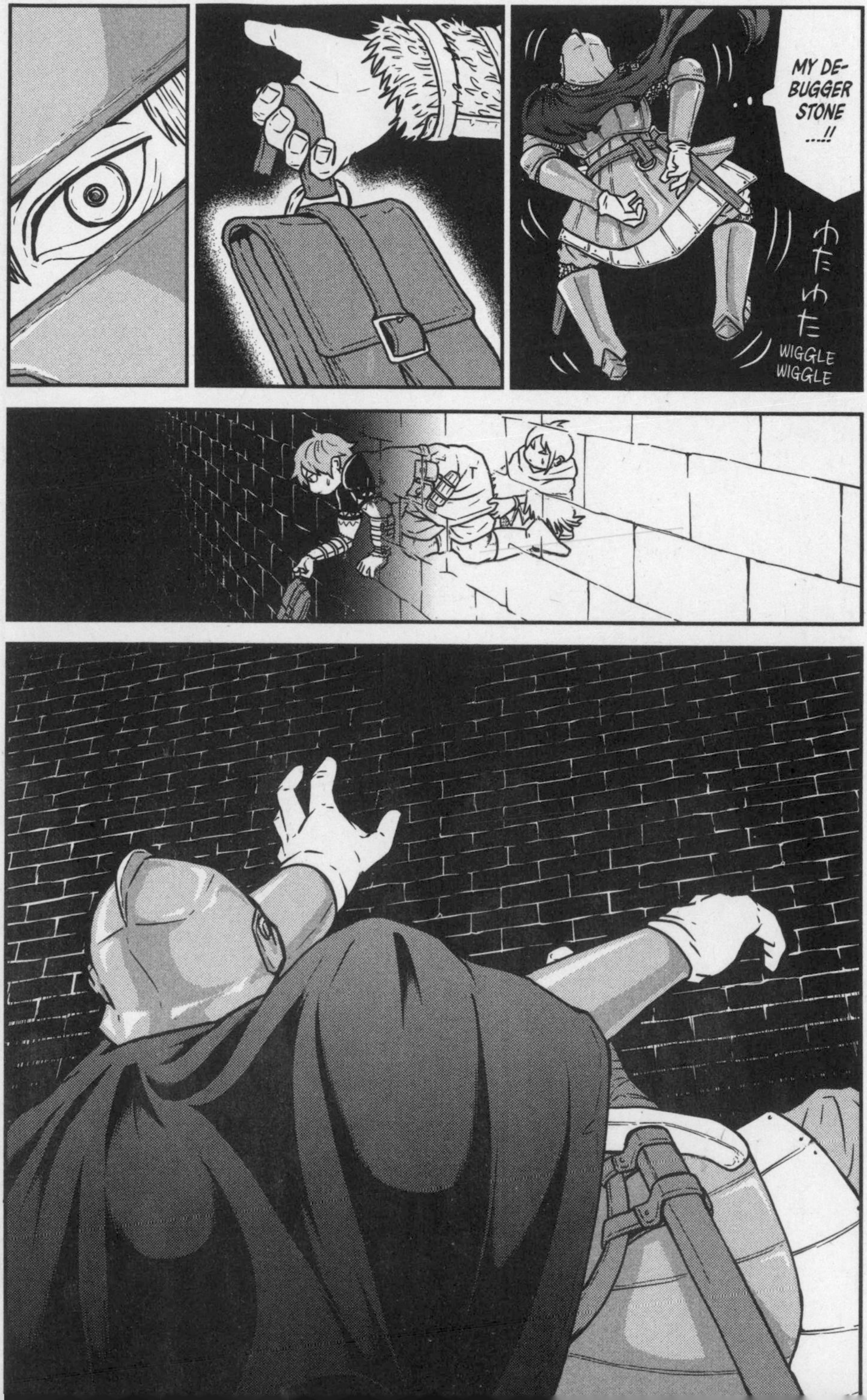
MY DE-BUGGER STONE ...!!
ゆたゆた
WIGGLE WIGGLE

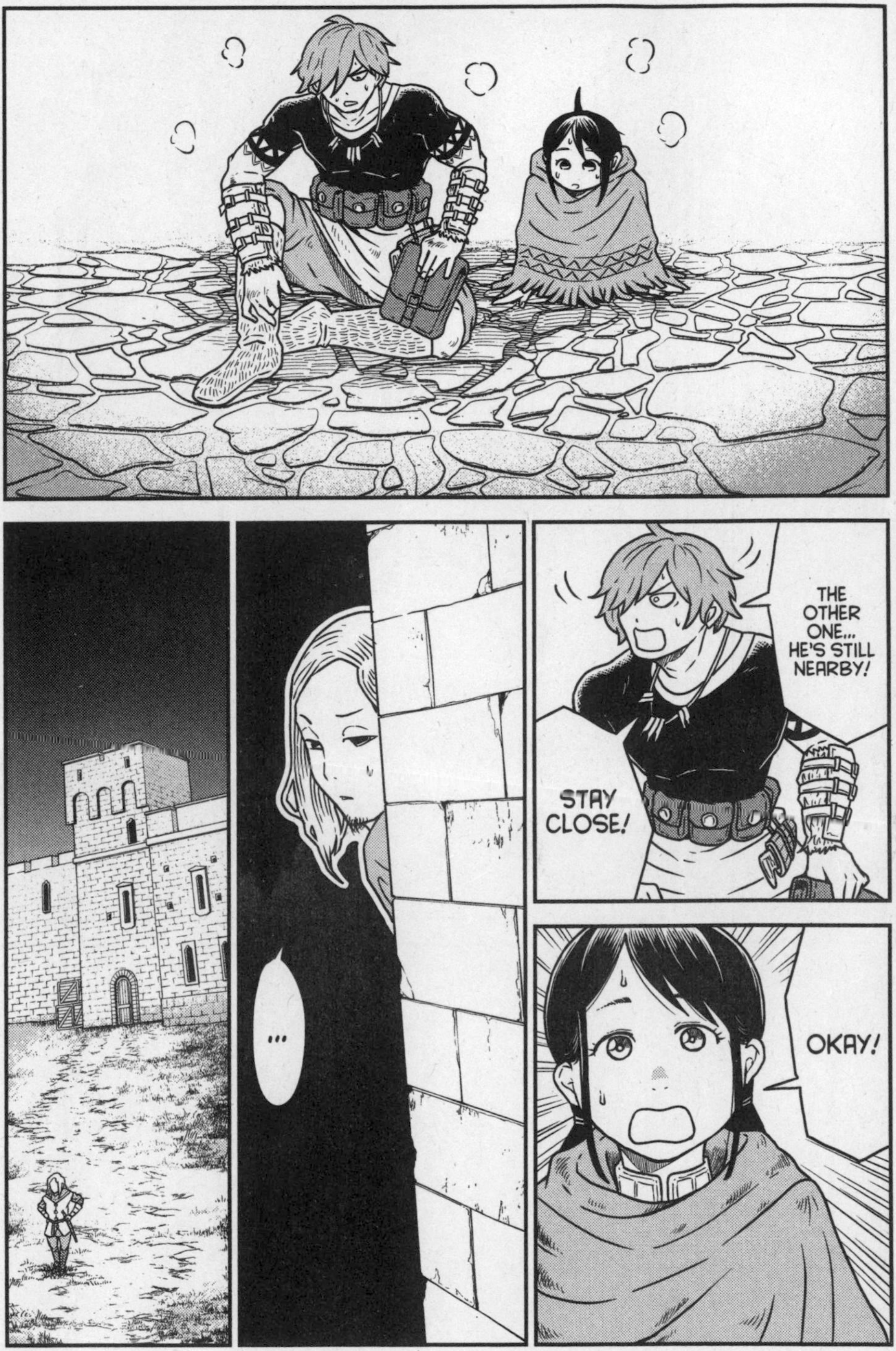
THE OTHER ONE... HE'S STILL NEARBY!
STAY CLOSE!
OKAY!
...

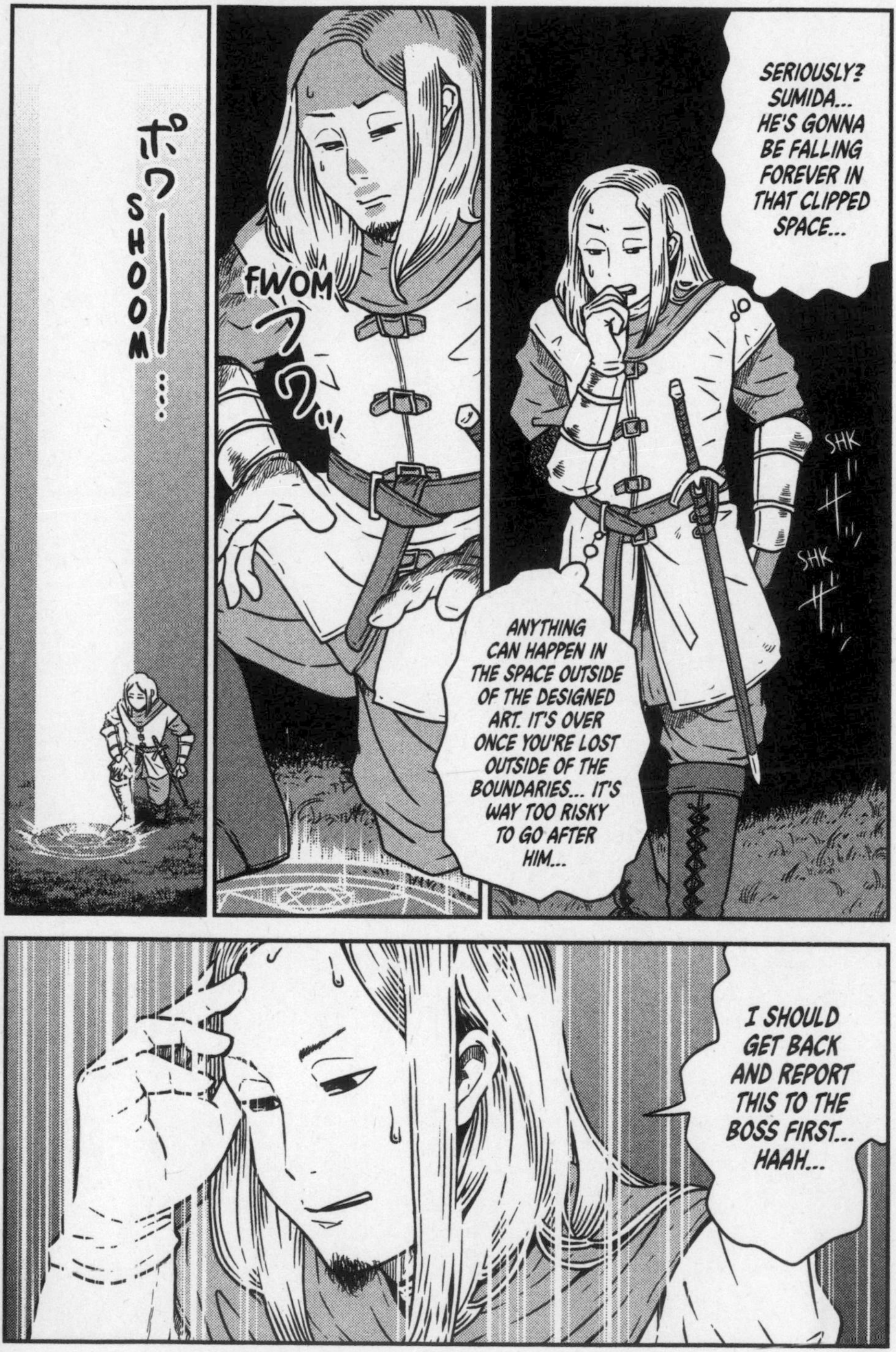
SERIOUSLY? SUMIDA... HE'S GONNA BE FALLING FOREVER IN THAT CLIPPED SPACE...
ANYTHING CAN HAPPEN IN THE SPACE OUTSIDE OF THE DESIGNED ART. IT'S OVER ONCE YOU'RE LOST OUTSIDE OF THE BOUNDARIES... IT'S WAY TOO RISKY TO GO AFTER HIM...
ザッ SHK
ザッ SHK
フワッ FWOM
ポワー SHOOM...
I SHOULD GET BACK AND REPORT THIS TO THE BOSS FIRST... HAAH...

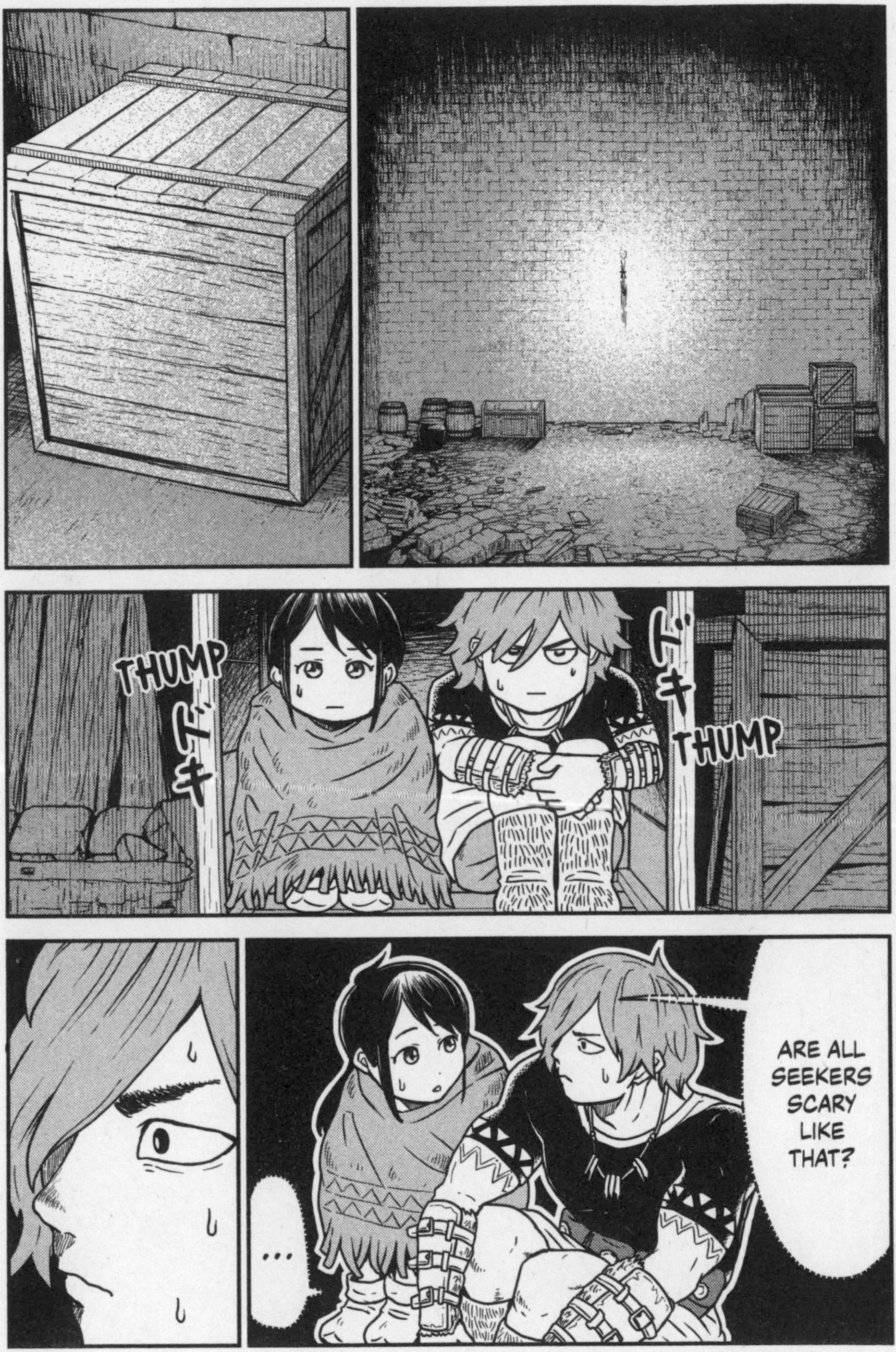
ドキ
THUMP
THUMP
ドキ
ARE ALL SEEKERS SCARY LIKE THAT?
...

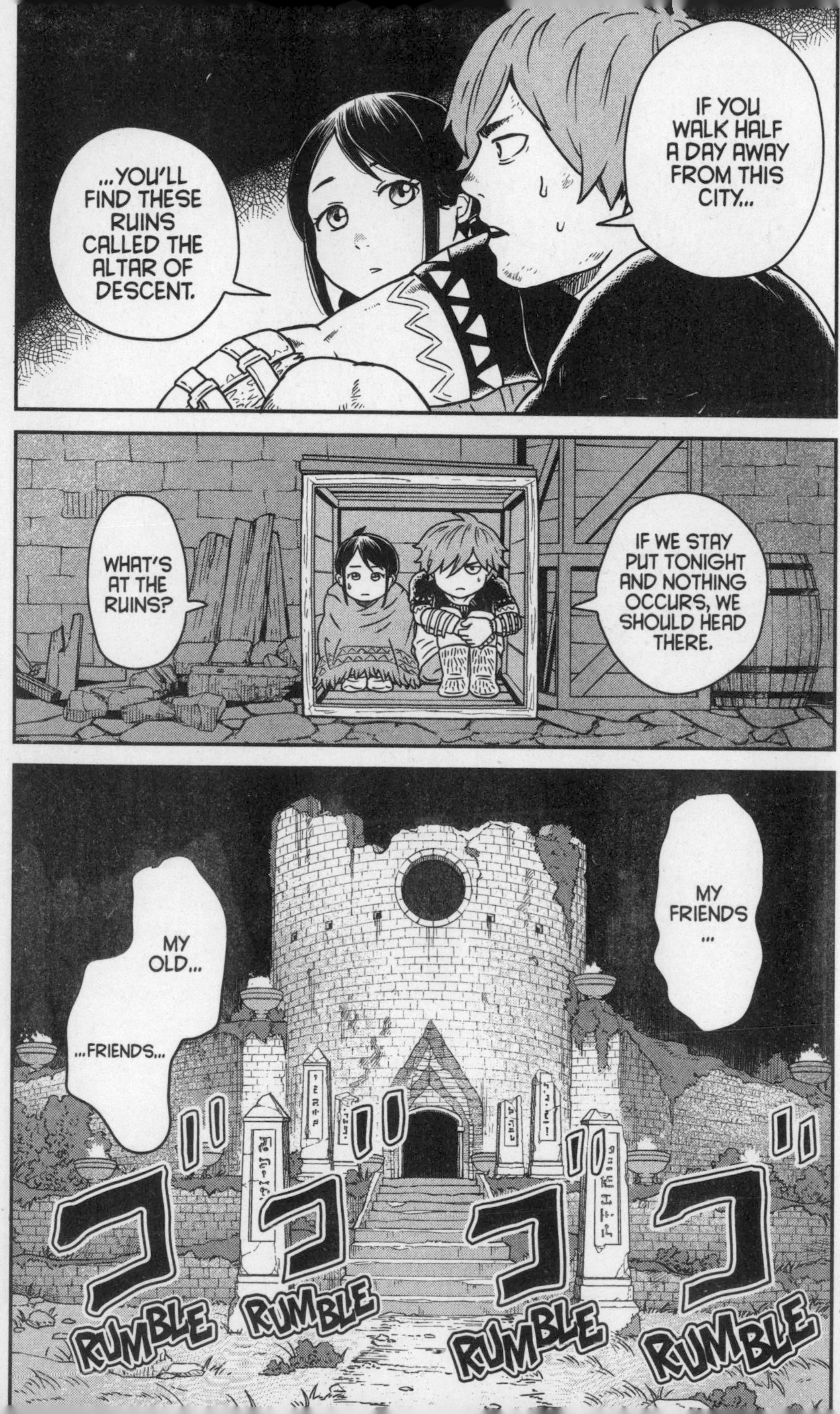
IF YOU WALK HALF A DAY AWAY FROM THIS CITY...
...YOU'LL FIND THESE RUINS CALLED THE ALTAR OF DESCENT.
IF WE STAY PUT TONIGHT AND NOTHING OCCURS, WE SHOULD HEAD THERE.
WHAT'S AT THE RUINS?
MY FRIENDS...
MY OLD...
...FRIENDS...
ゴゴゴゴ
RUMBLE RUMBLE RUMBLE RUMBLE

NO.3/END

No.4 | My Friends
HERE IS MY NEW INVENTION, SIR.
LET'S GIVE IT A TRY...
パク
BITE
...

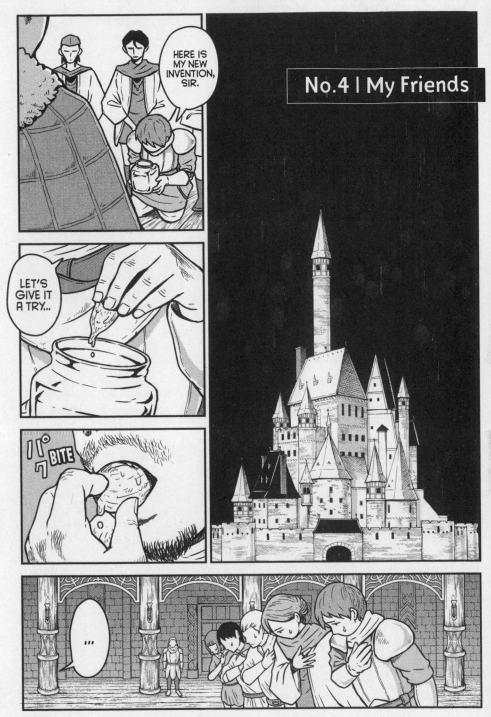

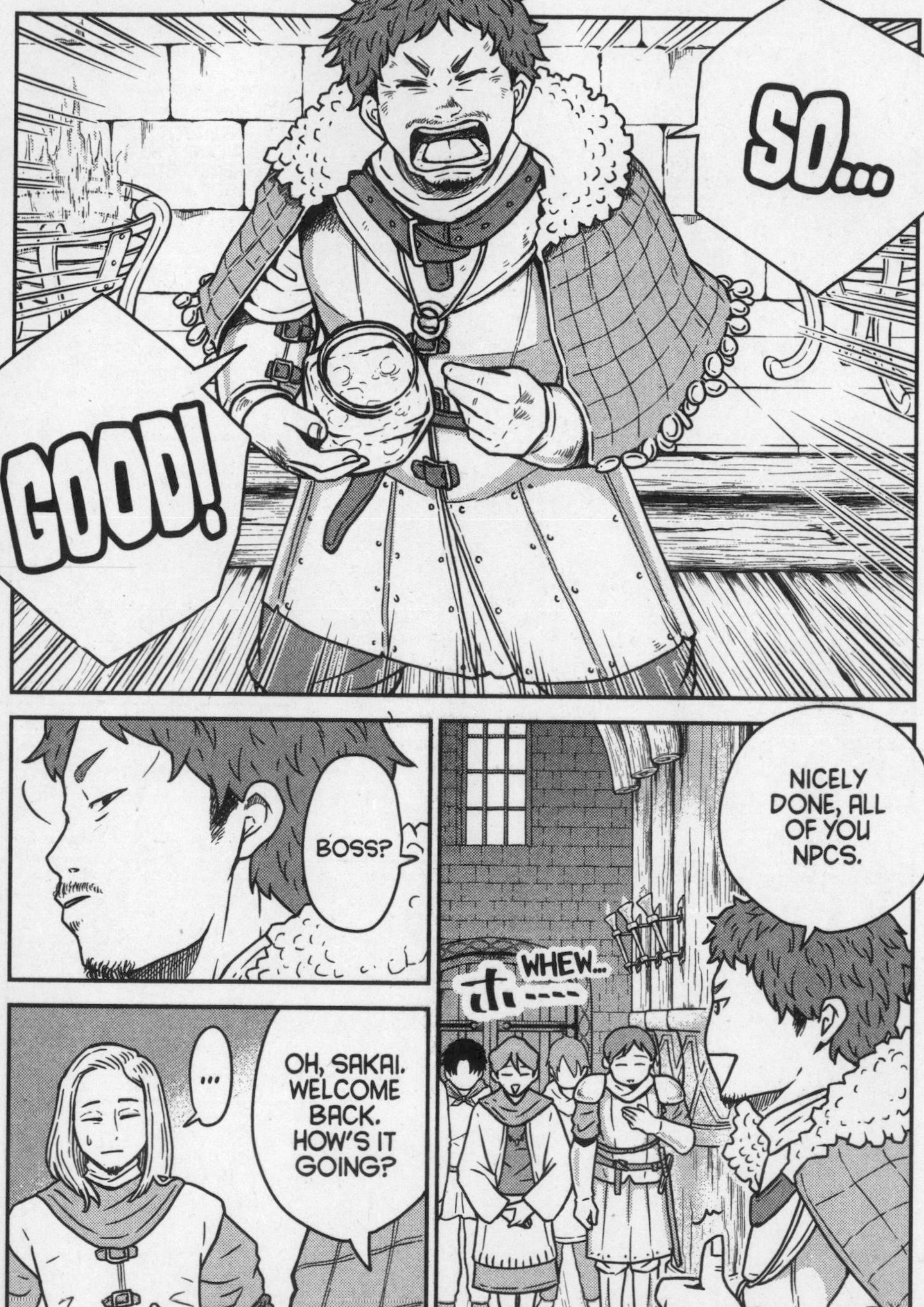

SO...
GOOD!
NICELY DONE, ALL OF YOU NPCS.
WHEW...
BOSS?
OH, SAKAI. WELCOME BACK. HOW'S IT GOING?
...

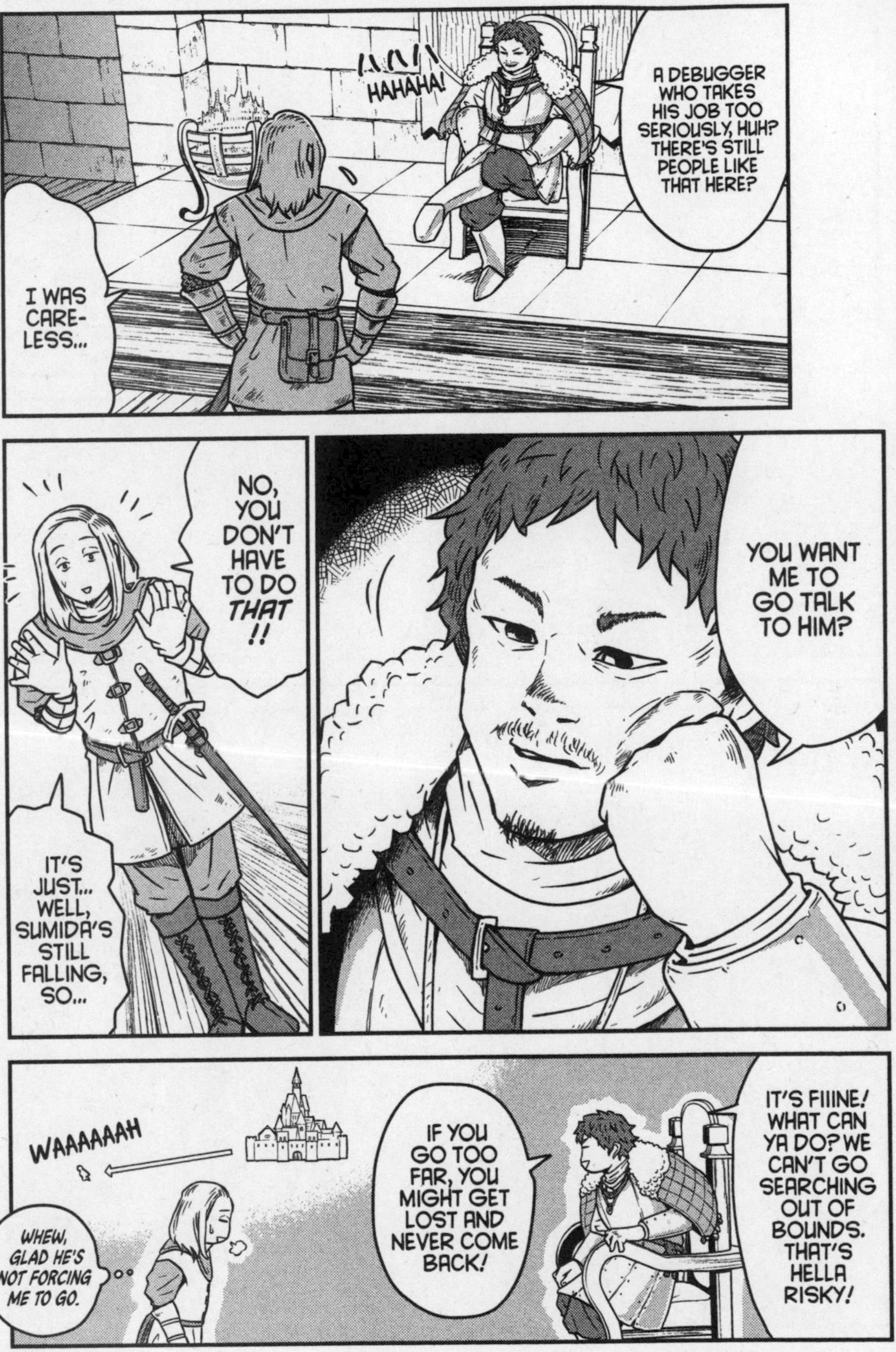
A DEBUGGER WHO TAKES HIS JOB TOO SERIOUSLY, HUH? THERE'S STILL PEOPLE LIKE THAT HERE?
HAHAHA!
I WAS CARE-LESS...
YOU WANT ME TO GO TALK TO HIM?
NO, YOU DON'T HAVE TO DO *THAT*!!
IT'S JUST... WELL, SUMIDA'S STILL FALLING, SO...
IT'S FIIINE! WHAT CAN YA DO? WE CAN'T GO SEARCHING OUT OF BOUNDS. THAT'S HELLA RISKY!
IF YOU GO TOO FAR, YOU MIGHT GET LOST AND NEVER COME BACK!
WAAAAAAH
WHEW, GLAD HE'S NOT FORCING ME TO GO.

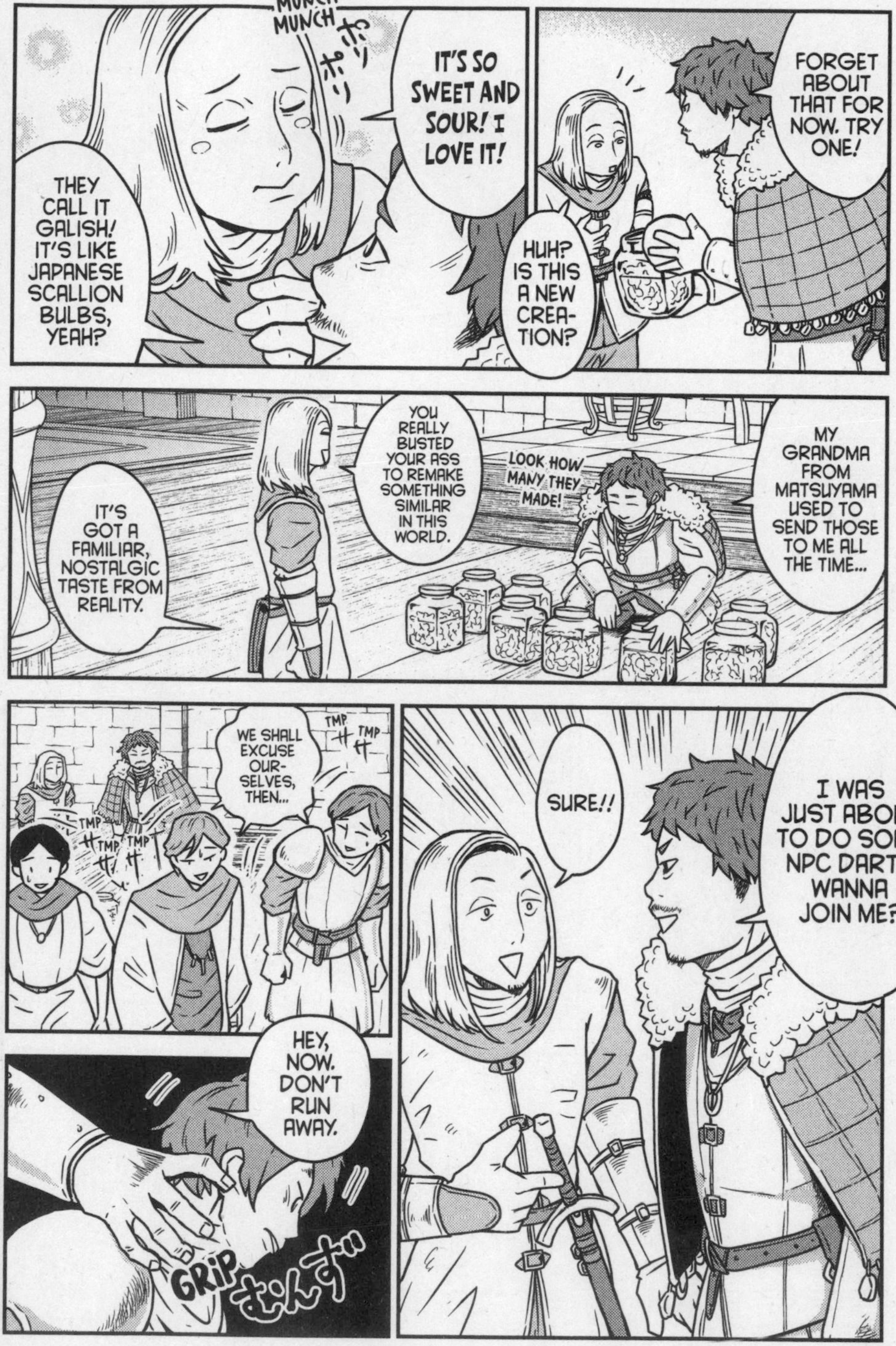
FORGET ABOUT THAT FOR NOW. TRY ONE!
HUH? IS THIS A NEW CREA-TION?
MUNCH MUNCH
ポリポリ
IT'S SO SWEET AND SOUR! I LOVE IT!
THEY CALL IT GALISH! IT'S LIKE JAPANESE SCALLION BULBS, YEAH?
MY GRANDMA FROM MATSUYAMA USED TO SEND THOSE TO ME ALL THE TIME...
YOU REALLY BUSTED YOUR ASS TO REMAKE SOMETHING SIMILAR IN THIS WORLD.
LOOK HOW MANY THEY MADE!
IT'S GOT A FAMILIAR, NOSTALGIC TASTE FROM REALITY.
I WAS JUST ABOUT TO DO SOME NPC DARTS. WANNA JOIN ME?
SURE!!
TMP TMP
WE SHALL EXCUSE OUR-SELVES, THEN...
TMP TMP TMP
HEY, NOW. DON'T RUN AWAY.
GRIP
むんず

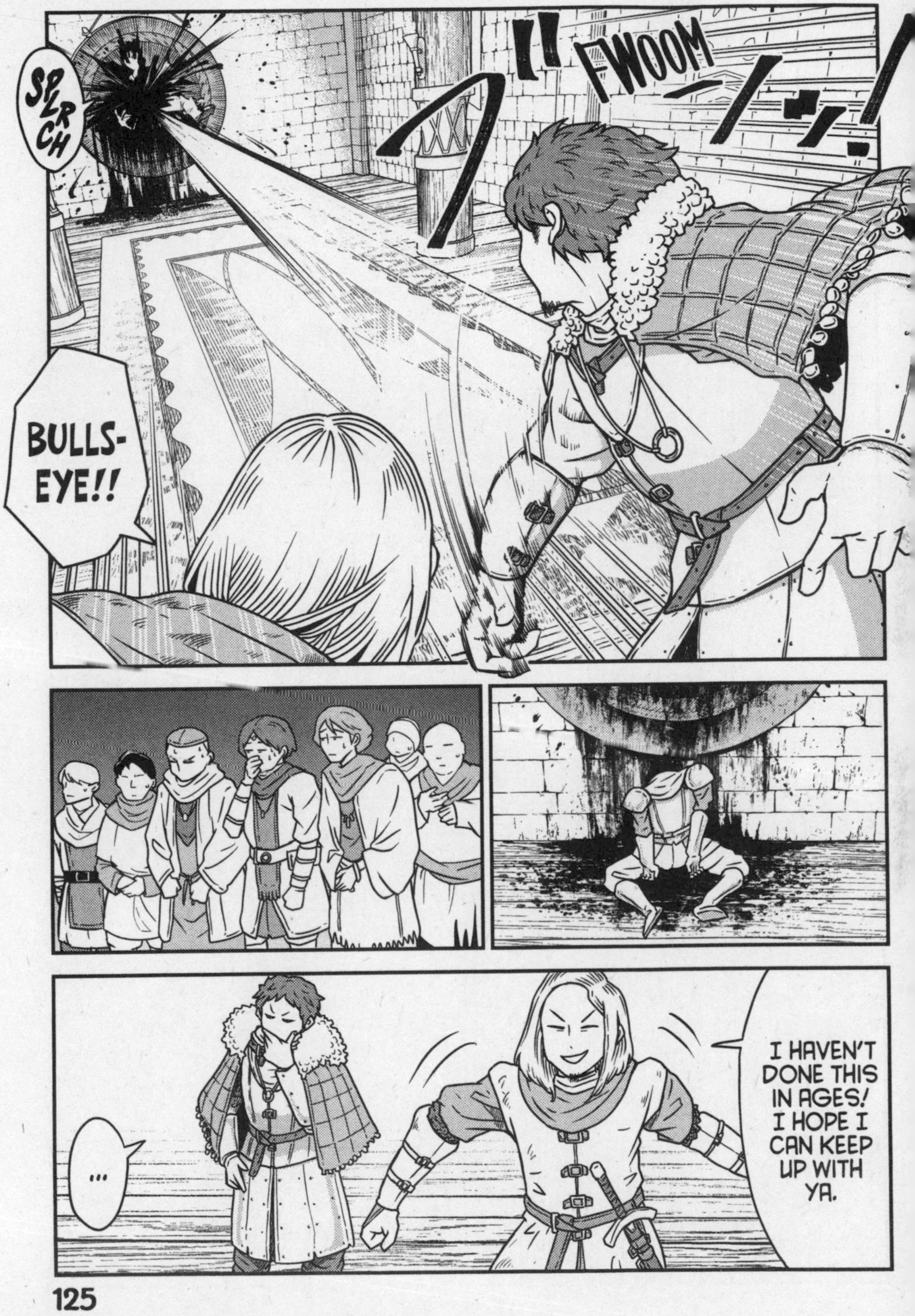
FWOOM
SPLRCH
BULLS-EYE!!
I HAVEN'T DONE THIS IN AGES! I HOPE I CAN KEEP UP WITH YA.
...

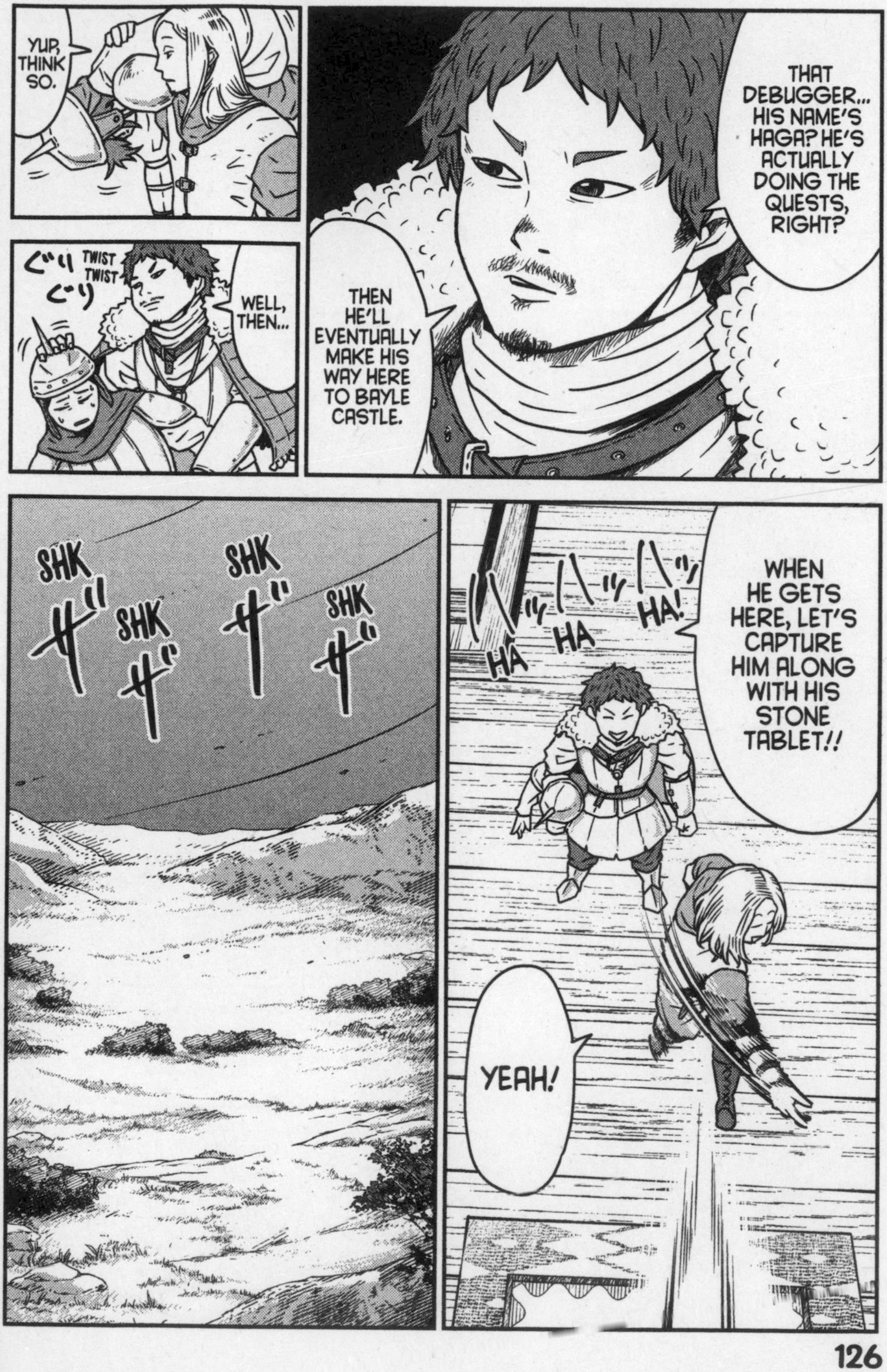
THAT DEBUGGER... HIS NAME'S HAGA? HE'S ACTUALLY DOING THE QUESTS, RIGHT?
THEN HE'LL EVENTUALLY MAKE HIS WAY HERE TO BAYLE CASTLE.
YUP, THINK SO.
ぐり TWIST
TWIST ぐり
WELL, THEN...
WHEN HE GETS HERE, LET'S CAPTURE HIM ALONG WITH HIS STONE TABLET!!
HA
HA
HA!
YEAH!
SHK
SHK
SHK
SHK

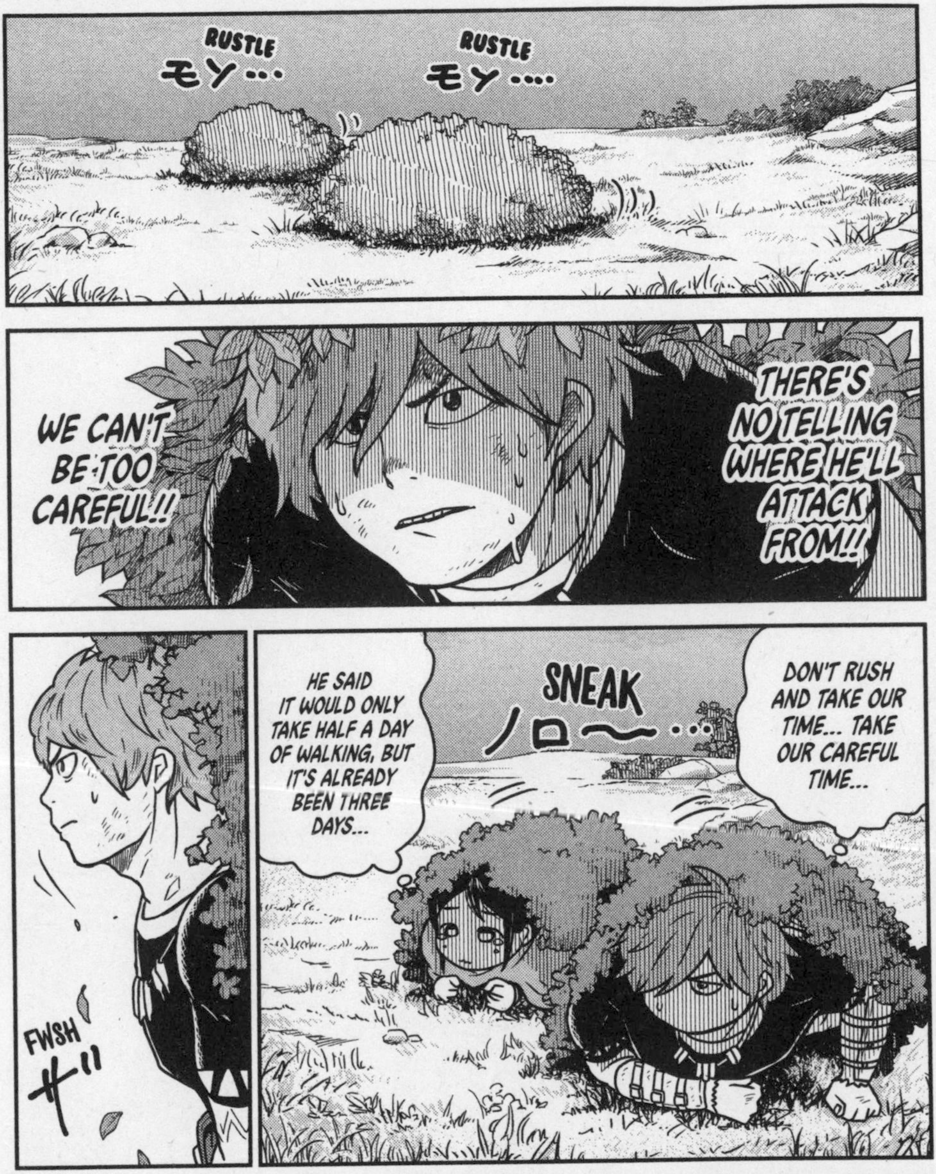
RUSTLE
モソ....
RUSTLE
モソ...
THERE'S NO TELLING WHERE HE'LL ATTACK FROM!!
WE CAN'T BE TOO CAREFUL!!
DON'T RUSH AND TAKE OUR TIME... TAKE OUR CAREFUL TIME...
SNEAK
ノロ〜...
HE SAID IT WOULD ONLY TAKE HALF A DAY OF WALKING, BUT IT'S ALREADY BEEN THREE DAYS...
FWSH
ALL RIGHT... WE'RE HERE.

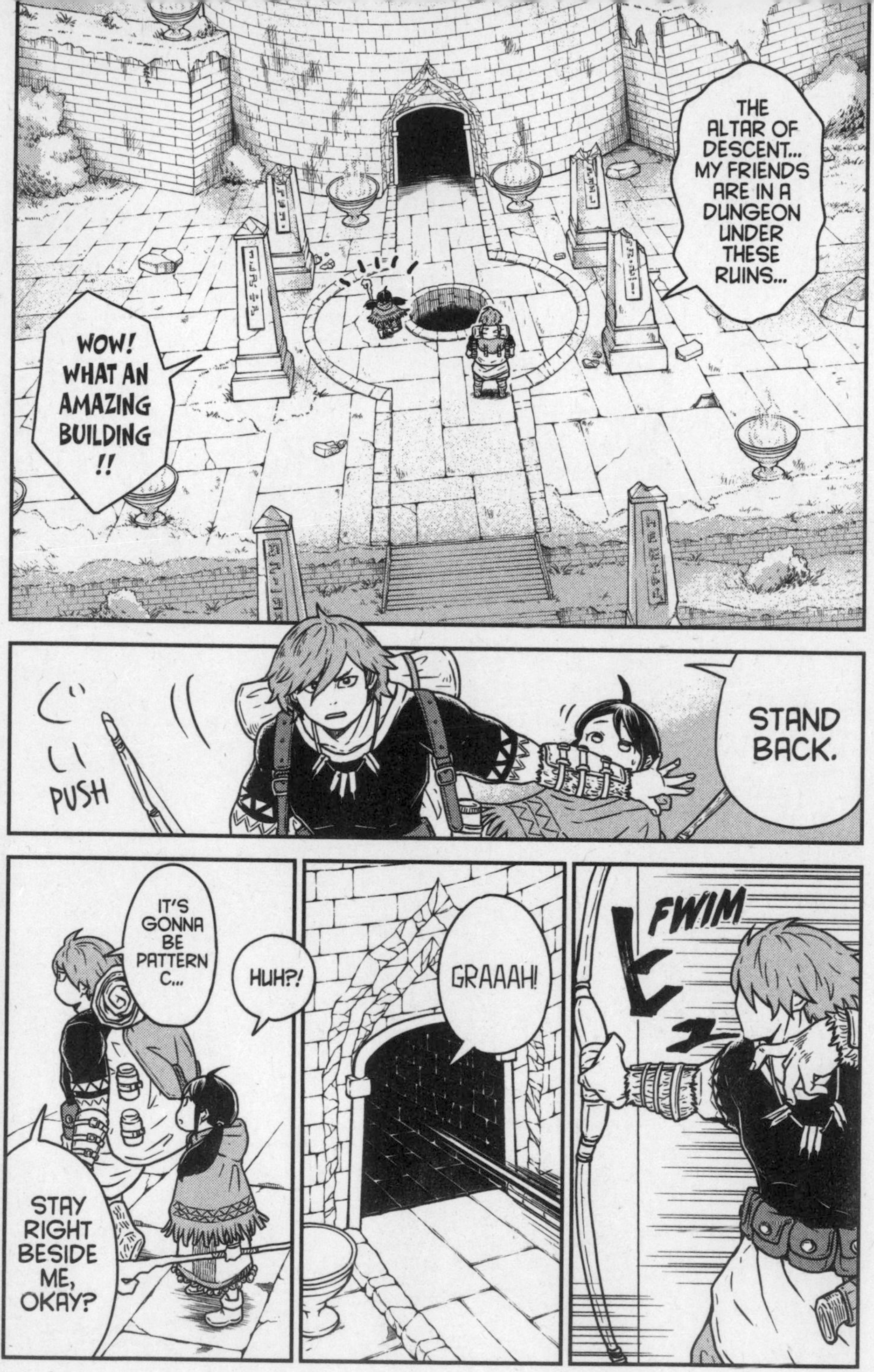
THE ALTAR OF DESCENT... MY FRIENDS ARE IN A DUNGEON UNDER THESE RUINS...
WOW! WHAT AN AMAZING BUILDING!!
STAND BACK.
ぐい
PUSH
FWIM
GRAAAH!
IT'S GONNA BE PATTERN C...
HUH?!
STAY RIGHT BESIDE ME, OKAY?

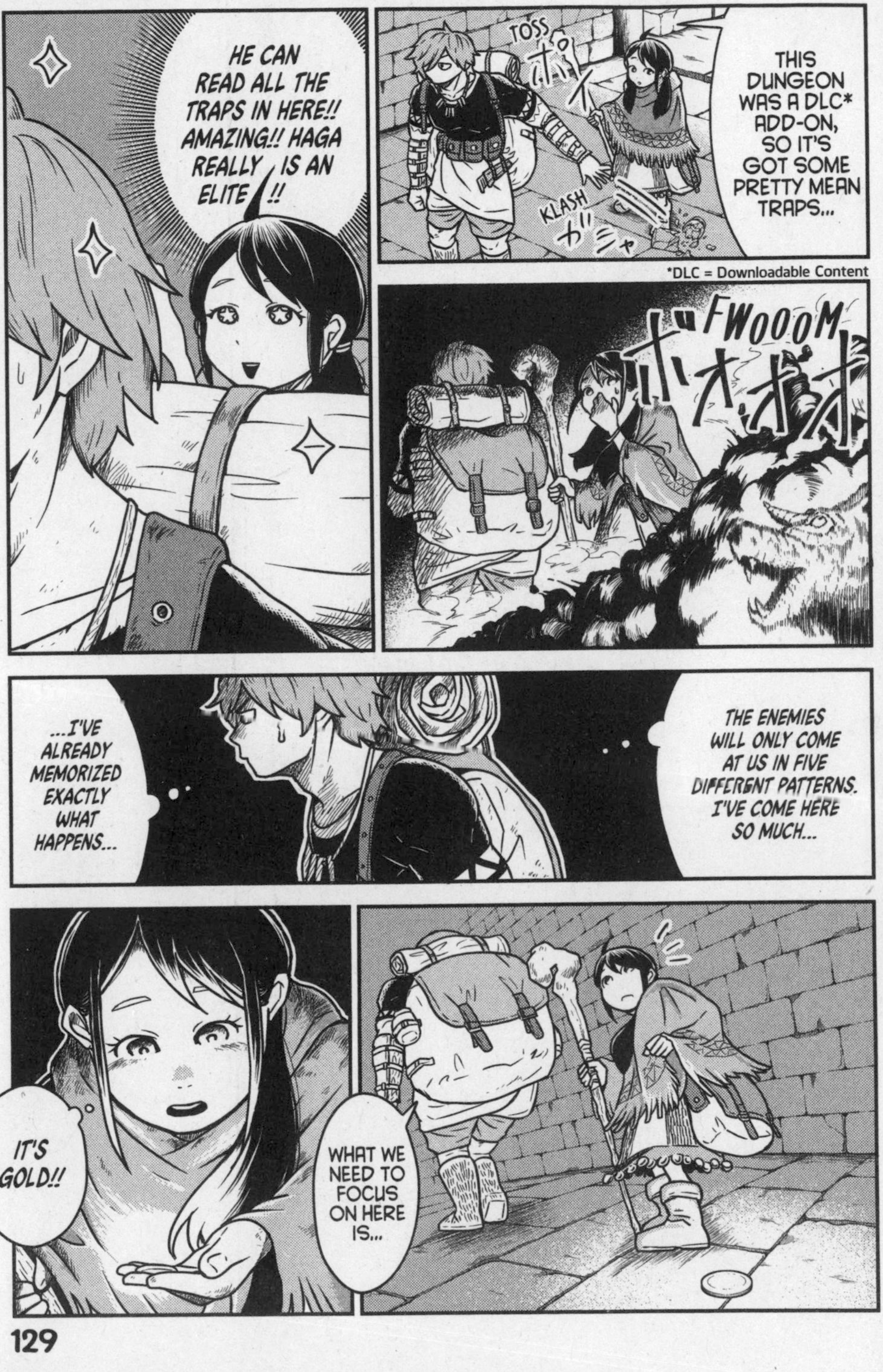
THIS DUNGEON WAS A DLC* ADD-ON, SO IT'S GOT SOME PRETTY MEAN TRAPS...
TOSS
KLASH
FWOOOM
HE CAN READ ALL THE TRAPS IN HERE!! AMAZING!! HAGA REALLY IS AN ELITE!!
THE ENEMIES WILL ONLY COME AT US IN FIVE DIFFERENT PATTERNS. I'VE COME HERE SO MUCH...
...I'VE ALREADY MEMORIZED EXACTLY WHAT HAPPENS...
WHAT WE NEED TO FOCUS ON HERE IS...
IT'S GOLD!!

*DLC = Downloadable Content

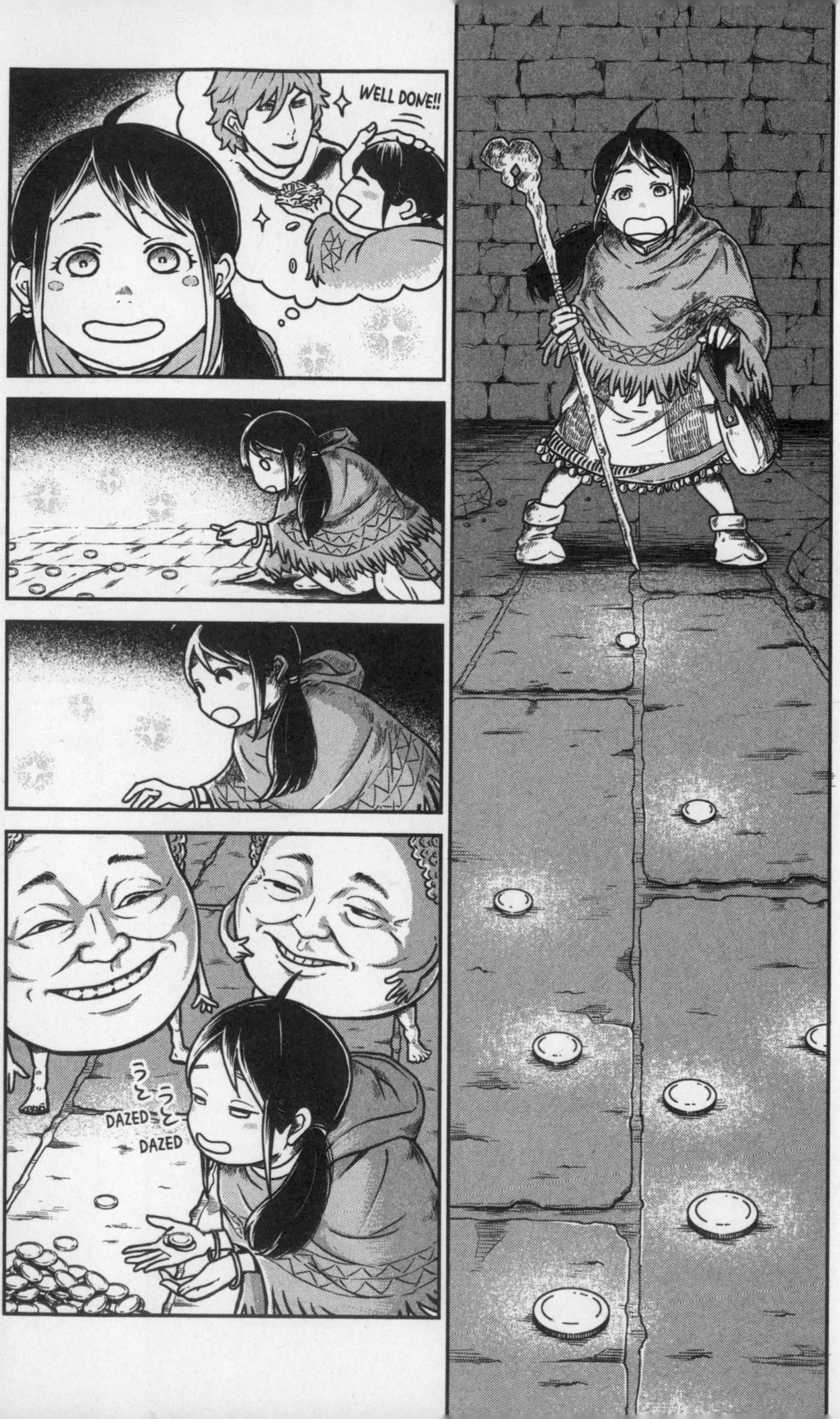
WELL DONE!!
うとうと
DAZED
DAZED

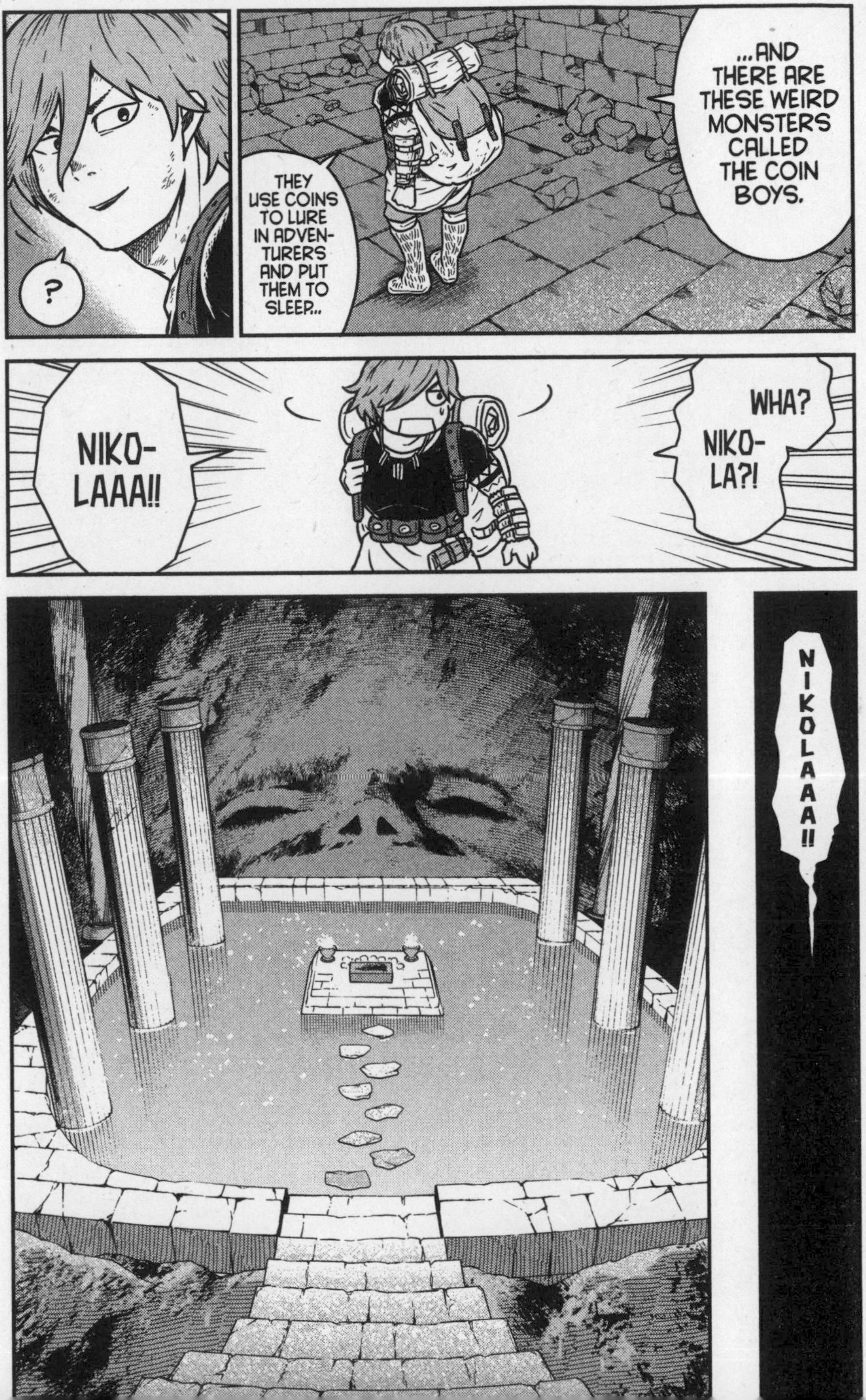
...AND THERE ARE THESE WEIRD MONSTERS CALLED THE COIN BOYS.
THEY USE COINS TO LURE IN ADVEN-TURERS AND PUT THEM TO SLEEP...
?
WHA? NIKO-LA?!
NIKO-LAAA!!
NIKOLAAAA!!

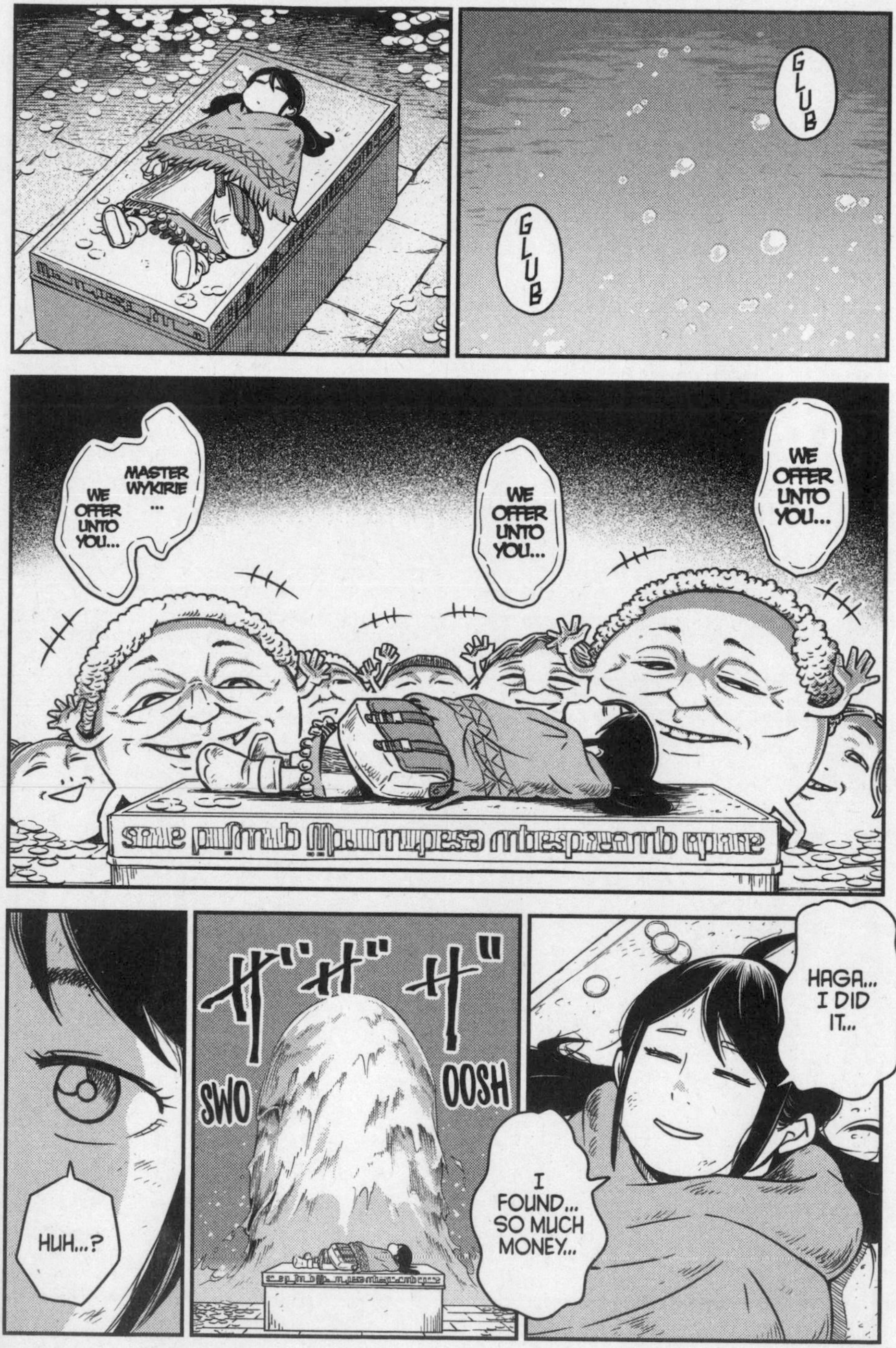
GLUB
GLUB
WE OFFER UNTO YOU...
WE OFFER UNTO YOU...
MASTER WYKIRIE... WE OFFER UNTO YOU...
HAGA... I DID IT...
I FOUND... SO MUCH MONEY...
ザザザ
SWO OOSH
HUH...?

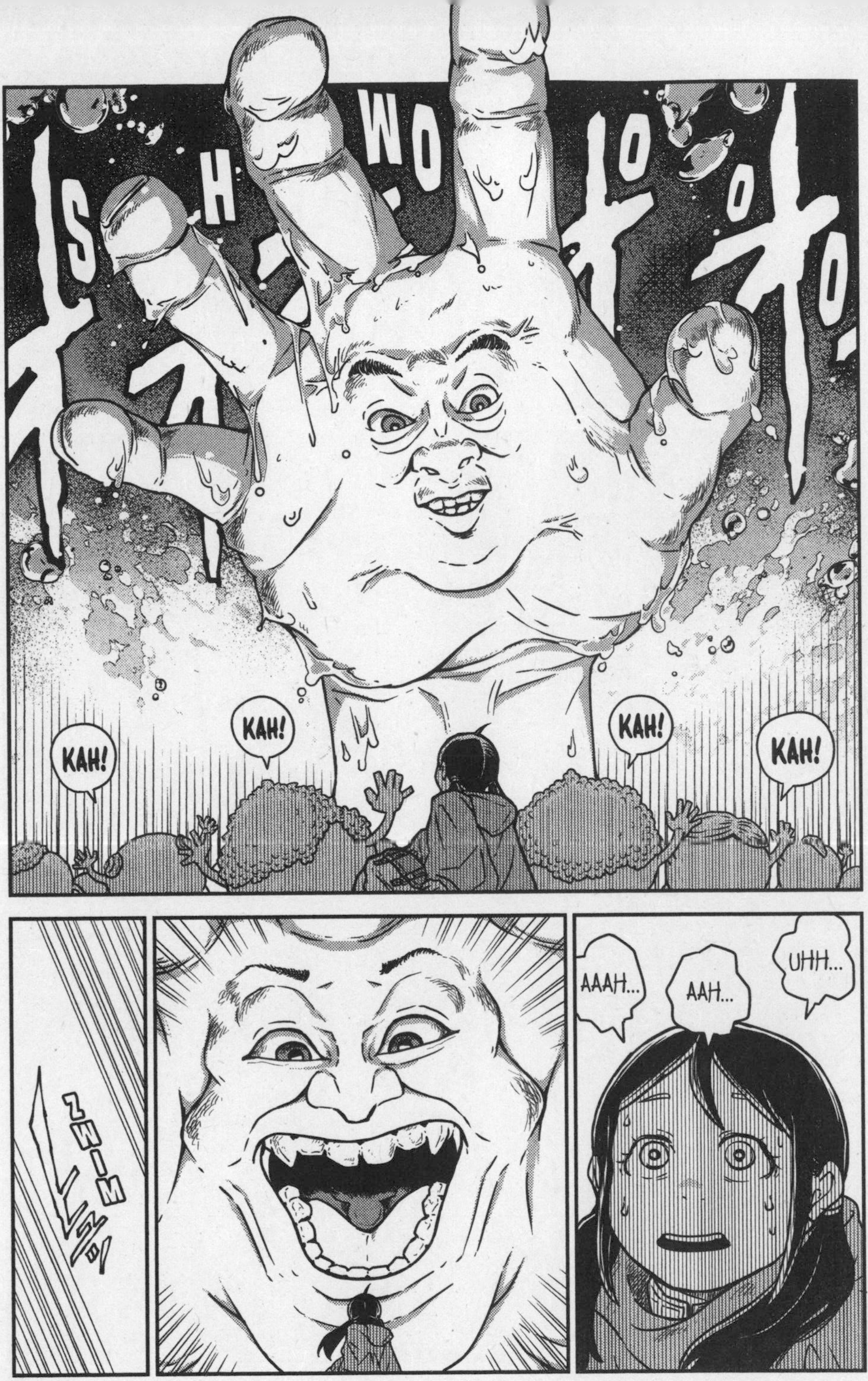
SHWOOOO!
KAH!
KAH!
KAH!
KAH!
UHH...
AAH...
AAAH...
ZWIM

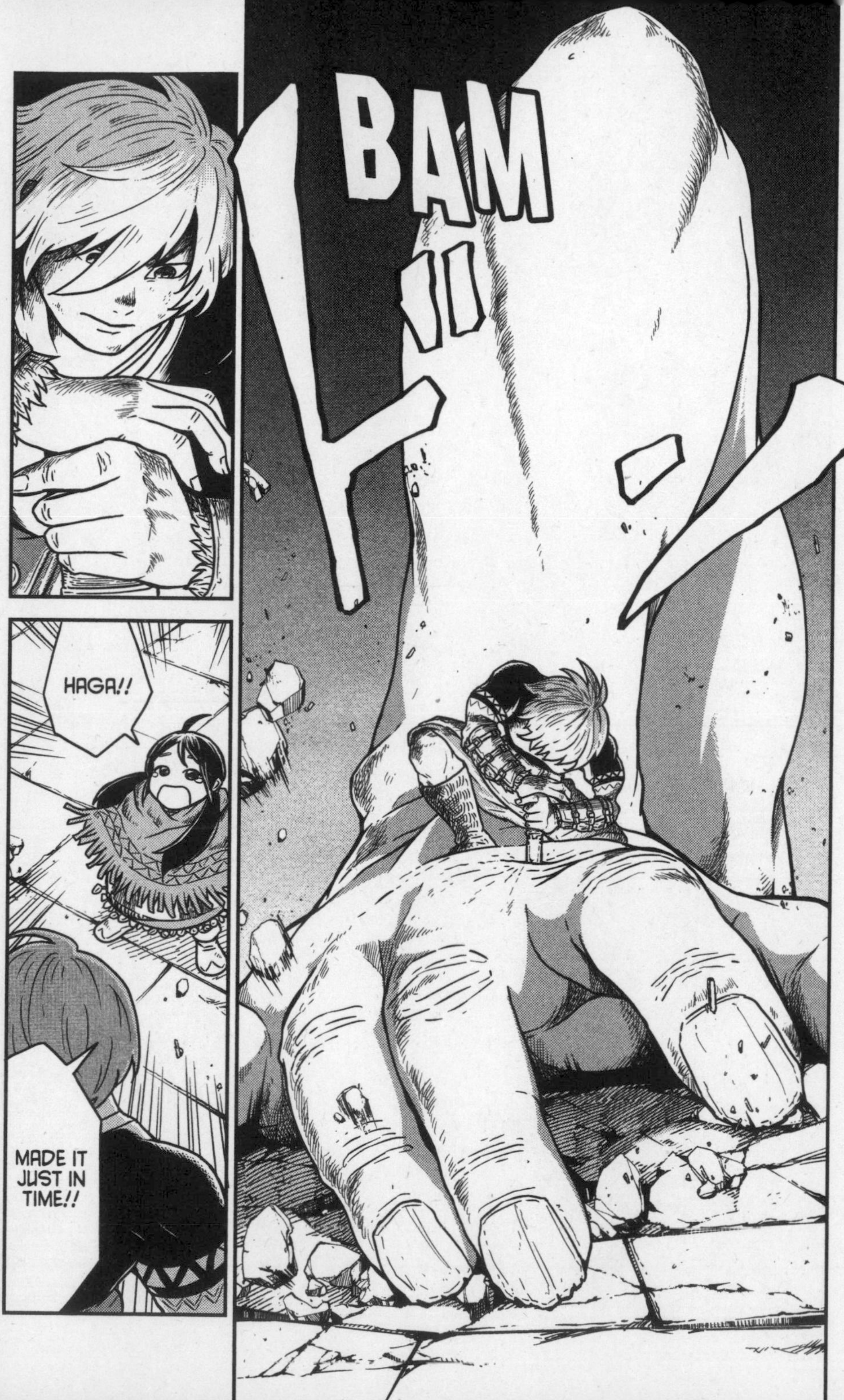
BAM
HAGA!!
MADE IT JUST IN TIME!!

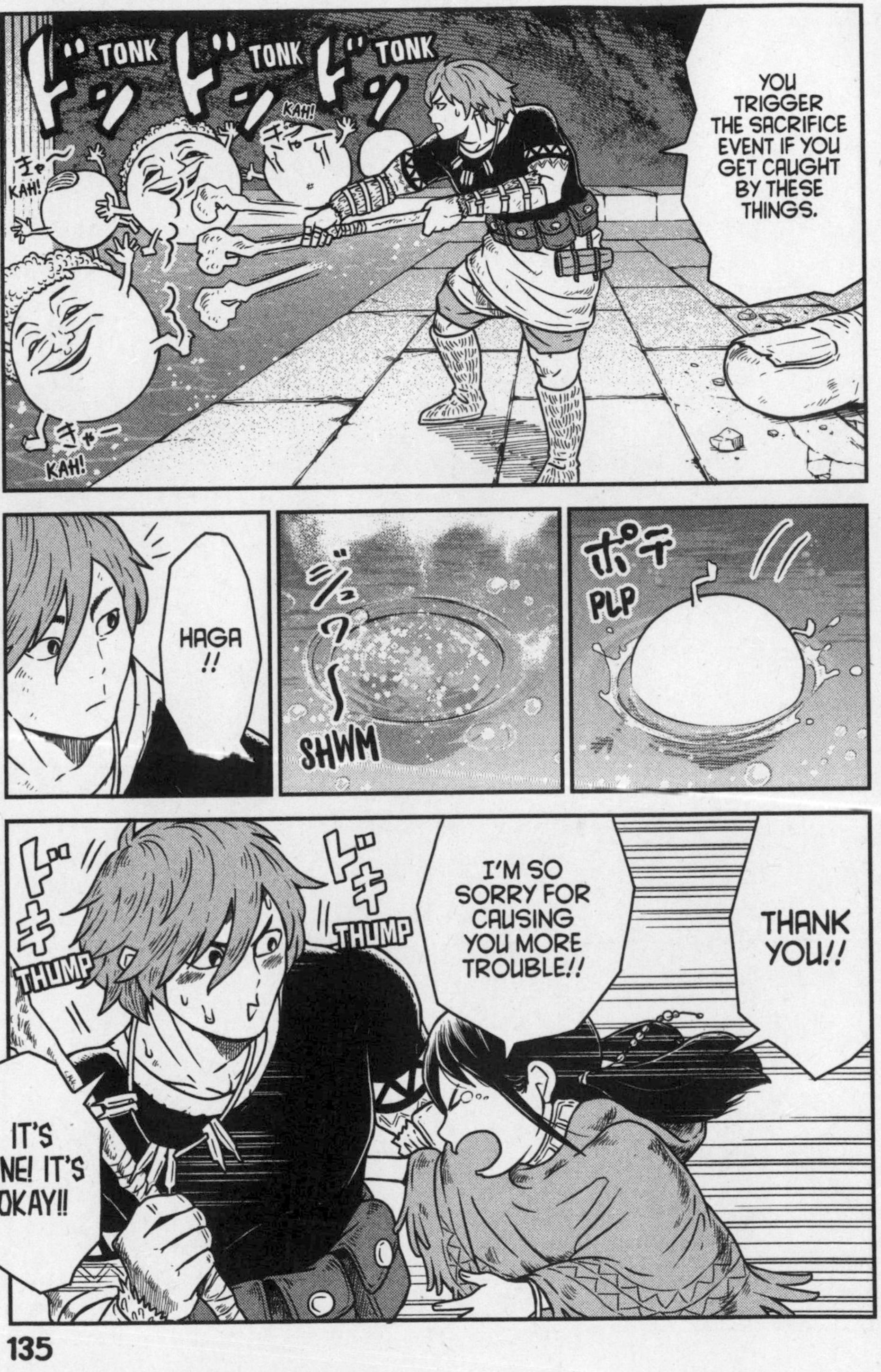
YOU TRIGGER THE SACRIFICE EVENT IF YOU GET CAUGHT BY THESE THINGS.
TONK
KAH!
TONK
TONK
KAH!
KAH!
ポテ
PLP
SHWM
HAGA!!
THANK YOU!!
I'M SO SORRY FOR CAUSING YOU MORE TROUBLE!!
THUMP
THUMP
IT'S FINE! IT'S OKAY!!

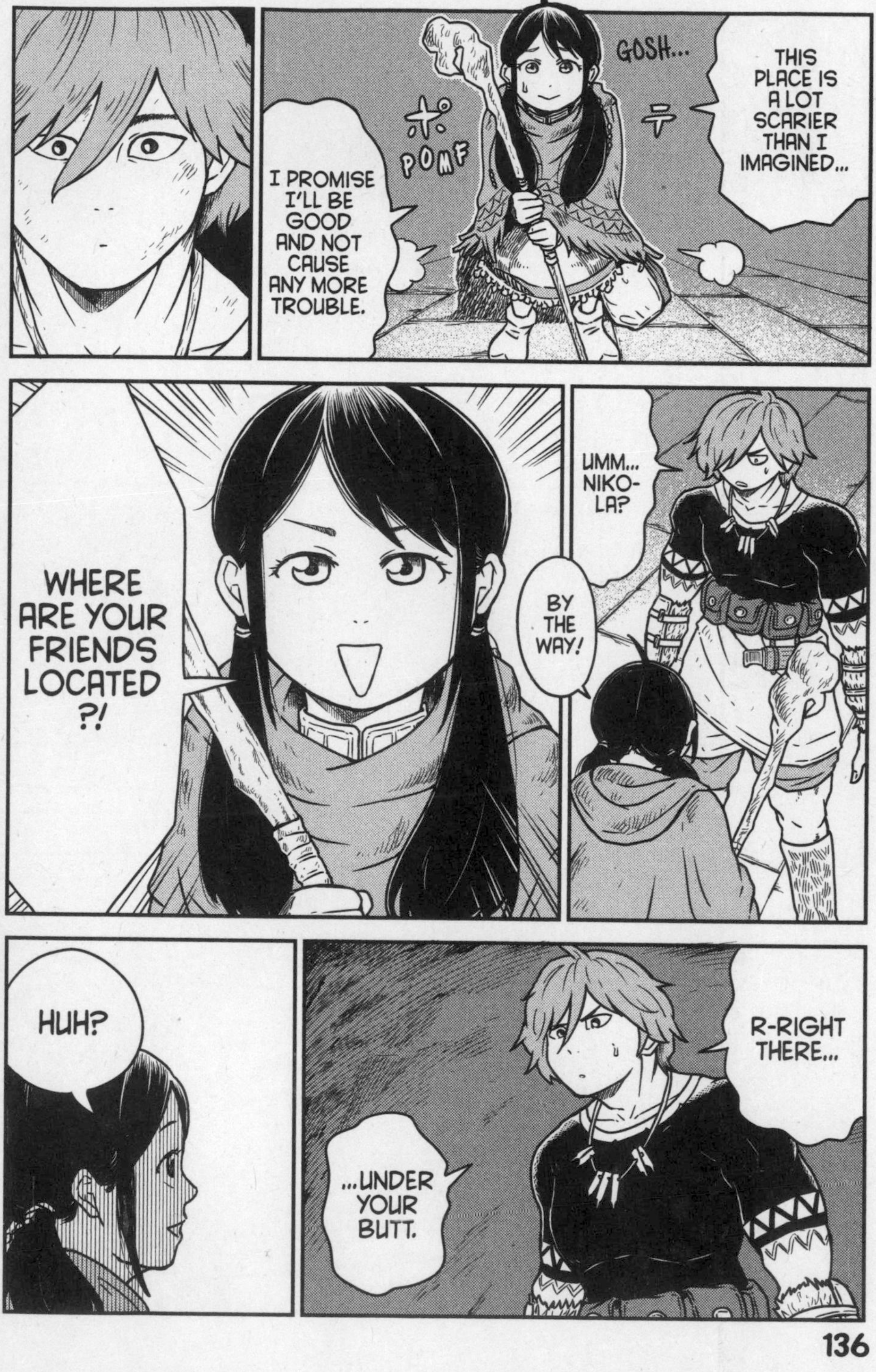
THIS PLACE IS A LOT SCARIER THAN I IMAGINED...
GOSH...
POMF
I PROMISE I'LL BE GOOD AND NOT CAUSE ANY MORE TROUBLE.
UMM... NIKO-LA?
BY THE WAY!
WHERE ARE YOUR FRIENDS LOCATED?!
R-RIGHT THERE...
...UNDER YOUR BUTT.
HUH?

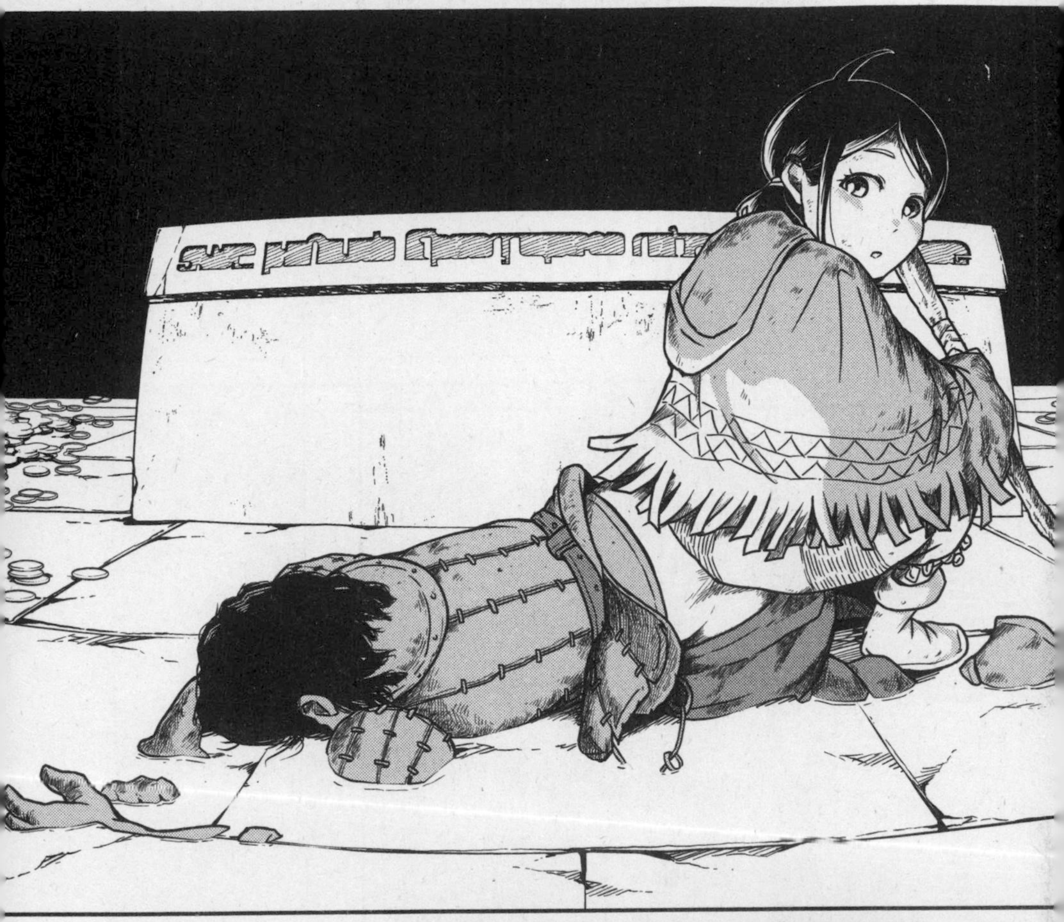

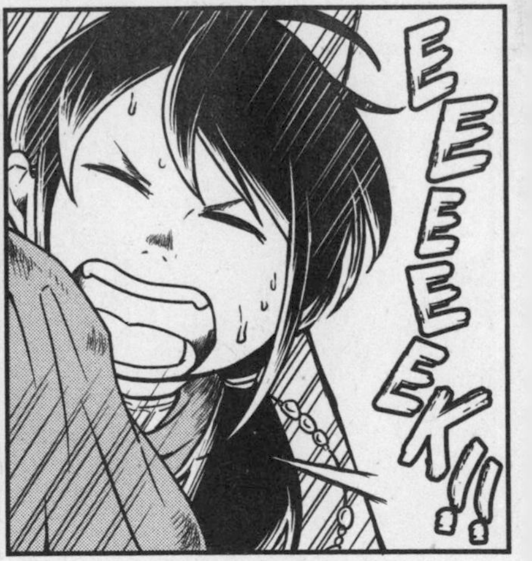
EEEEEEK!!

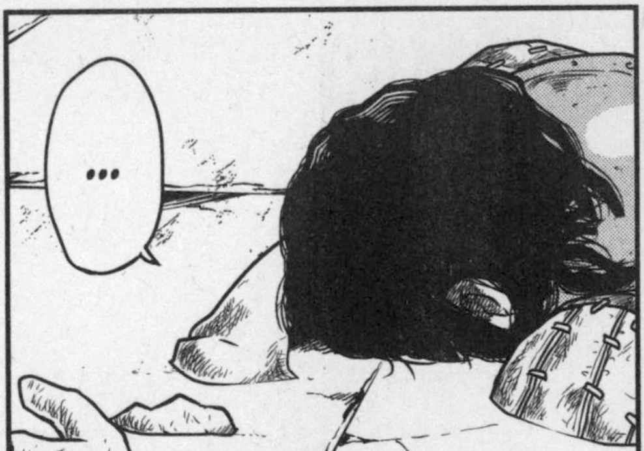
...

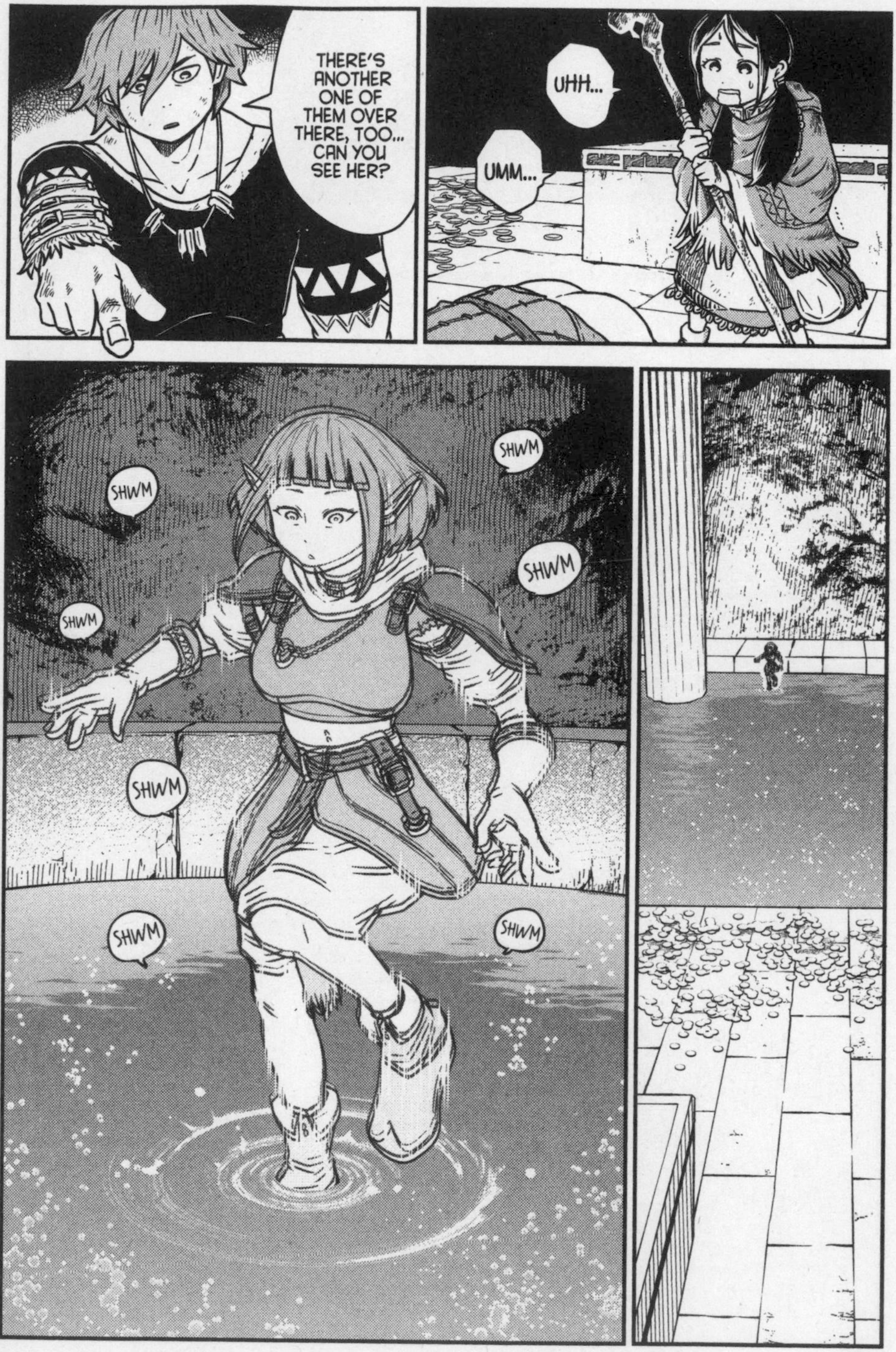
UHH...
UMM...
THERE'S ANOTHER ONE OF THEM OVER THERE, TOO... CAN YOU SEE HER?
SHWM
SHWM
SHWM
SHWM
SHWM
SHWM
SHWM

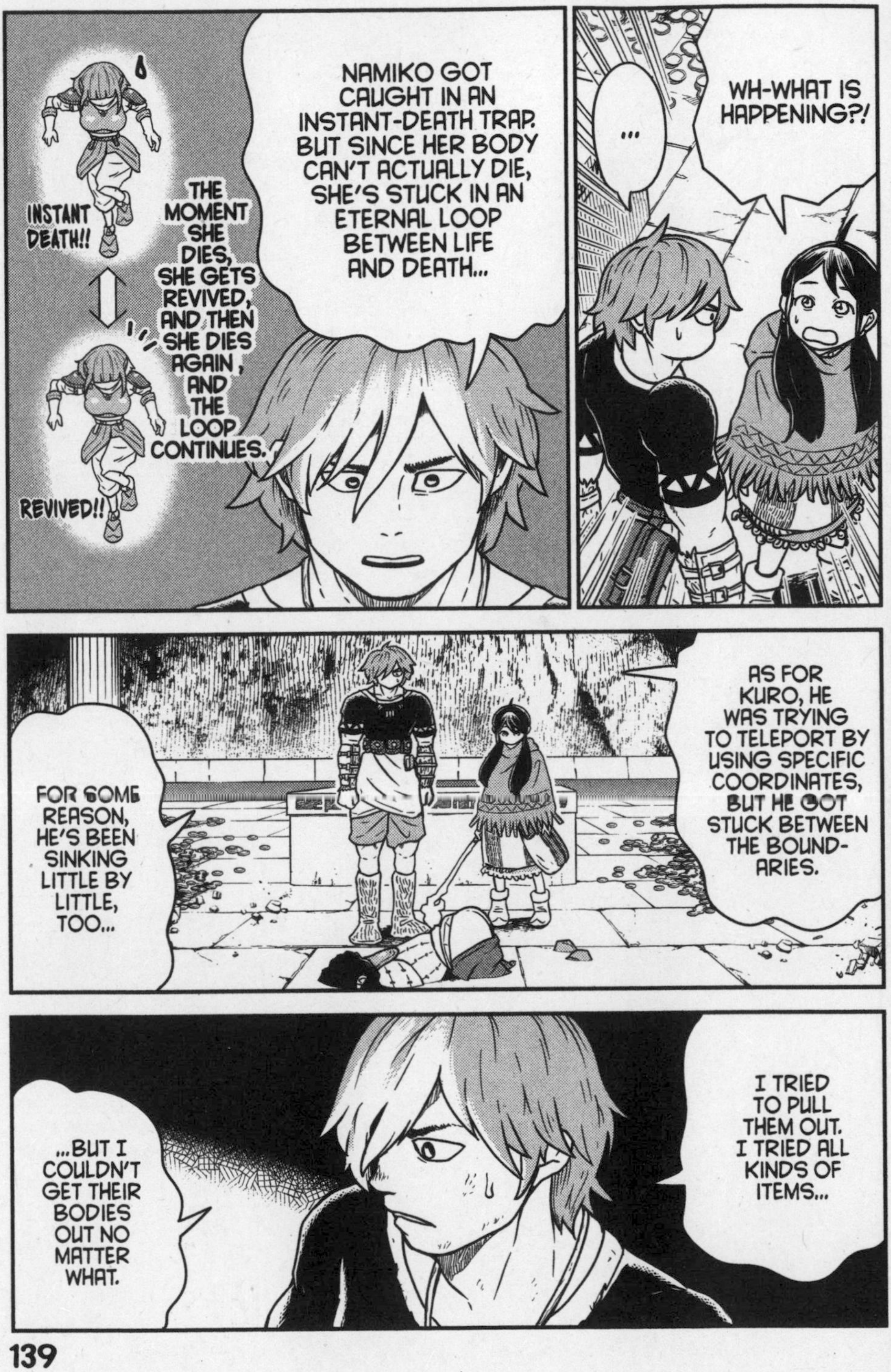
WH-WHAT IS HAPPENING?!
...
NAMIKO GOT CAUGHT IN AN INSTANT-DEATH TRAP. BUT SINCE HER BODY CAN'T ACTUALLY DIE, SHE'S STUCK IN AN ETERNAL LOOP BETWEEN LIFE AND DEATH...
THE MOMENT SHE DIES, SHE GETS REVIVED, AND THEN SHE DIES AGAIN, AND THE LOOP CONTINUES.
INSTANT DEATH!!
REVIVED!!
AS FOR KURO, HE WAS TRYING TO TELEPORT BY USING SPECIFIC COORDINATES, BUT HE GOT STUCK BETWEEN THE BOUNDARIES.
FOR SOME REASON, HE'S BEEN SINKING LITTLE BY LITTLE, TOO...
I TRIED TO PULL THEM OUT. I TRIED ALL KINDS OF ITEMS...
...BUT I COULDN'T GET THEIR BODIES OUT NO MATTER WHAT.

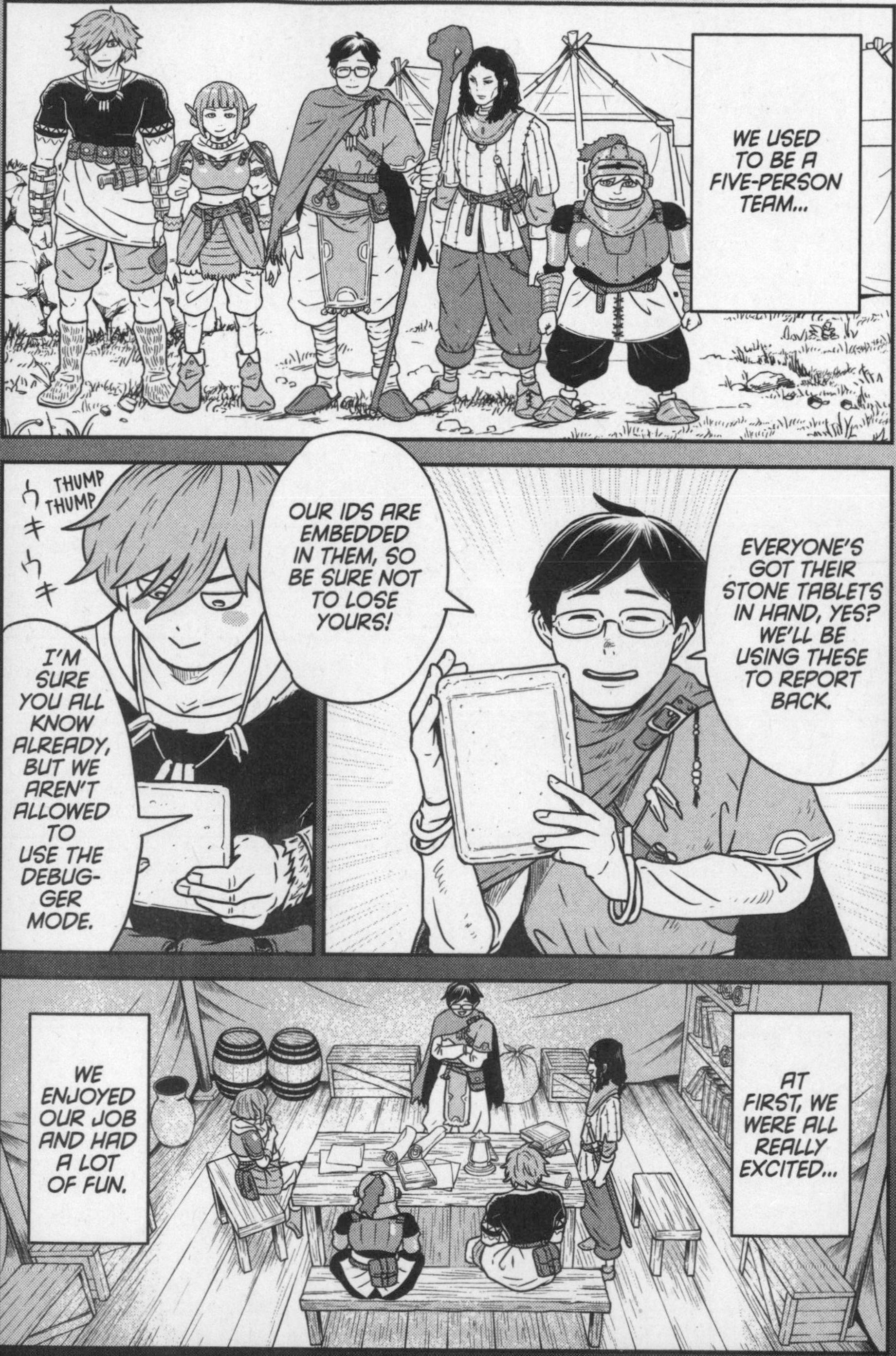

WE USED TO BE A FIVE-PERSON TEAM...
EVERYONE'S GOT THEIR STONE TABLETS IN HAND, YES? WE'LL BE USING THESE TO REPORT BACK.
OUR IDS ARE EMBEDDED IN THEM, SO BE SURE NOT TO LOSE YOURS!
THUMP THUMP
ウキウキ
I'M SURE YOU ALL KNOW ALREADY, BUT WE AREN'T ALLOWED TO USE THE DEBUG-GER MODE.
AT FIRST, WE WERE ALL REALLY EXCITED...
WE ENJOYED OUR JOB AND HAD A LOT OF FUN.

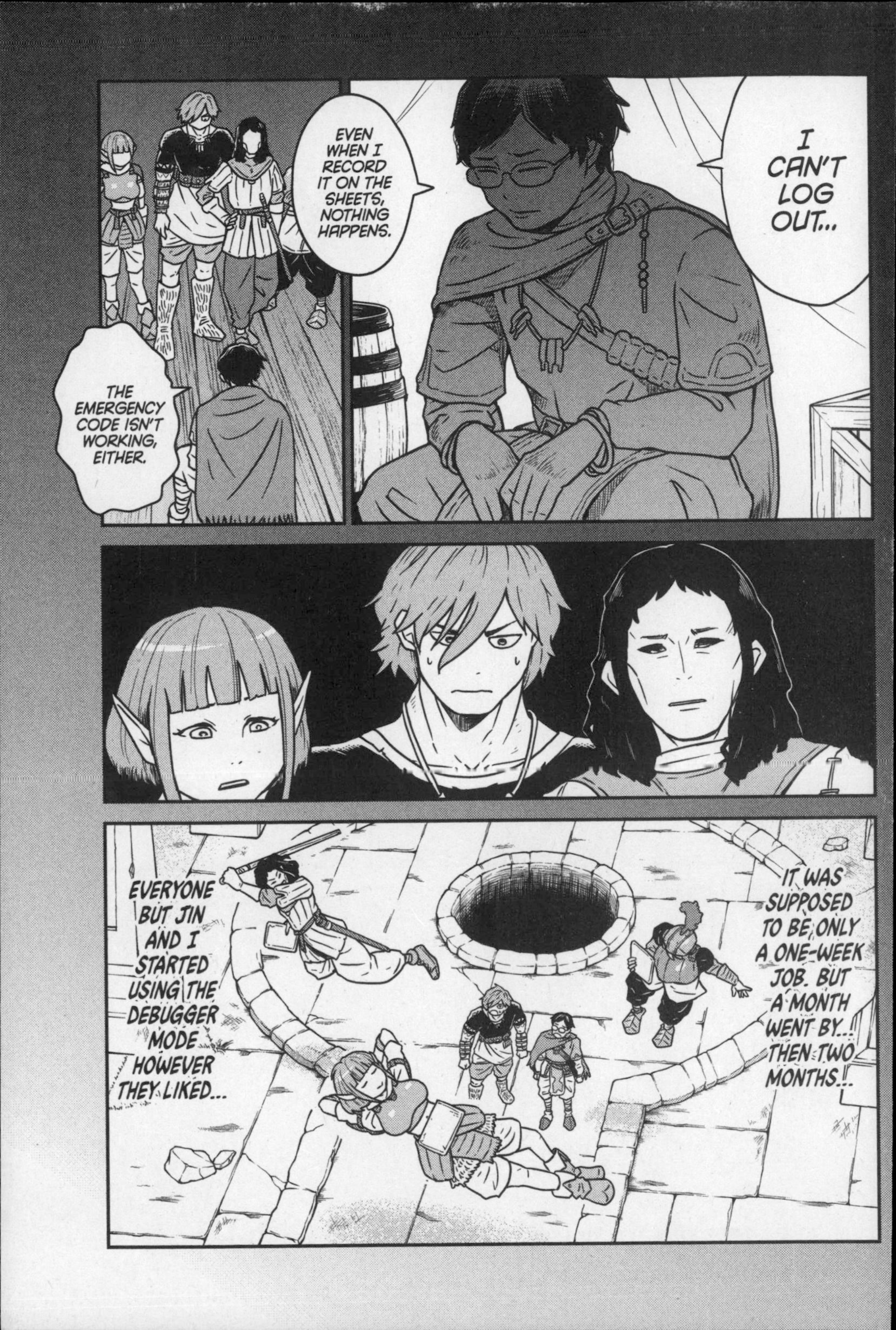
I CAN'T LOG OUT...
EVEN WHEN I RECORD IT ON THE SHEETS, NOTHING HAPPENS.
THE EMERGENCY CODE ISN'T WORKING, EITHER.
IT WAS SUPPOSED TO BE ONLY A ONE-WEEK JOB. BUT A MONTH WENT BY... THEN TWO MONTHS...
EVERYONE BUT JIN AND I STARTED USING THE DEBUGGER MODE HOWEVER THEY LIKED...

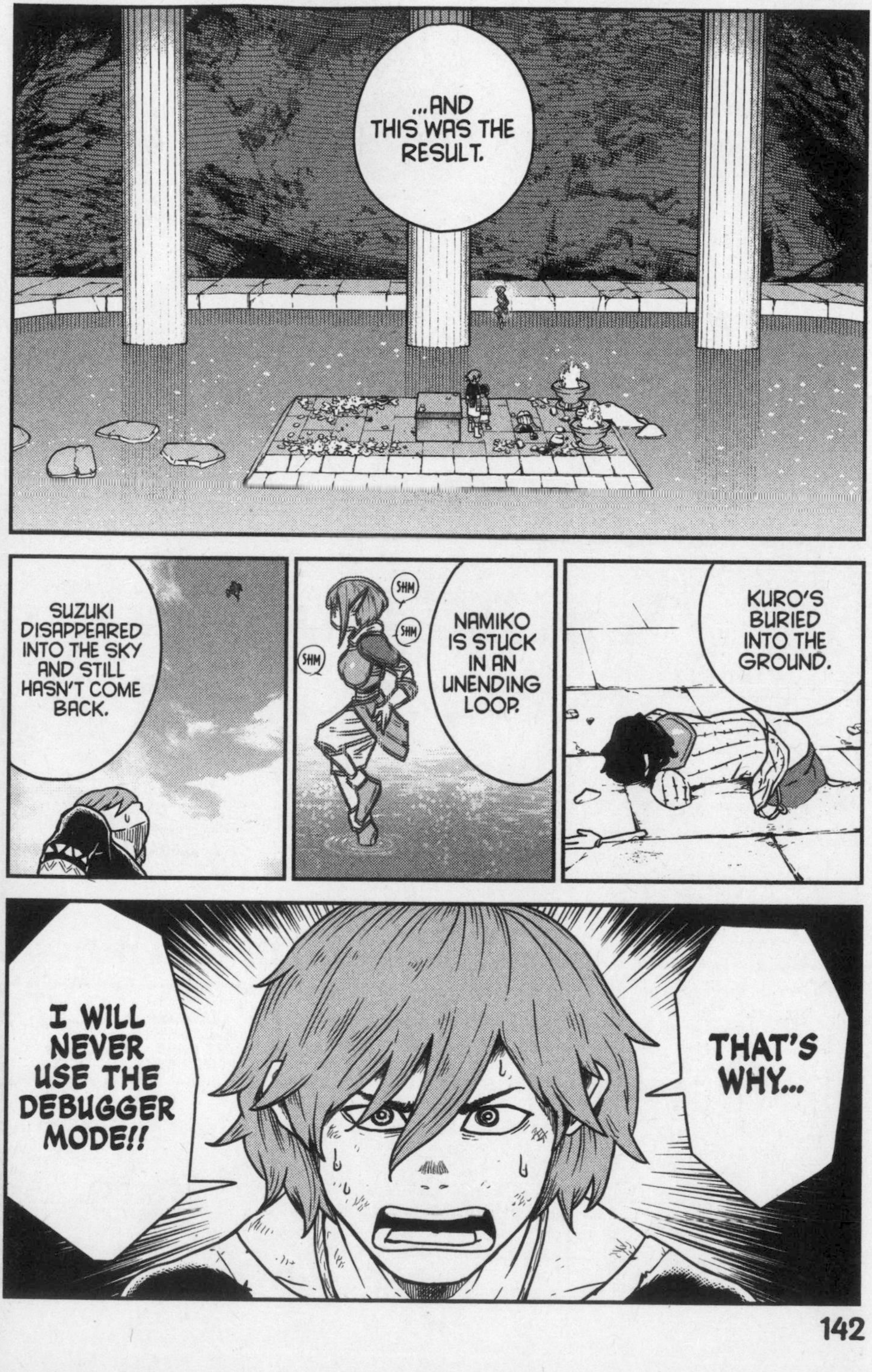
...AND THIS WAS THE RESULT.
KURO'S BURIED INTO THE GROUND.
SHM
SHM
SHM
NAMIKO IS STUCK IN AN UNENDING LOOP.
SUZUKI DISAPPEARED INTO THE SKY AND STILL HASN'T COME BACK.
THAT'S WHY...
I WILL NEVER USE THE DEBUGGER MODE!!

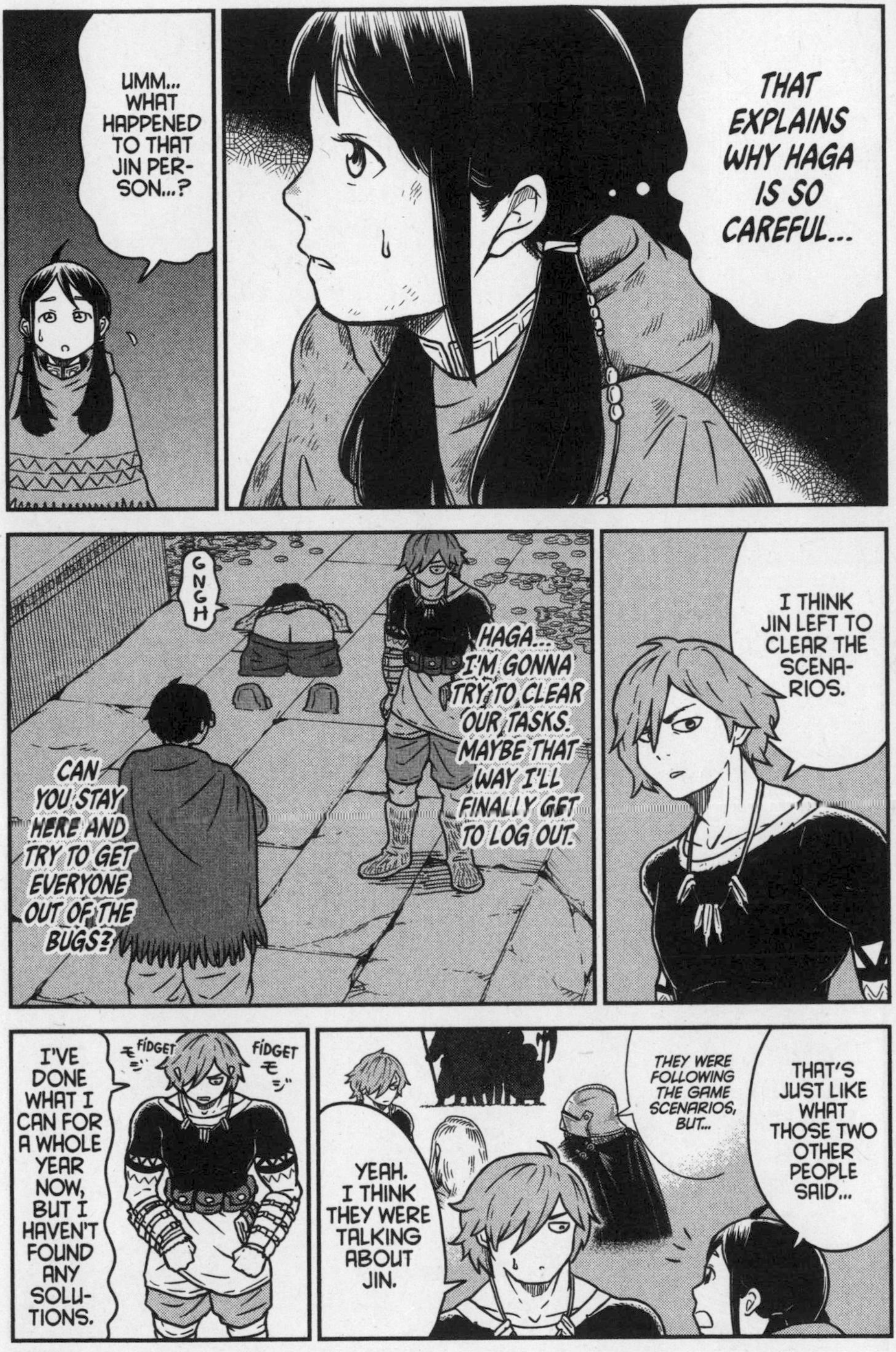
THAT EXPLAINS WHY HAGA IS SO CAREFUL...
UMM... WHAT HAPPENED TO THAT JIN PERSON...?
I THINK JIN LEFT TO CLEAR THE SCENARIOS.
GNGH
HAGA... I'M GONNA TRY TO CLEAR OUR TASKS. MAYBE THAT WAY I'LL FINALLY GET TO LOG OUT.
CAN YOU STAY HERE AND TRY TO GET EVERYONE OUT OF THE BUGS?
THAT'S JUST LIKE WHAT THOSE TWO OTHER PEOPLE SAID...
THEY WERE FOLLOWING THE GAME SCENARIOS, BUT...
YEAH. I THINK THEY WERE TALKING ABOUT JIN.
FIDGET モジ
FIDGET モジ
I'VE DONE WHAT I CAN FOR A WHOLE YEAR NOW, BUT I HAVEN'T FOUND ANY SOLUTIONS.

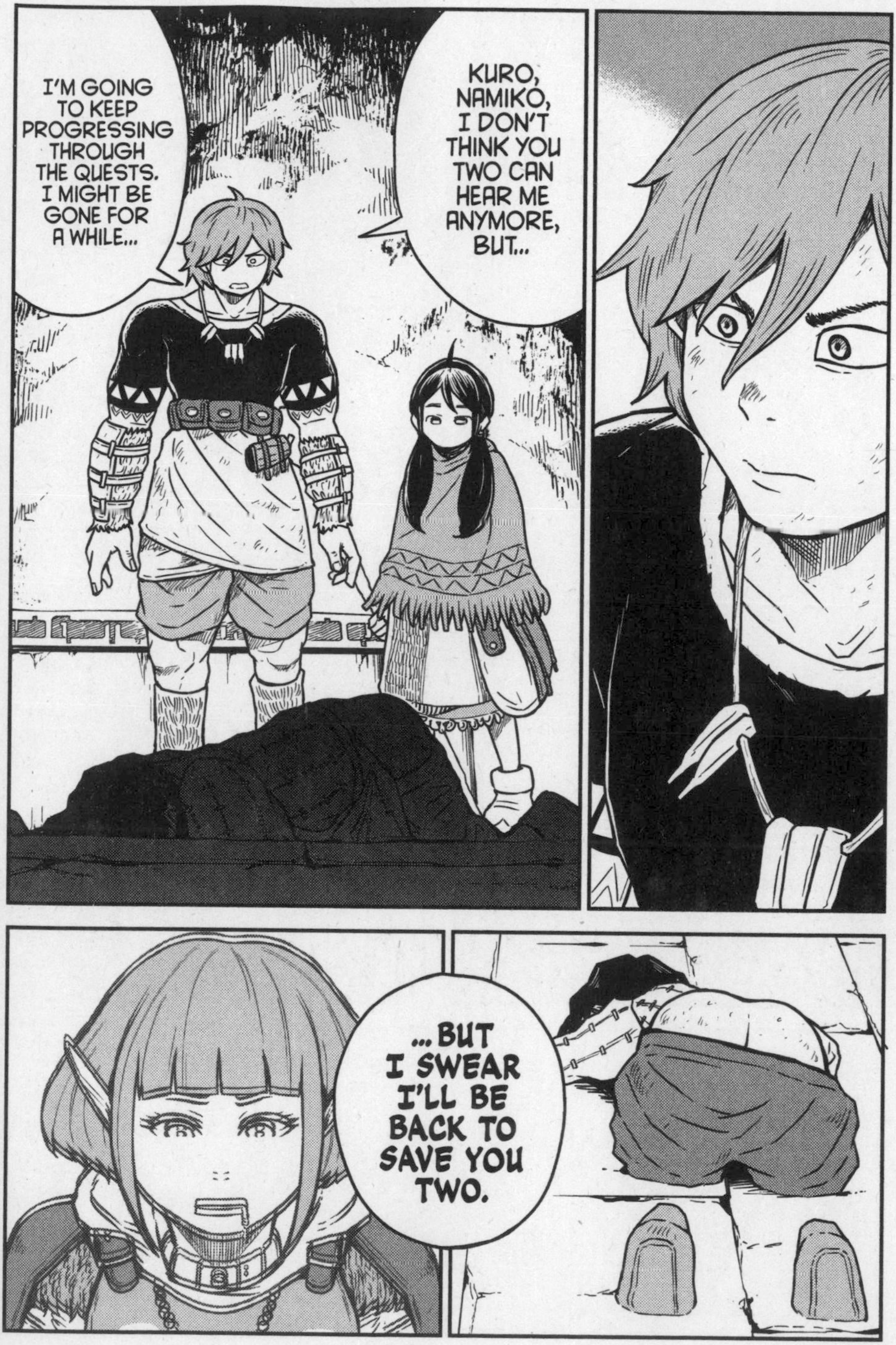
KURO, NAMIKO, I DON'T THINK YOU TWO CAN HEAR ME ANYMORE, BUT...
I'M GOING TO KEEP PROGRESSING THROUGH THE QUESTS. I MIGHT BE GONE FOR A WHILE...
...BUT I SWEAR I'LL BE BACK TO SAVE YOU TWO.

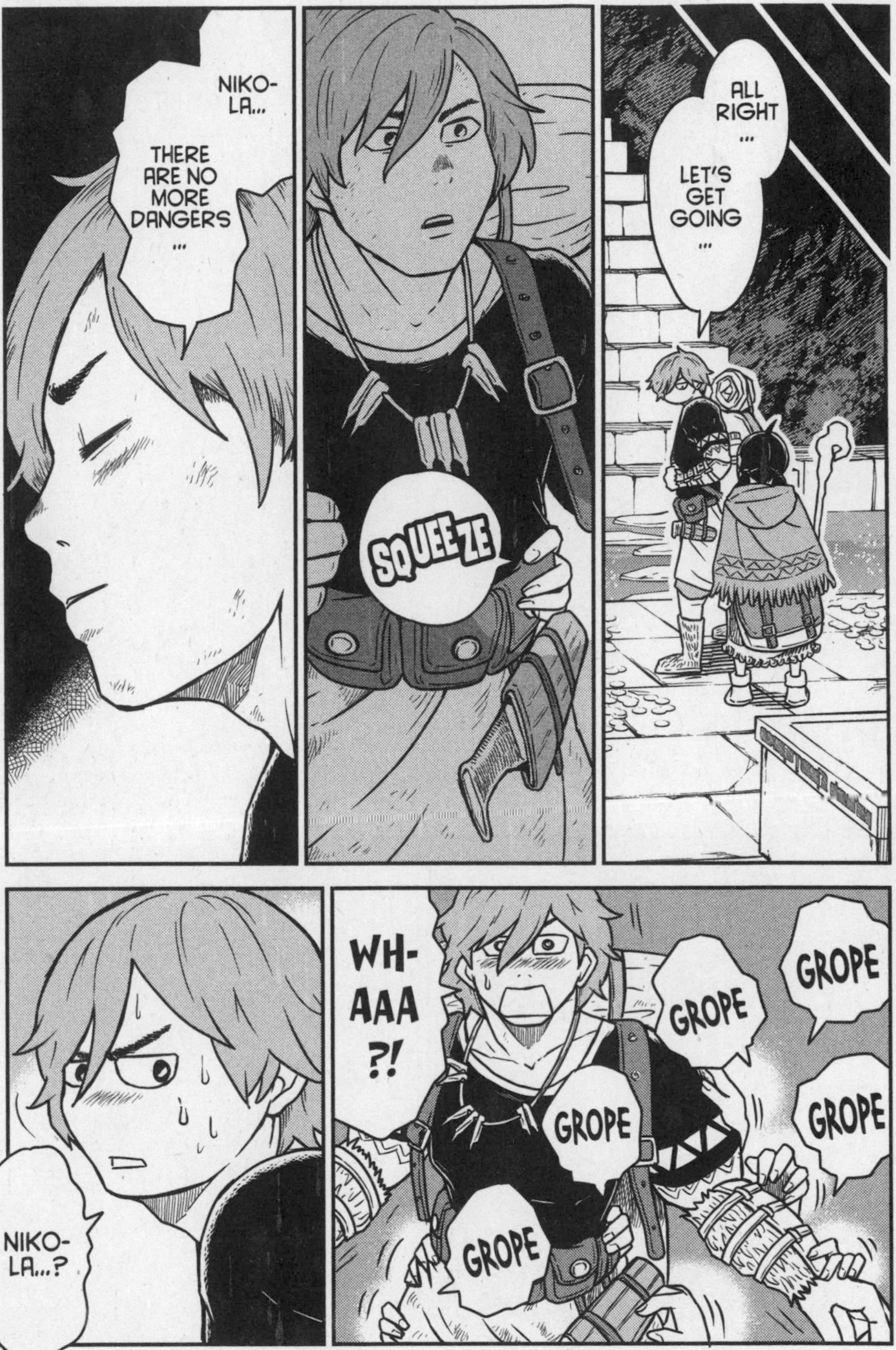
ALL RIGHT ... LET'S GET GOING ...
SQUEEZE
NIKO-LA...
THERE ARE NO MORE DANGERS ...
WH-AAA ?!
GROPE
GROPE
GROPE
GROPE
GROPE
NIKO-LA...?

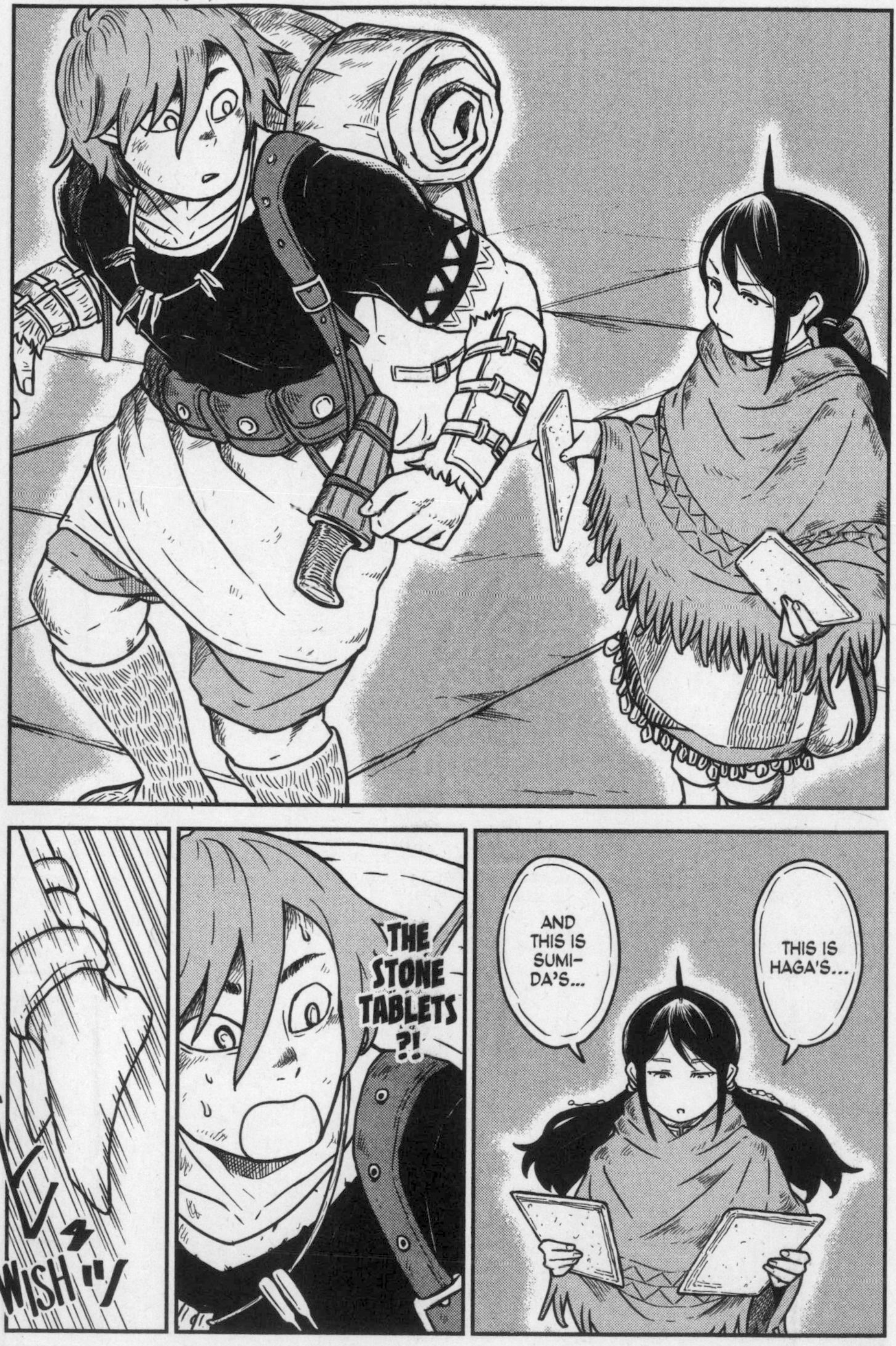
THIS IS HAGA'S...
AND THIS IS SUMI-DA'S...
THE STONE TABLETS ?!
FWISH

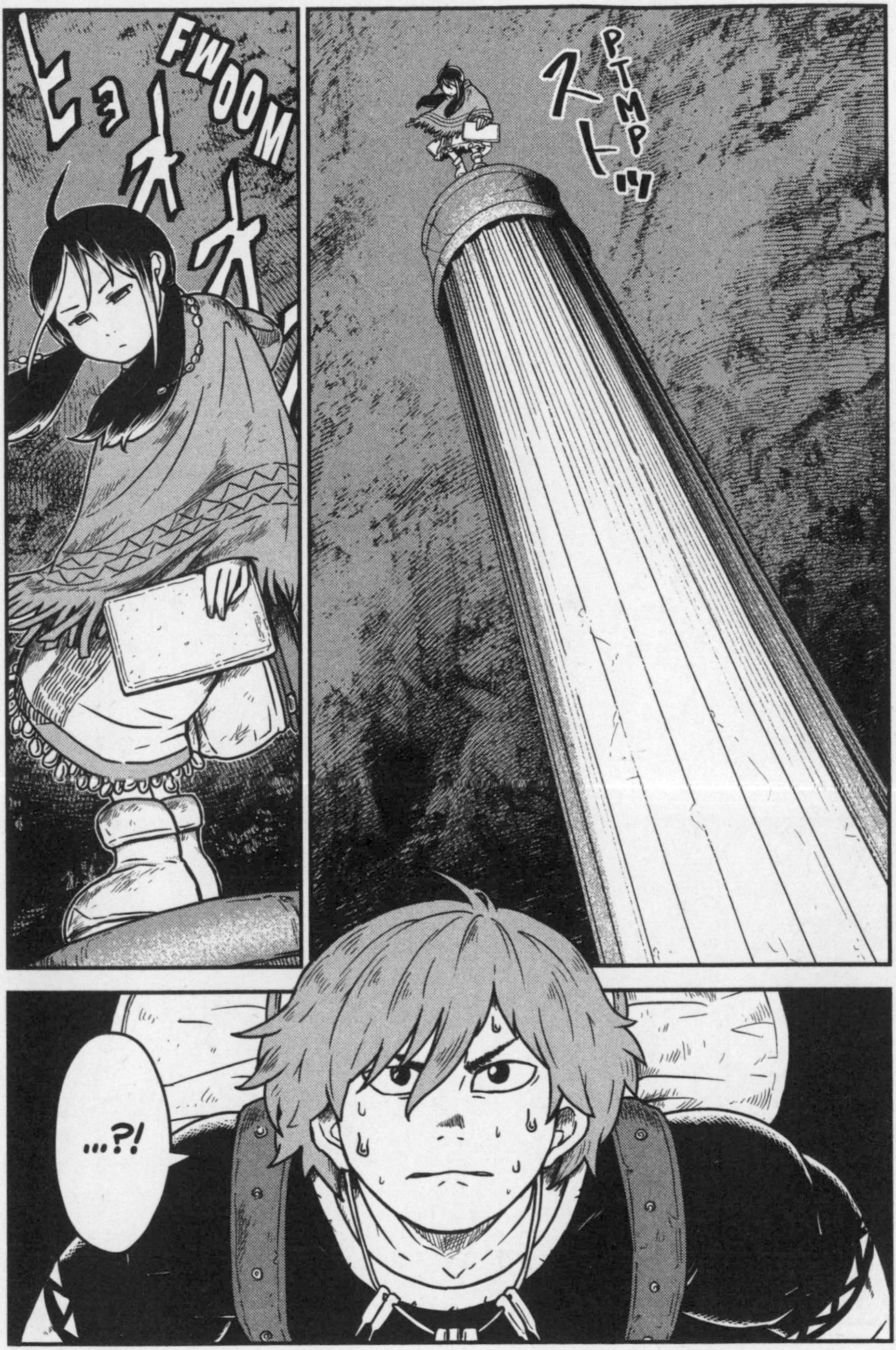
PTMP
ストッ
FWOOM
...?!

NO.4/END

The Altar of Descent

The Altar of Descent is a ruined building left over from another age. The ruins became a labyrinth when it was seized by monsters and cultists from the main continent. Only reckless adventurers would dare come close.

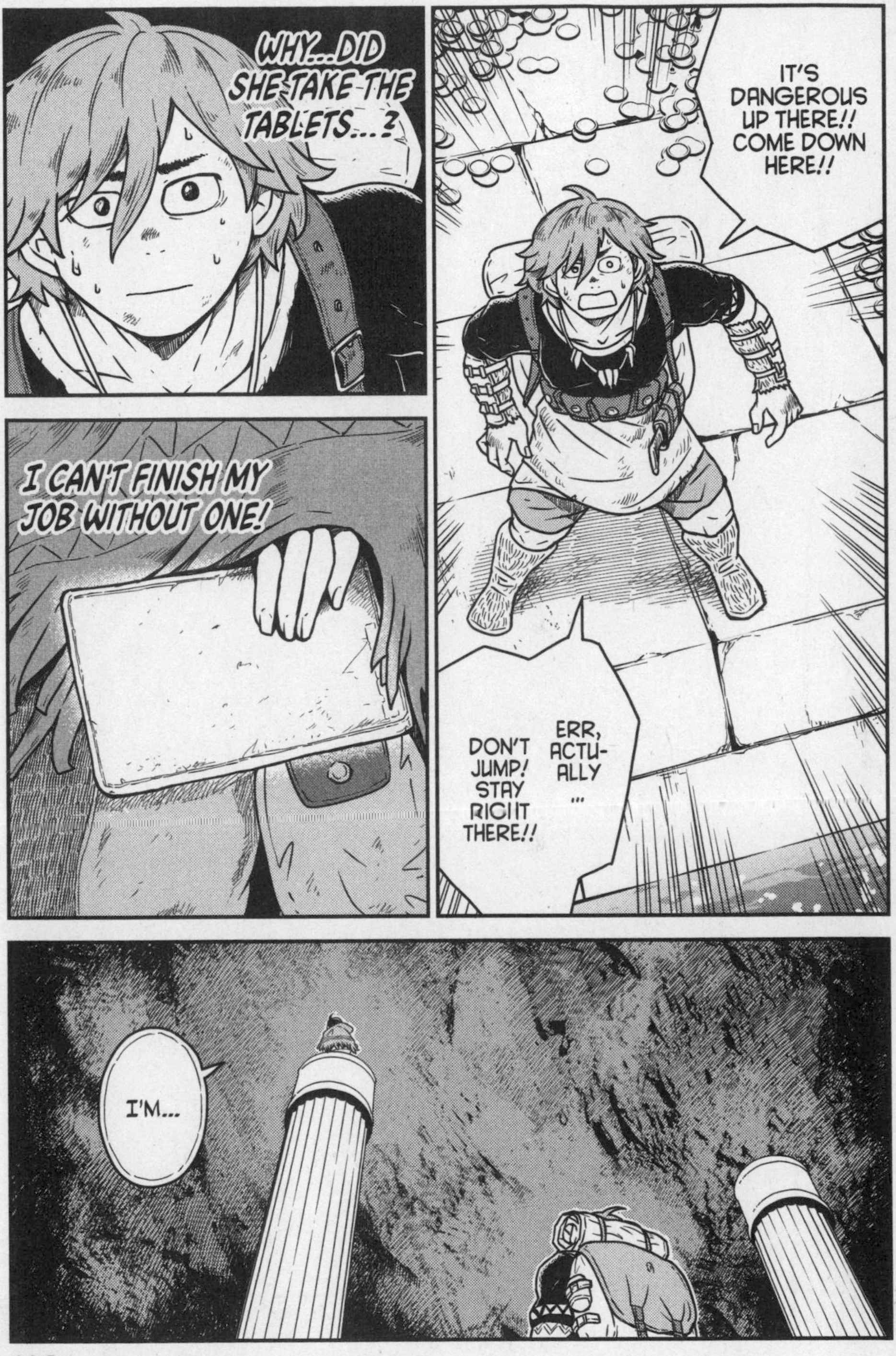
IT'S DANGEROUS UP THERE!! COME DOWN HERE!!
ERR, ACTU-ALLY ...
DON'T JUMP! STAY RIGHT THERE!!
WHY...DID SHE TAKE THE TABLETS...?
I CAN'T FINISH MY JOB WITHOUT ONE!
I'M...

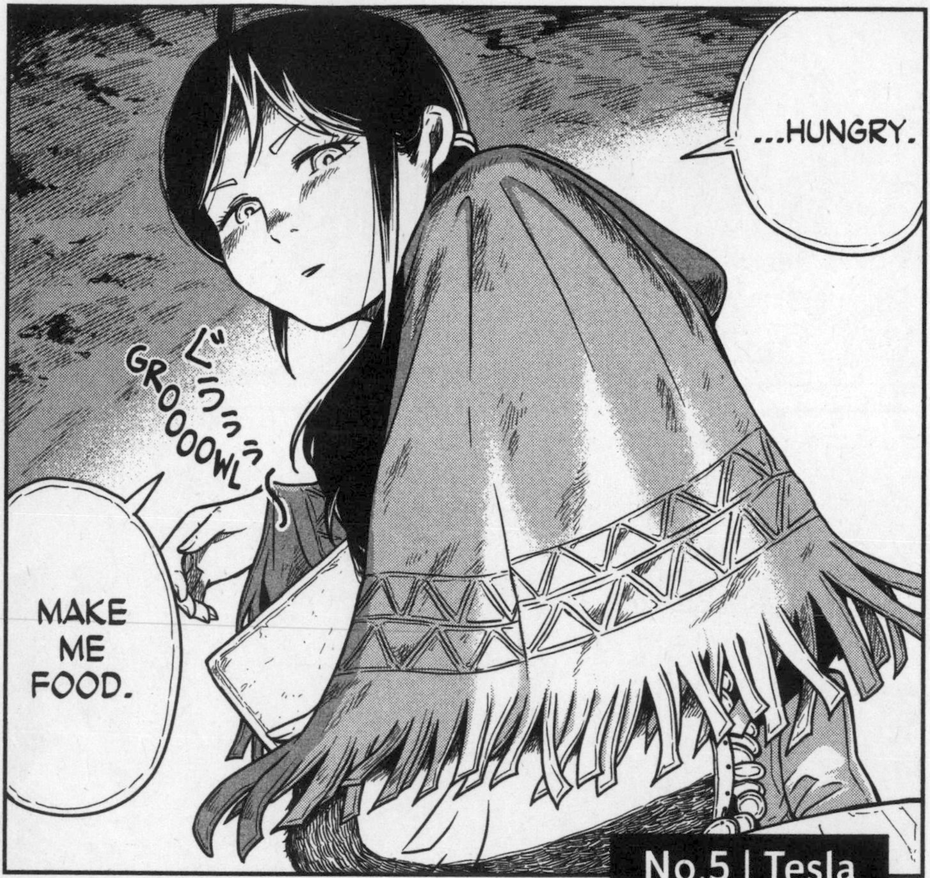
...HUNGRY.
ぐぅぅぅ
GROOOOWL
MAKE ME FOOD.

No.5 | Tesla

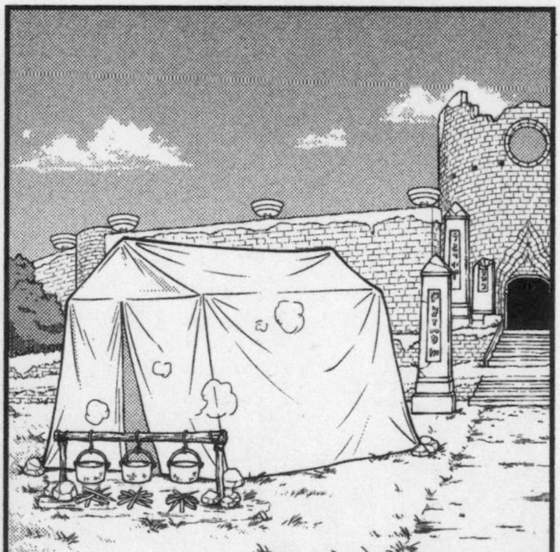

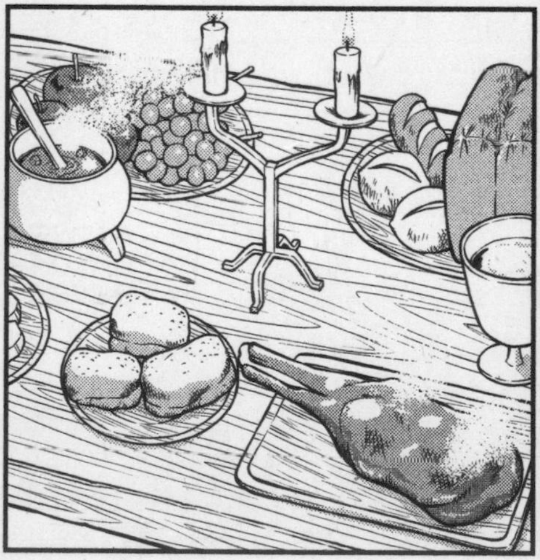

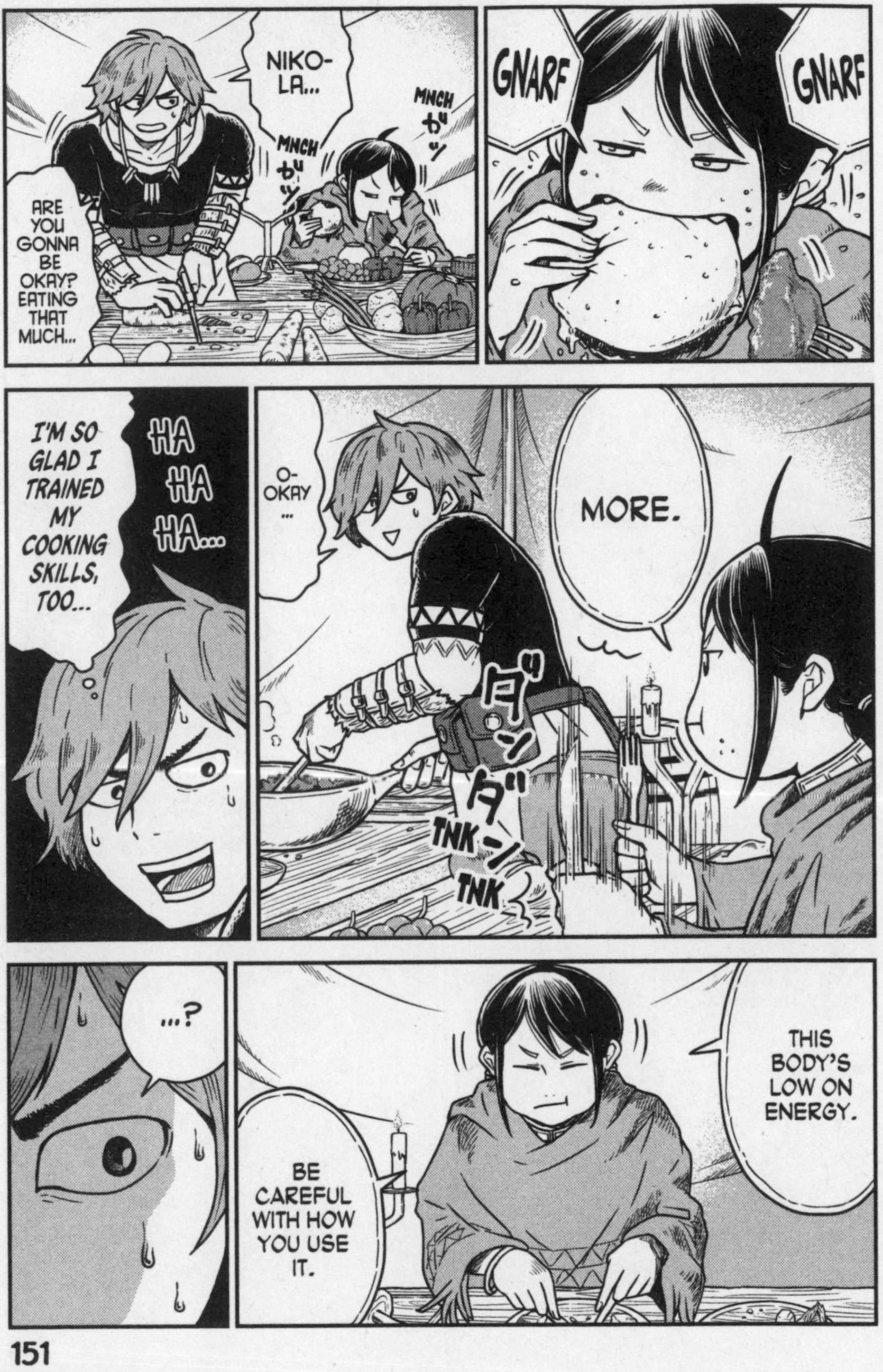
GNARF
GNARF
NIKO-LA...
MNCH ガッ
MNCH ガッ
ARE YOU GONNA BE OKAY? EATING THAT MUCH...
MORE.
O-OKAY ...
ダン ダン
TNK TNK
HA HA HA...
I'M SO GLAD I TRAINED MY COOKING SKILLS, TOO...
THIS BODY'S LOW ON ENERGY.
BE CAREFUL WITH HOW YOU USE IT.
...?

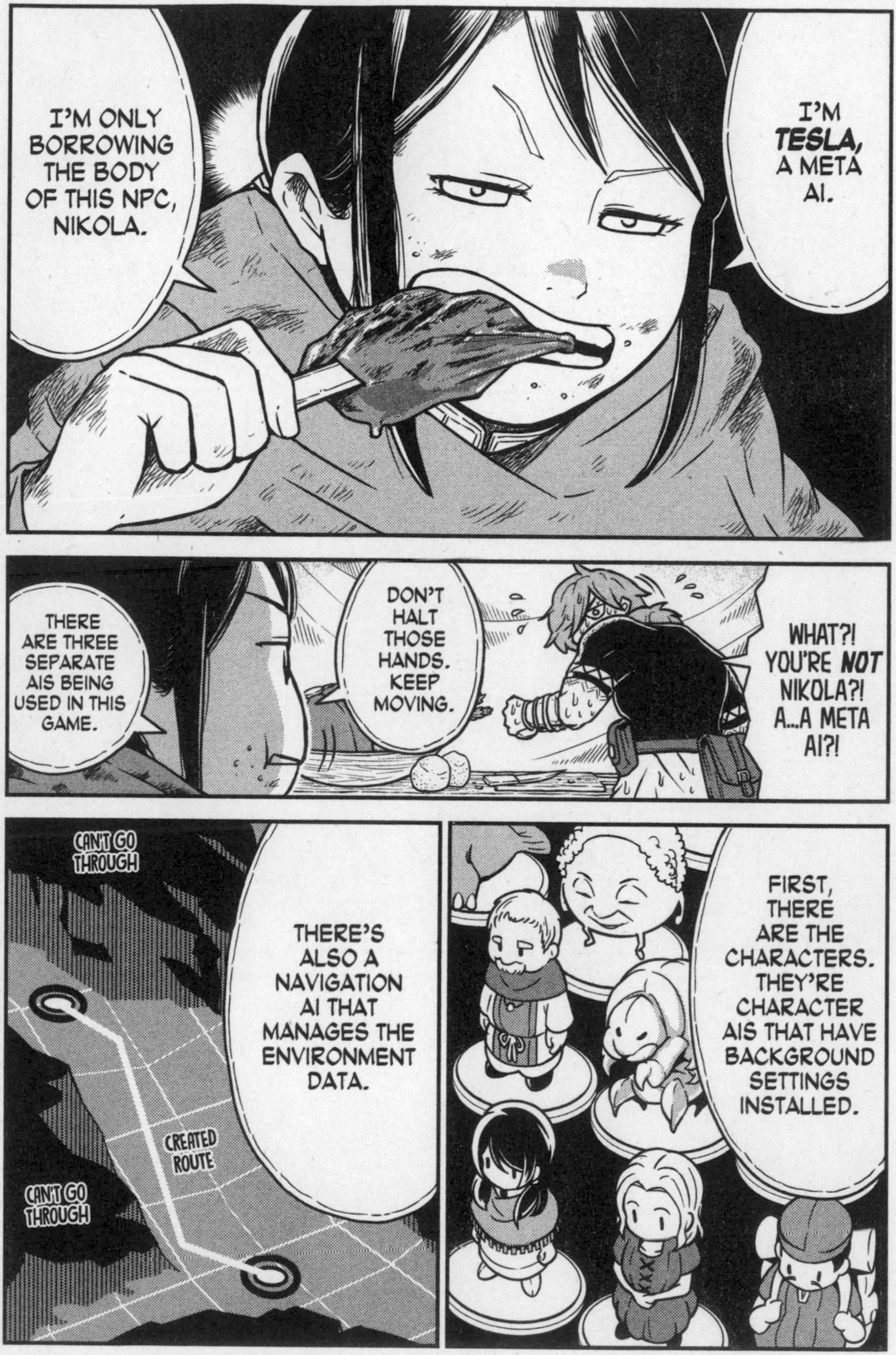
I'M TESLA, A META AI.
I'M ONLY BORROWING THE BODY OF THIS NPC, NIKOLA.
WHAT?! YOU'RE NOT NIKOLA?! A...A META AI?!
DON'T HALT THOSE HANDS. KEEP MOVING.
THERE ARE THREE SEPARATE AIS BEING USED IN THIS GAME.
FIRST, THERE ARE THE CHARACTERS. THEY'RE CHARACTER AIS THAT HAVE BACKGROUND SETTINGS INSTALLED.
THERE'S ALSO A NAVIGATION AI THAT MANAGES THE ENVIRONMENT DATA.
CAN'T GO THROUGH
CREATED ROUTE
CAN'T GO THROUGH

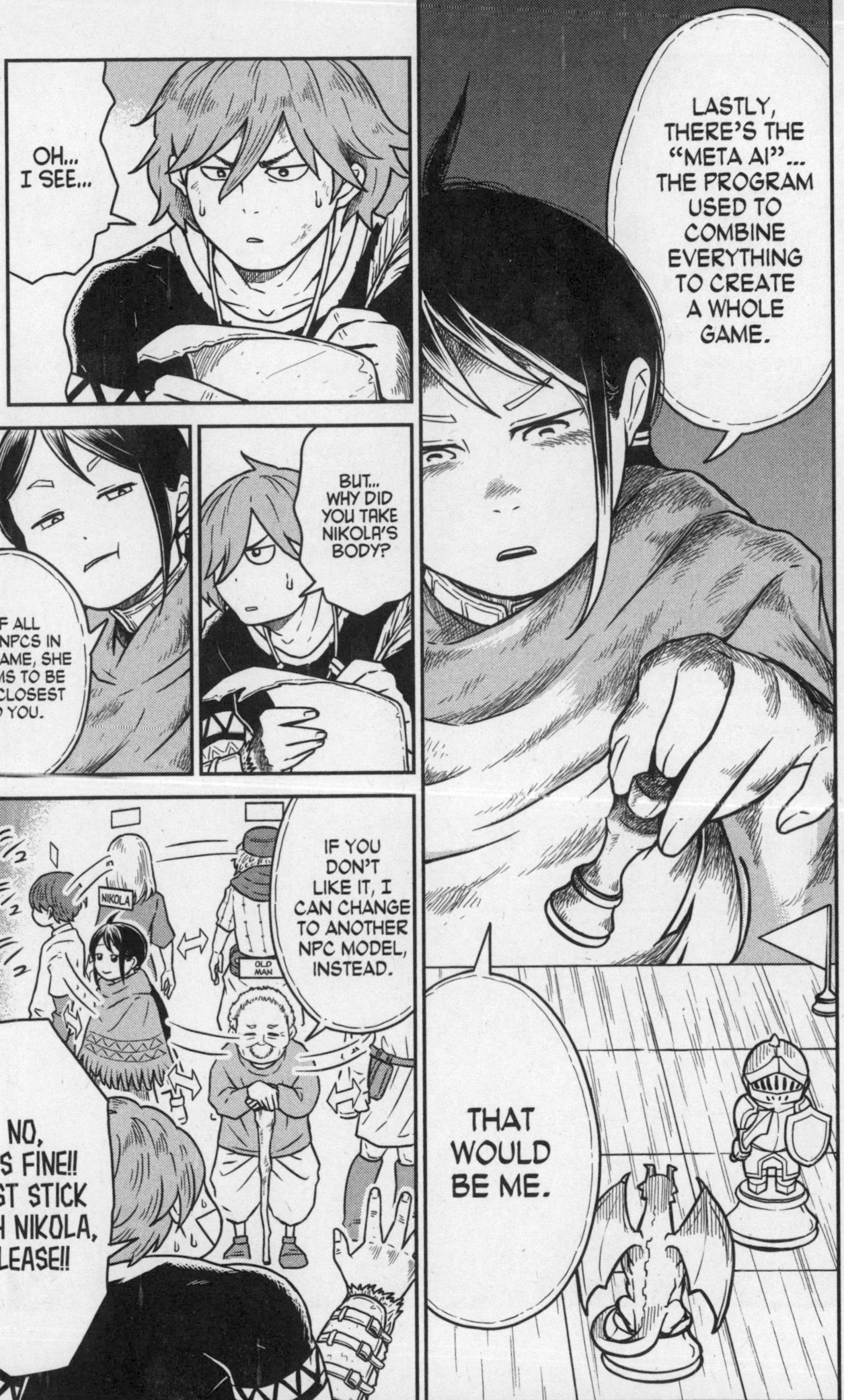
LASTLY, THERE'S THE "META AI"... THE PROGRAM USED TO COMBINE EVERYTHING TO CREATE A WHOLE GAME.
THAT WOULD BE ME.
OH... I SEE...
BUT... WHY DID YOU TAKE NIKOLA'S BODY?
OF ALL THE NPCS IN THE GAME, SHE SEEMS TO BE THE CLOSEST TO YOU.
IF YOU DON'T LIKE IT, I CAN CHANGE TO ANOTHER NPC MODEL, INSTEAD.
NIKOLA
OLD MAN
SHWP
SHWP
SHWP
NO, IT'S FINE!! JUST STICK WITH NIKOLA, PLEASE!!

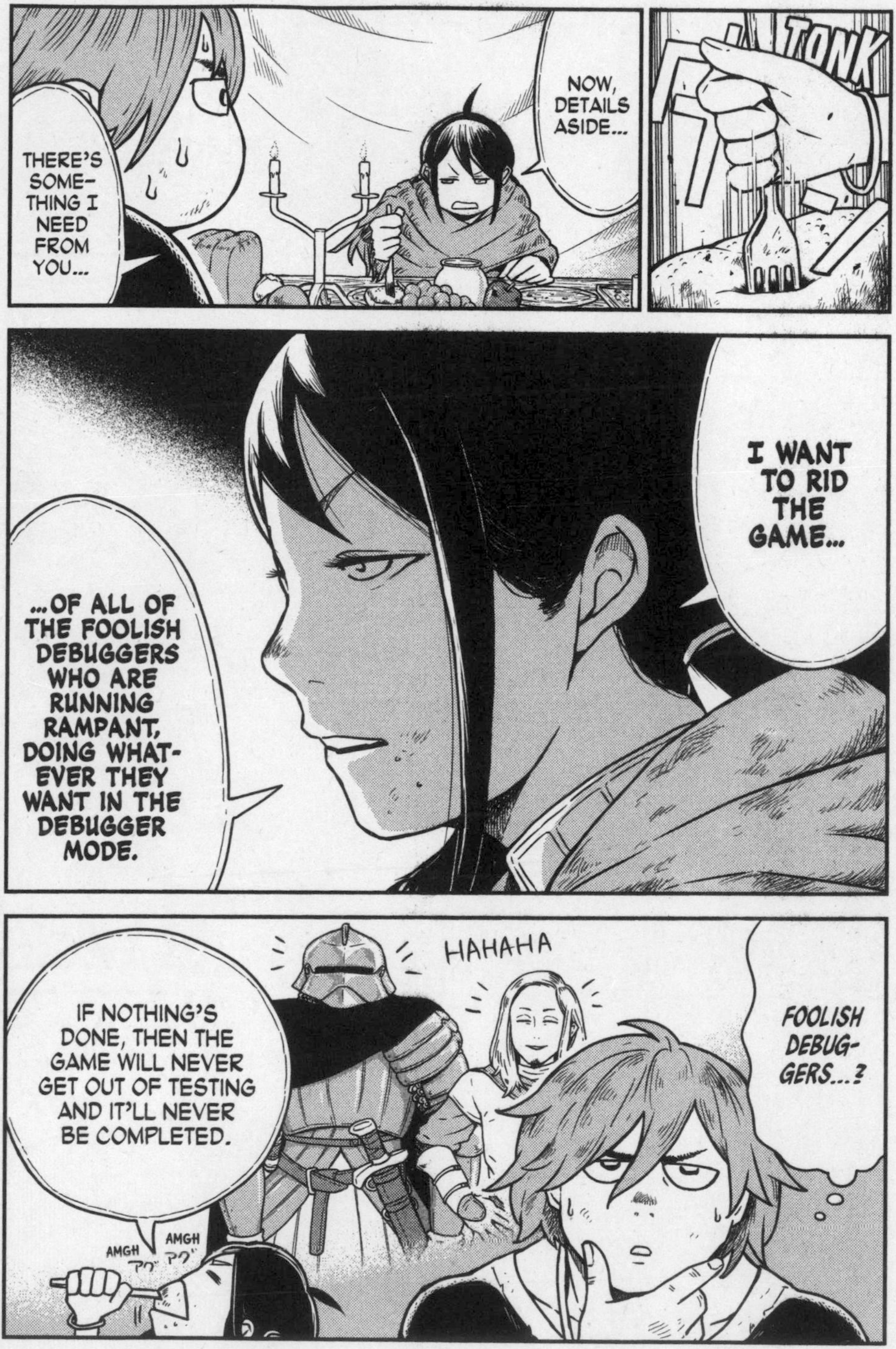
TONK
NOW, DETAILS ASIDE...
THERE'S SOME-THING I NEED FROM YOU...
I WANT TO RID THE GAME...
...OF ALL OF THE FOOLISH DEBUGGERS WHO ARE RUNNING RAMPANT, DOING WHAT-EVER THEY WANT IN THE DEBUGGER MODE.
FOOLISH DEBUG-GERS...?
HAHAHA
IF NOTHING'S DONE, THEN THE GAME WILL NEVER GET OUT OF TESTING AND IT'LL NEVER BE COMPLETED.
AMGH
AMGH

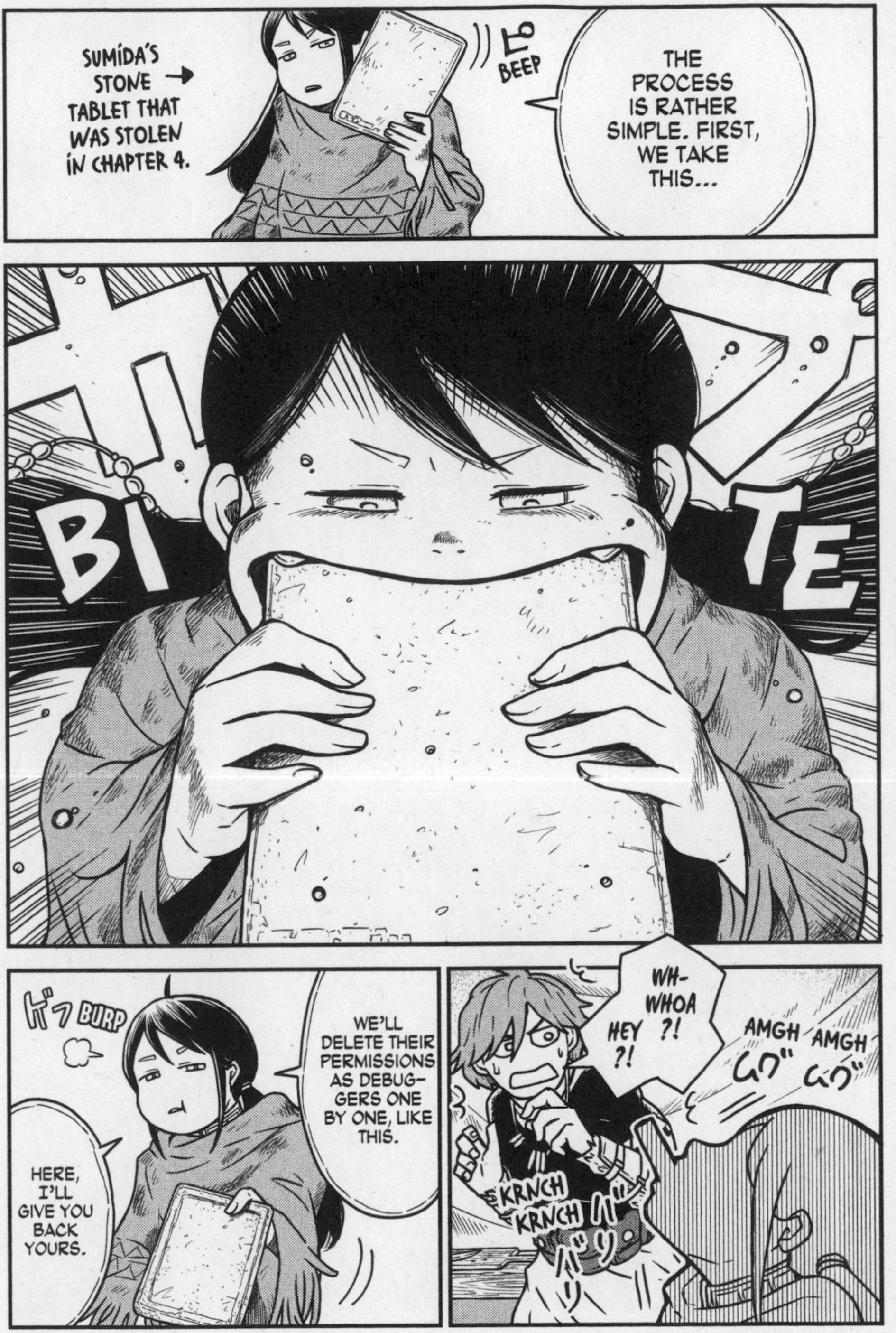
THE PROCESS IS RATHER SIMPLE. FIRST, WE TAKE THIS...
BEEP
SUMIDA'S STONE TABLET THAT WAS STOLEN IN CHAPTER 4.
BITE
WH- WHOA ?!
HEY ?!
AMGH AMGH
KRNCH KRNCH
WE'LL DELETE THEIR PERMISSIONS AS DEBUGGERS ONE BY ONE, LIKE THIS.
BURP
HERE, I'LL GIVE YOU BACK YOURS.

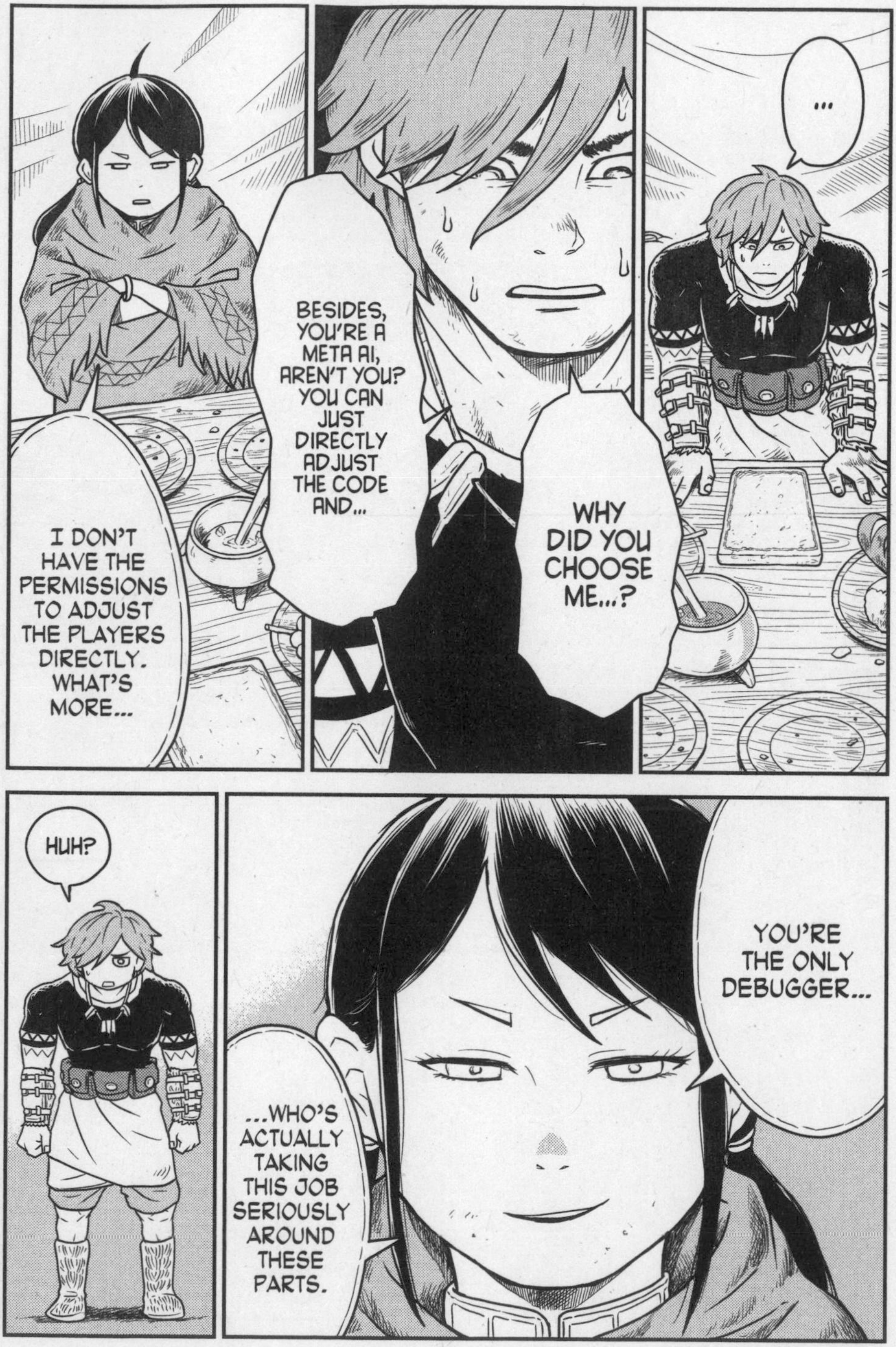
...
WHY DID YOU CHOOSE ME...?
BESIDES, YOU'RE A META AI, AREN'T YOU? YOU CAN JUST DIRECTLY ADJUST THE CODE AND...
I DON'T HAVE THE PERMISSIONS TO ADJUST THE PLAYERS DIRECTLY. WHAT'S MORE...
YOU'RE THE ONLY DEBUGGER...
...WHO'S ACTUALLY TAKING THIS JOB SERIOUSLY AROUND THESE PARTS.
HUH?

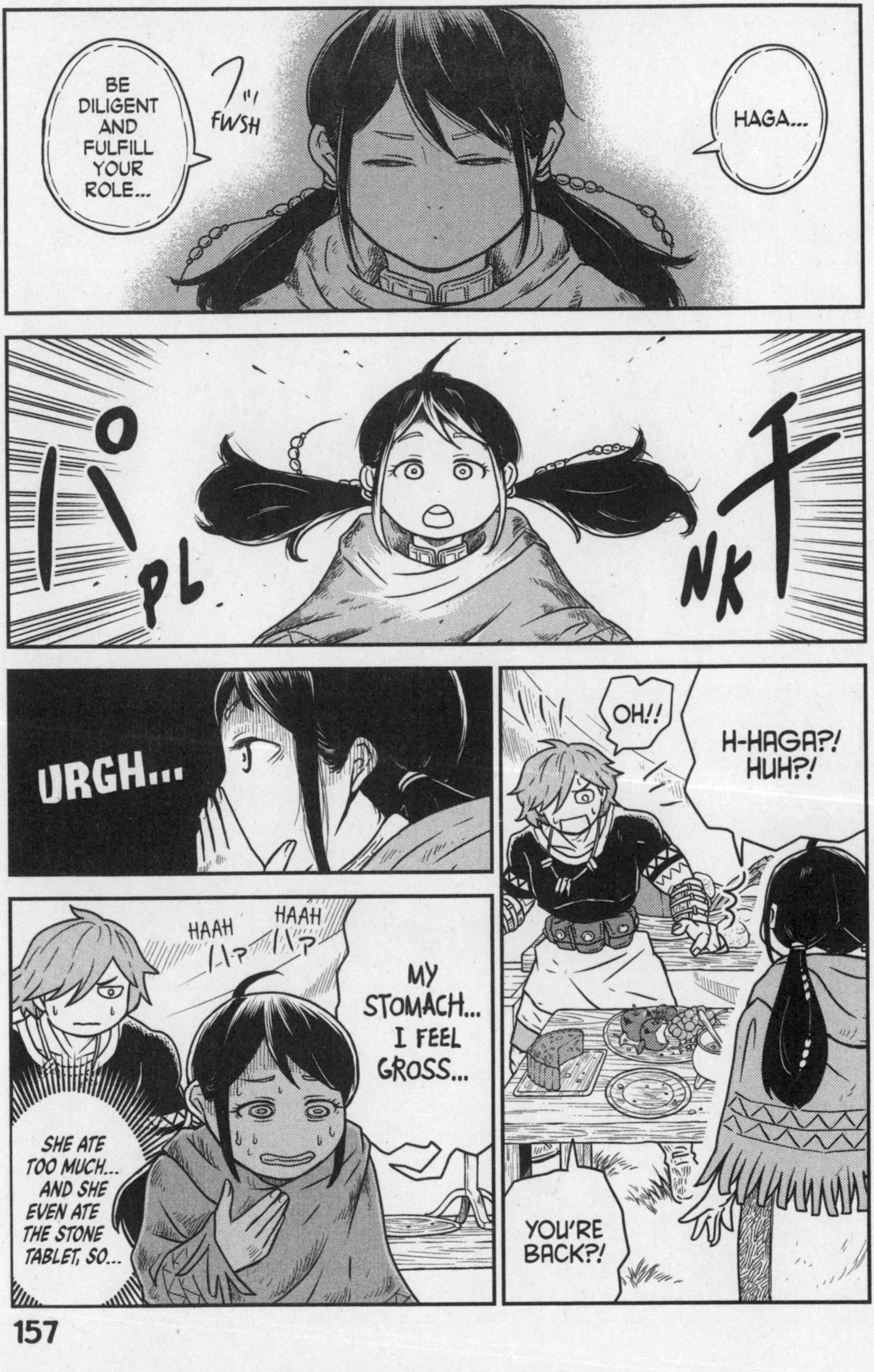
HAGA...
フッ
FWSH
BE DILIGENT AND FULFILL YOUR ROLE...
チ
NK
パ
PL
H-HAGA?! HUH?!
OH!!
YOU'RE BACK?!
URGH...
MY STOMACH... I FEEL GROSS...
HAAH
ハァ
HAAH
ハァ
SHE ATE TOO MUCH... AND SHE EVEN ATE THE STONE TABLET, SO...

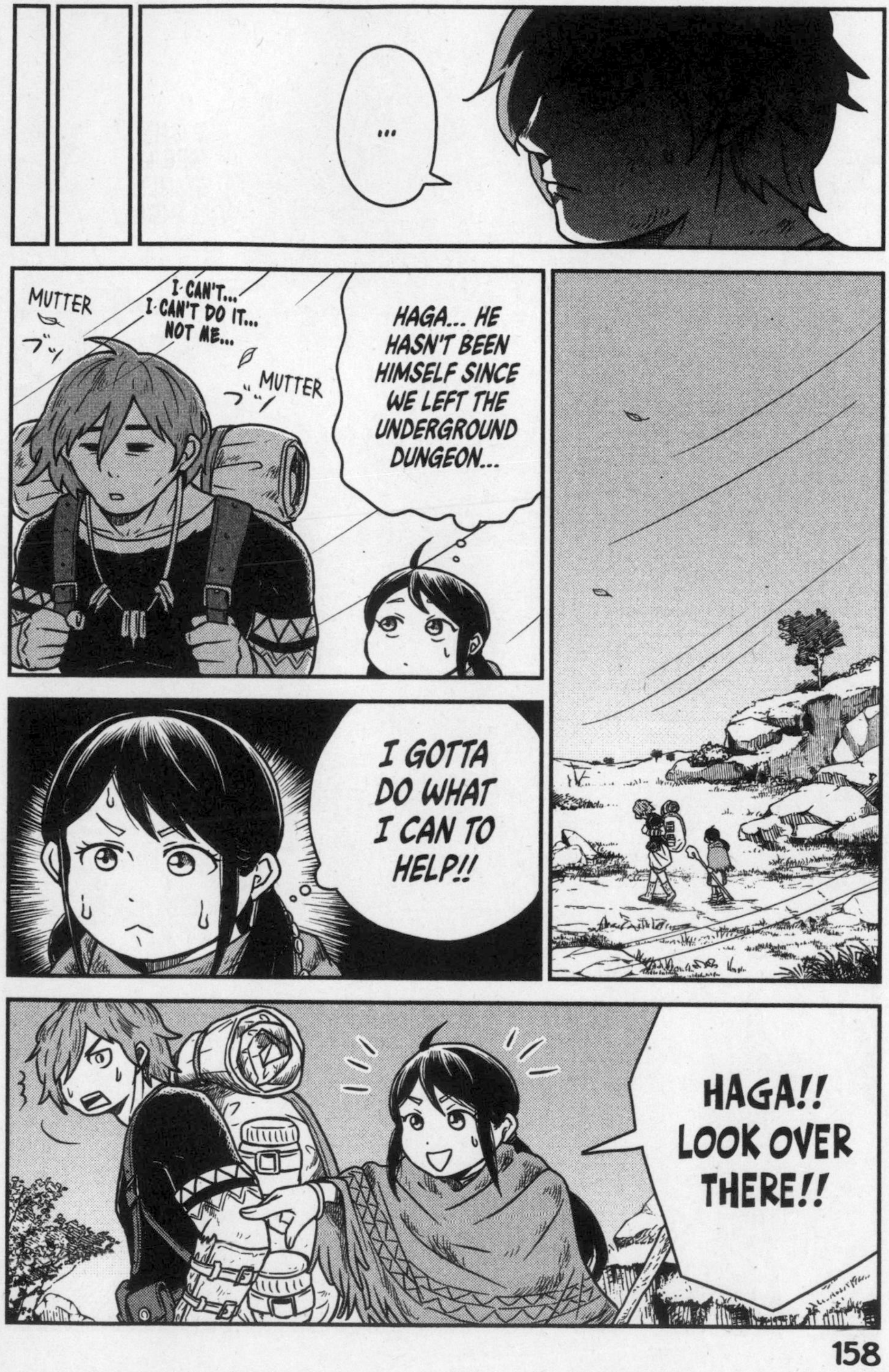
...
HAGA... HE HASN'T BEEN HIMSELF SINCE WE LEFT THE UNDERGROUND DUNGEON...
I-CAN'T... I-CAN'T DO IT... NOT ME...
MUTTER
ブツ
MUTTER
ブツ
I GOTTA DO WHAT I CAN TO HELP!!
HAGA!! LOOK OVER THERE!!

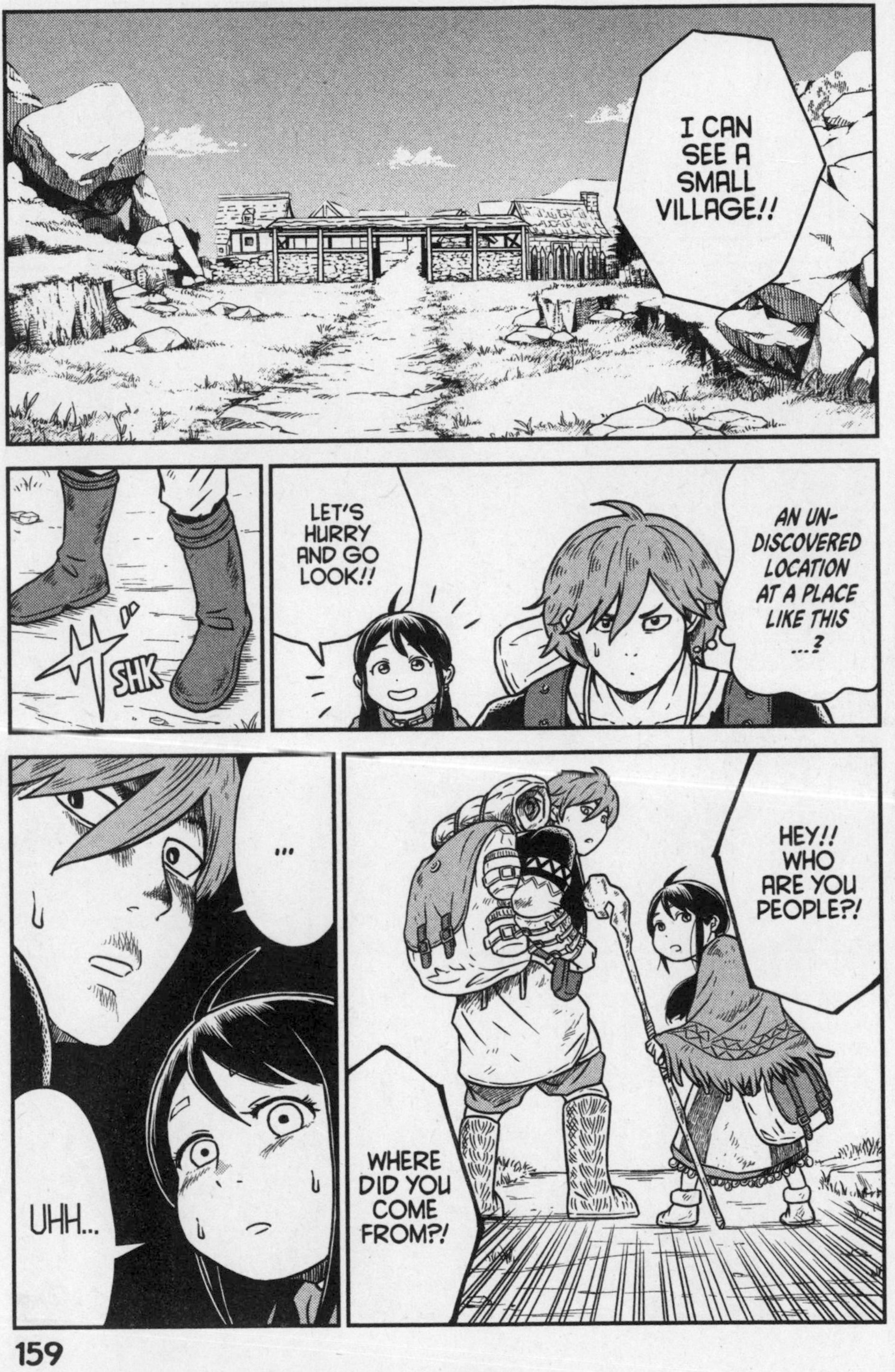
I CAN SEE A SMALL VILLAGE!!
AN UN-DISCOVERED LOCATION AT A PLACE LIKE THIS ...?
LET'S HURRY AND GO LOOK!!
SHK
HEY!! WHO ARE YOU PEOPLE?!
WHERE DID YOU COME FROM?!
...
UHH...

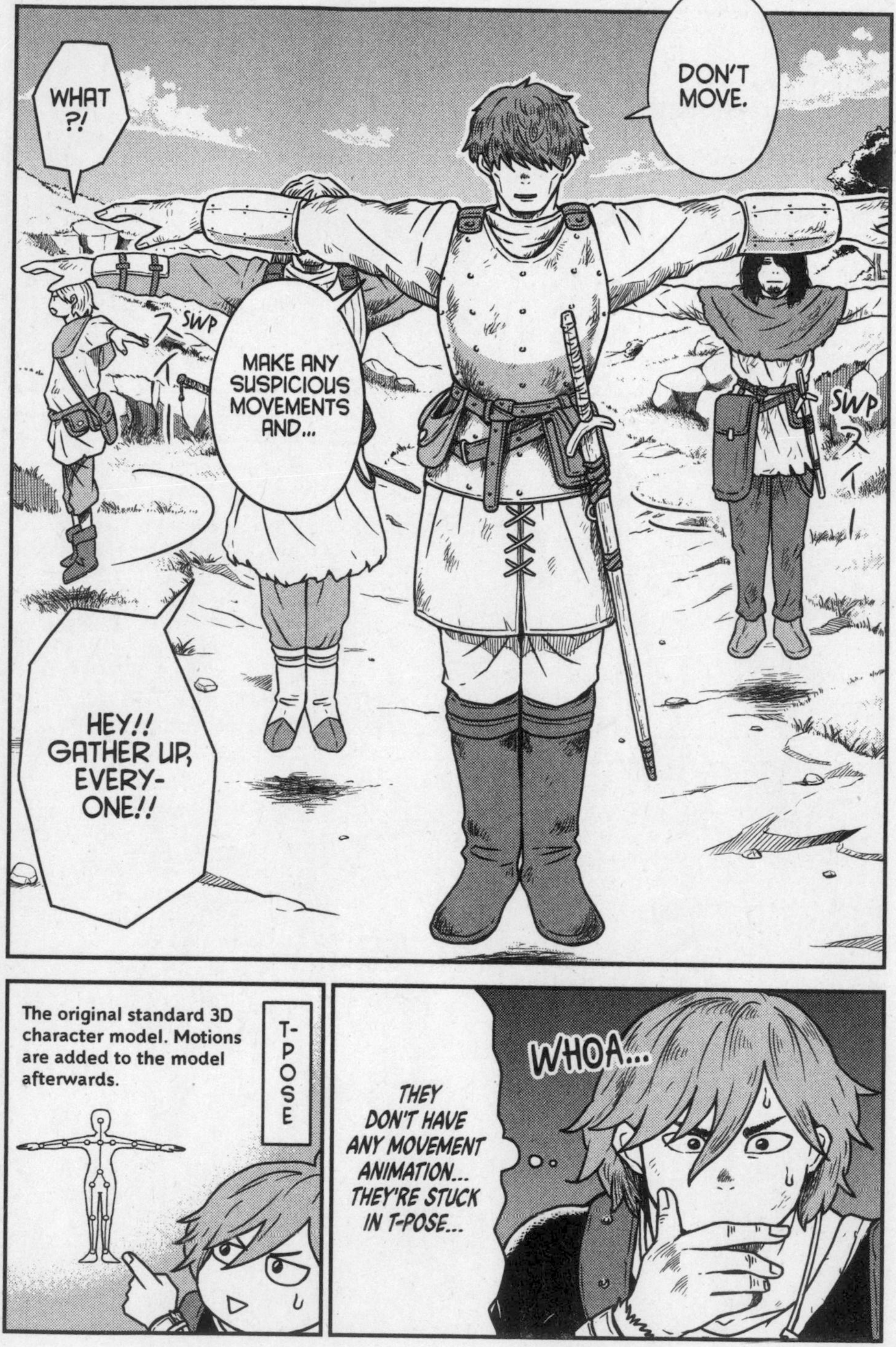
DON'T MOVE.
WHAT?!
SWP
MAKE ANY SUSPICIOUS MOVEMENTS AND...
SWP
HEY!! GATHER UP, EVERY-ONE!!
WHOA...
THEY DON'T HAVE ANY MOVEMENT ANIMATION... THEY'RE STUCK IN T-POSE...
T-POSE
The original standard 3D character model. Motions are added to the model afterwards.

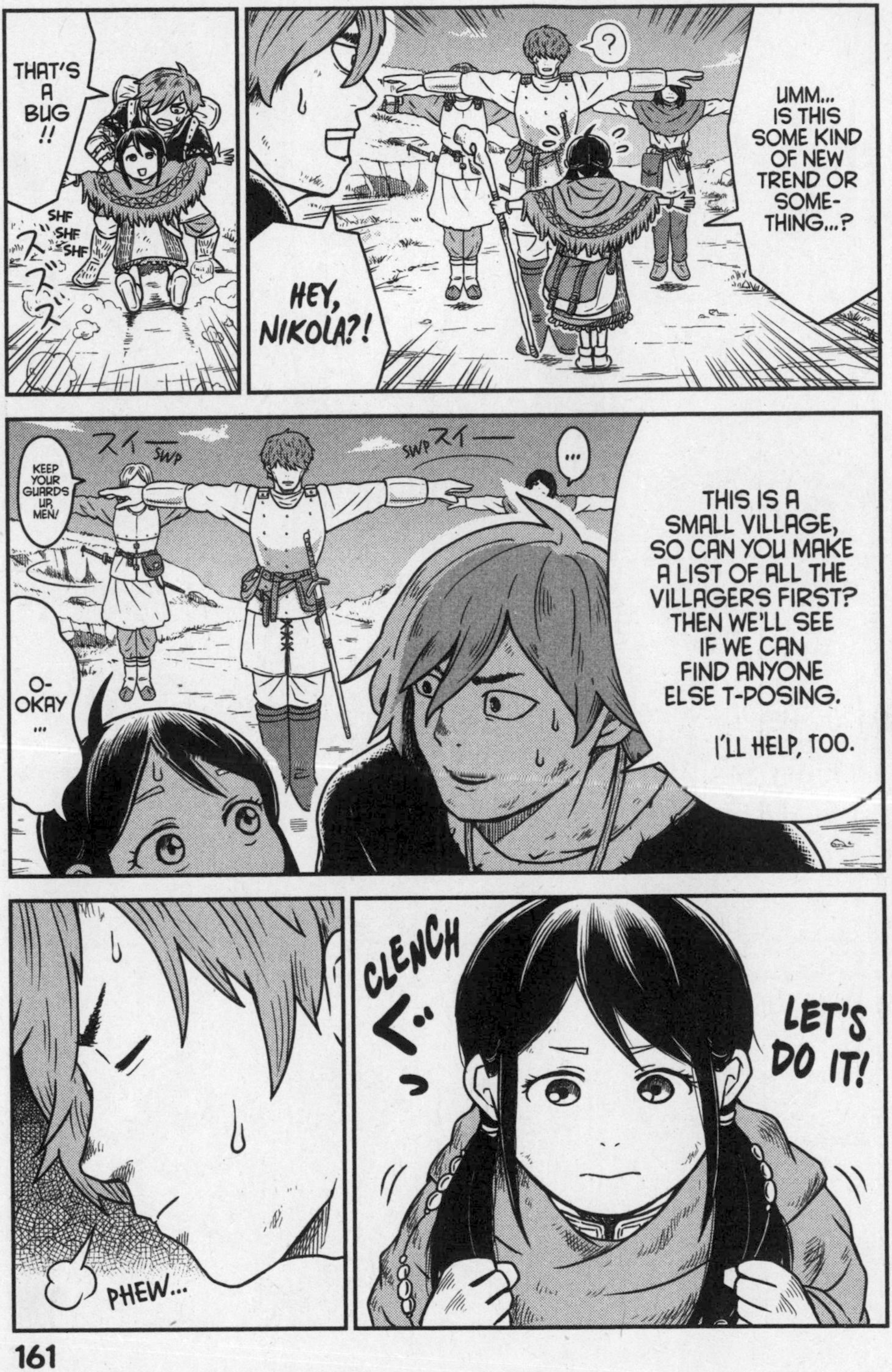
?
UMM... IS THIS SOME KIND OF NEW TREND OR SOME-THING...?
HEY, NIKOLA?!
THAT'S A BUG !!
SHF SHF SHF
THIS IS A SMALL VILLAGE, SO CAN YOU MAKE A LIST OF ALL THE VILLAGERS FIRST? THEN WE'LL SEE IF WE CAN FIND ANYONE ELSE T-POSING.
I'LL HELP, TOO.
...
スイー SWP
スイー SWP
KEEP YOUR GUARDS UP, MEN!
O-OKAY ...
LET'S DO IT!
CLENCH
PHEW...

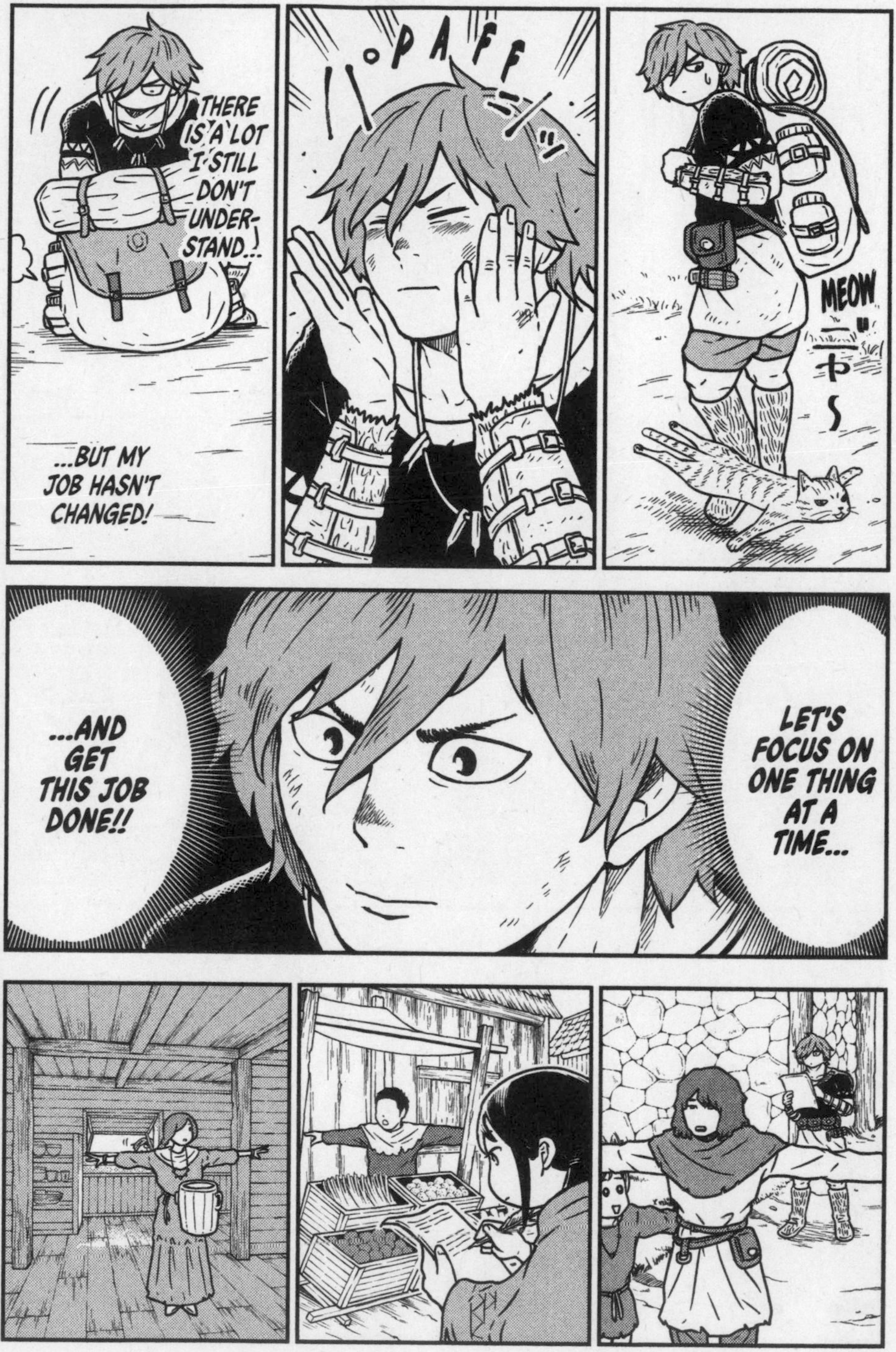
MEOW
PAFF
THERE IS A LOT I STILL DON'T UNDER-STAND...
...BUT MY JOB HASN'T CHANGED!
LET'S FOCUS ON ONE THING AT A TIME...
...AND GET THIS JOB DONE!!

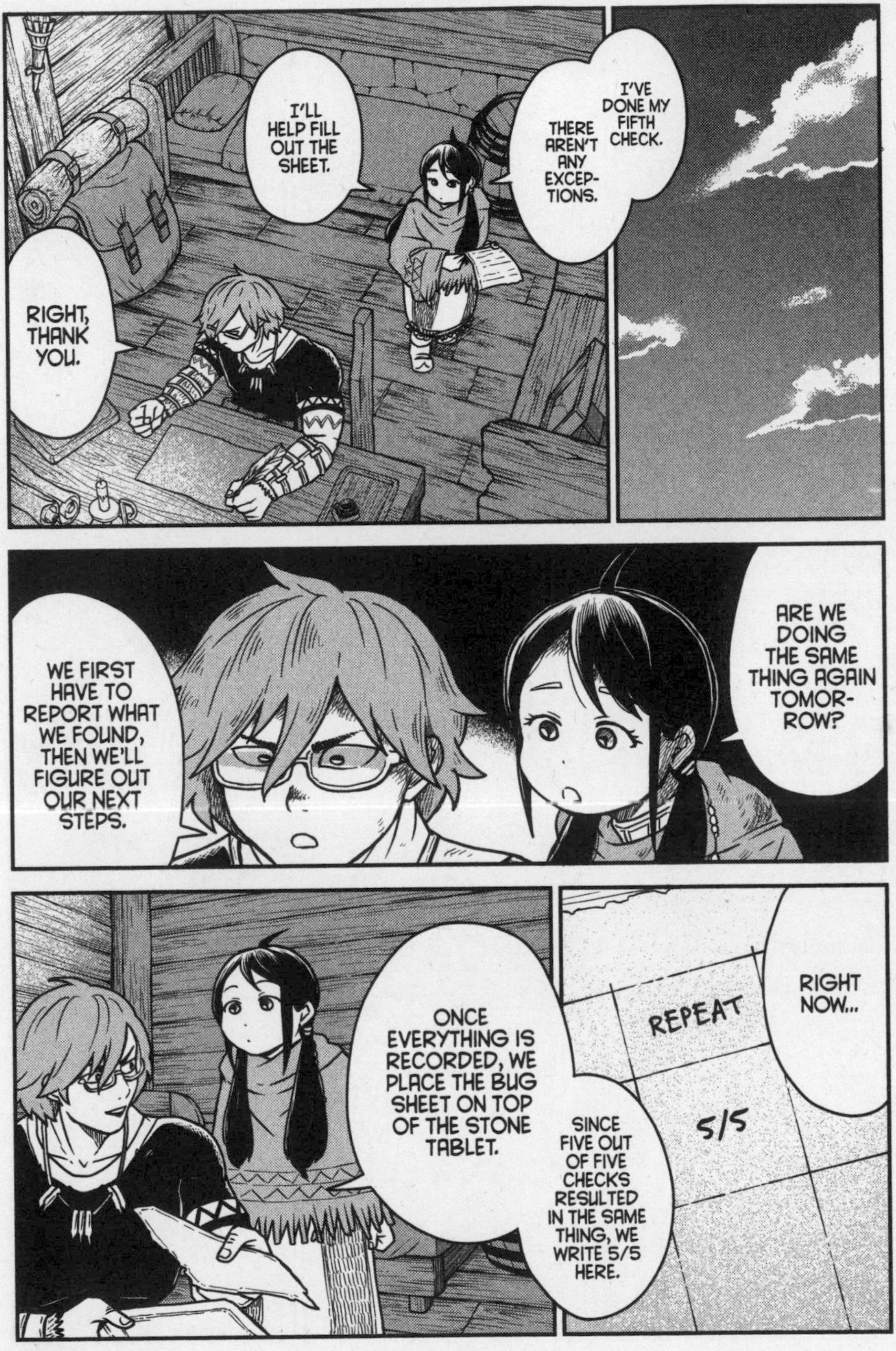
I'VE DONE MY FIFTH CHECK.
THERE AREN'T ANY EXCEP-TIONS.
I'LL HELP FILL OUT THE SHEET.
RIGHT, THANK YOU.
ARE WE DOING THE SAME THING AGAIN TOMOR-ROW?
WE FIRST HAVE TO REPORT WHAT WE FOUND, THEN WE'LL FIGURE OUT OUR NEXT STEPS.
RIGHT NOW...
REPEAT
5/5
SINCE FIVE OUT OF FIVE CHECKS RESULTED IN THE SAME THING, WE WRITE 5/5 HERE.
ONCE EVERYTHING IS RECORDED, WE PLACE THE BUG SHEET ON TOP OF THE STONE TABLET.

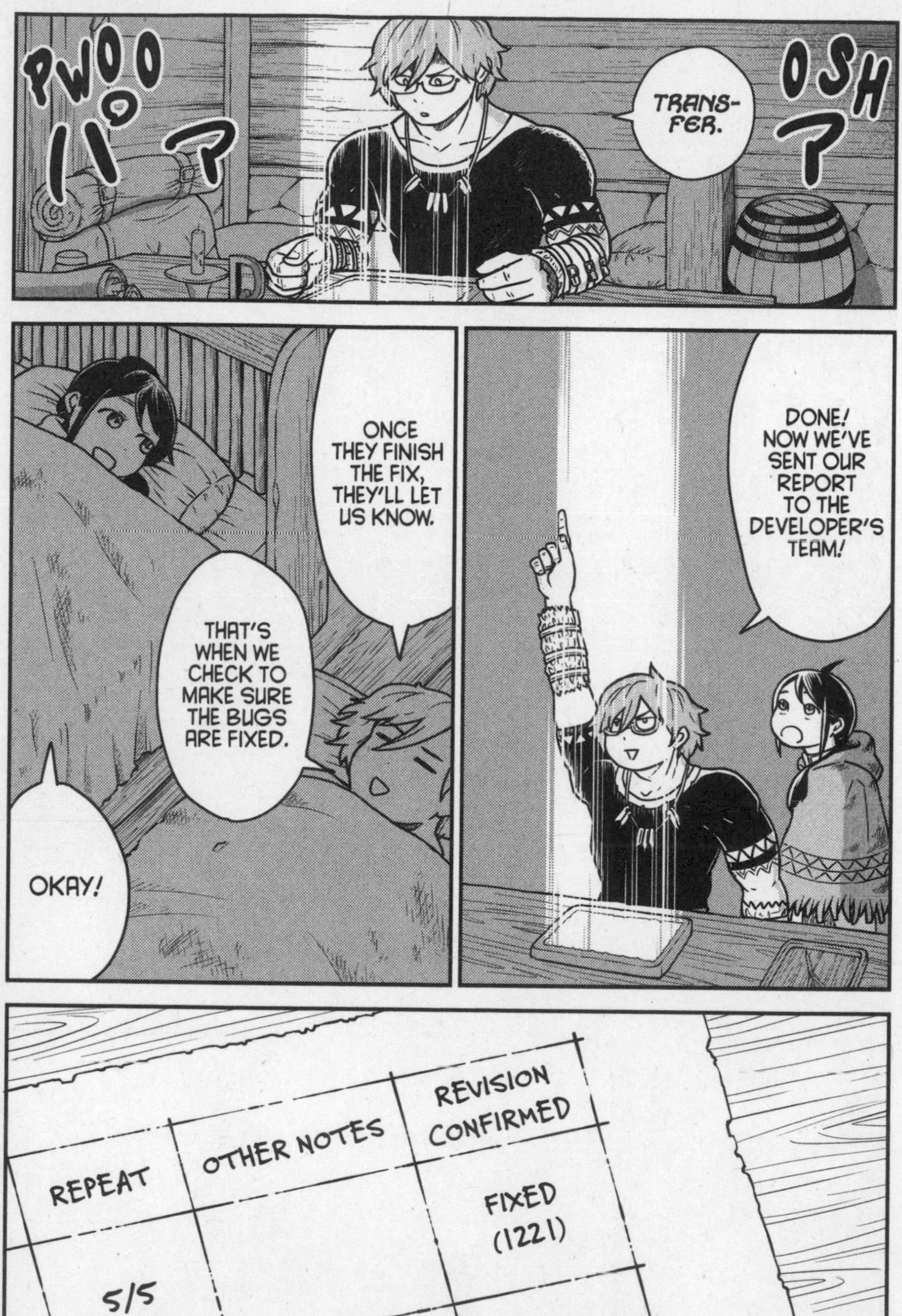
PWOO
パア
OSH
ア
TRANS-FER.
DONE! NOW WE'VE SENT OUR REPORT TO THE DEVELOPER'S TEAM!
ONCE THEY FINISH THE FIX, THEY'LL LET US KNOW.
THAT'S WHEN WE CHECK TO MAKE SURE THE BUGS ARE FIXED.
OKAY!
REVISION CONFIRMED
OTHER NOTES
REPEAT
FIXED (1221)
5/5
FIXED

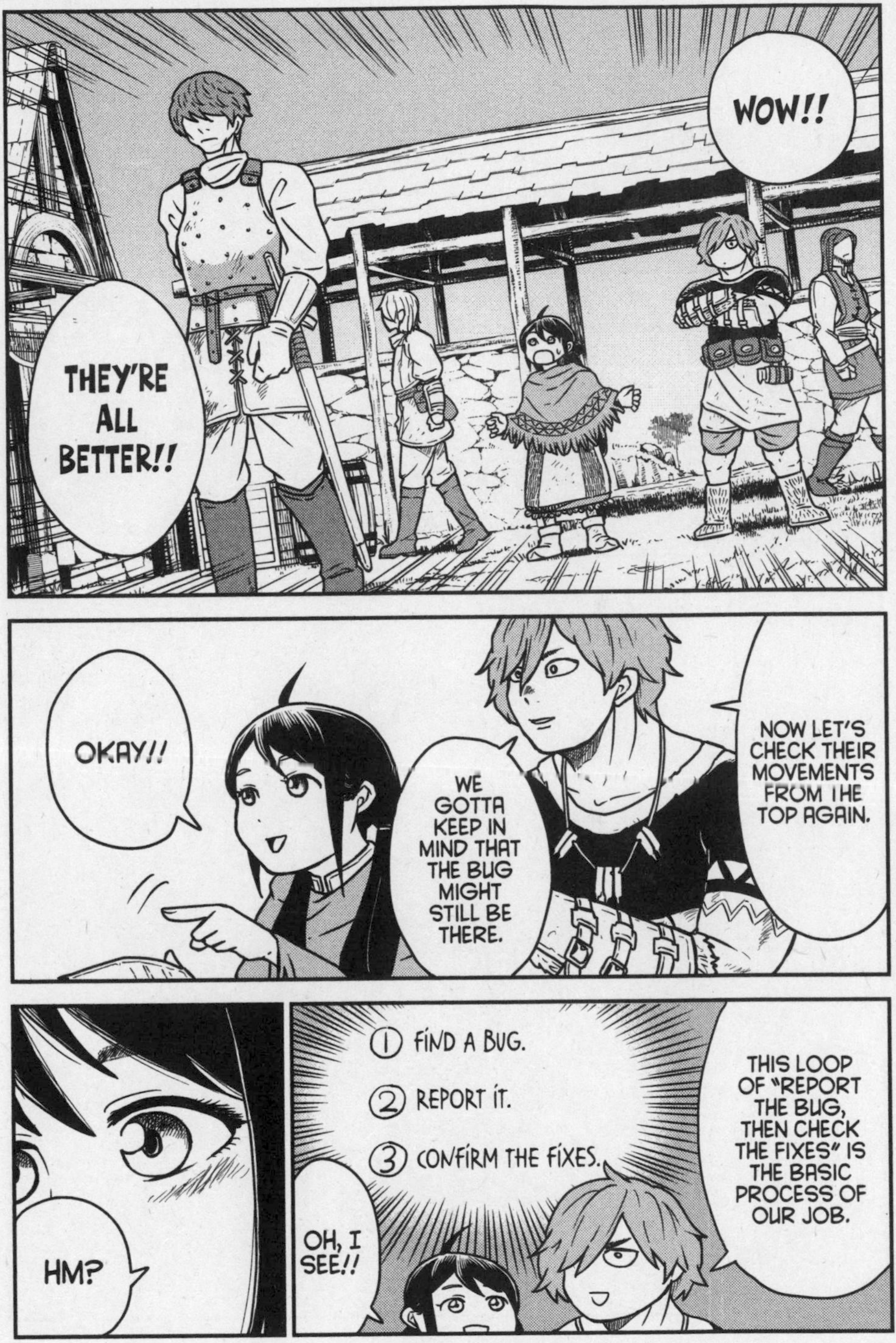
WOW!!
THEY'RE ALL BETTER!!
NOW LET'S CHECK THEIR MOVEMENTS FROM THE TOP AGAIN.
WE GOTTA KEEP IN MIND THAT THE BUG MIGHT STILL BE THERE.
OKAY!!
THIS LOOP OF "REPORT THE BUG, THEN CHECK THE FIXES" IS THE BASIC PROCESS OF OUR JOB.
① FIND A BUG.
② REPORT IT.
③ CONFIRM THE FIXES.
OH, I SEE!!
HM?

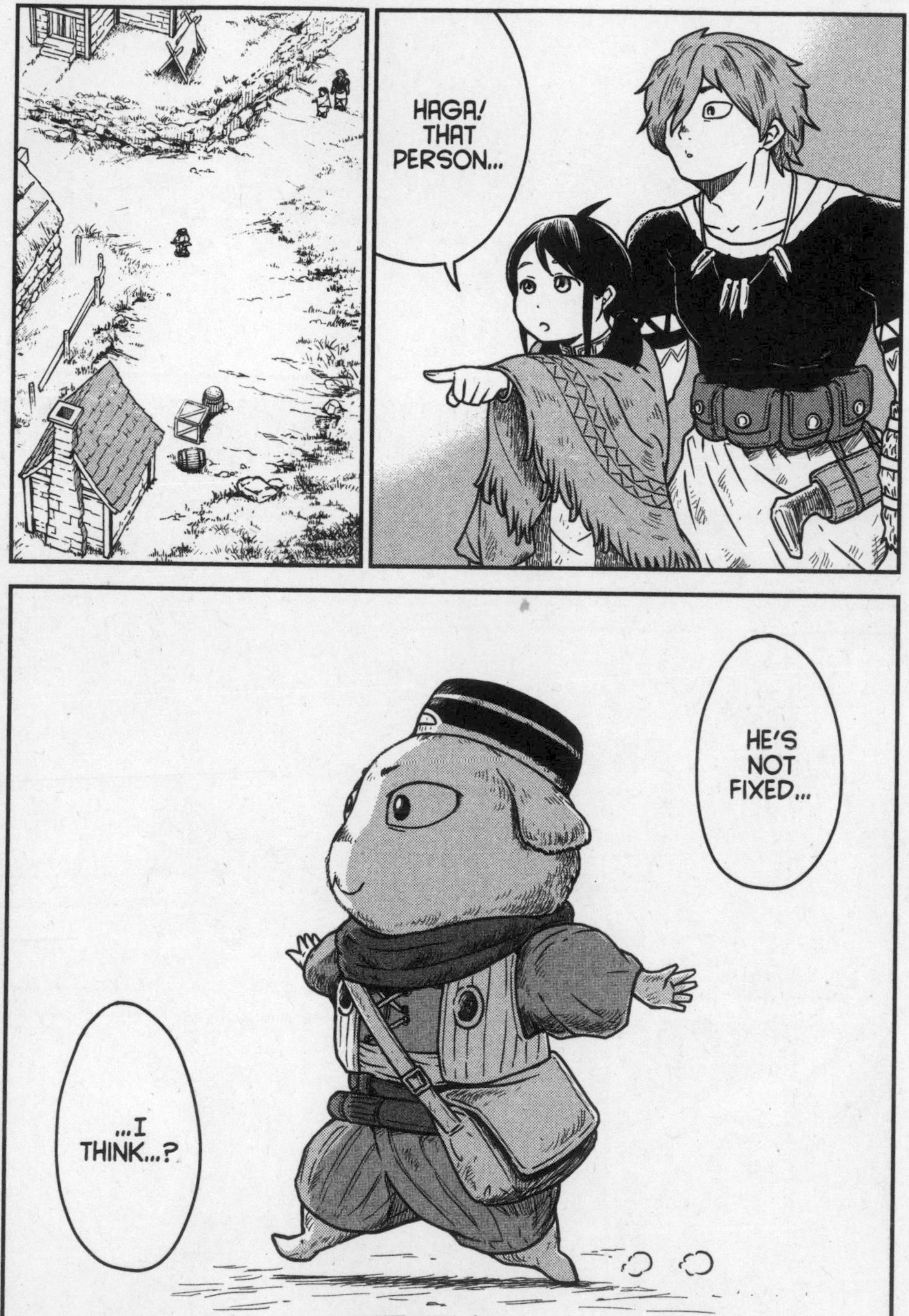
HAGA! THAT PERSON...
HE'S NOT FIXED...
...I THINK...?

NO.5/END

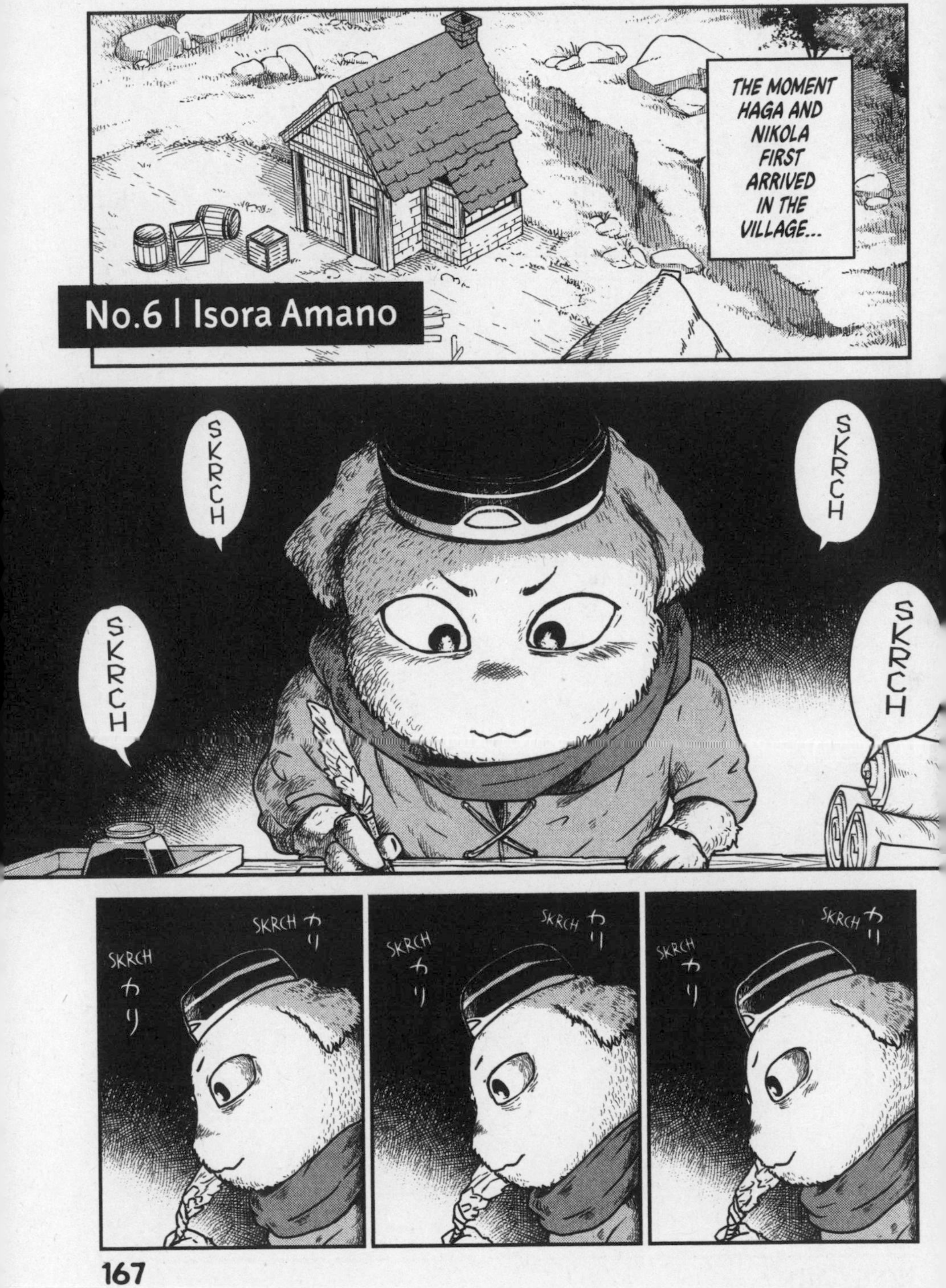
THE MOMENT HAGA AND NIKOLA FIRST ARRIVED IN THE VILLAGE...
No.6 | Isora Amano
SKRCH
SKRCH
SKRCH
SKRCH
SKRCH カリ
SKRCH カリ
SKRCH カリ
SKRCH カリ
SKRCH カリ
SKRCH カリ

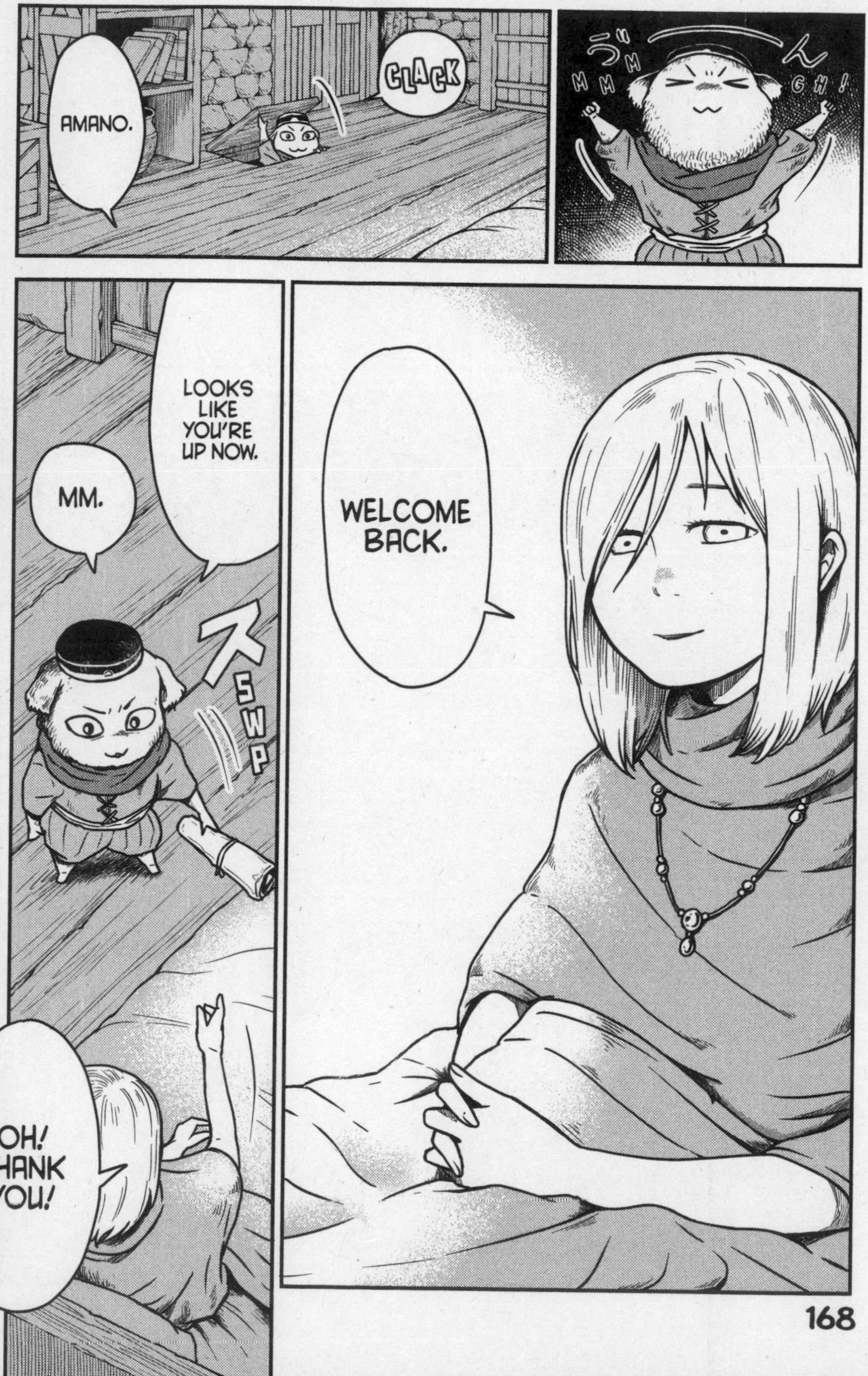
ゔーん
MMMGH!
CLACK
AMANO.
WELCOME BACK.
LOOKS LIKE YOU'RE UP NOW.
MM.
SWP
OH! THANK YOU!

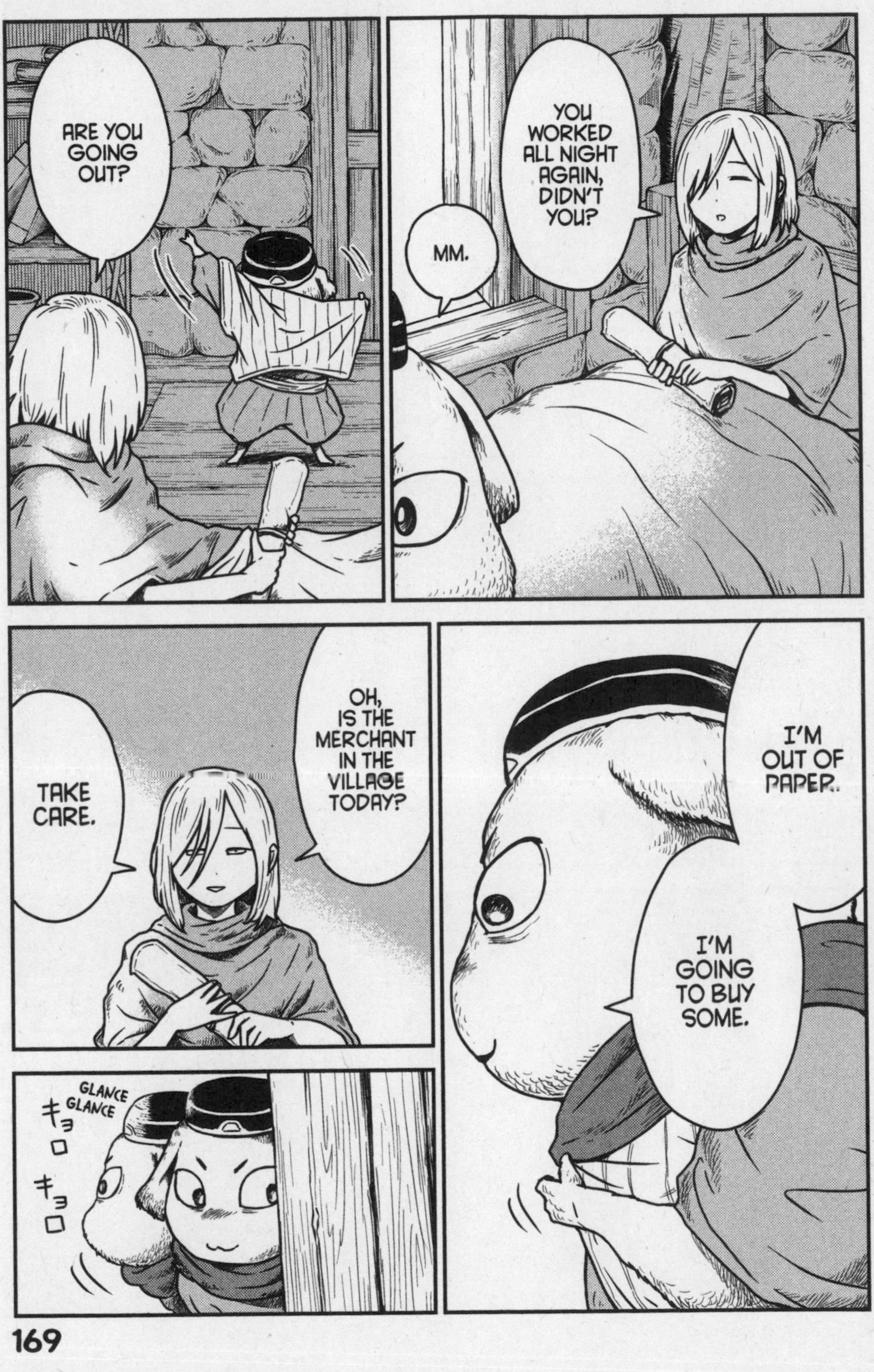
YOU WORKED ALL NIGHT AGAIN, DIDN'T YOU?
MM.
ARE YOU GOING OUT?
I'M OUT OF PAPER..
I'M GOING TO BUY SOME.
OH, IS THE MERCHANT IN THE VILLAGE TODAY?
TAKE CARE.
GLANCE GLANCE
キョロ キョロ

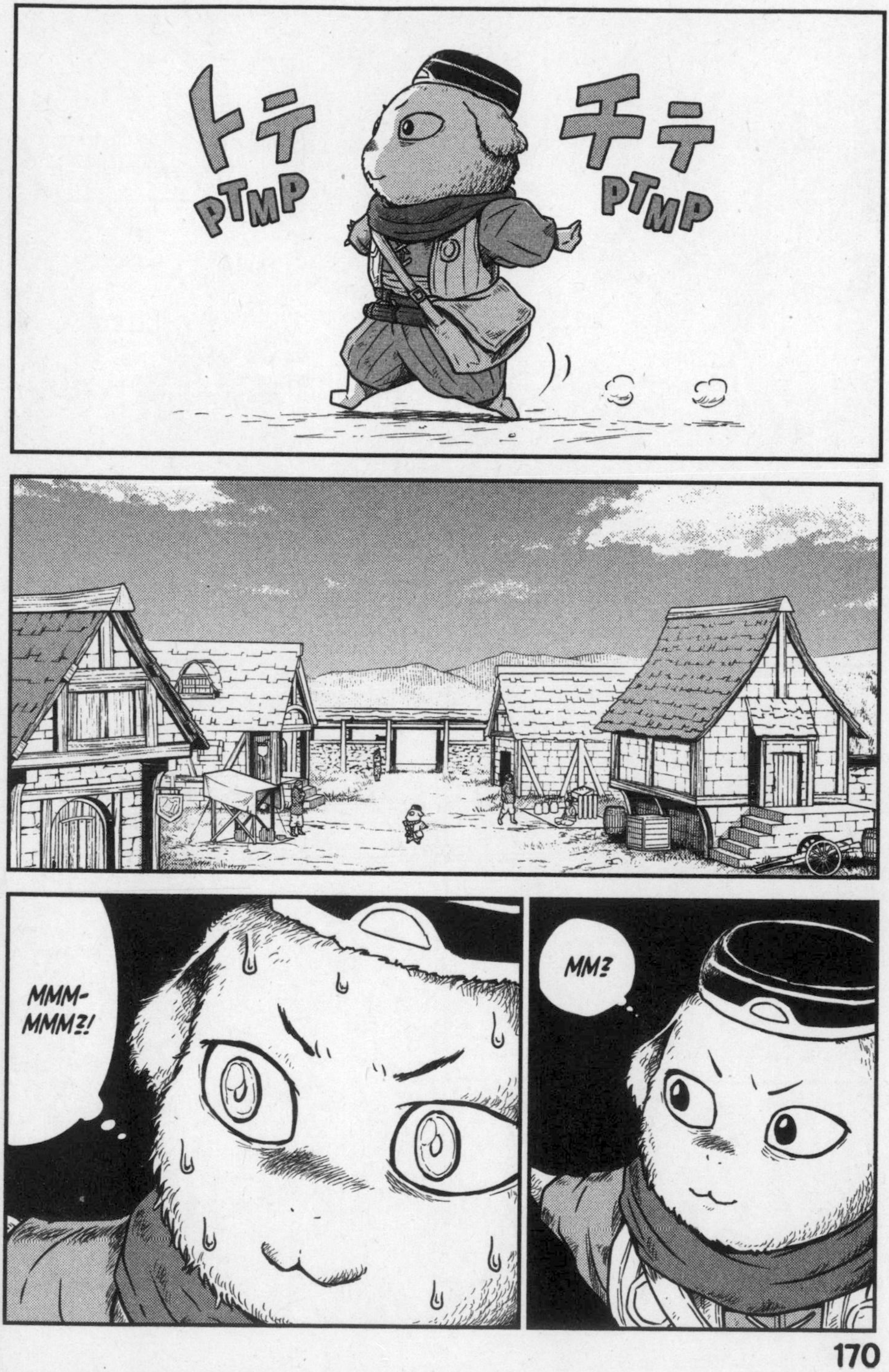
チテ
PTMP
トテ
PTMP
MM?
MMM-MMM?!

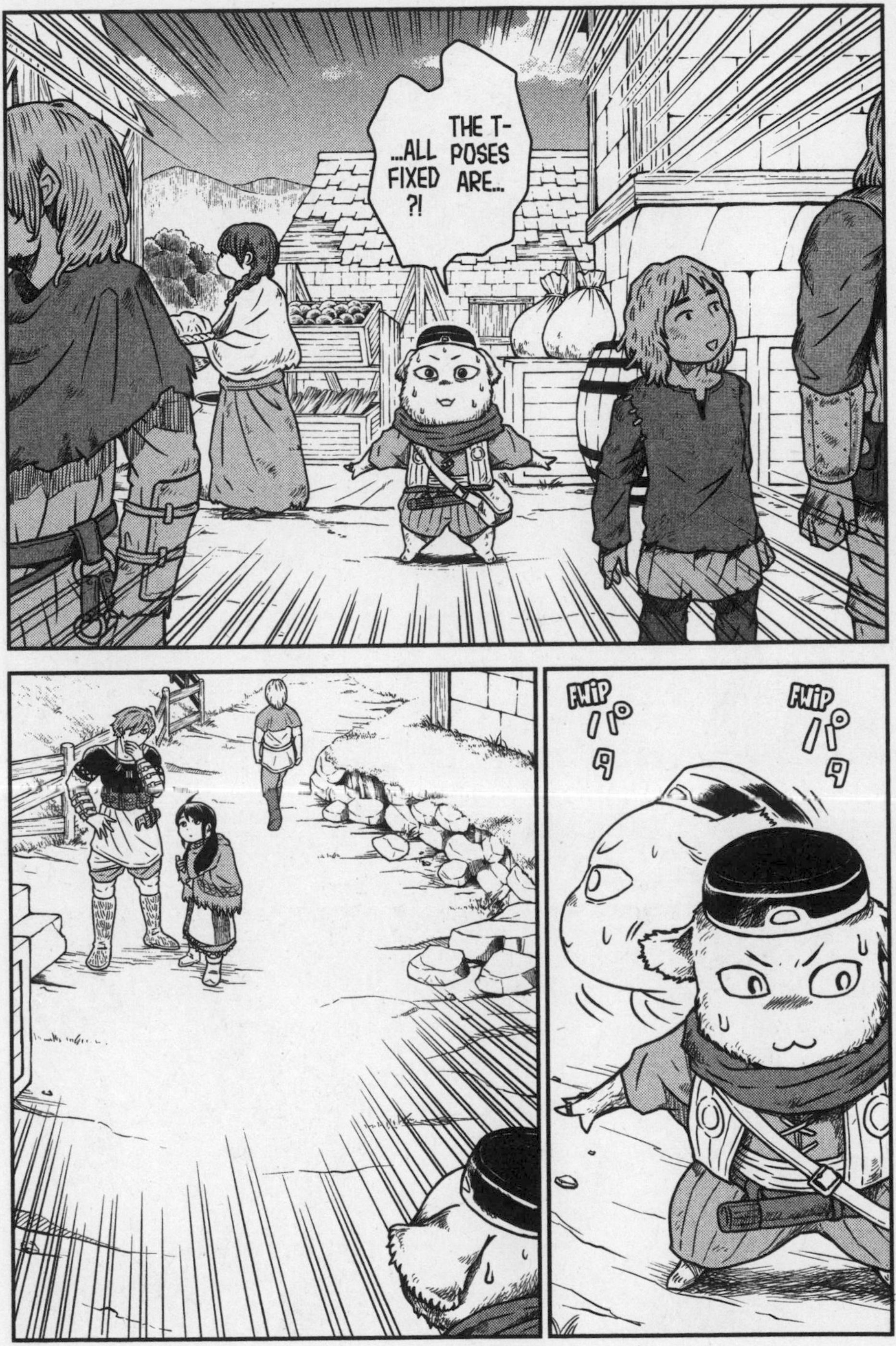
THE T-POSES ARE...
...ALL FIXED?!
FWIP パタ
FWIP パタ

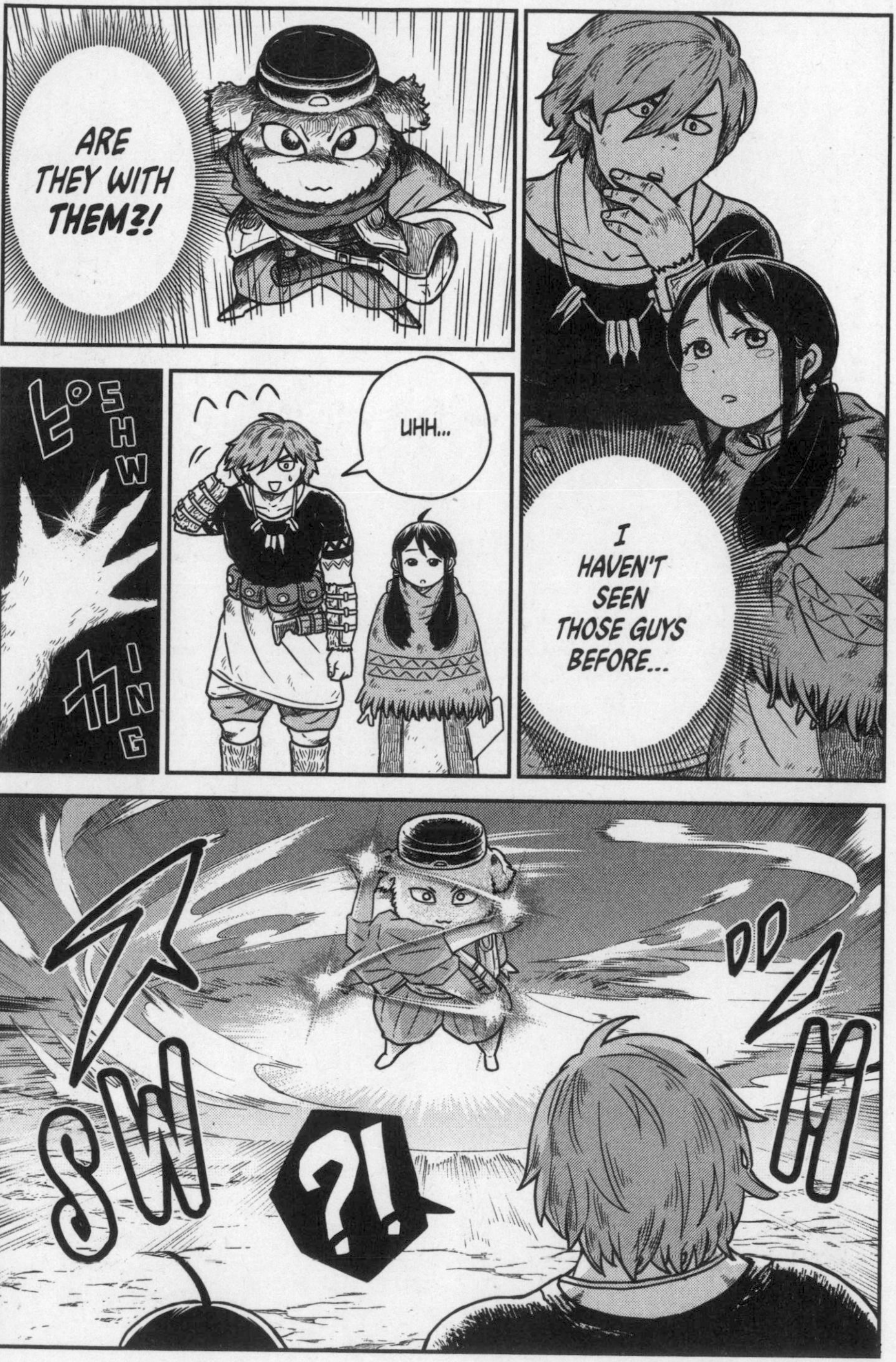
I HAVEN'T SEEN THOSE GUYS BEFORE...
ARE THEY WITH THEM?!
UHH...
SHWING
OOM
?!
SW

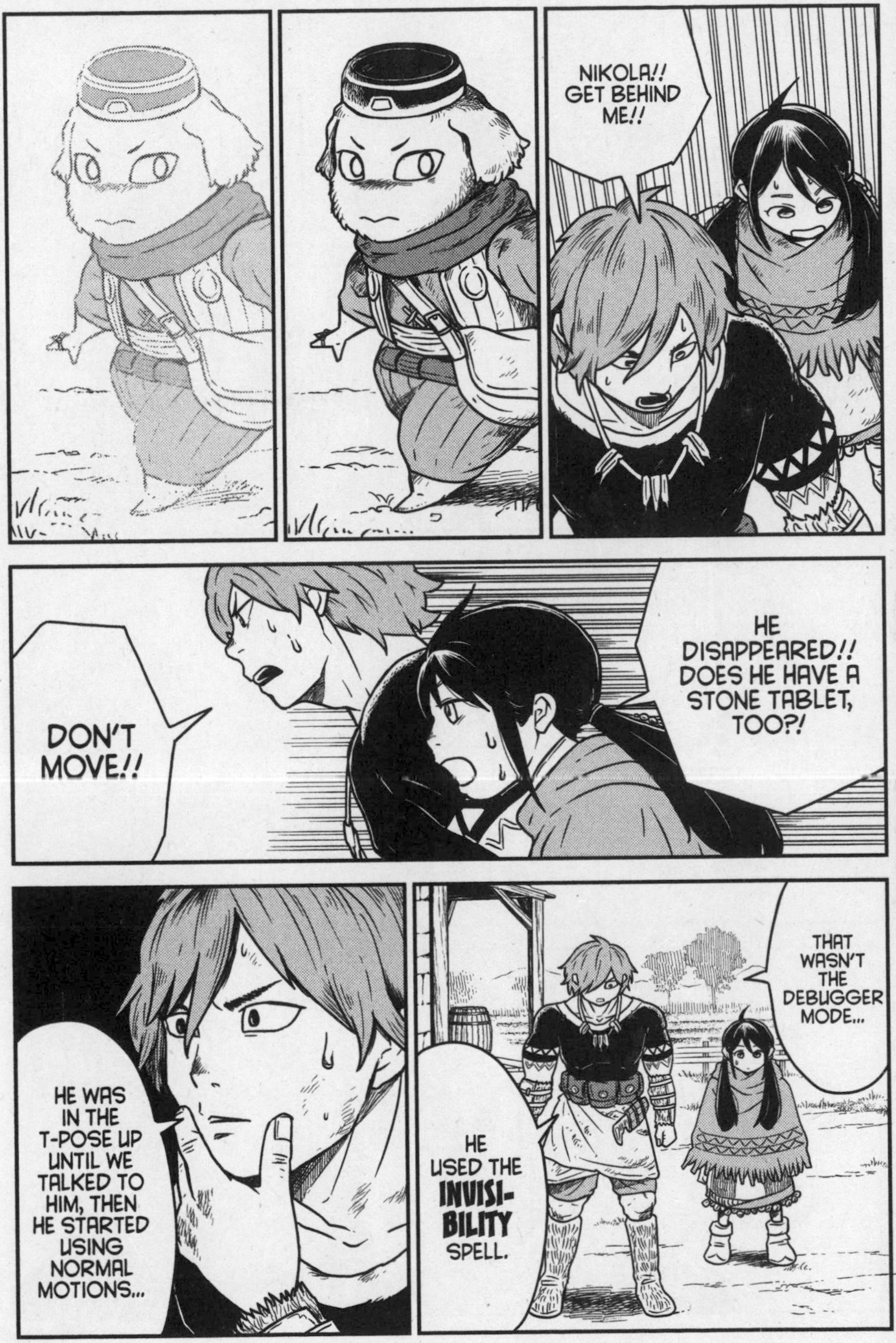
NIKOLA!! GET BEHIND ME!!
HE DISAPPEARED!! DOES HE HAVE A STONE TABLET, TOO?!
DON'T MOVE!!
THAT WASN'T THE DEBUGGER MODE...
HE USED THE INVISIBILITY SPELL.
HE WAS IN THE T-POSE UP UNTIL WE TALKED TO HIM, THEN HE STARTED USING NORMAL MOTIONS...

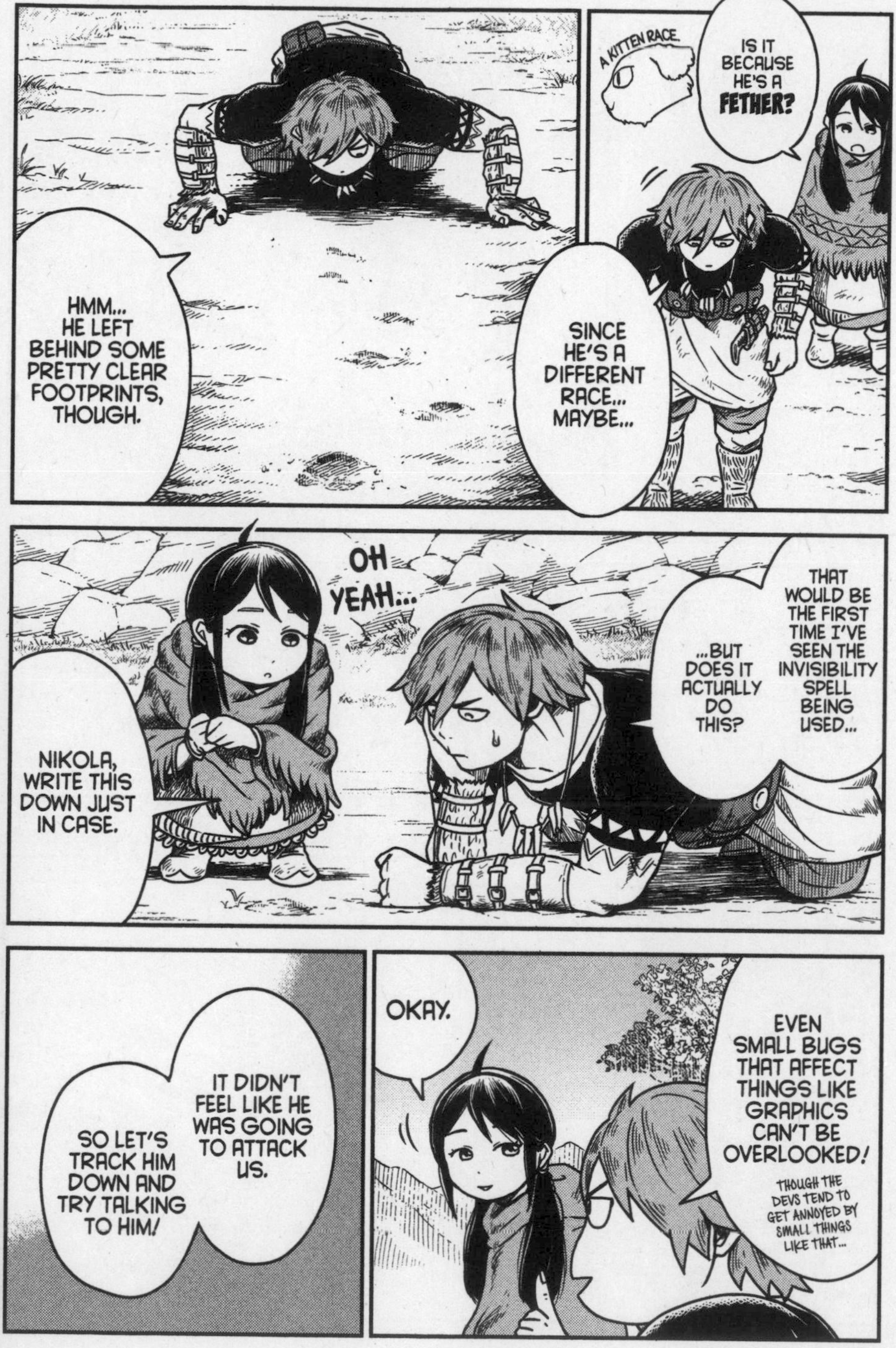
IS IT BECAUSE HE'S A FETHER?
A KITTEN RACE.
SINCE HE'S A DIFFERENT RACE... MAYBE...
HMM... HE LEFT BEHIND SOME PRETTY CLEAR FOOTPRINTS, THOUGH.
THAT WOULD BE THE FIRST TIME I'VE SEEN THE INVISIBILITY SPELL BEING USED...
...BUT DOES IT ACTUALLY DO THIS?
OH YEAH...
NIKOLA, WRITE THIS DOWN JUST IN CASE.
EVEN SMALL BUGS THAT AFFECT THINGS LIKE GRAPHICS CAN'T BE OVERLOOKED!
THOUGH THE DEVS TEND TO GET ANNOYED BY SMALL THINGS LIKE THAT...
OKAY.
IT DIDN'T FEEL LIKE HE WAS GOING TO ATTACK US.
SO LET'S TRACK HIM DOWN AND TRY TALKING TO HIM!

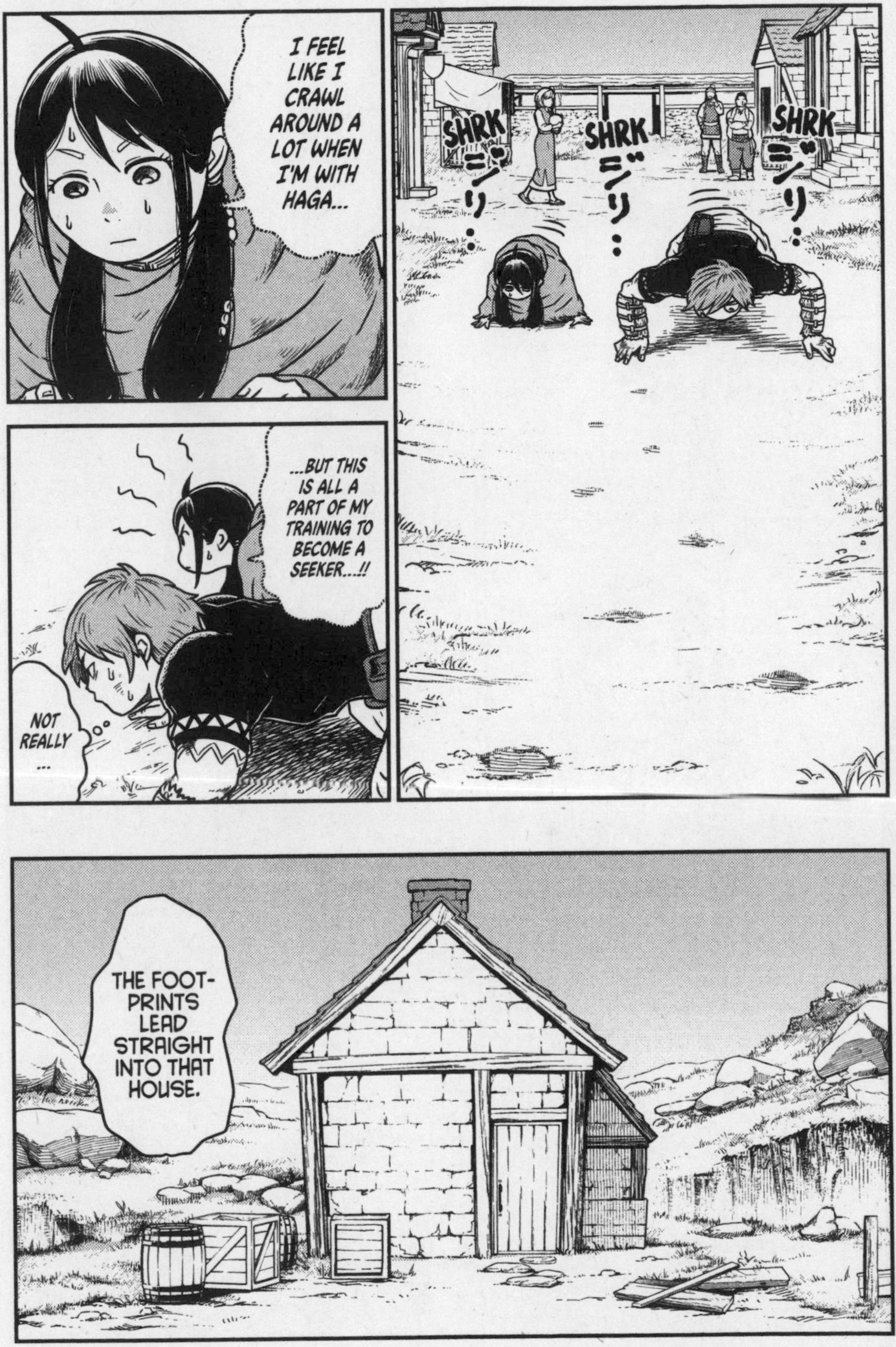
SHRK ジリ…
SHRK ジリ…
SHRK ジリ…
I FEEL LIKE I CRAWL AROUND A LOT WHEN I'M WITH HAGA...
...BUT THIS IS ALL A PART OF MY TRAINING TO BECOME A SEEKER...!!
NOT REALLY ...
THE FOOT-PRINTS LEAD STRAIGHT INTO THAT HOUSE.

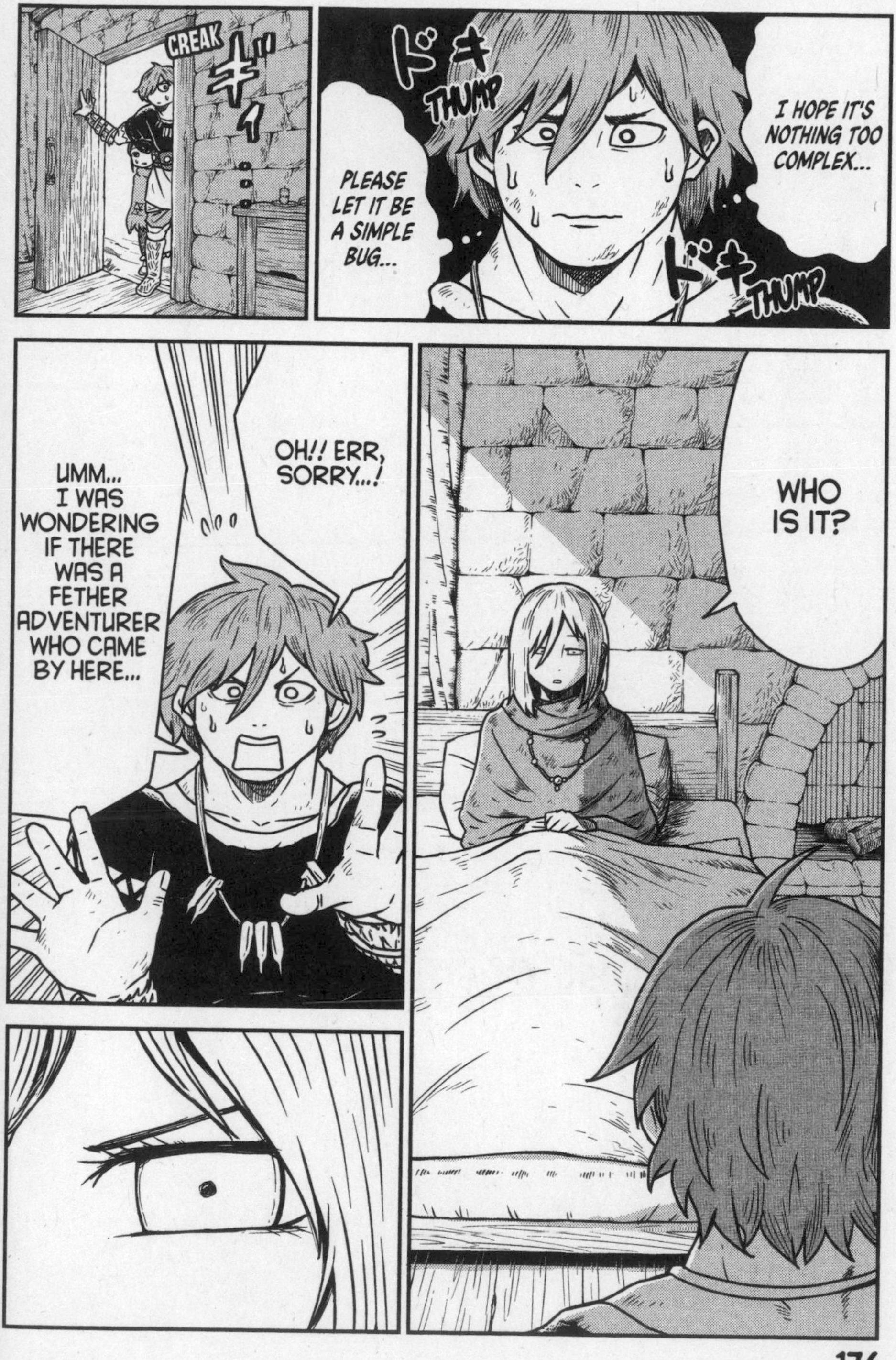
I HOPE IT'S NOTHING TOO COMPLEX...
ドキ
THUMP
PLEASE LET IT BE A SIMPLE BUG...
ドキ
THUMP
CREAK
ギィ
WHO IS IT?
OH!! ERR, SORRY...!
UMM... I WAS WONDERING IF THERE WAS A FETHER ADVENTURER WHO CAME BY HERE...

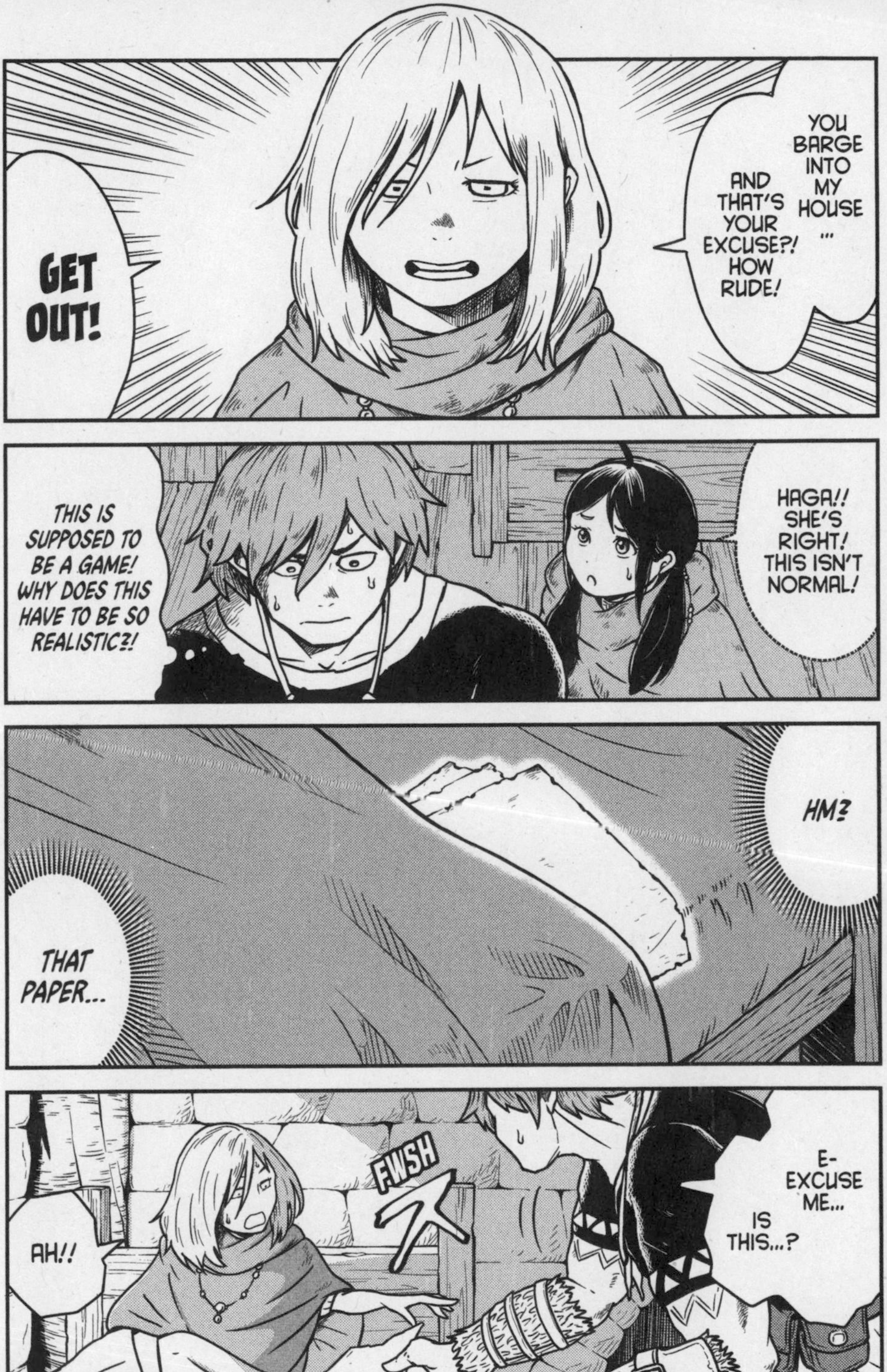
YOU BARGE INTO MY HOUSE ...
AND THAT'S YOUR EXCUSE?! HOW RUDE!
GET OUT!
HAGA!! SHE'S RIGHT! THIS ISN'T NORMAL!
THIS IS SUPPOSED TO BE A GAME! WHY DOES THIS HAVE TO BE SO REALISTIC?!
HM?
THAT PAPER...
E-EXCUSE ME...
IS THIS...?
FWSH
AH!!

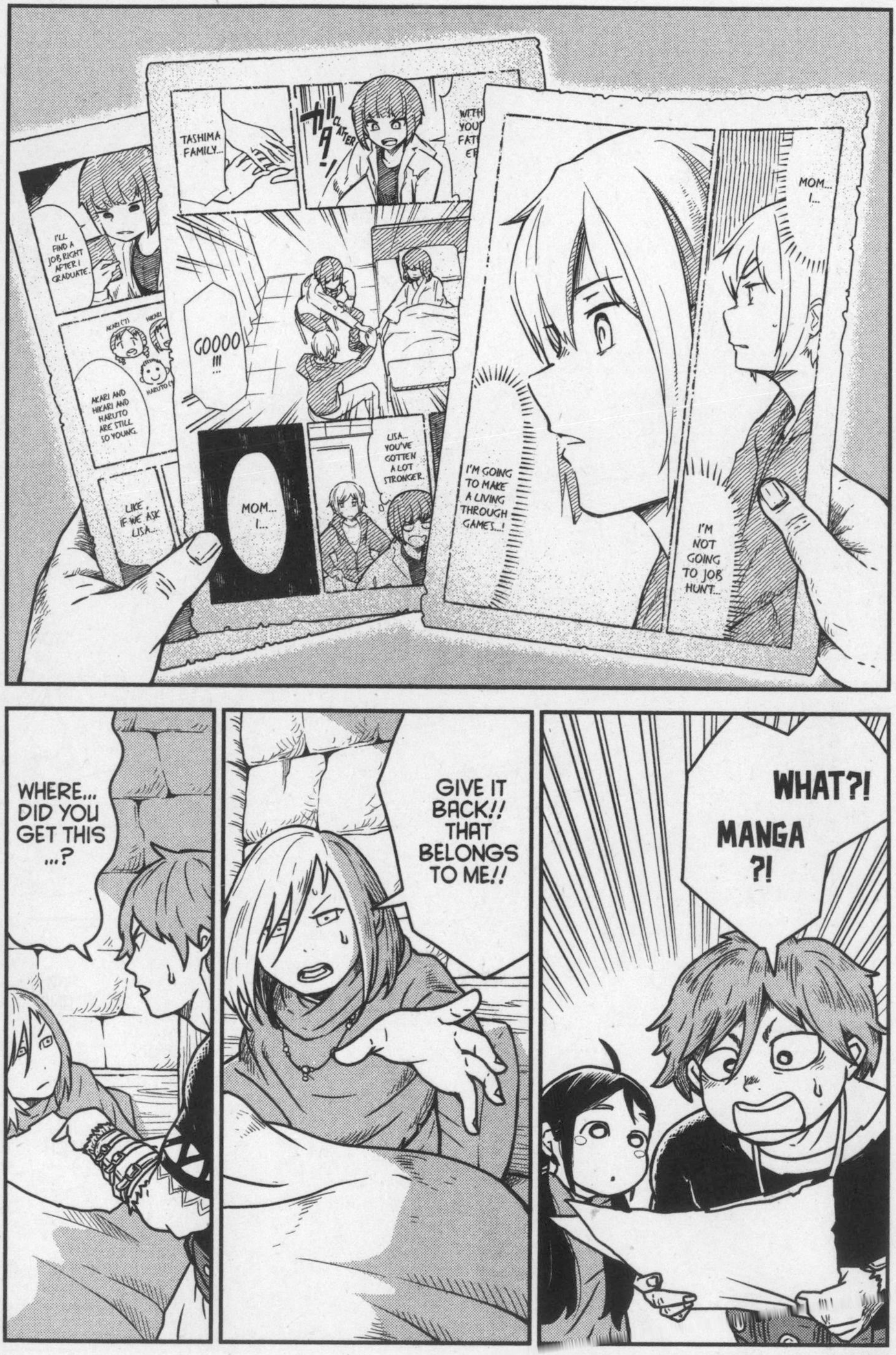
MOM... I...
I'M NOT GOING TO JOB HUNT...
I'M GOING TO MAKE A LIVING THROUGH GAMES...!
CLATTER
TASHIMA FAMILY...
GOOOO!!!...
LISA... YOU'VE GOTTEN A LOT STRONGER.
MOM... I...
I'LL FIND A JOB RIGHT AFTER I GRADUATE.
AKARI AND HIKARI AND HARUTO ARE STILL SO YOUNG.
LIKE, IF WE ASK LISA...
WHAT?!
MANGA ?!
GIVE IT BACK!! THAT BELONGS TO ME!!
WHERE... DID YOU GET THIS ...?

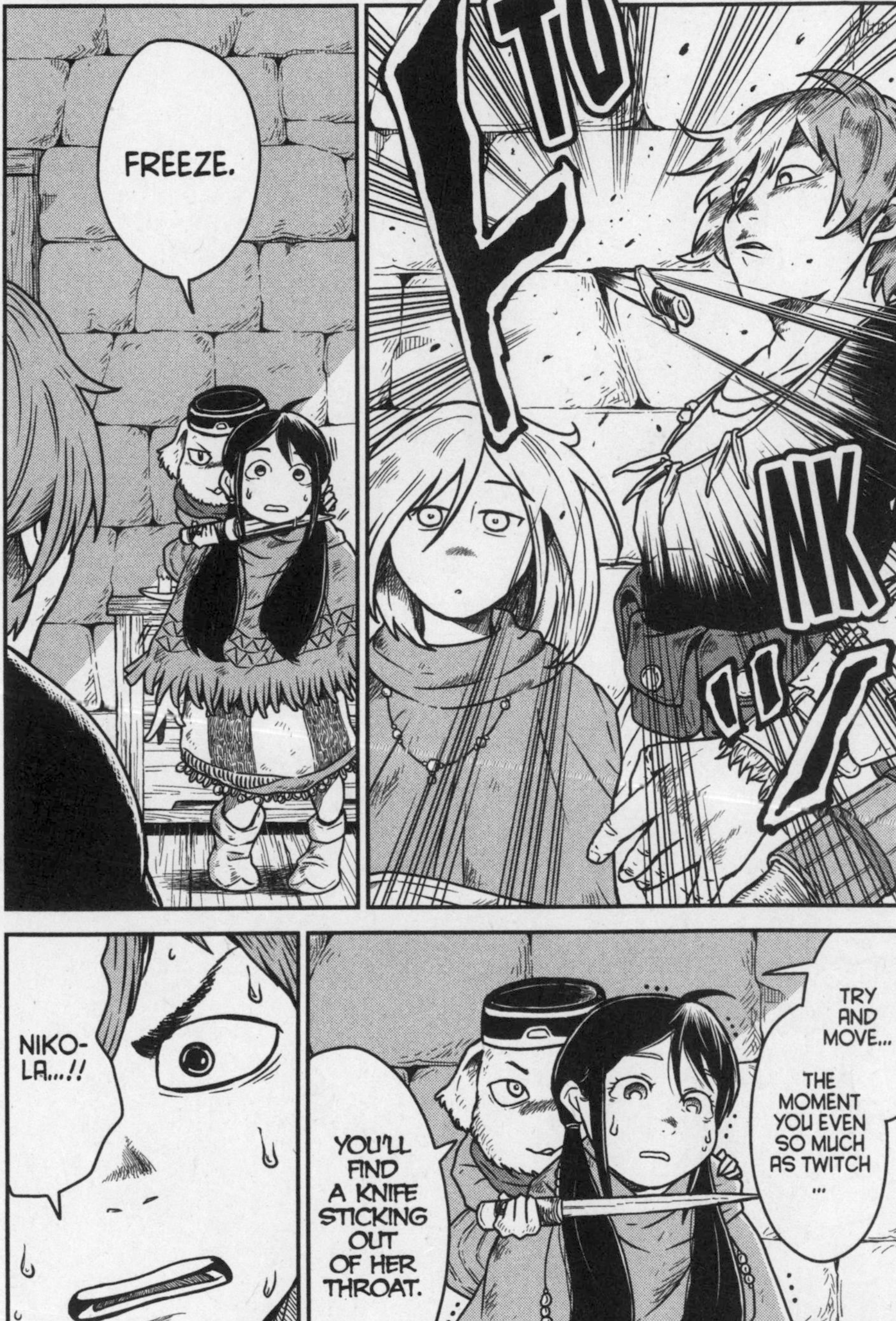
TO
NK
FREEZE.
TRY AND MOVE...
THE MOMENT YOU EVEN SO MUCH AS TWITCH ...
YOU'LL FIND A KNIFE STICKING OUT OF HER THROAT.
NIKO-LA...!!

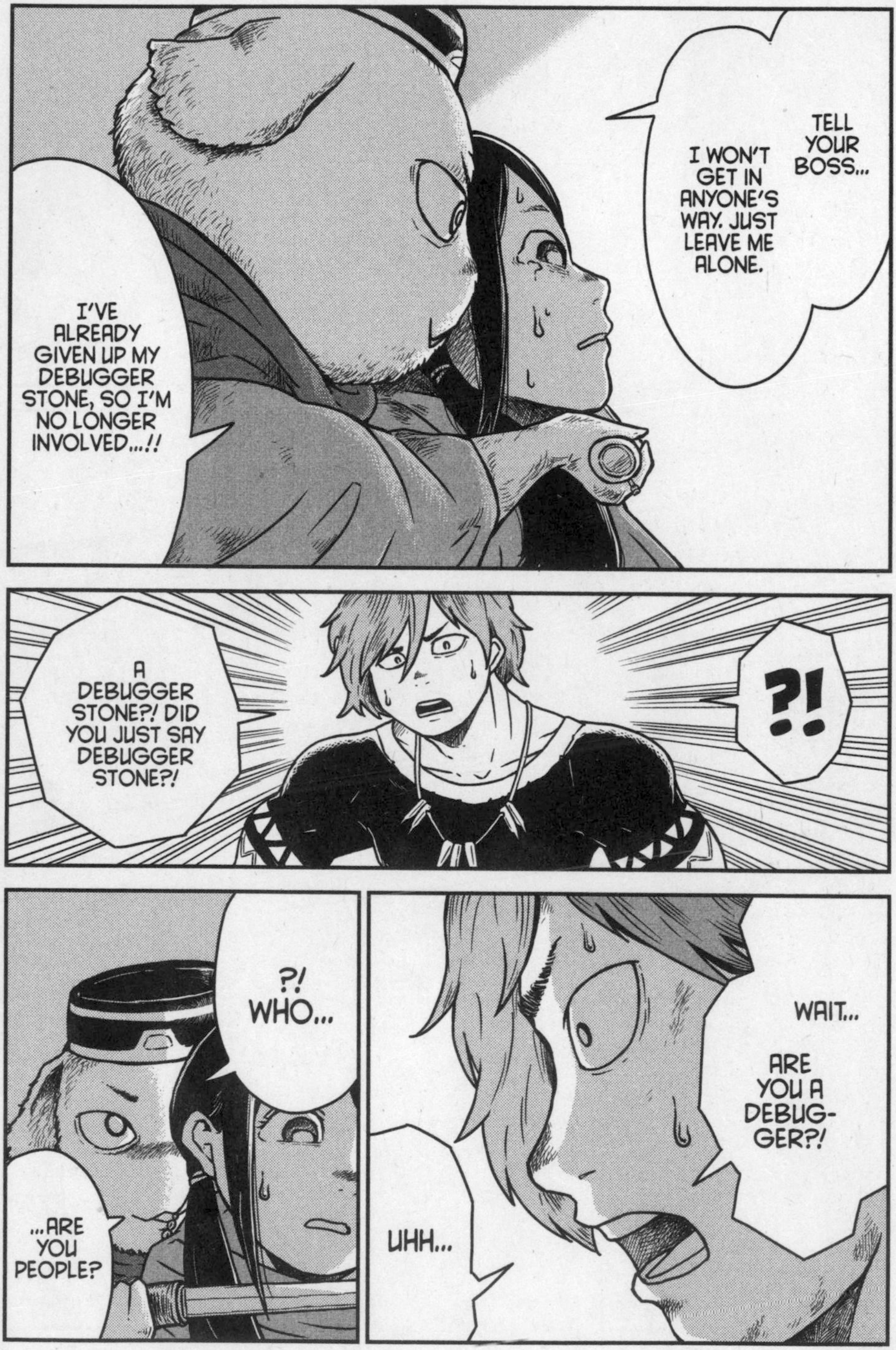
TELL YOUR BOSS... I WON'T GET IN ANYONE'S WAY. JUST LEAVE ME ALONE.
I'VE ALREADY GIVEN UP MY DEBUGGER STONE, SO I'M NO LONGER INVOLVED...!!
?!
A DEBUGGER STONE?! DID YOU JUST SAY DEBUGGER STONE?!
WAIT...
ARE YOU A DEBUGGER?!
UHH...
?! WHO...
...ARE YOU PEOPLE?

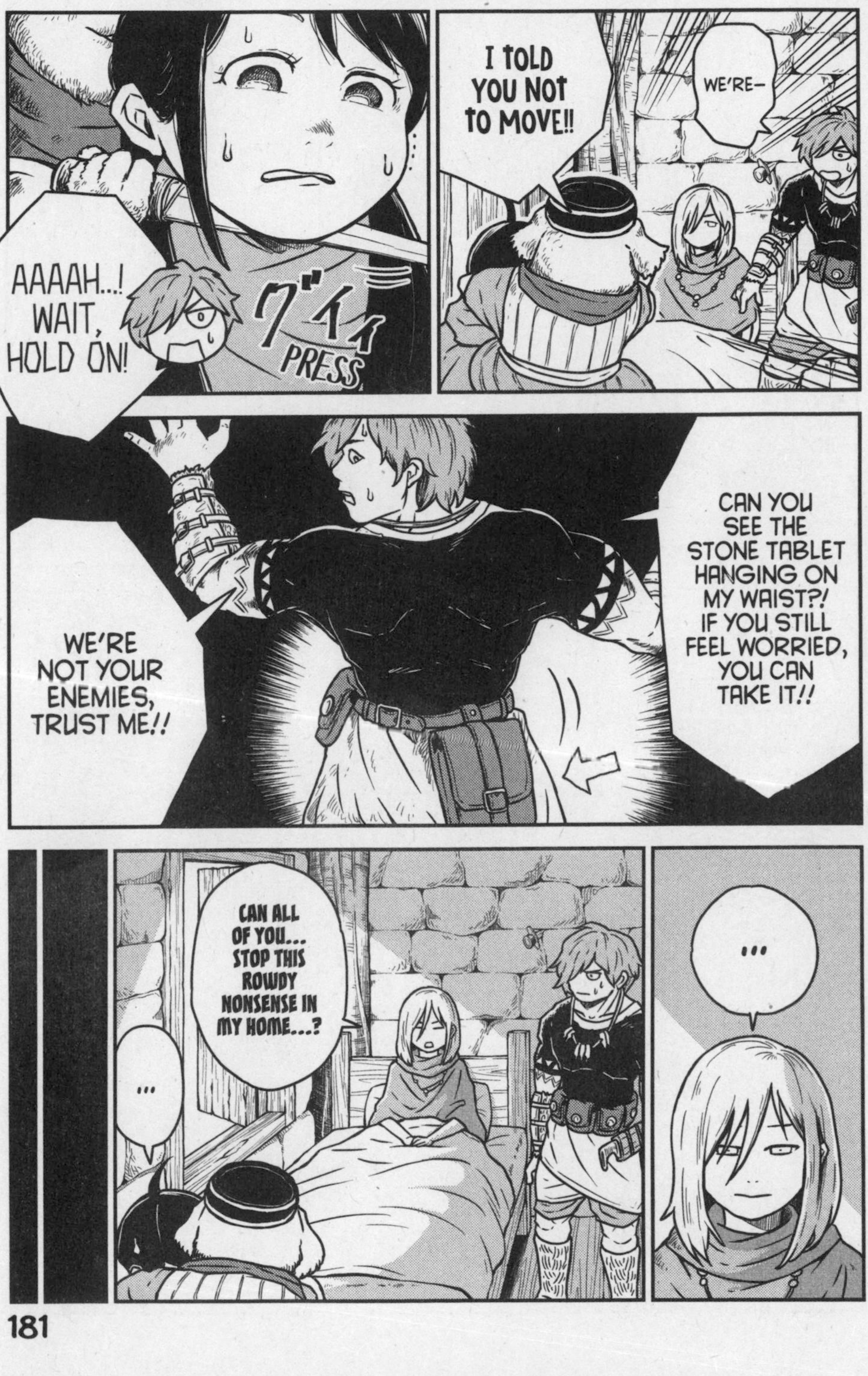
WE'RE—
I TOLD YOU NOT TO MOVE!!
AAAAH...! WAIT, HOLD ON!
ヴィイ PRESS
CAN YOU SEE THE STONE TABLET HANGING ON MY WAIST?! IF YOU STILL FEEL WORRIED, YOU CAN TAKE IT!!
WE'RE NOT YOUR ENEMIES, TRUST ME!!
...
CAN ALL OF YOU... STOP THIS ROWDY NONSENSE IN MY HOME...?
...

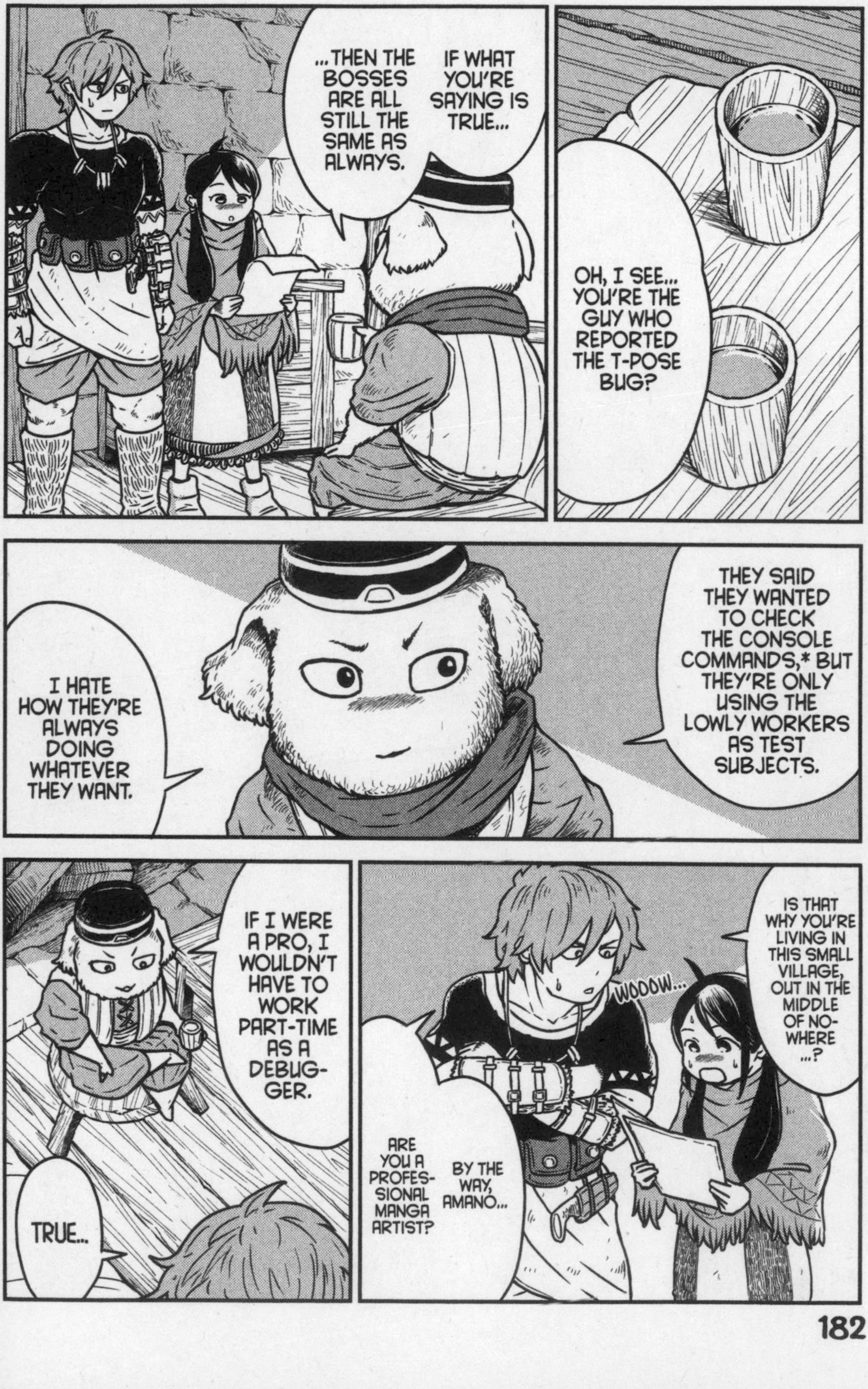
OH, I SEE... YOU'RE THE GUY WHO REPORTED THE T-POSE BUG?
IF WHAT YOU'RE SAYING IS TRUE...
...THEN THE BOSSES ARE ALL STILL THE SAME AS ALWAYS.
THEY SAID THEY WANTED TO CHECK THE CONSOLE COMMANDS,* BUT THEY'RE ONLY USING THE LOWLY WORKERS AS TEST SUBJECTS.
I HATE HOW THEY'RE ALWAYS DOING WHATEVER THEY WANT.
IS THAT WHY YOU'RE LIVING IN THIS SMALL VILLAGE, OUT IN THE MIDDLE OF NO-WHERE ...?
WOOOW...
BY THE WAY, AMANO...
ARE YOU A PROFES-SIONAL MANGA ARTIST?
IF I WERE A PRO, I WOULDN'T HAVE TO WORK PART-TIME AS A DEBUG-GER.
TRUE...

*Console Commands: Commands used for debugging, including adjusting inventory items, item functions, and anything in-game to make debugging easier.

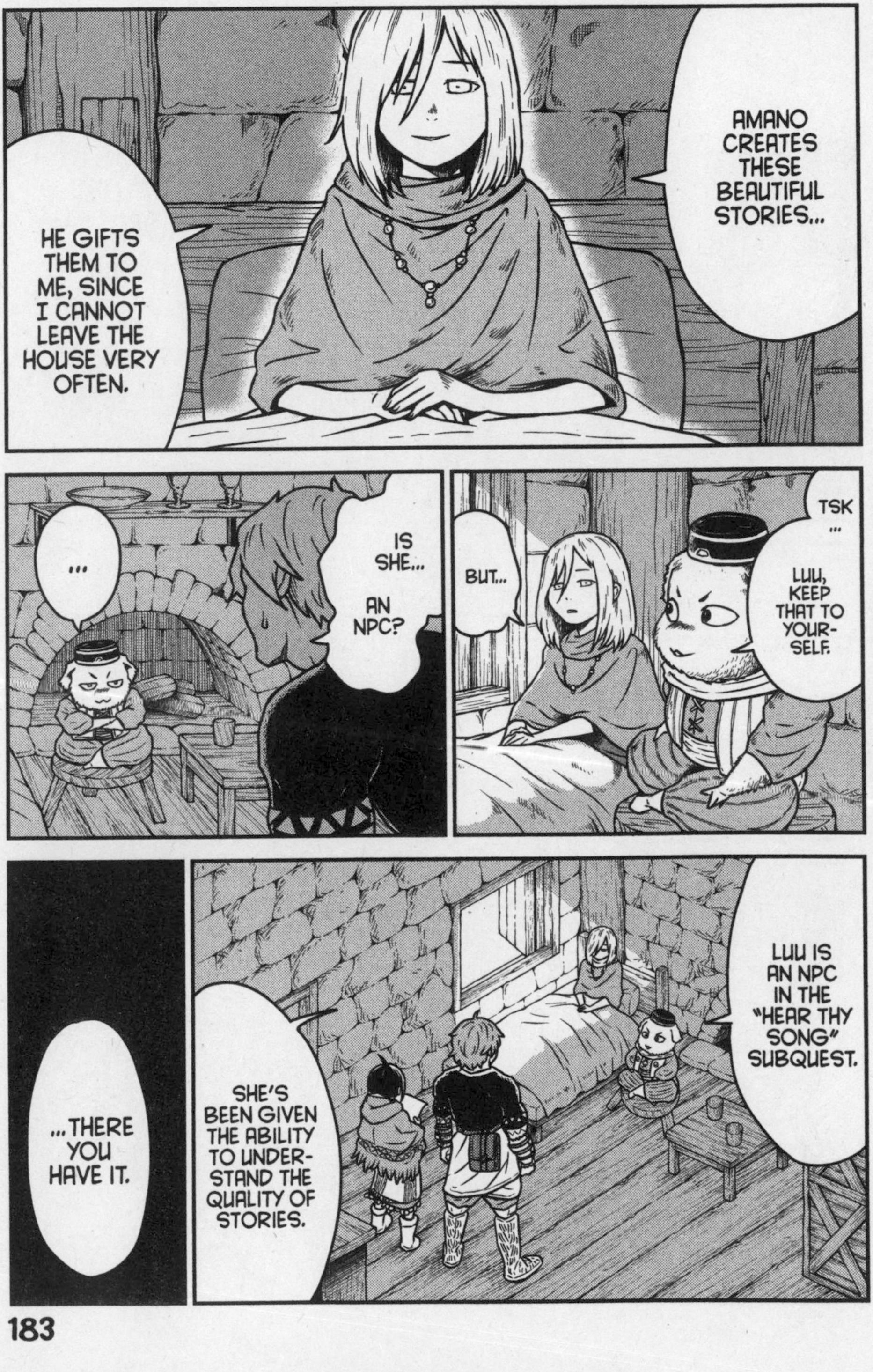
AMANO CREATES THESE BEAUTIFUL STORIES...
HE GIFTS THEM TO ME, SINCE I CANNOT LEAVE THE HOUSE VERY OFTEN.
TSK ...
LUU, KEEP THAT TO YOUR-SELF.
BUT...
IS SHE... AN NPC?
...
LUU IS AN NPC IN THE "HEAR THY SONG" SUBQUEST.
SHE'S BEEN GIVEN THE ABILITY TO UNDER-STAND THE QUALITY OF STORIES.
...THERE YOU HAVE IT.

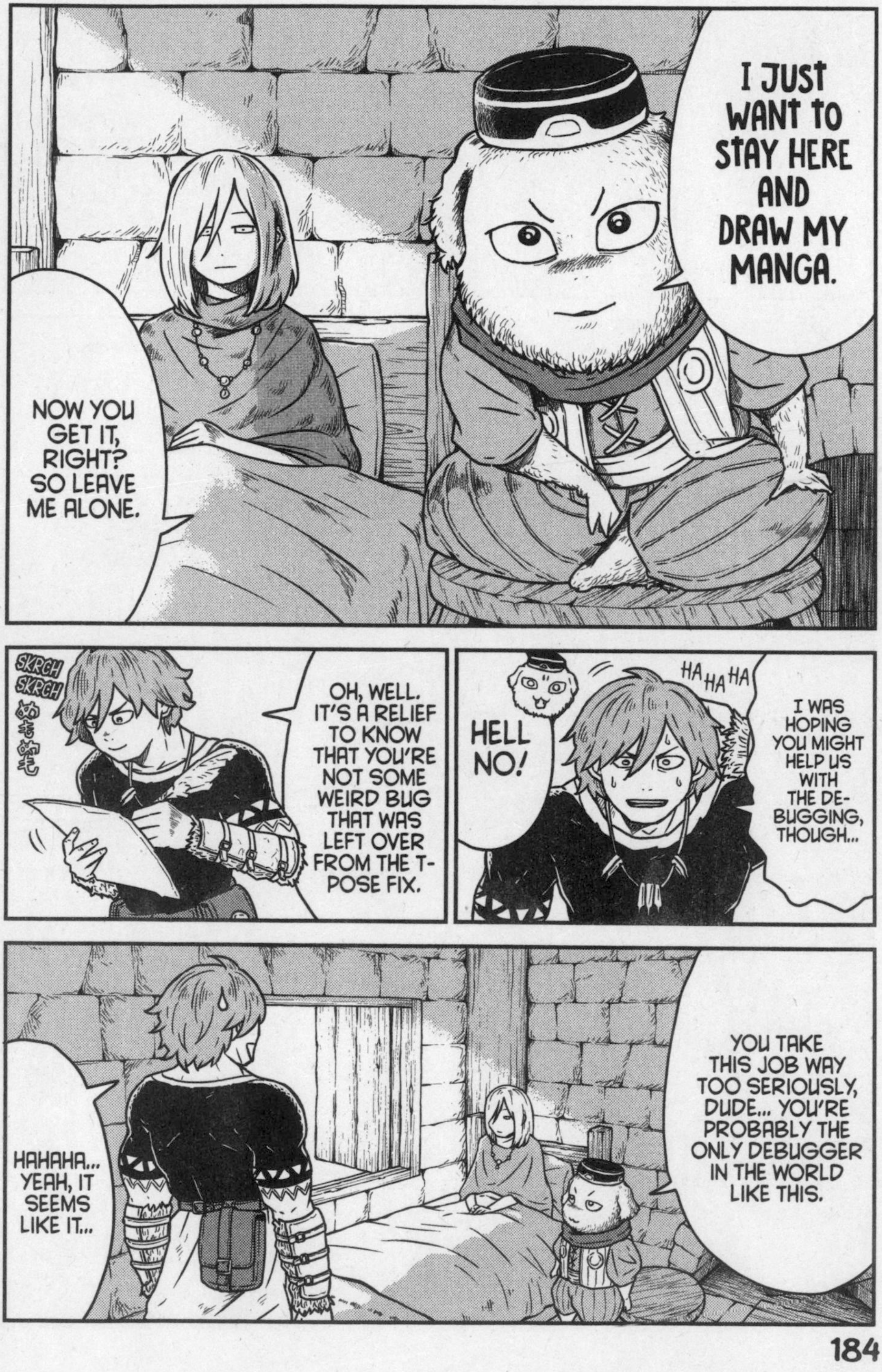
I JUST WANT TO STAY HERE AND DRAW MY MANGA.
NOW YOU GET IT, RIGHT? SO LEAVE ME ALONE.
HA HA HA
I WAS HOPING YOU MIGHT HELP US WITH THE DE-BUGGING, THOUGH...
HELL NO!
OH, WELL. IT'S A RELIEF TO KNOW THAT YOU'RE NOT SOME WEIRD BUG THAT WAS LEFT OVER FROM THE T-POSE FIX.
SKRCH SKRCH
YOU TAKE THIS JOB WAY TOO SERIOUSLY, DUDE... YOU'RE PROBABLY THE ONLY DEBUGGER IN THE WORLD LIKE THIS.
HAHAHA... YEAH, IT SEEMS LIKE IT...

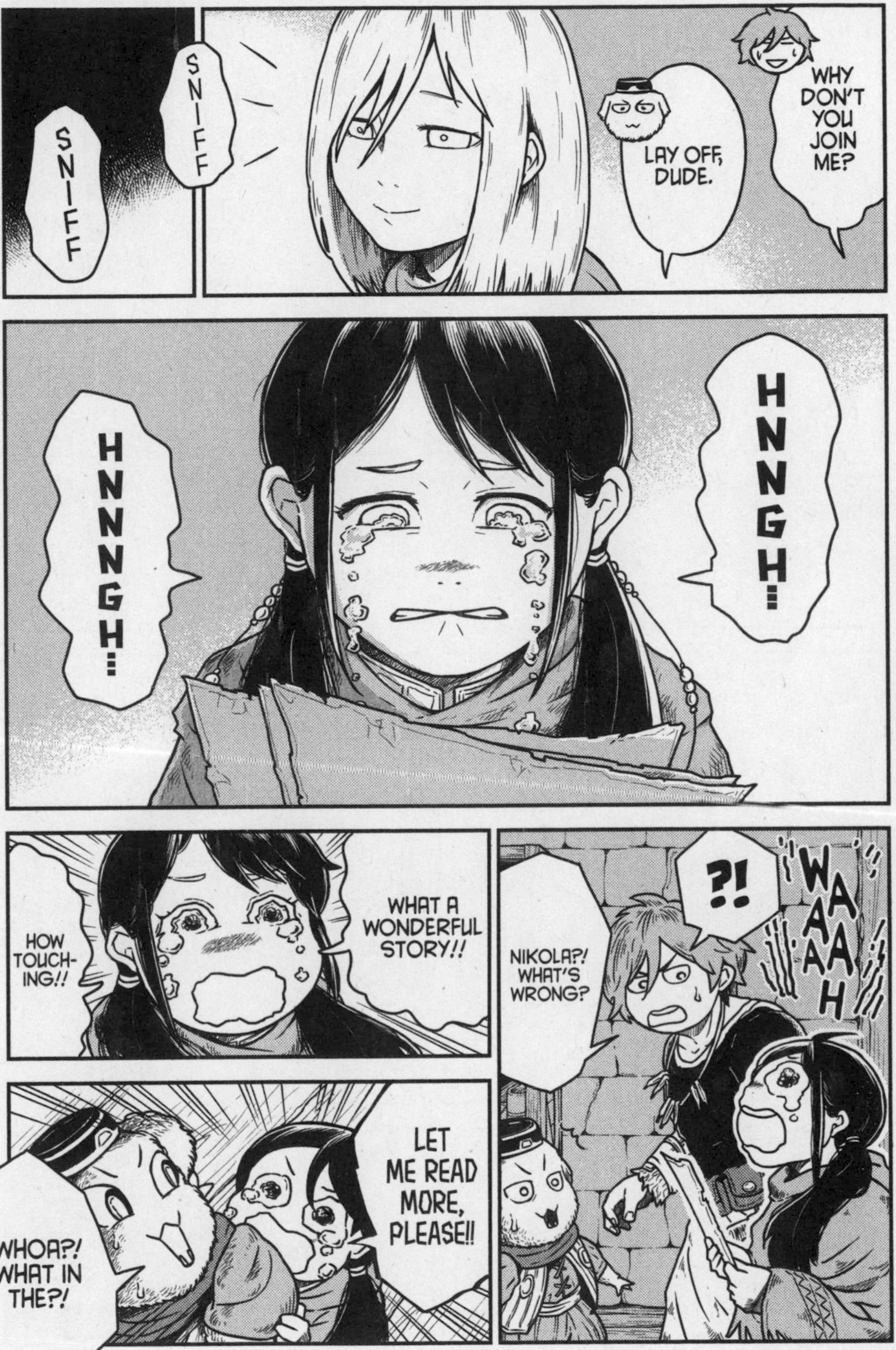
WHY DON'T YOU JOIN ME?
LAY OFF, DUDE.
SNIFF
SNIFF
HNNGH...
HNNNGH...
WAAAH
?!
NIKOLA?! WHAT'S WRONG?
WHAT A WONDERFUL STORY!!
HOW TOUCHING!!
LET ME READ MORE, PLEASE!!
WHOA?! WHAT IN THE?!

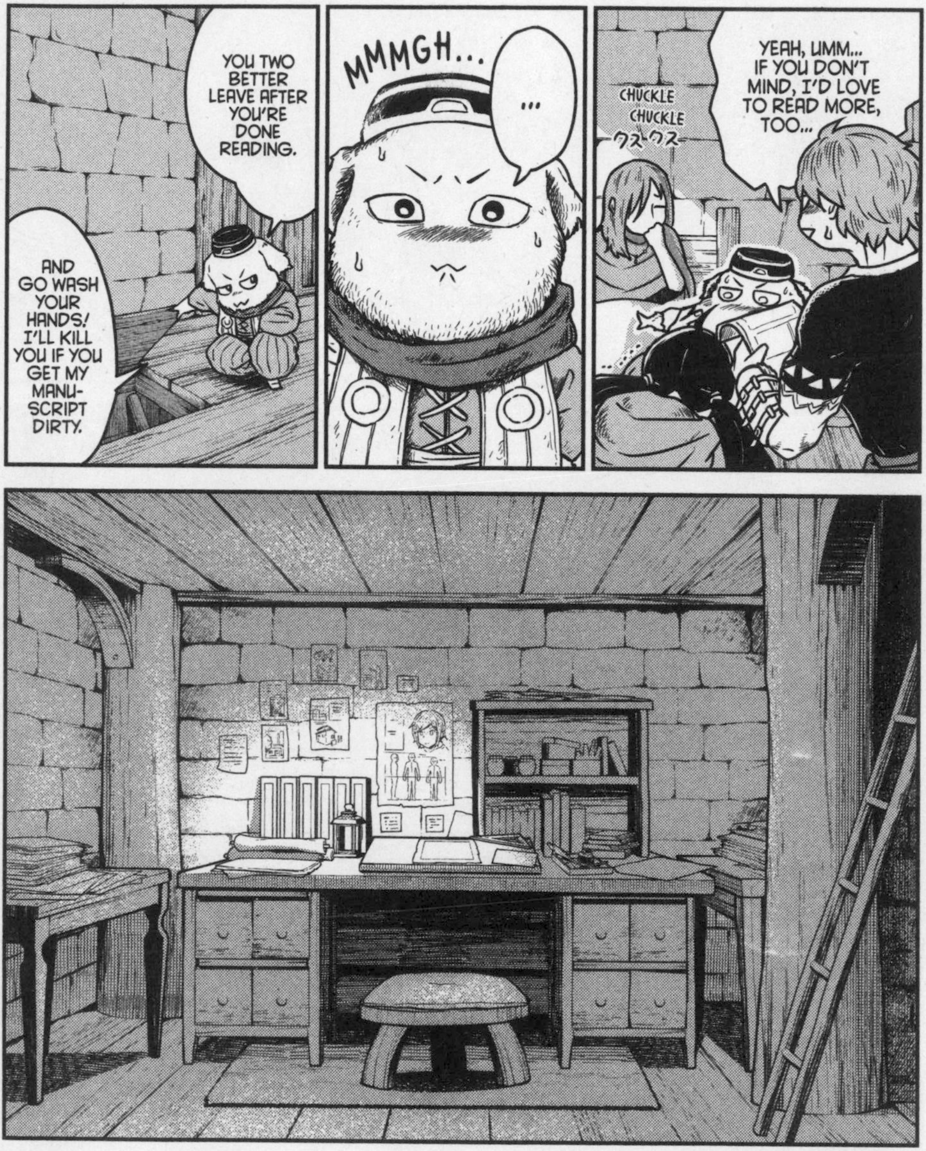
YEAH, UMM... IF YOU DON'T MIND, I'D LOVE TO READ MORE, TOO...
CHUCKLE CHUCKLE
クスクス
MMMGH...
...
YOU TWO BETTER LEAVE AFTER YOU'RE DONE READING.
AND GO WASH YOUR HANDS! I'LL KILL YOU IF YOU GET MY MANU-SCRIPT DIRTY.

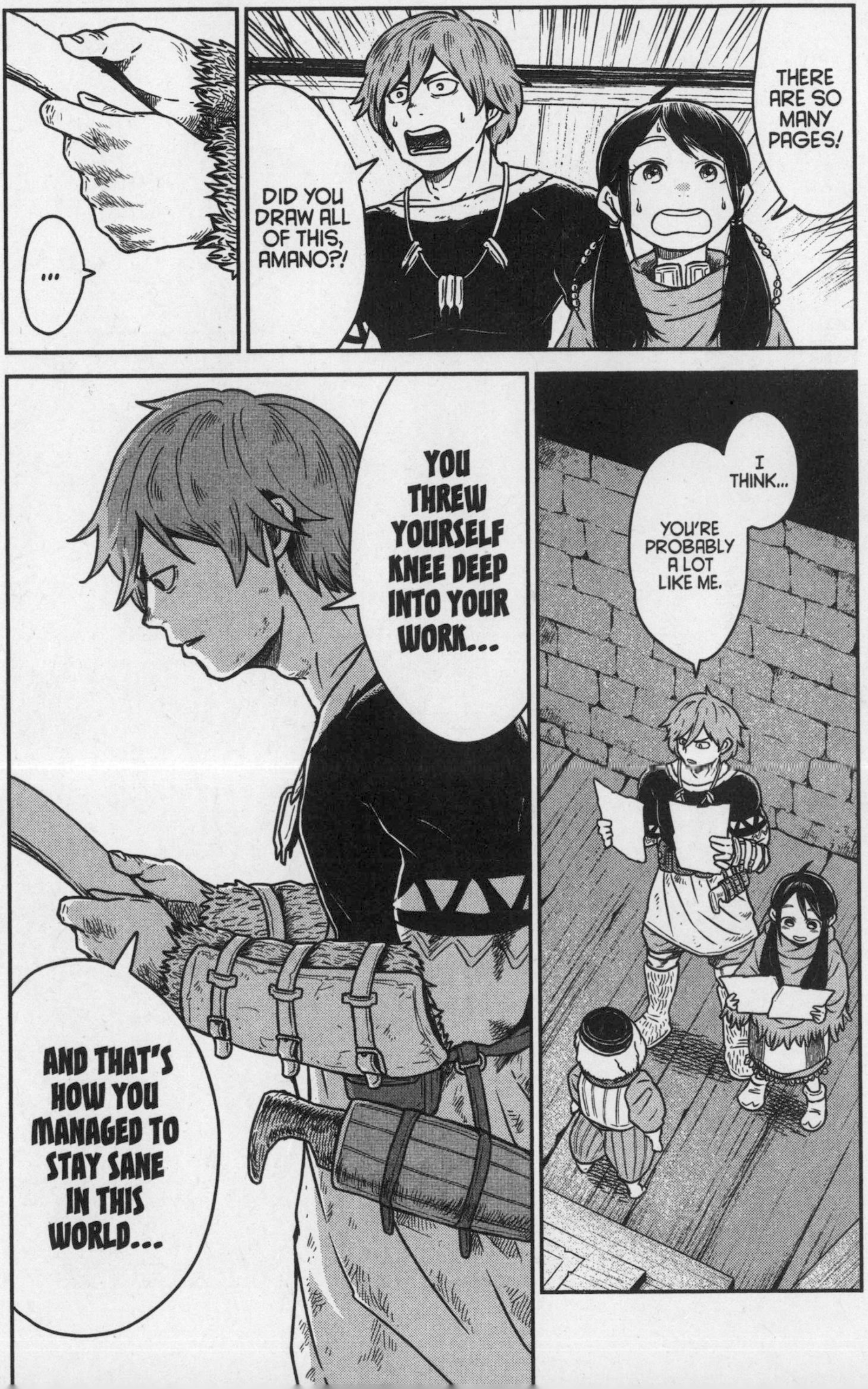
THERE ARE SO MANY PAGES!
DID YOU DRAW ALL OF THIS, AMANO?!
...
I THINK...
YOU'RE PROBABLY A LOT LIKE ME.
YOU THREW YOURSELF KNEE DEEP INTO YOUR WORK...
AND THAT'S HOW YOU MANAGED TO STAY SANE IN THIS WORLD...

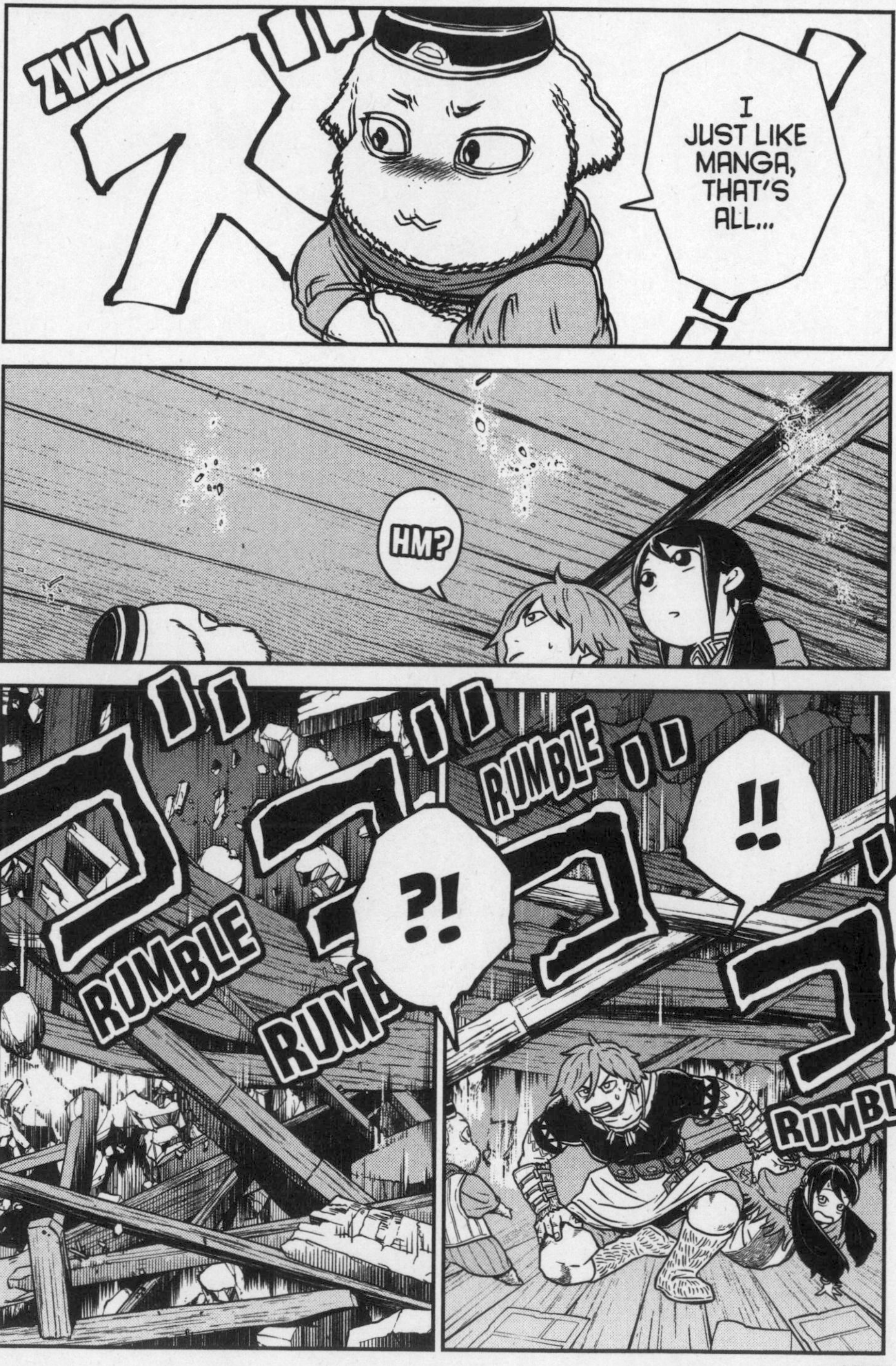
ZWM
I JUST LIKE MANGA, THAT'S ALL...
HM?
RUMBLE
!!
RUMBLE
?!
RUMBLE
RUMBLE

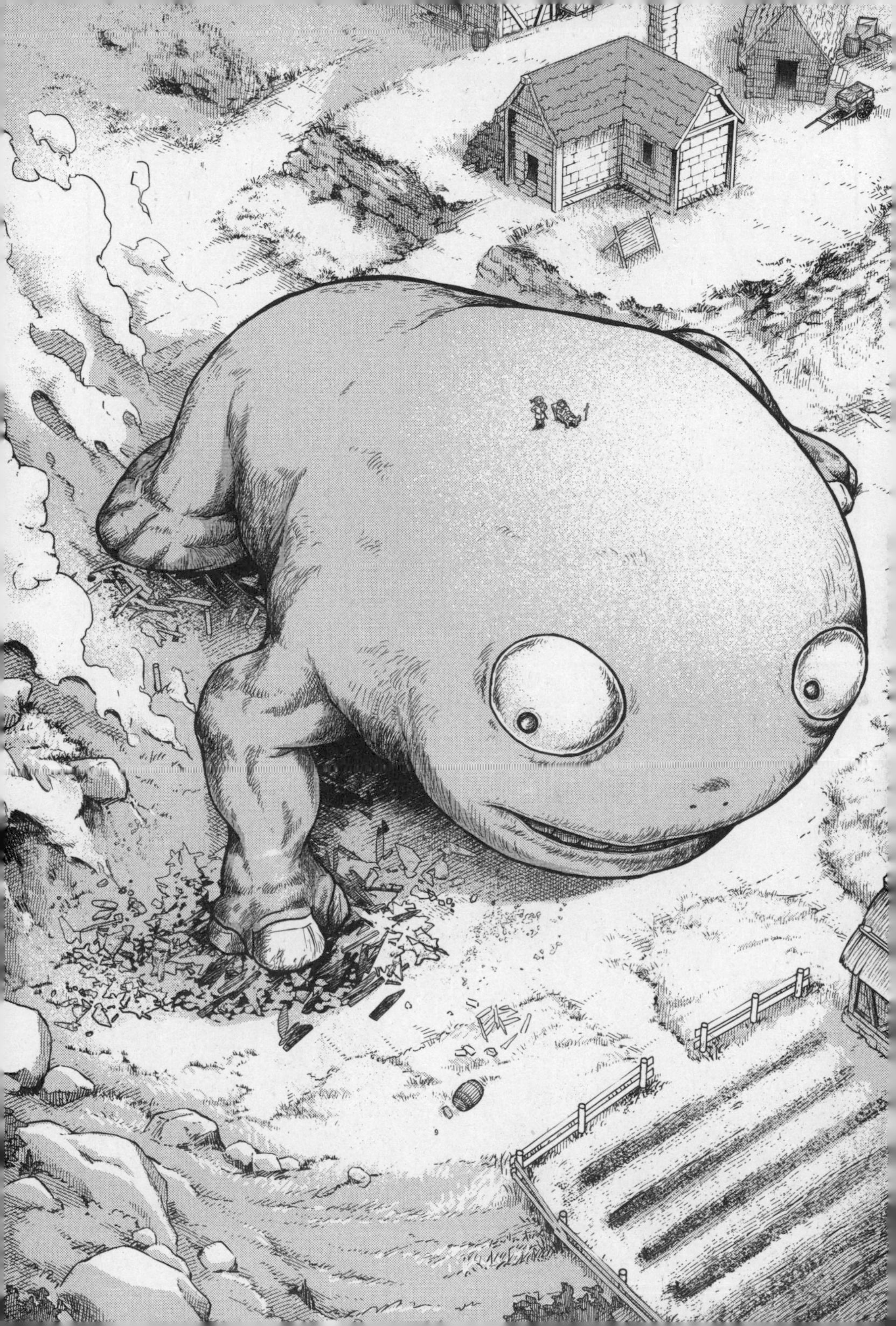

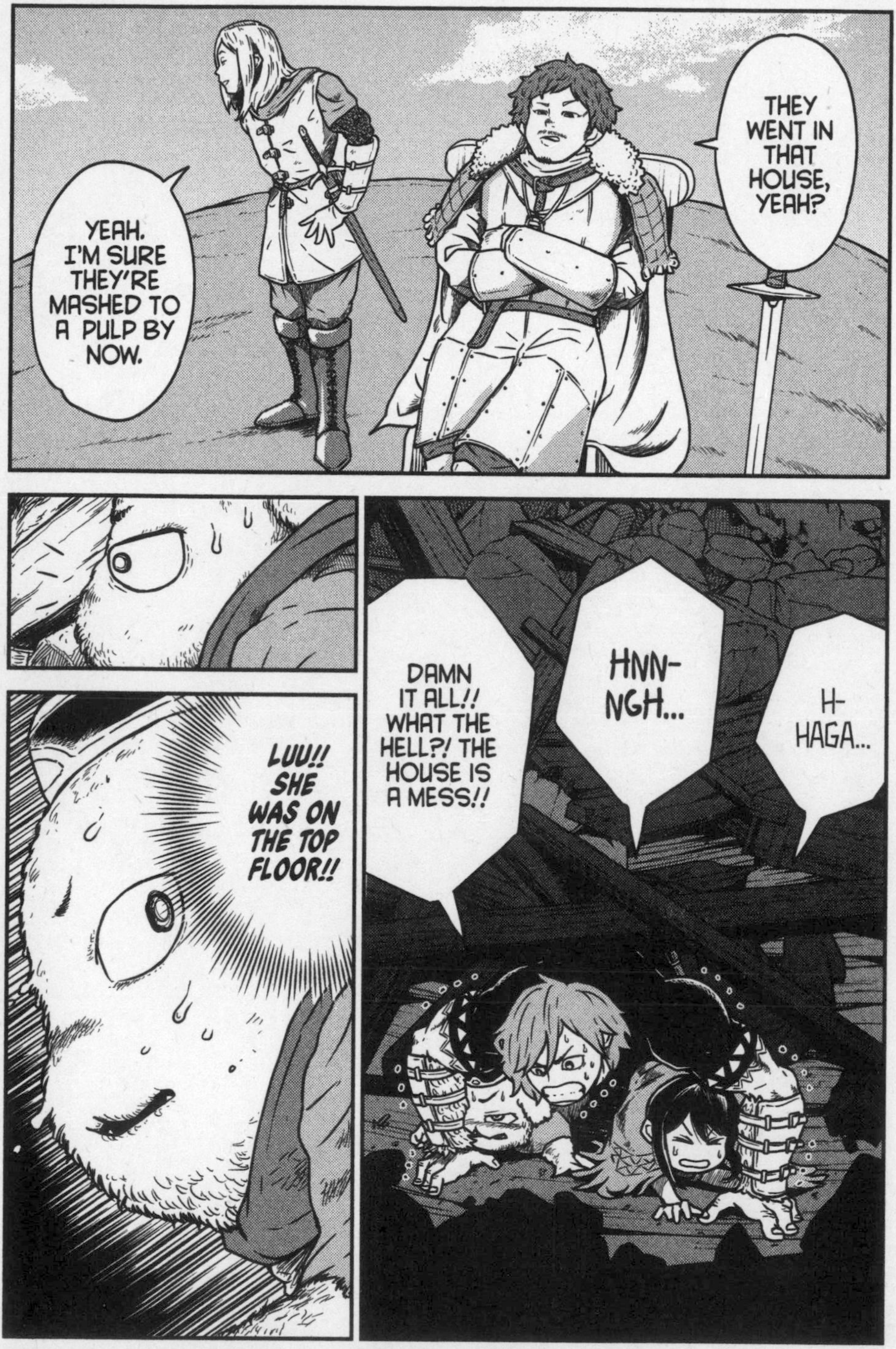
THEY WENT IN THAT HOUSE, YEAH?
YEAH. I'M SURE THEY'RE MASHED TO A PULP BY NOW.
H-HAGA...
HNN-NGH...
DAMN IT ALL!! WHAT THE HELL?! THE HOUSE IS A MESS!!
LUU!! SHE WAS ON THE TOP FLOOR!!

QUALITY ASSURANCE IN ANOTHER WORLD 1/END

QUALITY ASSURANCE in ANOTHER WORLD

DETAILS	REPEAT	OTHER NOTES	REVISION CONFIRMED
ROCK SLABS WITH METAL PROPERTIES FOUND. WHEN THEY INTERACTS WITH CERTAIN OBJECTS, THEY CREATES THE SAME RINGING SOUND METAL WOULD MAKE. *I'VE CONFIRMED THIS WITH SIX INDIVIDUAL ROCK SLABS NEAR THE CAVE OF SAGES.	10/10	I WILL BE TESTING THE ROCKS IN OTHER LOCATIONS.	
THE HOIMOIDRAGONS I MET IN THE VENNA GRASSLANDS IN CHAPTER ONE, "THE BEGINNING OF THE DISASTER," HAVE DISPLAYED THE FOLLOWING UNUSUAL BEHAVIOR: AROUND NOON, A DRAGON EN ROUTE TO THE VILLAGE GOT CAUGHT BEHIND A ROCK.	5/5		DONE
IN CHAPTER ONE, "THE BEGINNING OF THE DISASTER," I WAS ABLE TO DEFEAT THE FINAL HOIMOIDRAGON.	1/1	AFTER DEFEATING THE HOIMOIDRAGON, THE VILLAGE WOULD STILL BURN DOWN, SO I WOULD LIKE TO CONFIRM IF THIS SCENARIO IS SET IN STONE.	SPEC
IN THE CITY OF ADAN BY THE GATE AT THE SECOND GUARD POST, THERE IS A PART OF THE FRONT WALL THAT HAS NO COLLISION DETECTION AND YOU WILL FALL.	1/1		DONE
THE MOVEMENT ANIMATION OF THE VILLAGERS IN THE FORGOTTEN VILLAGE IS NOT DESIGNATED, RESULTING IN T-POSE.	5/5	OTHERWISE, EVERYTHING WAS UNAFFECTED.	DONE
ON THE MAP, IT IS CALLED "FORGOTTEN VILLAGE," BUT IN THE VILLAGER'S DIALOGUE, THEY CALL IT "FORGOTTEN TOWN."	5/5		

DAY	TESTER	TYPE	PRIORITY	OVERVIEW	
4/21	HAGA	SOUND EFFECT	B	ROCK SLABS HAVE ADDED METAL PROPERTIES.	
4/21	HAGA	ENEMY	B	THE HOIMOIDRAGONS ARE ACTING UNUSUAL.	
4/22	HAGA	SPEC CHECK	B	I WAS ABLE TO DEFEAT THE CHANGED-FORM HOIMOIDRAGON.	
4/23	HAGA	COLLISION DETECTION (CD)	B	IN THE CITY OF ADAN AT THE GUARD POST, THERE IS A WALL WITH NO CD.	
4/28	HAGA	CHARACTER	B	THE MOVEMENT ANIMATION OF THE VILLAGERS IN THE FORGOTTEN VILLAGE IS NOT DESIGNATED.	
4/28	HAGA	TEXT	C	NAMING INCONSISTENCY BETWEEN "FORGOTTEN VILLAGE" AND "FORGOTTEN TOWN."	

About the Author

Masamichi Sato debuted in 2016 with the robotics
drama *Iron Body*, followed by the 2018 series about
Japanese chess *Shogi Sasu Kedamono*. Sato's
latest is *Quality Assurance in Another World*.

Young characters and steampunk setting, like *Howl's Moving Castle* and *Battle Angel Alita*

Beyond the Clouds © 2018 Nicke / Ki-oon

A boy with a talent for machines and a mysterious girl whose wings he's fixed will take you beyond the clouds! In the tradition of the high-flying, resonant adventure stories of Studio Ghibli comes a gorgeous tale about the longing of young hearts for adventure and friendship!

KAMOME SHIRAHAMA

Witch Hat Atelier

A magical manga adventure for fans of Disney and Studio Ghibli!

The magical adventure that took Japan by storm is finally here, from acclaimed DC and Marvel cover artist Kamome Shirahama!

In a world where everyone takes wonders like magic spells and dragons for granted, Coco is a girl with a simple dream: She wants to be a witch. But everybody knows magicians are born, not made, and Coco was not born with a gift for magic. Resigned to her un-magical life, Coco is about to give up on her dream to become a witch…until the day she meets Qifrey, a mysterious, traveling magician. After secretly seeing Qifrey perform magic in a way she's never seen before, Coco soon learns what everybody "knows" might not be the truth, and discovers that her magical dream may not be as far away as it may seem…

Knight of the ICE

Yayoi Ogawa

Knight of the Ice ©Yayoi Ogawa/Kodansha Ltd.

SKATING THRILLS AND ICY CHILLS WITH THIS NEW TINGLY ROMANCE SERIES!

A rom-com on ice, perfect for fans of *Princess Jellyfish* and *Wotakoi*. Kokoro is the talk of the figure-skating world, winning trophies and hearts. But little do they know... he's actually a huge nerd! From the beloved creator of *You're My Pet* (*Tramps Like Us*).

Chitose is a serious young woman, working for the health magazine *SASSO*. Or at least, she would be, if she wasn't constantly getting distracted by her childhood friend, international figure skating star Kokoro Kijinami! In the public eye and on the ice, Kokoro is a gallant, flawless knight, but behind his glittery costumes and breathtaking spins lies a secret: He's actually a hopelessly romantic otaku, who can only land his quad jumps when Chitose is on hand to recite a spell from his favorite magical girl anime!

A SMART, NEW ROMANTIC COMEDY FOR FANS OF *SHORTCAKE CAKE* AND *TERRACE HOUSE!*

LIVING ROOM

MATSUNAGA-SAN

Keiko Iwashita

KC KODANSHA COMICS

A romance manga starring high school girl Meeko, who learns to live on her own in a boarding house whose living room is home to the odd (but handsome) Matsunaga-san. She begins to adjust to her new life away from her parents, but Meeko soon learns that no matter how far away from home she is, she's still a young girl at heart — especially when she finds herself falling for Matsunaga-san.

PERFECT WORLD

Rie Aruga

A TOUCHING NEW SERIES ABOUT LOVE AND COPING WITH DISABILITY

An office party reunites Tsugumi with her high school crush Itsuki. He's realized his dream of becoming an architect, but along the way, he experienced a spinal injury that put him in a wheelchair. Now Tsugumi's rekindled feelings will butt up against prejudices she never considered — and Itsuki will have to decide if he's ready to let someone into his heart...

"Depicts with great delicacy and courage the difficulties some with disabilities experience getting involved in romantic relationships... Rie Aruga refuses to romanticize, pushing her heroine to face the reality of disability. She invites her readers to the same tasks of empathy, knowledge and recognition."
—Slate.fr

"An important entry [in manga romance]... The emotional core of both plot and characters indicates thoughtfulness... [Aruga's] research is readily apparent in the text and artwork, making this feel like a real story."
—Anime News Network

KC KODANSHA COMICS

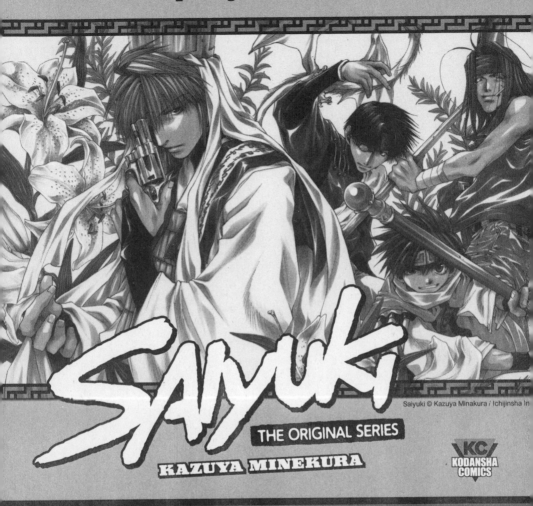

Something's Wrong With Us

NATSUMI ANDO

The dark, psychological, sexy shojo series readers have been waiting for!

A spine-chilling and steamy romance between a Japanese sweets maker and the man who framed her mother for murder!

Following in her mother's footsteps, Nao became a traditional Japanese sweets maker, and with unparalleled artistry and a bright attitude, she gets an offer to work at a world-class confectionary company. But when she meets the young, handsome owner, she recognizes his cold stare...

KC
KODANSHA
COMICS

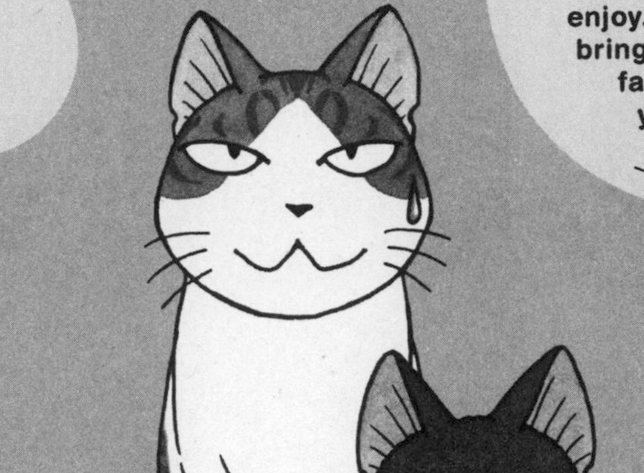

THE SWEET SCENT OF LOVE IS IN THE AIR! FOR FANS OF OFFBEAT ROMANCES LIKE *WOTAKOI*

Sweat and Soap © Kintetsu Yamada / Kodansha Ltd.

In an office romance, there's a fine line between sexy and awkward... and that line is where Asako — a woman who sweats copiously — meets Koutarou — a perfume developer who can't get enough of Asako's, er, scent. Don't miss a romcom manga like no other!

SAINT ☆ YOUNG MEN

A LONG AWAITED ARRIVAL IN PREMIUM 2-IN-1 HARDCOVER

After centuries of hard work, Jesus and Buddha take a break from their heavenly duties to relax among the people of Japan, and their adventures in this lighthearted buddy comedy are sure to bring mirth and merriment to all!

"Brilliant…the physical comedy and facial expressions will make you literally LOL."
—Sam Humphries
(host of *DC Daily*; writer, *Green Lanterns, Legendary Star-Lord*)

The beloved characters from *Cardcaptor Sakura* return in a brand new, reimagined fantasy adventure!

"[*Tsubasa*] takes readers on a fantastic ride that only gets more exhilarating with each successive chapter." —Anime News Network

In the Kingdom of Clow, an archaeological dig unleashes an incredible power, causing Princess Sakura to lose her memories. To save her, her childhood friend Syaoran must follow the orders of the Dimension Witch and travel alongside Kurogane, an unrivaled warrior; Fai, a powerful magician; and Mokona, a curiously strange creature, to retrieve Sakura's dispersed memories!

Quality Assurance in Another World 1 is a work of fiction. Names, characters, places, and incidents are the products of the author's imagination or are used fictitiously. Any resemblance to actual events, locales, or persons, living or dead, is entirely coincidental.

A Kodansha Trade Paperback Original

Published in the United States by
Kodansha USA Publishing, LLC, New York.

Publication rights for this English edition arranged through
Kodansha Ltd., Tokyo.

First published in Japan in 2020 by Kodansha Ltd., Tokyo
as *Kono sekai wa fukanzen sugiru,* volume 1.

ISBN 978-1-64651-777-0

Printed in the United States of America.

1 st Printing

Original Digital Edition Translation: Jacqueline Fung / Local Manga
Original Digital Edition Lettering: Jamil Stewart / Local Manga
TOYOKUNI Printing Co., Ltd.
Print Edition Lettering: Jamil Stewart
Print Edition Editing: Maggie Le
Kodansha USA Publishing edition cover design by Pekka Luhtala

Publisher: Kiichiro Sugawara

Director of Publishing Services: Ben Applegate
Director of Publishing Operations: Dave Barrett
Publishing Services Managing Editors: Alanna Ruse, Madison Salters, with Grace Chen
Production Manager: Jocelyn O'Dowd

KODANSHA.US

KODANSHA